WITHDRAWN

ARM THE SPIRIT

Arm the Spirit

A Woman's Journey
Underground and Back

by Diana Block

Arm the Spirit: A Woman's Journey Underground and Back
by Diana Block

ISBN: 978 1 904859 87 1

Library of Congress Number: 2008927316

© 2009 Diana Block
This edition © 2009 AK Press

Book Design & Layout: Brian Awehli

Cover Design & Layout: Suzanne Shaffer

Front cover photo "March in support of Inez Garcia's freedom in downtown San Francisco, 1974," by Cathy Cade, www.cathycade.com

AK Press
674-A 23rd Street
Oakland, CA 94612
www.akpress.org
akpress@akpress.org
510.208.1700

AK Press U.K.
PO Box 12766
Edinburgh EH8 9YE
Scotland
www.akuk.com
ak@akedin.demon.co.uk
0131.555.5165

Printed in Canada on 100% recycled, acid-free paper by union labor.

Advance Praise for *Arm the Spirit*

"Diana Block elaborates a true definition of solidarity—both in words and in deeds. As a life-long Puerto Rican *independentista*, I have struggled with many North Americans over this essential concept. This is a story of victory and the will to confront a difficult life without remorse or victimization. Block offers a snapshot of many pains, sufferings, and challenges, but most importantly, she articulates a powerful lesson: life is most fully lived, when lived for others." —José E. López, Executive Director, The Puerto Rican Cultural Center, Chicago

"*Arm the Spirit* is a tour-de-force through the revolutionary 1970s and turbulent 1980s, to our troubled state today. Poignant and personal, passionate and political, it demonstrates Block's enduring commitment to solidarity as a mechanism for liberation: of women, queers, colonized nations—the fury and future of all who are oppressed. This book is an eloquent testimonial to the lessons learned from a life in the struggle. Written with an urgent yet reflective beauty, it is an unforgettable story by an irrepressible radical." —Dan Berger, author of *Outlaws of America: The Weather Underground & the Politics of Solidarity*

"Diana Block's memoir *Arm The Spirit* is a riveting personal and political story by one of the founders of San Francisco Women Against Rape who went underground for over a decade with two of the FBI's "Ten Most Wanted" and came back to tell the tale. Diana's odyssey transports us into the midst of San Francisco's radical and revolutionary movements from the 1970's to the present day. Her clear and powerful voice provides the reader with invaluable insight into the debates and activities of the relatively little known, but remarkably dynamic, movements of those who carried on the struggle for self-determination in the wake of the 1960's. But this is also the powerfully poignant story of a mother balancing political commitment with raising children, knowing while underground that arrest and imprisonment could terminate the joys of parenthood in a heartbeat. This is a must read book that brims full of life, politics, love and poetry." — Robert Meeropol, Executive Director, Rosenberg Fund for Children

"Diana Block's *Arm the Spirit* is a stunning piece of work with pitch-perfect voice and strong writing. She gives voice to many of us who took up the vocation of revolution and have remained true to the vision of a radically transformed world. *Arm the Spirit* is honestly self-critical without renouncing the continuing long struggle to end capitalism, imperialism, exploitation, and oppression, which Diana Block remains an integral part of, a role model for us all. —Roxanne Dunbar-Ortiz, author of *Outlaw Woman*

"*Arm the Spirit* is one woman's tale of wanting a better world, struggling to bring that vision to fruition and then literally having to flee for her life. It is a story of internal exile that holds lessons for us all, particularly in these times when a 'war on terror' has so often become a war against our own best citizens. Block's telling is helped by beautiful poetry and resistance to dogma. This is truly a story for every reader." —Margaret Randall, author of *Stone Witness* and *Sandino's Daughters*

CONTENTS

PART TWO

With Eyes Not Yet Born

Now I Can Tell You

To Tony

Now I can begin to tell you
the tales that were locked up
all these years;
How we left the house unlocked
with everything in it
in four and a half hours.
Left your two-week old crib,
the carefully chosen changing table,
and all the blue
I had just trimmed
in your room.
How I packed two bags
stuffed with diapers, bears and tiny onesies,
but that was still too much
and I had to dump one in a dumpster
so we could travel light
through the huge L.A. heat.

Now I can picture for you
how we left the house
unlocked;
knowing they would come in
and take over everything –
strafe white detecting dust
over the plants and batiks,

the fish and the cat;
rifle our records,
brand our books,
pirating their proof,
constructing their clues –
who are they really,
how did they think
and where did they go?

Now I can begin to name
that huge L.A. heat,
rising from the floorboards,
infiltrating the windows,
enveloping the house
with bugs and voyeurs,
watching, listening, fabricating
our acts and our views.
That huge malevolent heat
that was insinuating itself into our lives,
fusing our dreams,
until we uncovered
and broke from it.
Driving away,
leaving everything
but you
behind.

Now I can let myself hear you
screaming in your car seat
as we drove round and round,
escaping cars
real and phantom
that were circling and taunting,
until I left the car, the car seat, the extra baggage
and shouldered you in your snugli,
cradling you within
the great pendulous fear of it all,
walking the downtown streets,
another mother and her baby,
out for a lifesaving stroll.

Now I can remember
how we wandered the malls
pretending to be shoppers
hauling their newborn
in their hunger for mall-made things,
and all the other women, mothers
would gaze at you and sigh –
such a little baby, such a tiny baby –
and after each polite encounter
I had to run to the bathroom,
convulsed with sobs

at the unspoken reproach –
Why have you taken
this ever so tiny baby
away from his home
and his blue-trimmed room,
his perfect changing table,
to mill blindly through streets and malls
away to where?

Now I can realize
that miraculously we did find where,
and you grew:
no longer a tiny voyaging oddity,
you changed name and form,
defying the search parties
and our own pulls toward despair.
You got round, even plump,
walked, talked
and fed our hope,
reflecting our will to keep on.

Now I can begin
not to dread
the moment of truth –
behind us now –
telling you the story,

explaining the best we could
why we risked so much,
why we burned to change
so much,
and even now, still do.
Because now I can see
that the truth was alive
inside you all that time –
your soul's warmth was fired
by that L.A. heat;
your spirit was tempered
in that precipitous flight;
and these unlocked tales
now stoke the passions
that fuse your blood.

—Winter 1995

INTRODUCTION

We must arm our spirits.
When the spirit is armed, the people are strong.

—Fidel Castro, 1971

THE DECISION TO WRITE A MEMOIR has been a complicated one for me. When I and my companions returned to public life in 1994, we were approached by various newspapers and magazines about our "stories," but we had no interest in talking with them about any of it. Yet shortly after we came back, journal entries and poems like "Now I Can Tell You" began to spill out of me. I became convinced that the process of return involved reflecting upon my history in written form.

When my sister first suggested I write a memoir, the idea immediately intrigued me, but I was wasn't sure how to deal with the problematic issues that the memoir form seemed to pose. On the simplest level, there were questions about how I would talk about the facts of our lives. Underground means out-of-sight. Just because we were now back in sight didn't mean that the nuts and bolts of how we functioned should be available on the printed page.

There were also complicated philosophical questions. A memoir is rooted in a description of personal experience. I saw my experience underground as intrinsically linked to a group of people, a larger movement, and a collective process. I worried that the memoir form would privilege my individual experiences and point of view at the expense of others who were involved.

Could I make it clear that this story was only my viewpoint of a complicated history; that I wasn't attempting to speak for others? Could I tell a compelling story without focusing on personalities and interpersonal relationships that would violate other people's history and privacy?

Many years after the idea first sparked, I decided that I could write my personal history as I have always perceived it—as part and parcel of a larger social process. I could tell my own particular story and at the same time shed light on political events that have not been previously narrated. I could bring a woman's voice and feminist perspective to a subject matter that has been largely dominated by a male discourse. I could go beyond an epoch frozen in the past. I remain politically engaged, working with a new generation to figure out how to reframe the struggle in this dystopic millennium, and I wanted to write a book that brought history forward into the present.

This is a "true" story, but that doesn't mean that every aspect is exactly how it happened. While I have tried to report historical facts as accurately as possible, some of the personal parts are essentially, but not literally, true. In most cases I have decided not to use other people's real names, and in many cases the characters I describe are amalgams. The integrity of the book does not depend on these details.

Writing a memoir about this complicated subject matter in the post-911 period poses additional challenges. In the wake of the September 11th attacks, the virulent anti-terrorist climate has driven discussion about armed resistance underground. In the sixties and seventies, this discourse was compelled by the international victories of wars for national liberation and by urban guerrilla activity in Europe, Latin America, and the United States. Now, the political terrain has shifted dramatically. The U.S. government and media have largely succeeded in putting the blame for all violence worldwide on terrorists and criminals. The role of the U.S. military/prison industrial complex as the global spearhead for war and violence has been conveniently disappeared. Homeland Security databases, right-wing internet sites, and repressive legislation have even branded spoken and written dissent as terrorist activity. Is it any wonder that the subject of armed resistance has become taboo?

"We must arm our spirits. When the spirit is armed, the people are strong," Fidel Castro exclaimed in a 1971 speech in Santiago, Chile after Salvador Allende was first elected president.[1] The Weather Underground used Fidel's phrase "Arm the Spirit" to introduce their political statement, *Prairie Fire,* published in 1974. In 1978, political prisoner Jalil Muntaqim called the revolutionary prison newsletter that he initiated at San Quentin, *Arm the Spirit.* In the nineties, a Canadian anarchist collective named itself "Arm the Spirit." There may be other uses of the phrase which I am not aware of.

What I do understand more with each passing year, is that the protracted struggle to win fundamental political change cannot be sustained unless we continually find ways to arm our spirits—creatively, theoretically, imaginatively, defiantly. Since I have returned to public life, my political work has primarily been focused on prisoners—women prisoners and political prisoners. I have witnessed the myriad ways in which people hone their capacity to resist through reading, writing, conversation, poetry, drawing, painting, story making, quilting, praying, meditation, music, thinking—the list goes on. Inside prison, all the contradictions of this society become magnified a thousand-fold. If they are to hold on to their humanity, if they are to retain hope, prisoners must envision something which is deliberately oppositional to the brutal, meaningless, humiliating structures that deform their reality and sap their humanity.

When former Panther and Black Liberation Army member Assata Shakur was in prison she wrote a poem called "Affirmation." In one stanza she writes:

> *I have been locked by the lawless.*
> *Handcuffed by the haters.*
> *Gagged by the greedy.*
> *And, if i know any thing at all,*
> *it's that a wall is just a wall*
> *and nothing more at all.*
> *It can be broken down.* [2]

Soon after she wrote this poem, Assata escaped from prison and found political asylum in Cuba where she has been able to live in freedom to this day. This book is dedicated to all those—known and unknown, inside prisons around the globe—who each day arm their spirits, fighting to hold on to the understanding that *a wall is just a wall/and nothing more at all*. Despite prisons, gulags, and detention camps, the struggle for a different world continues.

ACKNOWLEDGEMENTS

FIRST AND FOREMOST I acknowledge the global movements for liberation, especially Black Liberation, Puerto Rican Independence, and international feminism, as the groundspring for my political work and writing.

I thank my partner Claude, my children, Leila and Tony, and my four other companions and their children who were all underground with me—Donna, Jody, Karen, Rob, Ericka, and Zoe—for supporting my effort to write about our shared history.

My sister, Joyce, first suggested that I write this memoir, and she has continually encouraged me to complete the project over many years.

Many friends and political associates read the manuscript at different stages and gave important feedback.

AK Press responded quickly and enthusiastically (every first-book writer's dream) as soon as I submitted my manuscript to them. They are the model of a collective, activist press that is committed to disseminating radical writing and I am proud to be published by them!

Terry Bisson was luckily available to be my editor. He is a radical author of many books of his own, an experienced editor, and participated in much of the political history covered in my book. I am thankful for his political insight, the editorial skills he brought to this project, and for his wise perspective on which editorial issues are worth fighting over and which are not.

Finally, I am grateful for the women and men in prison I visit and correspond with. Their determination, courage, and hope under daunting circumstances fuel my belief in the power of the people.

PART ONE

CLAIM
NO EASY
VICTORIES

"Assata" (acrylic on canvas) was painted in 1997 by political prisoner Sundiata Acoli who was captured a few days after Assata Shakur in 1973. www.sundiataacoli.org

ESCAPE

IN HINDSIGHT, MANY DREAMS SEEM PROPHETIC. In my sleep, just before
Claude woke me, our back yard was exploding—our carefully planted garden disintegrating into shards of burnt leaves and incinerated flowers. So,
when Claude shook me out of *that* nightmare into another, my heart was already
racing. It took me a few minutes to register the palm-sized square box with wires
extending from its side which Claude held in one hand. The index finger of his
other hand was placed in warning over his mouth. Almost inaudibly he whispered that he had just found this ugly object while trying to fix the car radio of
our green Toyota. The object was a bug, a surveillance device for tracking movement. Dazed but awake now, I looked over on the floor at the right side of my
bed. Our two-week old son, Tony, was sleeping calmly in the handcrafted cradle
we had found at a garage sale a month before. He had finally fallen into a deep
sleep after a night of restless feedings. Now, as my mind began to assimilate our
transformed situation, I longed to return to the questions about the best breastfeeding schedule that Claude and I had been arguing about in the middle of the
night instead of dealing with the looming issue before us: *what were we going to
do now that the FBI had found us?*

While, we didn't know *how* they had found us, a bug in our car could
only mean one thing—the FBI had planted a tracking mechanism because they
knew who we really were and were watching us to gather more information
before arresting us. They weren't interested in the comings and goings of Lynne
Foster the hospital clerk or Ed James the short order cook, the underground
personas we had been carefully cultivating for some time. They wanted information on Diana Block, Claude Marks, and the four other people we were working

with in clandestinity, plus anyone else they could ensnare. Fear was rising inside of me, but another glance over at Tony helped click my mental discipline into place. I could not allow myself to dwell on the worst-case scenario. We had to figure out what to do.

We knew that our houses were likely to be bugged with other listening devices and watching contraptions, making it impossible to talk freely inside. Within an hour, Claude and I had contacted our four companions and gathered for a faux picnic in our local Van Nuys park. We wanted to act as normal as possible, to behave as if we had found nothing, to buy ourselves time so that even an observant FBI agent would not realize that we had discovered their bug. Instead, they would think we were merely continuing the strange daily routines we used to secure our clandestine lives. We constantly met in parks, in coffee shops, or in malls. We spoke in measured voices. We rarely used our home phones and, when we did, it was only to call the movie theater or library—never to communicate with each other. We watched for cars that were watching us—or at least we tried to. While we aspired to disciplined technique, in reality we were novices in clandestine methodology and were easily worn out by the constant pressure of our sometimes arbitrary rules. That June morning it seemed like all of our past shadowy efforts had been a poor dress rehearsal for this, the real thing.

It was June 11, 1985 in Los Angeles' San Fernando Valley and at 10 AM the heat was already building and the park, with its brownish grass and skimpy sprinklers, was filling with kids. The seven of us—myself, Claude, Donna, Jody, Karen, Rob, and Tony—spread out our pretend, hastily compiled picnic on a blanket and took turns walking and jiggling Tony to keep him content while we all tried to stave off panic and concentrate on the decisions at hand.

As I looked around, I absurdly noted how each one of us was gravitating toward his or her typical comfort food. Claude had cornered the bag of tortilla chips, Jody was chomping the raw vegetables, Rob had cut off a huge hunk of gouda cheese, Donna was nibbling a chocolate bar, Karen hugged the box of triscuits, and I was gobbling cherries. These people had been my close friends and political comrades for over ten years, and we had already been in many tough political situations together. But most of those years we had worked together as public activists. We had never faced the type of cataclysmic decision that was now ominously staring us in the face. Still, the consistency of their food preferences reassured me. I knew them all well enough to trust their instincts beyond food.

Usually we debated issues and decisions at great length. We each had our own, different ways of coming at problems and it could take hours before we could hammer out a common approach to a challenge. This time there was little argument. We all agreed that the only possible solution was to leave as rapidly as possible with as much normalcy as we could muster. Over the past couple of years, other clandestine groups had been caught because they downplayed possible evidence of entrapment or didn't act decisively enough once they understood they were compromised. We could not make the same mistakes. Our only hope lay in getting away.

Our consensus on this necessity propelled us forward even though it seemed almost impossible that we could be successful. Although we had never rehearsed a sudden departure like this, we quickly figured out the basics of a getaway plan, the division of our small stash of money (kept expressly for a situation like this), and the framework for communication via public pay phones that could take us through the next two weeks without the need for further collective discussion.

Returning to our house, I put Tony down in his carved cradle and began the task of weeding through our accumulated papers in order to burn or dump what we didn't absolutely need to take with us. I wanted to be systematic and reasoned in this process, but my mind kept fixating on scenes of catastrophic capture.

In the beginning of May, little more than a month before, Claude and Donna had made a trip to Louisiana to pick up explosives with the intention of turning them over to Puerto Rican *independentistas*. They weren't sure what the explosives would be used for—maybe to attack a symbol of U.S. colonialism or perhaps to liberate a Puerto Rican political prisoner; there was no "need to know"[1] the specifics. It was enough to know that they were acting in solidarity with forces fighting to end the colonial stranglehold that the United States held over Puerto Rico.

The trip to Louisiana was difficult and exhausting. The prearranged contacts, whom Claude met in a parking lot, dragged him out to the bayou swamps filled with live "chiggers" that stuck to his shirt and pants. They kept him in the bayous for hours, while Donna waited anxiously in the hotel. Finally, he came back with the boxed explosives in the trunk of his car, worried that the people he had connected with were fools or worse. But after he and Donna had driven around for several hours, checking to make sure that they weren't being followed, they began to believe that they were safe.

While Claude and Donna took a circuitous combination of trains and buses back to L.A., I drove thirty miles to a pay phone to wait for the call that would tell me they were okay. As Tony kicked inside of me, less than a month away from his due date, I pondered what I would do if the call didn't come. If they didn't return, if I had to leave the area I was living in, what hospital would I go to, what story would I manufacture to explain to a brand new doctor my sudden appearance in my ninth pregnant month?

The call came, Donna and Claude returned to L.A., and I allowed myself to focus on the baby whose kicks were becoming more insistent each day. Yet, my happiness about what was going on inside my body coexisted with an escalating sense of dread. Soon after Claude and Donna returned, the city of Philadelphia bombed the house of MOVE, a Black revolutionary naturalist organization, on Mother's Day, May 13. The powerful military explosive killed eleven men, women, and children, and burned sixty other houses on an entire city block. We watched on TV as Ramona Africa, the only surviving adult, ran from the house, her hair lit up by the fire. The scene was horrifying, shocking. For years we had witnessed the ways in which Black lives were considered dispensable in twentieth-century America. Still, we were unprepared for the naked, massive brutality of this assault.[2]

The bombing was supposedly a response to MOVE's naturalist life-style, which Philadelphia claimed was a nuisance and a hazard. Allegations were made that the MOVE family allowed garbage to accumulate in their house, were noisy, and that they were armed and prepared to resist any police intervention. For years, MOVE had challenged the oppressive conditions for Black people in Philadelphia—the poor housing, the mis-education, and the constant brutality of the police force which occupied their community.[3] They were not polite or careful about their accusations, and the police had come to hate MOVE. In 1985, the police were backed by an African-American mayor, Wilson Goode, who was prepared to demonstrate his capacity to repress dissent regardless of its color.

In the aftermath of the bombing, there were endless media commentaries debating the extent of Mayor Goode's "blunder," as the bombing came to be described, at the same time as these pundits dissected MOVE's "fringe" philosophy as an excuse for what had happened. Listening to this blather as I finished painting the blue trim in what was soon to be Tony's room, I felt in my gut that this was why I was living underground. Beneath the many complicated ideological reasons that led to our decision was the burning desire to build militant resistance to a government that asserted its power through the bombardment of people from Viet Nam to Central America—and now in the backyards of the city of brotherly love. Our tiny effort to organize clandestinely might be an impossible undertaking, but what we had just witnessed in Philadelphia heightened my conviction that it was worth trying to figure out a counterforce to out-of-control state terrorism.

The smell of smoke and burning hair lingered in my pores during that month, filtered through the blooming smells of L.A. in May. A week later, on May 21, we read in the *New York Times* that anti-imperialists Susan Rosenberg and Tim Blunk had been sentenced to fifty-eight years for the possession of explosives and weapons.[4] They were white people who, like us, were trying to figure out what armed resistance should look like in this era of history. Now they were facing decades in prison for possessing explosives while right-wing abortion clinic bombers, who had actually attacked clinics, were receiving sentences of just a few years.

Late in the evening of May 24, Claude came back from his job cooking in a gourmet café with the *New York Times*. There on the front page was a picture of Alan Berkman, another political activist. He had just been arrested near Philadelphia and charged with a long list of offenses.[5] After spending a few tense minutes wondering to each other what dreadful thing would happen next, we went to bed.

Images of disaster wound through my sleep. I woke up gripped by the pain of my first contractions. For the next hours of labor, at home and at the hospital, I focused on my body, on the tangible physical agony that I knew I had to get through. Jody and Claude were my birthing coaches, and together we joked with the orderlies and argued vehemently with the nurses who were trying to keep me lying in bed, tied to a fetal monitor, despite the fact that this was not part of our natural birthing plan. We won the fight about the monitor, and at 5 AM Tony emerged whole and unscathed, five hours after my labor had begun. We were ecstatic and Jody quickly found the nearest pay phone to tell the others about his arrival. This new person arriving at such a dark moment felt like a small but precious collective victory.

It wasn't until later in the day after Tony (named Alex at the time) had all of his reflexes tested and scored and my body began to come out of its laboring state, that my thoughts returned to the people who had just been arrested. As Claude and I ate the hospital's celebratory after-birth dinner, the disturbing disjunction hit me. Here we were eating lobster and cuddling this miraculous new person, while Alan Berkman and others were experiencing their first day behind bars.

My sense of surrealism would have been complete had I realized that while we enjoyed our dinner, the FBI was parked outside our house waiting for us to return and resume the work that they were so eager to track.

For the first two weeks of Tony's life, before we discovered the bug, most of our energy was taken up with him. Maybe that's why we didn't pay much attention to the guys lounging in parked cars, the cable TV truck making frequent customer service stops on the block, and the static on the car radio that I kept asking Claude to try and fix. I pushed to the back of my mind all the deep-

ly disturbing occurrences of that cruel May while I figured out breastfeeding
and sleep schedules, and took time to absorb the reality of having a baby. Sitting
in our backyard, watching him sleep in the sun, his peaceful presence made me
forget that all of this could implode on us at any moment. But as soon as Claude
woke me that June morning, when I saw the bug in his hand, I remembered all of
the various cosmic and microcosmic warnings of the past month.

⸺∞⸺

Now, on June 11, just two weeks after Tony's birth, I was going through
the things we needed to do to leave our home, as if we were preparing for a
weekend trip, sorting clothes, tossing unnecessary papers, looking through the
drawers and closets to make sure we wouldn't leave some critical thing behind. I
counted out onesies, bottles, stuffed animals for Tony; shirts, pants, and a swimming suit for doing laps for me. Claude argued that I was taking too much, but I
insisted (as I always did on weekend trips), that I needed every item, especially
the green velour bathrobe that I had hauled with me when we left San Francisco.
Yet, when it came to packing my treasured earrings—the cornelians, turquoises,
amethysts, and malachites collected over the years from family, friends, and
lovers—I decided to leave all but one plain pair of studs behind. All of the earrings could have fit into a small pouch, but I left them sitting in their lacquered
box, waiting for the FBI to finger and file.

In the same disjointed spirit, I spent forty-five minutes going through all
my journals and poetry, only to decide to tear up everything but two poems. In
that paranoid moment, I felt that any forms of self-expression could provide the
FBI with a psychological window that I didn't want opened up.

*Time and again over the years I have mourned these drastic decisions,
to leave my cherished jewelry and shred my only written history. Looking back, I
believe that it was not only driven by panic but also by some subliminal, supersti-
tious sense that this sacrifice was necessary for us to get away.*

We were all operating on too many levels at once. We knew we couldn't talk in the house about anything that was really going on, but we tried to keep up normal, daily conversation. In some ways our effort to seem normal kept us on track and focused on the tasks at hand. But at points it contributed to my mental confusion, blurring the reality of what was happening. I called my pediatrician to cancel the appointment for Tony's check-up and found myself getting out my datebook to reschedule before I realized that I would be tossing out the datebook for good in another few hours. I spent an hour paying a jaywalking ticket, even though I had no intention of using the same identity after we left L.A.

Questions about where I would spend the night with Tony, how I would deal with his infant jaundice, and which snugli would work best for prolonged carrying evaded the basic question of whether I would still be with him at all the next hour or the next day. As soon as my mind would start to bring this awful doubt into focus, I would quickly shift to another detail on my getaway list.

As the day went on, I began to feel more ambivalence about our plan. Where were the hidden cameras, the other tracking devices, the suspicious car watchers? We had looked but discovered nothing. Maybe the bug we had found was just a fluke, a mistake, a mechanism intended for someone else's car that accidentally ended up in ours. Maybe we were overreacting and leaving so precipitously would in fact be our downfall. But every time I followed this line of reasoning to its desired conclusion—that we should stay put instead of packing up and heading off to nowhere—my rational sense, enhanced by my fear, took over. There really couldn't be any other explanation for the bug besides FBI entrapment. We had to go.

We were convinced that their surveillance was not just about us; they hoped that we would lead them to others. We understood that all the decisions we made could impact other people living underground, no matter how indirectly, and that we had a responsibility to limit as much as possible what the FBI would learn about us after we left. We were juggling endless unknown variables. Did we need to get rid of all our books on the chance that a stray fingerprint of a friend found on a random page could somehow associate them with us? But how could we get rid of the books? By burning? By shredding? By hauling them off in suspicious sacks to a dumpster? We finally decided to leave them right where they were, and moved on to the next task.

Had we fully understood the quantity of forces that were ranged against us at that point, it probably would have paralyzed us. In fact, we found out years later, the FBI was watching us closely that entire day and were aware that we had discovered their device. Did they spend the day debating what to do? Were they waiting for instructions from above? Or did they continue to gamble that we would never just leave everything and they had time to continue their watch without jeopardizing their larger goals of ensnaring more people in their net? We never found out for sure.

By the middle of the afternoon, I was ready to load three nondescript bags into the car, strap Tony into his car seat, and say a casual good-bye to Claude and Donna, as if we were going out grocery shopping rather than making a great escape. We had decided that I should leave first with Tony, so as to minimize the possible attention on the two of us. Everyone else would follow in ones or twos to force the would-be trackers to divide up their forces. Later that afternoon, I would meet up with Karen and the two of us would proceed together from that point. Claude and I, we reasoned, were too identifiable as a couple to risk traveling together. I shoved aside the image of Tony leaving his father at two weeks old, perhaps for years to come. If we stuck to our plan and followed our security procedures, maybe, just maybe, we would all reconnect as scheduled in two weeks.

With Tony dozing, calm and secure in his seat, I drove off in hyper-focused gear, checking my rearview mirror every few seconds, trying to concentrate on the color and make of the cars behind me, something which was always difficult for me to do because I knew (and cared) so little about cars.

My plan was to weave through the Valley streets, making lots of turns which would give me a chance to check for tails. I drove for blocks without any car at all behind me, took a main thoroughfare to another quiet neighborhood, and repeated the process. The lack of any hint of danger was unsettling, even though that was what I had hoped for. Once again, the doubts about our course of action surfaced, though now, wending through the scorching, silent streets, they became louder and harder to contain. Had we somehow made the whole thing up? How could we leave behind an entire house full of furniture, books, records, quilts, batiks, clothes, and lives that had real connections to jobs, doctors, bank accounts, people? Where were we off to?

Driving around had made me car-sick and dizzy. I knew I was starting to lose it, the vast void before me now more palpable since I was away from the house and the support of other people. Tony started to cry. I imagined him dehydrating from his tears and lack of mother's milk. I pulled over at one of the thousand cookie cutter strip malls that make up the outer reaches of L.A., and before I could get the key out of the ignition I was weeping, awash in the loss and fear and hardness of the day. For a couple of minutes, Tony stopped his cries for whatever coincidental or empathic reason. But he only gave me those two minutes before he began again, pushing me to push it all down and get on with the business at hand.

By the time I had finished feeding Tony, I had recovered some sense of purpose. I decided that I had spent enough time weaving car circles, and after a couple of more brief checks I headed to the freeway. I got off in downtown L.A., drove the car into a parking lot, unloaded my unwieldy baggage from the trunk, loaded Tony into the snugli, and took off for a rush hour stroll. Catching a glimpse of my cumbersome figure in the store window, I almost burst out laughing at this consummate lack of "low" profile appearance which flew in the face of clandestinity's rules. Who could this woman be with her three suspiciously stuffed bags and a tiny baby's head peeking through the web of straps? As I walked, I began to relax a little. I overheard a fragment of intense conversation, smelled a mix of appealing foods, and saw another mother frantically trying to cope with her three kids. Most reassuringly, no one gave me and Tony a second glance.

At McDonald's, where I was supposed to meet up with Karen, I settled into a corner table, and as discreetly as possible I began to breastfeed Tony. As I nursed, my mind wandered and I found myself thinking of Black Panther Assata

Shakur and what she must have felt like the day of her escape from a New Jersey prison in 1979. [6] Assata's courage had always inspired me. During one of her six trials, she dared to conceive a child with a co-defendant, Kamau.[7] She gave birth shackled to the delivery table with dozens of armed guards standing watch throughout the hospital. She then developed a bold plan to escape from the maximum security wing of the prison where she was serving a sentence of life plus 33 years. How had she found the determination and the vision to believe escape was possible? How had she been able to turn that vision into a reality?

Thinking of Assata helped balance me. True, I was sitting in a Hollywood McDonald's nursing my baby without knowing where I would sleep that night. But I was here because of a conscious decision, because of my solidarity with revolutionary movements around the world. I had to rise to the challenges we were facing.

That visionary moment passed and there were rare times in the next few weeks when I was able to focus on the political context for our desperate situation. Karen and I met up at McDonald's and took a long sequence of buses out of central L.A. We found a 7-11 for disposable diapers and a motel that seemed adequate for the night. Though we had arrived at this room randomly, we double locked the door and carefully checked for any signs that the FBI had somehow anticipated our arrival. It was an absurd exercise, but we went through the motions to be as vigilant as possible. As I lay down next to Tony, a tiny misfit in the queen size motel bed, I flashed on the cradle we had left behind in the house that was now *theirs*.

Tony slept like he was drugged. I was used to waking up every two hours, but during this haunted night he slept without interruption. Several times, waking from my broken sleep, I leaned over and put my ear over his mouth, to make sure that he was still breathing. I needed to know that no one had planted an invisible bug deep inside of him that could suck his baby breath away.

During that next crazed week Karen, Tony, and I did everything we could to physically distance ourselves from L.A. We had all set a time to meet in Portland, Oregon two weeks later. In the meantime, each group was to change locales, appearances and names to make as much of a break as possible with our L.A. identities. Until then, I had rarely stepped inside a shopping mall. The metastatic proliferation of buyable things literally made my skin crawl, and since I preferred thrift store goods anyway, there was no need to go near these consumer casinos. Now, malls became our haven, offering anonymity, resting places, fast food, and bathrooms. Tony was a helpful cover as we pushed him along the congested mallways in the collapsible stroller we had hurriedly bought. His small, cheerful form attracted *oohs* and *aahs* from every other passerby who focused on him and happily ignored us. Yet with each innocent question—"He's so tiny, he's like a newborn, how old is he?"— I felt my defenses collapse and could only gulp out a half-answer before leaving him with Karen and bolting to the bathroom, convulsed with sobs. What kind of mother hauls her two-week old from mall to mall, exposing him to the noise, germs, and capitalist karma of these mega-marketplaces? Not the kind of mother I had hoped to be. Only Karen's patient perspective that Tony was really doing fine helped me stop my dramatic cycling. And eventually the mall's mission began to win me over as I focused on all the goods that were conveniently available for our identity makeovers.

When we had first gone underground a few years before, changing our appearance had been an intriguing challenge. But having to change everything once again, in the midst of our total disorientation, was much more wrenching. Red hair vs. blonde, curly vs. straight, Jean vs. Jane became subjects of elaborate arguments. I became obsessed with the question of what colors I could safely wear. I had already given up wearing the purples and greens that I so loved, settling into burgundy, rust and teal blue in L.A. *I draw the line at wearing pastel pink and yellow* I raged to Karen as we searched for pieces of a new wardrobe. And she had to remind me that pastels just couldn't be where I drew the line.

Tony seemed blissfully unaware of all this, not noticing when his mother came back from the beauty parlor a strawberry blond or when we stopped calling him *Alex,* the name we had given him at his birth. After his first night of exhaustion, he settled into his baby routine almost as if he were back home in his blue trimmed room, even though he was sleeping in a different place almost every night, and his crib was often a dresser drawer. His adaptability encouraged ours, and his presence forced us to make time for walks and parks.

There were magic moments, strolling around a lake in a city park, when we felt like our lives were ordinary, like those of all the people who were walking around us. But, in those crystal moments, I could see more clearly than ever how this society afforded the casual expectation of normalcy, sufficiency, and simple pleasures to a privileged sector of its population, while an ever larger group of others lived on the edge—without green parks, enough food for themselves, or even a house to sleep in at night. We were staying in motels with families who were living packed together in tacky single rooms for months on end because welfare would pay for temporary housing but not for anything long term. We were waiting endlessly at bus stations with mothers who traveled with four and five kids for days to visit a husband, father, or brother in prison whom they hadn't seen for years.

We were dislocated but we were still able to assimilate ourselves into the pockets of calm that dotted the whiter areas of most cities. Our skin color and our upbringing had taught us to expect and claim secure, relaxed spaces in our lives. In the midst of our turmoil, on some level we maintained the expectation that this marginalized period would come to an end and that someday our lives would return to "normal."

While we moved away from L.A. physically, mentally we kept being pulled back to the scene of our tumultuous departure and to the imagined mayhem that was taking place since we had left. In the absence of any answers, endless questions became our means of processing what had happened. How long had it taken for the FBI to break into our houses and ravage through them? Had we inadvertently left any clues as to where we were going in our frenzied race to get away? Was the FBI interrogating our bosses, our coworkers, the other parents in our birthing class, the women in my writing group? We had been deliberately vague about our lives with our acquaintances to protect ourselves and them. But even in this restricted framework we had built relationships. We were

worried that our friends were being harassed even though they had no knowledge of any of our political activities.

Well into the week, we still hadn't noticed any signs of being followed.
We struggled with ourselves not to relax our guard. The FBI was clever enough
to cloak their voyeurs. Their hired hands included women and men of different ethnic backgrounds and different ages with a wide costume repertoire. It
was crucial that we pay attention to a person's behavior and not just their looks.
During one circuitous Greyhound bus trip, the same unobtrusive guy sat behind
us on three legs of our journey. As I watched him take his seat for the third time
directly in back of me, my body tensed and I gripped Tony. Why was this guy
with his t-shirt, jeans, and face empty of discernible prejudices, taking the exact
same route if he didn't have a deliberate interest in us? In a whispered bathroom
huddle at the next stop, Karen and I decided to reverse directions to smoke him
out. He didn't follow us further, this man whom I had vested with state powers.
We knew this didn't conclusively prove anything, but we still felt like we had
done something to secure ourselves that day.

We combed the newspapers, searching for some mention of our escape,
some external confirmation that we had recognized a real threat and made the
right decision by leaving: TERRORISTS FLEE, LEAVING HOUSE FULL
OF SUSPICIOUS BATIKS AND PLANTS BEHIND or SIX ADULTS AND
BABY USE PRIMITIVE METHODS ELUDE FBI'S ELITE TEAM. But
there was nothing. Finally, we realized that the FBI had no desire to give us clues
through the press. We stopped looking, relieved that our pictures were not on
the front pages of newspapers up and down the West Coast.

———— ∞ ————

As the days passed, our worries began to mount about our friends and
lovers who were traveling their parallel paths. Each time I turned on the evening
news, a foreboding scene would pass through my mind: Claude and Donna with
handcuffs chafing, trying to look strong, passing a silent message to us across air
space—"We're okay, stay strong, send our love to Tony." To keep from crying, I
made myself envision an alternate picture: Claude and Donna, Jody and Rob all

turning on the evening news just like we were doing, worrying like we were worrying, but still miraculously free.

The closer it came to our designated meeting time, the harder it
was to believe that everything would work out as planned. Even if the worst-
case scenario hadn't occurred, there were so many other things that could go
wrong—train delays, accidents, loss of money, loss of memory, sickness, global
catastrophes, petty cataclysms. We had picked Portland as our destination point
arbitrarily. It was on the West Coast and so seemed a manageable distance from
L.A. And from afar it had an aura of calm and greenness, alternative culture and
livability that seemed to offer sanctuary. But when we walked off the plane into a
scorching, record-breaking heat wave and checked into yet another motel room
with cigarette burns on the carpets, sagging beds, and the sound of family fights
straining through the walls, it was hard to feel like we had reached our hoped for
asylum. Then I heard Karen describing in her special, matter-of-fact story voice
the various features of the room to Tony: "And here is your new crib in this great
big dresser drawer made just for you!" Seeing Tony gaze up at her with all the
trust and love he could muster at three weeks old, I realized how lucky we were
to have made it this far. And how glad I was to have someone like Karen as a
travel-sister, living through this together.

The first step, before the whole group got together, was for me to meet
Claude. By the time I left the next morning for the restaurant we had picked at
random out of a phone book, I had compressed all the uncertainties of the past
week into one question: would he be waiting for me when I got there? Claude
was always compulsively early for everything—a mandatory ten minutes early for
movies, twenty minutes early for dentist appointments, a half an hour early for
work. If he wasn't there waiting when I got to the restaurant, I knew he wouldn't
be coming. I would have to turn around and make my way back empty-handed
to the motel where Karen and Tony, watching endless hours of soap operas,
were waiting expectantly for my return.

He was there, early of course, but I almost walked right by him. He
no longer had a beard or mustache, his hair was shorn, and what was left was
slicked down with a grease that I couldn't imagine ever touching. For a moment

I was more disoriented seeing this reconstructed Claude than I would have been by his absence. Then it registered—he hadn't been arrested! He was really here and this meeting had, against all odds, worked on the first try.

We hugged, and for a little while we let stories from the past couple of weeks tumble out in no particular order: Tony's love for his newly acquired bottle, the endless hours of wandering we had all done since we last saw each other, the news that Leonard Peltier had once again been denied a new trial, our anxieties about each other and about Jody and Rob with whom we still had to hook up. Neither of us could let our layered emotions spill through the constraints of this time and place. I couldn't think, let alone say, "I've been aching with worry that you would never hold Tony again." We couldn't afford to have a waiter overhear a part of our talk which might identify us. We didn't know who the woman sitting alone at the table across from us really was, as she looked at us out of the corner of her eye. Hundreds of miles away from L.A., we still felt that we could be picked out of a crowd at any time, and that interrupted the connection between us. We cut the conversation short, making arrangements for all of us to meet later at a park away from the center of town.

Claude left first and as I watched him walking away, his feet characteristically pointing outwards, I clutched, realizing all the little things he/we had not altered about ourselves. How terrible to see all our small and often endearing idiosyncrasies as vulnerabilities for the FBI to seize upon. Did we need to put more time and energy into makeovers for each one of us? At the same time, I began to wonder what deeper-than-hair changes Claude might have gone through this past week. How was he looking at what had happened to us? What did it make him think about our future? Of course, these weren't just questions for me and Claude, but for all of us in these new circumstances. After years of doing public organizing, we had gone underground together because we believed that it was necessary at this stage of history to develop clandestine political work. Now, on the run, with little money, resources, or support, and no idea about the larger ramifications of this FBI encirclement, what could we hope to accomplish? At this critical juncture shouldn't we reexamine the ideas, the feelings, and the history that had brought us here? On the other hand, should we let one setback dismantle a commitment that had been developing for years? Should we step back, or push on?

I was startled when the waiter presented the check, panicked that he had been watching me, reading through the worry lines on my face to the content of my concerns. I left him an extra large tip and hurried to the bus stop. I couldn't wait to tell Karen and Tony that the reunion had succeeded!

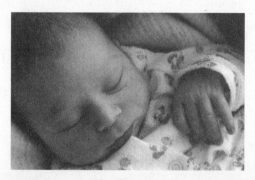

Top—Tony a day after he was born. Middle—Tony at three months.
Bottom left—Tony at his second birthday. Bottom right—Tony at a lake
in Minneapolis.

FUGITIVE DECONSTRUCTIONS

I T'S THE FOURTH OF JULY, 1985. Tony is a month-old, wizard-faced baby in a sky-blue snugli. I'm a thirty-something, face-painted mother in a Goodwill dress that is trying to look fresh off the rack at Penney's. We sit sedately together, Tony's eyes hungrily taking in lights, patterns, the shapes of smiles. My eyes are focused downward on the *Newsweek* in my lap. Its headline glares: *"TEN WAYS TO FIGHT TERRORISM."* The story continues, "Once again from Beirut to San Salvador, it was America the Vulnerable," decrying the attacks on Americans in El Salvador by the liberation forces. Reagan pledges military aid to the right-wing Salvadoran government and declares, "We must act against those who have so little regard for human life and the values we cherish."[1]

"Regard for human life," I fume, thinking of the eleven MOVE people recently killed in Philadelphia and the thousands being killed in El Salvador by paramilitary forces backed by the United States. If I could, I would write a letter to the editor of *Newsweek* that explained the absurd disjunction between Reagan's words and the reality. I begin to shape the letter, choosing the compelling examples which could convince people…

But part of my mind remains unabsorbed, and so I hear a name, "my" name, the one I constructed expressly for this trip, booming across the crowded ticket waiting area, "Sandra Hopkins, Sandra Hopkins." I try to suppress my reflexive fear, as I gather Tony up and casually approach the ticket counter.

"Ms. Hopkins," the attendant drawls and with relief I recognize tones of attentiveness and feel my hunched shoulders relax. "We just wanted to make sure since you're traveling with a baby that you have an opportunity to board before the other passengers. What a sweet baby. Is this his first flight?"

The question catches me by surprise, since it should be such a little baby's first time in the air, but in fact it's his third. "Yes, this is his first flight. We're going to see my parents. They've never seen him. They live in Minneapolis, that's where I'm from, and this is our first chance to visit." Already, I realize that I've gone too far. Suppose she asks what part of Minneapolis they live in, or what school I went to. I have glanced at a Twin Cities map but haven't yet memorized any street names. This is one of my weaknesses, elaborating stories that I can't back up, getting into the performance, the pleasurable side of lying, without doing my homework beforehand. I cut the conversation short and bustle Tony on to the plane.

In fact, all I knew about Minneapolis was that it was the place we had chosen to settle in for now. In their complicated trajectory between L.A. and Portland, Rob and Jody had taken a train to the Twin Cities, where none of us had ever been before. They found Minneapolis and St. Paul beautiful, with low rents, cheap restaurants, and abundant signs of alternative politics and culture. It was a place where we could blend in, two thousand miles away from the West Coast minefield.

With Tony slumped on my lap, I watched the clouds speed by, imagining us settling into a large, rambling house in the University neighborhood. He would have a real crib instead of the pulled out dresser drawers that we had been lining with blankets each night for his makeshift cradle. Claude and I would go to the movies. Jody and I would go for walks. Donna, Rob, and I would talk over tea in the afternoon. And we would all be able to focus on something besides getting away.

―――❦―――

It was a time of settling in. It was a time to scrutinize our every move. It was a time of building new routines. It was a time when every routine we began to build seemed threatened by the arm of the law. It was a time to enjoy Tony as he grew from infancy to babyhood. It was a time when such joy was constantly eroded by the fear of permanent loss.

Our new home wasn't large and rambling, but it was in the University neighborhood and had a large kitchen as well as two bedrooms and a walk-in closet with a window where we fit a crib for Tony. It was the first apartment we looked at and the landlord didn't require anything except the first month's rent. Our cash was dwindling and motel rooms were wearing very thin.

We tried to limit our vulnerability. We divided the seven of us between two apartments at opposite ends of town. If the people in one house were caught, those in the other might possibly get away. We took careful, circuitous routes when we all got together or visited each other's homes, we never made telephone calls directly to and from our apartments, and we definitely never discussed "significant issues" inside our houses.

Still, we managed to find ways to talk and talk about what had transpired. In parks while the weather was still warm, in walks around the sparkling lakes, in cafés and in empty classrooms at the nearby University, we desperately tried to figure out what had gone wrong and what we could possibly do differently in the future. Each of us admitted to lapses in security procedures back in L.A.—phone numbers and addresses we hadn't put in code, inattention to cars or people who could have been tails, conversations in our cars that probably were bugged. We recognized that the trip to New Orleans was the most likely security breach, but we were reluctant to accept that this was how the FBI had discovered us; because if it were, the implications were enormous.

We knew we couldn't only look at "technical" security issues but also needed to reevaluate the history and political strategy that had brought us here. We had gone underground in the early eighties, not a high-tide period for revolutionary activity in the U.S. Unlike the white people who had formed the Weather Underground Organization in the sixties,[2] we were not swept into clandestinity as a response to the Vietnam war or the militancy of the Black Panthers.[3] Instead, we were part of a small but active tendency within the movement that continued to support armed resistance within the U.S. even after the Vietnam war had ended in 1975 and the Black Panther Party had largely been destroyed by the FBI's COINTELPRO program.[4] As we saw it, armed struggle was still a necessary component of every revolutionary movement, and the

movement within the United States was not an exception. Most of the white left
had distanced themselves from the efforts of Blacks, Native Americans, Puerto
Ricans, and Chicanos to develop clandestine organization and activity, denouncing these endeavors as "ultra-left" and out of touch with the social reality of the
masses of Americans. We argued that a social reality dominated by electoral politics, unions tied to the Democratic party, white supremacy, debilitating cynicism,
and an increasing right-wing backlash had to be contested on many different
levels in order for any significant political breakthrough to occur.

The debates went on for years and in the end we had to put our theoretical commitments to the test. We owed it to the Third World forces we worked
with and to our own political integrity. And so, as Ronald Reagan embarked on
his effort to consolidate counter-revolution worldwide, we went underground.

*It would have helped if we hadn't been so polarized with those who
disagreed with us; if we hadn't been so young/arrogant/sure of our opinions even
when the uncertainties were raging inside our heads. It would have been better
if we had been able to engage our own reservations and questions about whether
clandestine organization was sustainable at this point in history or about what
types of activities were feasible at this stage of struggle. It would have been more
useful to the political debate about strategy inside the United States if we had
not laid claim to the recipe for revolution, but instead had suggested clandestine
activity as one contribution, one building block in the enormous task of taking
on the empire, which would ultimately require huge, collective leaps of strategic
and tactical imagination, the embrace of radical experimentation on all levels,
and unavoidable, enormous risks. It would have been better…but we made our
mistakes, took stock, and tried our best to carry on.*

Since we had gone underground, we had been able to develop some
concrete support mechanisms, clandestine methodology, and infrastructure.
However, even before our entrapment in Los Angeles, we were spending a
disproportionate amount of time on security procedures, and it had been difficult to preserve our connections to public political work, an integral part of our

initial conception. We wanted our activities to complement mass work for Puerto Rican independence, work against police brutality in Third World communities, work to expose and isolate the apartheid regime in South Africa. We didn't want to do disconnected actions, and we were worried about undertaking militaristic activities beyond our capacity. As time passed, we were losing our grasp on how our daily, invisible efforts to build clandestine infrastructure linked to a larger vision of revolutionary change.

We had watched as other clandestine groups were infiltrated, encircled, arrested, and imprisoned. We had escaped thus far by the skin of our teeth, but if we tried to resume even limited activity now that we were fugitives, wouldn't we too end up in prison very quickly? We cautioned each other not to be defeatist, but when we looked at the larger social picture, it was hard to find many positive signposts. Since Reagan had come into office in 1981, every type of social program that had been a result of working-class, civil rights and liberation struggle was facing systematic attack. Internationally, Reagan was gunning not only for the Nicaraguan revolution with his paramilitary contra strategy, but also was determined to eliminate the entire "communist" bloc, starting with the Soviet Union.

Given this state of affairs, what possible political work could we now undertake?

Amidst the political soul searching, our efforts to establish new identities, our work schedules and childcare schedules, and the pressing need to buy winter clothes before the looming Minneapolis winter set in, my best moments were when I quietly watched Tony lying on the floor on a blankie, voraciously claiming this mottled world with his eager eyes. He took it all in—the fading autumn sun designing recessive patterns on the wall, the hairline cracks crisscrossing the linoleum in the kitchen, and the bright rainbow colors of the mobile we had scrimped to buy. One day, I scribbled down a poem, the first one since we left L.A.

The eyes have it –
engulfing
flaming reds, purples,chartreuses
volatile dots, stripes, plaids
but also
simple surfaces
worn edges
complex cracks.
Adding, splicing
an angle here,
a curve there,
puzzle piecing together
not only
face, smile, scowl
but also
box top, dust pan, even door hinge.
Feeding his baby mind,
constructing with care
the vision
that will be his.

The scrawny, slightly jaundiced infant we had originally named Alex was now a plump, energetic baby. We needed a new name that we hoped he could keep for awhile. Juan Antonio Corretjer, the former Secretary General of the Puerto Rican Nationalist Party and renowned poet, had died six months previously in January, 1985 at the age of 77. We had met Don Juan, as his associates fondly called him, during trips he and his wife made to San Francisco in the seventies. They were an unforgettable couple—Don Juan with his black beret, large white mustache, and dignified bearing, and Doña Consuelo, a small wellspring of vitality. Both were poets, both had served time in prison for their passionate support of Puerto Rican independence, and both were still obviously in love after decades of marriage. Alex was rechristened Tony in Juan Antonio's honor, and he stubbornly held on to this name.

In a stroke of luck, we found a progressive day care center a short walk from our house which happened to have an opening for an infant. The center was bright, the walls were covered with fabrics from Africa and Indonesia, and it was home to children of many different races. The staff was friendly and knowledgeable and reflected the nationalities of the children they cared for. Although this daycare center definitely stretched our budget, we all agreed that it was worth it. Mornings, when I dropped Tony off before going to work at my unappealing new job at a nearby plasma center, I felt like things were definitely moving forward, at least for him. When I picked Tony up from the Center and walked the seven blocks to our apartment in the below-zero weather, I could ignore the fact that my hands were turning numb, even with gloves on, by thinking about the glowing, detailed notes that Tony's teacher had given me about the exciting things he had done that day. Or I would ponder the casual way another teacher told me that her church was giving Salvadoran refugees political sanctuary and asked if I wanted to bring by some canned food as a way of supporting them.

As we found jobs and began to know other people in Minneapolis, we were constantly reevaluating our security measures, urging one another not to become complacent just because it felt like we were safe. At one of our weekly meetings, the six of us were rehashing the security mistakes other groups had made in the past, when someone mentioned an article they had recently read about the search for the Ohio 7, a clandestine anti-imperialist group.[5] The FBI had posted the adults' wanted pictures in daycare centers up and down the East coast because they knew they had small children.

Before anyone could say anything more, I froze. "Maybe it's politically correct to take Tony out of the daycare center," I snapped defensively, "but we have to think of him also. He's moved so many times already in his short life and he's just started feeling comfortable there, and we can't put security above everything, and…"

A chorus of voices told me to back off, calm down, and try and look at things more objectively. I tried to listen to the reasoned arguments others were

presenting: "This is about Tony's safety. If we get caught what will happen to
him?" "What about the teacher at the daycare center who is involved with the
Sanctuary movement? That could be a source of heat." "We could find a daycare
home that would be much less risky." "Remember how the FBI interrogated
the children of the Ohio 7 about the activities of their parents after they were
arrested. They stop at nothing!"

I struggled to contain my tears. The specter of the FBI using Tony
against us was so cruel, yet it was exactly what we could expect. Someday Tony
could easily be vulnerable to this type of abuse. Yet, how could we know what
would really jeopardize us and him? "Let me think about it," I finally said to the
group, and everyone was happy to leave this particular battle for the time being
and move on to something else.

For the next couple of days, I went over and over the problem. Every
time I was at the point of saying yes, I would relapse into tears and anger. I didn't
want to feel pressured into accepting something I had reservations about. When
I had decided to go underground, I was wracked with indecision for months.
In meetings, I would embrace our political logic and vision, but when I thought
about giving up my life, my lover, my job, and my plans for the future, I was
thrown into turmoil. The final decision was mine, but it was also inextricably
bound up with the collective dynamic of the group.

In the months since our escape, our lives were more enmeshed than
ever before. At the same time, we each had a greater need to think things through
independently. The question of Tony's childcare had simply crystallized this
contradiction for me.

A few weeks before, I had bought a used copy of Margaret Randall's
Sandino's Daughters, which I had read once before. [6] In my search for a spiritual compass, I sometimes used books like many people used the Bible. So now
I opened up *Sandino's Daughters*, looking for a framework to help me work
through my painful dilemma.

I leafed through the pages, struck by the pictures of the Nicaraguan
women. Some looked like women I could have known, and they had in fact
studied in the United States and lived as urban intellectuals before deciding to

become full-time revolutionaries. While much of our experience was vastly different, we were also peers, having come of age and into political consciousness during the same historical epoch.

I reread the story of Nora Astorga who had lured a murderous Somocista General, Perez Vega, to her house where other members of the FSLN (Frente Sandinista de Liberación Nacional) then executed him. Nora's role in this action, which took place on March 8, 1978, International Women's Day, had made headlines worldwide and had inspired me and many other women around the world. Now, Nora's observations about her two daughters had a special resonance: "It may seem ironic, but part of my decision was precisely because of my children. I believed that by doing my part I would be helping to bring about a better world for them and other children like them."[7] She went on to talk about how her older daughter, age six, had resented the fact that Nora went underground after Vega's execution. Nora described the difficulties in their relationship honestly as one of the most difficult prices she paid for her revolutionary commitment.

Sandino's Daughters didn't offer a simple answer to my own contradictions, but it pushed them towards resolution. I was losing patience with my own vacillations, drama, and self-pity. I was elevating this small issue about Tony's daycare to the level of principle, and turning my frustrations on the others in our small, besieged collective.

I agreed to the change, and we all began looking for a daycare home which would be less accessible to an FBI sweep. Within a few weeks, we found a place run by an interesting woman who had a daughter of her own, just a few months older than Tony. We soon became friends with her entire family. Even in our overcast circumstances, it was possible to find a silver lining. I just had to be open enough to look for it.

—⸙—

Throughout the fall of 1985, the newspapers seemed to yield nothing but bad news. In the beginning of September, eleven Puerto Ricans, associated

with Los Macheteros were arrested in connection with a $7 million expropria-
tion from a Wells Fargo bank in Hartford, Connecticut.[8] In 1983, when this
unprecedented expropriation had occurred, we had seen it as a sign of the growing capacity of the Puerto Rican clandestine movement. The capture of these
independentistas, including long time leaders Filiberto Ojeda Rios and Juan
Segarra Palmer, was one more indication that the movement was suffering.

Then in February, 1986, two international upheavals gave us new hope.
On February 7, 1986, a popular movement in Haiti overthrew Jean Claude
"Baby Doc" Duvalier, forcing him to flee the country aboard a U.S. Air Force jet.
This ended the dictatorship of the Duvalier family which had been tormenting
Haiti with U.S. backing since 1957.[9] Just a couple of weeks later, on February
25, Ferdinand Marcos who had ruled the Phillipines for twenty years on behalf
of the U.S., snuck out the back door of the Malacañang Palace, fleeing a popular
democratic movement that had been building for decades.[10]

It was thrilling to watch the story unfold on the news and to hear
Reagan, who had been one of Marcos' key backers, call upon him to resign. We
realized the situation was very complicated and wished that we could discuss the
revolutionary potential of the moment with radical Filipinos we had known in
the Bay Area. I also wished I could share my happiness about Marcos' departure with a Filipina nurse I had worked with in L.A. Her name was Imelda,
just like the infamous first lady of the Phillipines, Imelda Marcos. "My name is
held hostage by the *Dragon Lady,*" Imelda confided in me. "She and her ugly
husband bring nothing but misery to my friends, my family, and my whole
country. No one will be safe until they are gone." As soon as the words were out
of her mouth, Imelda swerved around to see if anyone could have overheard our
conversation. "Marcos has trained spies everywhere," she explained in a nervous
whisper.

Now that Marcos had fled, I wanted so much to call Imelda and
celebrate. Instead I wrote her a letter that she would never see. It began: "The
Dragon Lady is gone, my friend. You can reclaim your name."

⋙⋘

Karen and Jody moved to St Louis. After a year in Minneapolis, we all felt the need to branch out. We decided it would be better for our collective security if we weren't all living in the same city, and besides it would be positive to explore new areas to evaluate their potential for political work. I was sad to see Karen and Jody go, but I trusted that we would preserve our political relationship and friendship, perhaps more so when there was some distance between us all.

A few weeks after Jody and Karen moved, on July 4, 1986, we read a short but chilling article buried on the sixth page of the *New York Times*. Three Puerto Ricans, whom the government claimed were part of the FALN, had been arrested in Chicago for being part of a plot to free *independentista* Oscar Lopez from the federal prison at Leavenworth, Kansas.[11] The article also mentioned that warrants had been issued for six unnamed others. It wasn't hard to guess who those warrants were for.

The next day, more details emerged that threw us into deeper tumult. According to these stories, a 1985 plot to free Oscar Lopez from prison had, from the beginning, involved undercover FBI agents and prisoner informants. FBI agents had sold Donna and Claude phony explosives in New Orleans and then followed them back to Los Angeles. Now they were named in the indictment along with the three arrested Puerto Ricans. The rest of us were being sought as material witnesses.

A year after we left L.A., we finally had printed proof that the surveillance we had detected was real and in direct connection to the New Orleans trip, validating our suspicions and our precipitous departure. But the picture was much worse than we had imagined. Three Puerto Ricans were now in jail, informers and government agents had worked their way into the *independentista* movement, and rather than sinking into dormancy, our case was now generating attention in media across the country. Why had the Government waited so long to make these arrests or put warrants out for us when they must have had all the necessary information the year before, when our trail was still hot? Our most convincing theory was that the FBI had been caught off guard by our quick flight from L.A. and they were hoping that we would slip up in our panicked exit and lead them to others. A year later, they finally decided to arrest those that they could. [12]

In a rushed, tense visit with Karen and Jody, who had barely settled into a small apartment in St. Louis, we reviewed our situation, trying to evaluate what, if anything, we should do in response to this news. Struggling to keep panic at bay, we decided that proceeding with our lives as we had constructed them so far was the best, indeed the only thing, we could do.

Our lives settled into a routine rhythm. We bought a car. I found a new job as a secretary at a non-profit agency, took up the guitar for the first time, and went to aerobics classes in my lunch break. Tony developed a fascination with buses, trucks, and anything that moved. I made a friend with one of the program coordinators at the agency where I worked. Our friendship centered on a shared love of "ethnic" cuisine and foreign movies, the attention I gave to her search for "Mr. Right," and her interest in my stories about Tony. But when I tried to open up conversations about the contra war in Nicaragua or the budding sanctuary movement in the Twin Cities, I could see her eyes glaze over, so I would switch to funny tales about Tony's latest tricks.

Our second spring in Minneapolis was breathtaking after the winter's deep freeze. One weekend, Claude and I drove to Wisconsin, leaving Tony with Donna and Rob. Our day-to-day conflicts over small child-rearing issues often mushroomed into tense fights about politics and our plans for the future. We badly needed time away to just be together. After a relaxing Saturday, we were planning to spend our Sunday morning like thousands of others around the country, reading about difficult but distant events in the *New York Times*. A few minutes into his read of the first section, Claude shoved the paper over to me, pointing to a small article. Claude and Donna had just been placed on the FBI's "Ten Most Wanted" list.

I felt dizzy with panic. One minute we were ordinary folks enjoying a reclusive weekend, and the next we were most wanted fugitives, spotlighted all over the country. I could feel eyes on us everywhere, although for the moment nothing had really changed.

In some ways the lack of any explanation for this sudden alteration in our status was the most disorienting part of this news. It was two years since we had left Los Angeles; did the FBI keep an anniversary calendar so that each summer they could up the ante as payback for slipping out of their grasp on June 11, 1985? This designation meant that something must have happened, but what could it be? Was it a development in the Puerto Rican movement, or something more internal to the dynamics of the FBI that made them want to "front burner" this case now?

We cut our trip short and got back to Minneapolis only to find a crisis brewing at Claude's job. He had been working for a year and a half at a home improvement store, where he had quickly worked his way up from retail clerk to manager of sales. Claude had a gift for selling, listening attentively to what customers wanted and enticing people with his ample knowledge of the comparative features of many items, making a perfect match between customer and product. His forte was hot tubs, a big money item, and he easily had outsold all the other salespeople for the last six months, earning hundreds in commissions and a promotion to the manager position. The crisis was not, however, about hot tubs but about a large amount of money that had been missing from the cash register several days in a row during the last week. There was no particular suspicion on Claude, but a major investigation was underway, and everyone who handled money would have to undergo a police detective interview and a lie detector test.

The four of us were hysterical imagining a lie detector test where a baseline answer to "what's your name?" would send the needle skyrocketing into the falsehood ozone. After reading up on lie detectors in the library, we discarded that particular worry and focused on the more insoluble problem. Claude would have to face a Minneapolis police detective at the very moment he had become one of the FBI's most wanted. We discussed leaving Minneapolis immediately with a story of deathly family illness, but that course of action would only signal that we were people who should be investigated further.

Still, we packed our bags before the police interview. It was held in a suburban detective office close to a mall. After I dropped Claude off, I went to wander through the mall. Over the past couple of years, I had developed a disturbing interest in shopping. I found myself looking forward to weekend expeditions to buy sheets, toddler clothes, or a new shirt for myself. The thought that my life could unfold as an endless series of mall excursions made me queasy. I sat down amidst the plastic plants and tried to read the South African novel I had brought with me.

After a couple of hours, I went to stand by a narrow window overlooking the parking lot and began to watch for Claude. When he emerged, the relief on his face was visible even from the window. He thought the lie detector test had gone smoothly, and by the end of the interview the detectives had dropped their formal approach and had become positively chatty.

The next day at Claude's job, they announced they now knew "whodunit." That night we took the opportunity to celebrate with a bottle of champagne, turning up Bob Marley, and dancing around the room with Tony. He never questioned what had caused this uncharacteristic spirit of release among the four adults in his life who usually spent their time enveloped in talk, talk, talk whenever they were all together.

Our relief was short-lived. We began to receive warning letters from the Social Security Administration about problems with our social security numbers. Then we read in the local papers that a grand jury had been convened in Minneapolis to investigate leftist connections to the clandestine Puerto Rican independence movement. The thought of uprooting and starting all over again was daunting, but the Twin Cities no longer offered the neutral space we needed. For the next few weeks we debated where to go. After a quick trip to compare Cleveland and Pittsburgh, we chose Pittsburgh which the year before had been voted America's "most livable city" in a magazine poll. While this designation seemed rather over-blown, Pittsburgh did have diverse neighborhoods, cheap rents, a relatively good transportation system, and two major universities. And we didn't think that it had much connection to the Puerto Rican independence movement.

Our first two weeks in Pittsburgh, it rained every single day. We hadn't realized that Pittsburgh also had the distinction of being the second wettest city

in the country, right after Seattle. As I unpacked our boxes in the humid damp-
ness, feeling disoriented, isolated, and depressed, my thoughts kept sliding back
to my move fifteen years before, from New York City to San Francisco. It had
been a time of great opening and expectation in my life. It had been a time that
set in motion all the changes that had now brought me, strangely enough, to
Pittsburgh.

March in support of Inez Garcia's freedom in downtown San Francisco, 1974. Diana is holding the bullhorn and Karen is on the far right front holding a sign. Photo by Cathy Cade, www.cathycade.com.

New World Coming

There's a new world coming
and it's just around the bend,
there's a new world coming,
this one's coming to an end.

—Nina Simone [1]

MY FIRST VISIT TO SAN FRANCISCO was on my way back from Mexico in 1971. I was following a common youth travel trajectory that spanned the continent and crossed borders in the quest to stretch personal boundaries. I was hesitant about including San Francisco in my trip because hippie-flowerchild hype was not my style, but I couldn't help but be curious about the many enthusiastic stories which other travelers had told me. After just a couple of days, I felt my carefully honed New York cynicism dropping away. The brilliance of the sun burning through the fog, the multicolored, eccentrically shaped houses, the burgundy bougainvilleas which cascaded with abandon down staircases and across door fronts, the breathtaking dynamic of hills and valleys that reflected an even more dramatic energy below the earth's surface, and the Pacific ocean which was so preciously close—all this converged in what I couldn't help feeling was geographic near-perfection after growing up amidst the towering, aging skyscrapers of Manhattan's Upper West Side which cut off the light and laid claim to all the space.

Then there were the hundreds of posters which lined the streets of the Mission district where I was staying with a friend, announcing political happenings of every sort—anti-war rallies, the San Francisco Mime Troupe, women's self-help health groups, support rallies for the Soledad Brothers—an enormous array of activities that all seemed to fit together to create the kind of political community that I longed to be part of. In New York, political posters were stuck up sporadically and dwarfed by their inhospitable surroundings, but in San Francisco the posters declared that something radically different was possible.

Intellectually, I knew that beneath the surface of San Francisco lay the same fault lines of poverty, racism, sexism, and violence that shaped the life of every urban area in the country. But in my journey around this city, I couldn't stop the new Nina Simone song from racing through my head *"there's a new world coming and it's just around the bend, there's a new world coming, this one's coming to an end...."*

I had never been an impulsive person, but within the first week I decided I had to move. I was slightly embarrassed when I called David, my boyfriend back in New York who wore his leftist-tinged skepticism like a badge of honor. I tried to explain that this wasn't just a California dreaming fantasy, but was about finding the type of collective political community we had both been talking about for the year we had been together. Although David responded with characteristic disparaging humor, I could tell that he believed that something real was sparking this new exuberance in me. Besides, we were in love and we wanted to pursue our dreams together.

It took another year for us to make the break with New York. A few weeks after I returned from my trip, George Jackson was murdered at San Quentin prison, thirteen miles away from San Francisco. I had read *Soledad Brother* the year before and had been gripped by all that George Jackson had to say about what it was like to be a young Black man growing up in America's ghettos, which funneled increasing numbers of youth directly into prison. In his book, George had written *"I know that they will not be satisfied until they've pushed me out of this existence altogether."*[2] And then, on August 21, 1971, he was killed.

George's assassination shook me deeply, especially because I had just been in San Francisco, a few miles from San Quentin, and yet I had been oblivious to that other murderously repressive side of California that co-existed with the culture of excitement and possibility that had been so seductive to me. George's death made me question my motives for wanting to move. Maybe it was just an escapist fantasy to want to get away from the aching contradictions of life in New York—family drama, constant street hassles, competition for everything, old ruts and cliques which, after twenty-two years, felt suffocating. I had started to become involved with different political groups in New York, but at the end of each meeting people went back to their separate apartments and separate lives. I yearned for something different. So, despite vaguely guilty feelings, David and I decided to leave. There was no harm in exploring. We could always move back.

In summer 1972, we drove cross-country with our belongings jumbled in the back of a drive-away. Within a week after reaching San Francisco, we found a room the two of us could share for $50 a month in a household of women and men in Bernal Heights. We started martial arts classes together. I began working part-time as a teacher's aide and David got a job as an aide in a residential treatment center. I joined a women's self-help health group and we both looked at the Liberation School catalogue to find ways to connect with other people politically.

I could feel the weight of skyscrapers lifting, I could sense the unraveling of years of embedded self-censorship and cynicism. I was opening up to radical possibility on all levels, resonating with the energy of the city and the thousands of other young people who had moved to the Bay Area to push their limits. The women's movement vision—the personal is political—had aroused my political consciousness a few years before. Now I wanted to build on that vision to be part of a movement that linked personal and social transformation, that put George Jackson, women's liberation, gay liberation, and Vietnam all together. I wasn't sure exactly what that meant, but I was determined to figure it out.

I put out a call in a Liberation School catalogue for women who were interested in starting an anti-rape group. A few months later the group that came together founded San Francisco Women Against Rape.

*Looking back at that move to San Francisco, I remember a whirlwind
of experience and emotion, an amazing period when my life and those of many
people around me changed irrevocably. The memories are infused with nostalgia,
a longing for the seventies and my twenties, when the youthful expectations that
I had were reflected in a movement belief that we could create revolution, a new
world, in our lifetime. But if I dig beyond the nostalgic, panoramic view, coupled
with the exhilaration, I remember the difficult, concentrated work we had to do
to map out new realms of political activity; the alternately thrilling and wracking emotions involved in dozens of new relationships; and the critical, wrenching
choices we each ended up making.*

The women who came to the first meeting of the anti-rape group that
was to become San Francisco Women Against Rape had a variety of political
backgrounds and motivations for answering an announcement about an issue
which, at that time, was still at the outer radical edges of the women's movement. Several of them had been in consciousness-raising groups, a few were
self-identified as lesbians, one had been part of SDS and considered herself a
socialist. All of them had experienced some type of sexual assault in their lives—
date rape, stranger rape, husband rape, child rape—the terminology naming
these distinct aspects of this widespread experience had not yet been developed.

My own involvement had begun a couple of years before with New
York Radical Feminists, the first political group I had ever been involved with.
At one of the first meetings I attended, Susan Brownmiller presented her
groundbreaking theory that rape was a politically constructed, deliberately controlling patriarchal act.[3] Initially, I rejected the analysis as an overstated interpretation that didn't coincide with my perception of rape as an individual violent
sexual act. But as I turned the idea over, I kept coming back to an incident
which I had pushed back into the recesses of my memory for years.

When I was eleven, a man had sexually assaulted me and my sister in
our apartment building stairwell, holding a knife to my sister and ordering me
to pull up my dress. Instead of complying, I started screaming and pushed my

sister out of his reach. Startled, he ran down the stairs while I, my sister and assorted neighbors all ran after him. He disappeared into the cavities of the Upper West Side and my sister and I returned to the seeming safety of our fourth-floor apartment, physically untouched but shell-shocked. That evening, my mother didn't applaud me for having resisted assault and averted danger. Instead, she scolded me for wearing such a tight belt on my dress since it obviously emphasized my hips and attracted men. I argued with her, but she had planted a seed of doubt and guilt. I put the belt away in my closet and never wore that dress again.

Thinking about that buried experience, Susan Brownmiller's theory began to make sense. It wasn't only one childhood incident, but the accumulated experience of daily catcalls, come-ons, and near assaults that I had been contending with since I was eleven. When I finally went to sleep that night, my dreams were punctuated with scenes of sleazy and aggressive seduction. By morning, it all clicked: understanding rape was pivotal to exposing the totality of sexism's operation in our society. A few months later, in January 1971, I testified at the first Rape Speak Out in the country organized by NY Radical Feminists. [4] Soon after that, I joined the newly formed New York Women Against Rape.

When I moved to San Francisco, I wanted to continue to do anti-rape work, but I wanted to go beyond a narrow feminist framework. From the beginning, the San Francisco group was determined to integrate our analysis of the patriarchal function of rape with our developing understanding of race and class in the U.S. There were few models for us to draw upon, so we had to hammer out our own.

Laurie had been at the University of Wisconsin and came with tales of SDS and the fractious split into Weatherman, a group of which she vociferously disapproved. She had been groped and mauled by countless leftist men before she found an anti-sexist man who was now her boyfriend. She was also attracted to women and was in the process of figuring out whether she was a lesbian or not. She brought her first tentative girlfriend, Marianne, to the first meeting of the group.

Marianne was a beautiful, thoughtful redhead who had been raped during high school by a man she was dating. She was only now beginning to process politically and emotionally what that rape had meant to her during the last six years.

Gina had moved to San Francisco from a small town in Wyoming where her Catholic family struggled to make ends meet. One day, she had overheard her mother telling her father about how her boss had assaulted her, and listened in horror while her father cautioned her mother to put the incident aside in order to keep the job. Gina was filled with simmering anger at the dominance of middle-class women in the women's movement, who arrogantly ignored class differences, unwilling to recognize that for working-class and poor women sexism was compounded by problems of poverty.

Kathleen had been a champion swimmer in her Virginia high school. When she had been raped after school one night and called the police to report it, the gossip at her high school implied that somehow this was just desserts for her independence and athleticism. Now she was fierce about the need for women to be trained in self-defense.

Then there was Jacqueline, who was one of my new roommates. Jacqueline was observant and witty and the poem she had written about her sexual assault at the hands of her favorite uncle brought me to tears. Jacqueline had been in a relationship with a Black man for a couple of years in college. She didn't want us, a group of white women, to play into the racist myths and lies that had framed Black men as rapists since the end of slavery and had more often than not resulted in lynchings, life-term prison sentences, or the death penalty.[5]

Celine was my friend since junior high school who had moved to San Francisco a few months after I did. In New York, we'd been in a Marxist study group together. Celine was the person I often talked to after the meetings and the retreats, making fun of Laurie's continual boasting and grappling with Gina's challenges to middle-class women.

These are the women I remember best, the core of the group. We forged our vision in meetings in each other's houses, in women's bars that were springing up all around the city, and on weekend retreats to Mount Tamalpais, where we hiked and sang and fought with each other but ended up, for that time period, as a cohesive group. Our words from that period have a bulldozing tone, but still largely ring true to me today:

> The fear of rape touches every woman—working class, middle class, and across racial lines. Men in society have a stake in perpetuating rape—aggressive sexuality keeps women dependent on men in the home and family, and limits the types of jobs women can take. The act of rape and the myths about rape are part of the social structure of this country. The myths that are perpetuated about rape help reinforce the racism and classism of the society. Police, laws, and courts all have been set up to serve the ruling men in power in the country, so it doesn't make sense to put a lot of energy into reforming them, we need to come up with community alternatives.[6]

We developed a three-pronged program to embody the different aspects of what we thought needed to be done. Our first priority was to set up an actual physical space, a protective center where we could house a rape crisis hotline and which could serve as a temporary shelter for women needing to get away from aggressive situations. Unless we could offer support to real women experiencing violence, our theoretical efforts to fight rape would be empty and ungrounded.

At the same time, we believed that education was crucial. We didn't want to merely help women after-the-fact; we wanted to prevent rape by educating about the embedded male supremacist attitudes and structures which supported rape in the society. Through education, women would raise their consciousness and become empowered to develop collective strategies for ending rape.

Finally, we envisioned community self-defense as a militant, collective alternative to reliance on the police. This meant everything from escort services where women would accompany other women from BART and bus stops late at night, to teams of women who would plaster the neighborhoods with pictures of men who had been identified as rapists (husbands, boyfriends, or acquaintances) in an effort to shame the men and warn other women.

The education part was the easiest. We reached out to college class-rooms, radio programs, and held community meetings to analyze and discuss this long secret but now publicly emerging issue. The response was overwhelmingly positive. What we said clicked with many women's experiences and soon we had many new volunteers eager to join the group.

Setting up a rape center was more challenging. We each committed a sizable amount from the salaries of our part-time jobs but still we didn't have enough to pay for rent, security deposit, and a phone for our center. The recently formed Vanguard Fund came to the rescue with an enormous $5,000 for seed money.

We found a small funky apartment in the Mission District. We told the landlord we were starting a secretarial service to cover the fact that many women would be coming in and out. We didn't dare admit our real purpose for fear he wouldn't rent to us. Besides, the secretive aspect connected with our sense that we were setting up a truly radical, alternative space.

We did admit to the phone company that we were setting up a rape hotline, however; we wanted our phone number to have the letters R-A-P-E in it. Once we started advertising our 647-RAPE number in free papers and on bulletin boards around the city, we quickly began to get a steady stream of calls. We were jubilant at first, but soon the reality of what we had undertaken began to hit us. We had committed ourselves to staffing not only a hotline but a shelter when necessary. None of us had formal training as counselors—we had believed that our political consciousness and empathy would be enough to carry us through. However, the women who were calling were usually in a state of great upheaval. Some had been subject to years of abuse, which had taken their toll on their physical and mental health. None of our members spoke Spanish, yet we were getting lots of calls from women who lived in the majority Latino Mission district.

Then there was the problem of our relationship with the police. We had to come up with a way to balance a woman's right to determine her own options with our own political distaste for the police as the enforcement arm of a system we abhorred. We decided to explain what a woman's options were and, if she decided to go to the police, we would accompany her in order to assure that she was correctly treated. Many women ended up choosing this option and inevitably this drew us into dealing more and more with the police. Since male officers were usually the ones to do the initial police interview of rape victims, we demanded that the police department form a special unit of women officers to deal with women who had been raped. The local precinct was cautiously open to our requests, and so we were drawn into extended negotiations, and inevitable compromises, about what the policies guiding this new unit should be.

As SF WAR grew rapidly, our on-paper unity began to fray. Women who had joined saying they were in agreement with our analysis of the racist and sexist function of the police were now arguing that we had to work with them in order to improve the conditions women faced after having been raped. Many of us original members felt ourselves being sucked into a type of direct service work that not only placed the police at its center, it also left little time and energy for the education or community defense aspects of our program.

As we were trying to sort out our various priorities, a case emerged that crystallized the contradictions among us. In 1974, Inez Garcia, a Chicana woman, was charged with killing a man who held her down while his friend raped her. In response, Third World women, the radical lesbian community, and a feminist lawyer, Susan Jordan, rallied to Inez's support. The issues seemed clear cut to me. A Latina woman was being threatened with a long prison sentence because she had defended herself against rape. She was being targeted because of her race, her class, and her assertion of her right to self-defense.[7]

Her case encapsulated all the principles that SF WAR claimed to espouse and it seemed logical to me that SF WAR would join the mobilization for Inez. However, many members were now engrossed in the task of providing services to rape victims and were reluctant to take on another issue. Others feared that involvement with Inez's case would jeopardize the fragile working relationship that was being built with the police, which could directly help the women who called us for support. Others said they agreed with supporting Inez, but never came to any of the meetings or rallies that were being organized.

The debates we were having in SF WAR mirrored those brewing in the anti-rape movement nationally. In 1975, Susan Brownmiller published, "Against Our Will: Men, Women, And Rape" which received much acclaim ranging from the New York Times *to* Ms. Magazine, *but was vehemently critiqued by women of color and some white anti-racist feminists. They sharply disagreed with the way that Brownmiller justified the racist use of the rape charge against Black men and deplored her advocacy of law enforcement as the key to fighting rape.[8]*

In SF WAR, our disagreements about Inez overlapped with other disagreements that had begun to polarize the group. We argued about the relationship of direct service to women who had been raped versus the need to organize a more militant self-defense network. We disagreed about whether SF WAR should join the new socialist-feminist women's union or whether an association with such an organization would turn off women who were not leftists. And we debated whether we should focus exclusively on anti-rape work or also involve ourselves with community coalitions to fight police brutality and end the war. Our personal relationships grew more and more tangled, charged, and tense. The original energy of collective purpose had evaporated.

In 2003, SF WAR held a 30th anniversary event which several of us founding members attended. Having been out of touch with each other for years, it was wonderful to come together again for this memorable occasion. Afterwards, four of us got together to reminisce. We all remembered the emotional meeting in early 1975 when the majority of the original group decided to leave the organization. I remembered the political struggles and the feeling that I couldn't continue to compromise my politics by belonging to a group that was working with the police. Gina remembered that everyone had wanted to move on with their lives either to new, more exciting political activities or to school and full-time jobs. Celine remembered how overwhelming and difficult the work of the hotline had become—

none of us knew or wanted to figure out how to keep up with the demands of a full fledged rape crisis center. And Marianne remembered the newer women who along with her had committed themselves to figuring out how to be a transition group that could be a bridge between the original core and a new grouping that could carry on the work.

It jolted me to realize how oblivious I had been back then to the group of women who had pledged themselves to continue SF WAR. I was losing patience with the approach of feminists who could not identify with other critical political issues—I wanted women's liberation work to be integrated into the breadth of left movement. The different approaches seemed irreconcilably polarized to me, and consequently I didn't see any value in maintaining my connections to the group.

Over the next twenty years, immersed in other political struggles, I hardly even thought back on the significance of the experience or wondered what had happened to SF WAR.

It wasn't until I returned to the Bay Area in the nineties that I learned that SF WAR had gone through various metamorphoses and had survived many upheavals. It was now self-consciously led by women of color and, unlike many other rape crisis centers across the country, it was committed to racial justice as a fundamental principle. The organization continued to grapple with some of the same contradictions we had confronted decades before. Thirty years later, I could take pride in the political foundations we had originally laid out and respect the creative methods that a new generation was undertaking to advance a radical vision of anti-rape work in another era.[9]

When David and I were looking for a home in San Francisco, the first ad we answered led us to a bright yellow house on Eugenia St., a hilly block at the foot of Bernal Heights. Jacqueline answered the door and I was immediately attracted by her long tangled dark hair and her friendly, matter-of-fact manner. She was living with her best friend Sarah and Sarah's boyfriend, and they needed to rent out the secluded room in the back of the house. Sarah and Josh were a little hesitant, but Jacqueline insisted that David and I were perfect for the room because of our similar political interests and some other indescribable copasetic qualities.

As soon as we moved in, Jacqueline and I began to spend hours on end in her room talking in the evenings while David was out working late shifts in a residential treatment center. Our talk was free form and wide ranging—about books, poetry, childhood, and sexual politics, with a heavy emphasis on sexual politics. Once we began working in SF WAR together, we added a running analysis of what was going on in the group to our nightly discussions.

From the moment that SF WAR started, the political dynamic among the women in the group was electrified by our collective probing of our sexual identities. Some of the women in the group were already out as lesbians and the rest were actively questioning, a common situation among radical feminists at the time. The argument that women loving women was the only real way to break with patriarchy and the constraining privileges of heterosexuality pushed every woman who was committed to the fight for complete liberation to examine her own ties to men.

Jacqueline and I both agreed theoretically—being in a heterosexual relationship inevitably involved divided loyalties and compromises that eroded women's solidarity. We told each other stories from our past which indicated our lesbian tendencies. I described my sleepover dates with Ginger, my friend in elementary school, when we would "pretend" to be having sex with our first boyfriend by rubbing our bodies together for exquisite hours on end. And I told her about my seventh grade crush, Ronnie, and how I ardently hoped her hand would brush up against mine when we did homework together. In turn, Jacqueline shared memories of her inseparable best friend in high school and her lack of enthusiasm for sex with a variety of boyfriends. Jacqueline had broken up with her last boyfriend a year before and didn't seem to be looking for another.

One evening, as Jacqueline and I were dissecting the complicated undercurrents going on in SF WAR, she sat up abruptly and asked me in a stilted voice if I would consider sleeping with her. I was startled, not because the possibility had never occurred to me, but because the question was so direct, without any of the romantic trappings that I had come to expect leading up to sex. I liked Jacqueline a lot, maybe even loved her, yet I didn't feel the hot spark which I was used to feeling when I was interested in a man. But maybe that was because I was brainwashed by a Hollywood-defined, romantic model of sexual relationships. Or maybe it was because the bedroom where David and I made love most nights was right down the hall.

"I don't know… I need some time to think about it," I answered lamely as I began to pick at my thumbs, a habit that Jacqueline had noted was a sure gauge of my stress level in our SF WAR meetings.

In the following weeks, I pored over my history, trying to sift out what was real and positive about my relationships with men from what were culturally ordained responses. In many ways, I felt like I was betraying feminist principles by being with David, but I wasn't ready to give him up. When David and I moved to San Francisco together, we had both agreed that we both wanted to be open to exploration on every level. I quickly became immersed in the women's movement, while David was having a harder time finding his place in the San Francisco political scene. He now seemed to be more dependent than ever and demanding of my time.

One evening, Jacqueline and I went to a poetry event at the Metropolitan Community Church in Noe Valley where lesbian poets Judy Grahn and Pat Parker were reading. I was thrilled by the poems and by the intense chemistry between the two of them. Judy read her poem "Carol, in the park, chewing on straws" (from *The Common Woman* series), and for the next few days her words echoed through my head:

> *She has take a woman lover*
> *whatever shall we do*
> *she has taken a woman lover*
> *how lucky it wasn't you…*

She walks around all day
quietly, but underneath it
she's electric;
angry energy inside a passive form.
the common woman is as common
as a thunderstorm. [10]

I couldn't continue walking around all day quietly with all of these conflicting feelings bursting within me. I told David that I wanted to sleep with Jacqueline though I still cared for him. David was shaken, but said he wanted to support me in figuring out my sexual identity. Jacqueline agreed that this needed to be a gradual process. And so, for a time, I was sleeping with both of them.

After all the months of talking and discussing, it was a relief to be with Jacqueline, to be exploring another woman's body, to be interspersing hours of talk with actual touch. Both of us felt good that our politics and our personal lives were now more integrated, and it was satisfying to be able to sit next to each other at meetings and brush our hands or exchange a quick kiss. Yet well after the first couple of months, the sex still felt awkward and strained, and for me the flare of love was missing.

I was growing more distant from David, but more distant from Jacqueline too. Jacqueline and David were both jealous of each other, I was disliking sex with both of them, and I was tormented by my conflicting ideas and feelings about whether I was or wasn't a lesbian.

In June of 1973, Jacqueline and I, along with several other women from SF WAR and hundreds of women from the Bay Area, drove down to Los Angeles for the first West Coast Lesbian Conference, held at UCLA. The energy among the two thousand women who participated was immense, and the disagreements were furious— ranging from the definition of lesbianism to the lack of childcare. My very first memory of Karen (who later was part of our underground collective) was when she took the mike at the conference and berated the organizers for not providing childcare and implicitly equating motherhood with patriarchal cooptation. I was impressed by her willingness to publicly challenge this disturbing but prevalent bias, and afterwards I went over and thanked Karen for her comments. I was happy to discover that Karen, her girlfriend Jody and another friend, Lynne, lived together in Bernal Heights, not far from me. The three of them explained that together they were parenting a girl whose mother wasn't able to take care of her. This was an unusual arrangement in those days, and they were adamant that lesbians needed to create new types of families and parenting structures. What's more, they expected other lesbians to support them!

Stimulating debates occurred in all of the Conference workshops about patriarchy, heterosexist privilege, class, and race, but I felt buffeted by the attacks on women who could not fully commit to being lesbians. Robin Morgan,[11] a prominent feminist author, was sharply criticized for living with a man and considering herself bisexual. Bisexuality was seen as a cover for playing both sides of the fence and being unwilling to give up men once and for all.

By the time the major political crisis of the conference occurred, I was feeling unsure and disoriented about everything. A transgender woman (male to female) had been invited to play the guitar at a conference plenary. When one group of lesbians discovered that she was "transsexual" (sic), they stormed the stage and demanded that she leave the conference. This debate split the conference, but in the end the transgender woman was asked to leave.[12] It was difficult to regain the high energy and feeling of togetherness after this incident.[13] I was not comfortable with the absolute designations about who was a real lesbian and who was not, but I was too unsure about my own identity to take a side.

After the conference, I broke up with both Jacqueline and David. Non-monogamy might work for others, but it was too emotionally draining for me. The sexual aspect of my relationship with Jacqueline wasn't working and all our discussions and efforts to be honest were not making it better. I still loved David in certain ways, but I had become detached from him; it wasn't fair to him, or my own efforts to come out, to stay together while I was looking for other women to become involved with.

Besides, I had begun to have nightly dreams about another woman, Janice. She was part of a group called Women Arise and their mission was to build solidarity with women in Viet Nam. During the meetings I began to attend, I would find myself staring at Janice's lush, dark hair and her breasts underneath her embroidered shirts while I listened to her evocative descriptions of the strength and courage of the Vietnamese women she had met in Cuba. I thought Janice was brilliant, voluptuous, and very complicated. Soon I was thinking about her and her stimulating politics all the time. Although I was unsure I could ever have a sexual relationship with her, I was now feeling a real spark for a woman and felt more sure than ever that I was in the process of coming out.

For ten years of my life I was a lesbian and being a lesbian became a core aspect of my identity. I loved individual women and I loved the lesbian community as it gathered in the women's coffee houses and bars that could be found in almost every neighborhood of San Francisco. I loved the early beginnings of the Gay Pride parade, marching proudly and defiantly down Market Street, feeling like we were all about to take over the world. And I loved various women, going through a process, over the years, of figuring out what mix of sex, emotion, and politics would create the kind of lasting, new world relationship that I was ultimately looking for.

Cover of the book *Women of Viet Nam* by Arlene Eisen-Bergman. Cover illustration by Jane Norling, www.janenorling.com.

RIDING THE TEMPEST

I FIRST MET JANICE AT AN ANTI-WAR RALLY IN GOLDEN GATE PARK where Women Arise had set up a photo exhibit about women in Viet Nam. One picture stood out to me: a small woman holding a rifle against the back of a large, American man, the captured pilot of a B-52 bomber. The woman looked resolute and serious, yet showed no sign of bravado.

As I was staring at the picture, Janice who was sitting at a leaflet-covered table next to the exhibit commented, "Impressive, isn't she?" When I nodded, she went on to say how she thought that Vietnamese women had much to teach us in the United States about women's liberation. My first reaction was skepticism, feeling that she was stretching the truth about the role of peasant women in a Third World country to make a point. But Janice seemed to antici-pate my response and went on to say that it made her angry how most American feminists thought that they had invented women's liberation and how it was a national chauvinist perspective to think that an American model of liberation, fo-cused on breaking with the nuclear family and supporting gay liberation, was the only approach to the fight against patriarchy. I was a little taken aback that she came on so strong, but I was also interested in what she had to say since it jibed with my own growing frustrations with much of the women's movement.

Janice saw that I was listening, so she continued. She had just gone through a painful divorce and was convinced that most of the left was sexist to the core. But this didn't mean that the Vietnamese had to define women's libera-tion in the same way as we did in America. I liked the boldness of her overview and the unabashed way in which she spoke about her own personal issues. When she invited me to the next meeting of Women Arise, I agreed to come.

Over the next few months, my political attraction to Janice evolved to include a passionate physical attraction. I was able to persuade her to have a sexual relationship with me which lasted on and off for three years with many ebbs and flows. However, in the long run it was our political connection which proved to have the most lasting significance in my life. Janice introduced me to an anti-imperialist politics that was rooted in international solidarity and a global perspective on women's liberation.

Before joining Women Arise I had been against the war, but in many respects the Vietnamese were faceless to me. I had not been part of SDS in college and had only been on the fringes of the anti-war movement previously, so the history of the Vietnamese struggle and the background of U.S. geopolitical interests in Indochina were eye-opening. What I learned made me realize that it was one thing to be against the war for moral, humanist, or pacifist reasons and it was another to support the Vietnamese because they were playing a critical, strategic role in the worldwide fight against U.S. imperialism, a system that had a political-economic stranglehold on Third World nations around the globe.

Shortly after I joined Women Arise, another member of the group, Arlene Eisen-Bergman, asked Janice, me, and a few others to become part of an editorial collective for a book she was writing about the women of Viet Nam and I jumped at the chance. Not only would such a project use my writing skills, it would also involve a collective process that seemed like a positive alternative to my experience with the individualized, proprietary approach of the academic world.

Over the next year, our editorial collective met almost weekly, reviewed each sentence of the book, and argued about the style, politics, and graphics. A gifted political artist, Jane Norling,[1] illustrated the book with original drawings that reflected the theme of each chapter, and the editorial collective helped to paste up the copy on the layout tables of the San Francisco publisher, Peoples Press. The collective method turned out to be less ideal in some ways than I anticipated. Differing editorial opinions, personalities, and work styles created repeated conflicts, and by the end of the intense production period the relationships in our group were considerably strained. Still, to me it was an exciting, collaborative process and I was very glad to play a role, working with Arlene, to produce a beautiful, groundbreaking book that was received very enthusiastically by the Vietnamese and by some sectors of the U.S. women's movement.

Editing the book, I began to absorb the stories of Vietnamese women until they became a part of me. I learned about the Trung Sisters, national heroines, who led an insurrection against the Chinese invaders in 40 A.D. Two hundred years later in 248 A.D., another peasant woman, Trieu Thi Trinh led thirty battles against the Chinese, declaring:

"My wish is to ride the tempest, tame the waves, kill the sharks. I want to drive the enemy away to save our people. I will not resign myself to the usual lot of women who bow their heads and become concubines." [2]

I loved that Trinh was able to express in this simple statement how the fight against foreign control and exploitation of her country was linked to the fight against patriarchy.

When we discussed the chapter "The Politics of Rape in Viet Nam," I began to understand how rape was used as a tool of military domination as well as psychological and cultural humiliation. The chapter contained searing testimony from Viet Nam Veterans Against the War (VVAW) that exposed how rape was not only a logical outgrowth of male upbringing in American society but was also a deliberate aspect of military training and a tactic of terror in a genocidal war. When GI's who had participated in mass rape and brutality of all sorts in Viet Nam returned to the U.S., their experiences spilled out in many destructive ways on to the women they had relationships with back home.

The message that we were trying to put across was not just about the victimization of women across international borders. We wanted to make it clear that the resistance of Vietnamese women was an example to emulate, and the transformation of women's gender roles in Viet Nam was intimately bound up with their participation in a people's war. The Vietnamese struggle was truly rooted in the hearts and minds of the people fighting—there was no other way to explain how such a small, poor country with limited military resources could be successfully resisting the United States' juggernaut.

And women were involved at every level. They formed the "Long-Haired Army," which had responsibility for persuading people to join the struggle, and they held key leadership roles, including that of Madame Nguyen Thi Dinh, who was the Deputy Commander of the People's Liberation Armed Forces in the South.

The last chapter of the book was titled "No Going Back" and we believed what one Vietnamese woman writer expressed: "None of the women are prepared to yield what they have gained from the revolution." [3] By the end, any skepticism I had at the beginning of the project about the leading role of Vietnamese women had disappeared, and I fully agreed with the book's conclusion that "Vietnamese women have moved closer to their emancipation than women anywhere else on the planet."[4]

As part of Women Arise, I also did presentations with a slide show about Vietnamese women at women's group meetings, schools, community centers, and churches. We usually were received with enthusiasm, polite questions, and occasional hostile arguments, but few responses compared to the one we received when we showed the slide show to a large group of women prisoners. Under the auspices of the Santa Cruz Women's Prison Project, which brought arts and education programs into the state prison for women,[5] Arlene, Karen, and I went on a memorable trip to the California Institution for Women (CIW) in Southern California. Luckily for us, our workshop was scheduled for the same weekend as a writing workshop conducted by poet Judy Grahn, and so we all had a chance to participate in an amazing outpouring of written creativity. I was blown away by the weight of brutality and grief the women prisoners expressed, and by their capacity to describe their experiences in mind altering words.

After the intensity of the writing workshop, we were a little worried that our slide show about Vietnamese women would seem distant and abstract. But in fact, the experience of sharing our own stories provided a bridge to our presentation about women in that far-off land. The women laughed uproariously at the traditional Vietnamese patriarchal saying: "one hundred women are not worth a single testicle." They were angered by the slides showing women being raped by American GI's, and they cheered at the picture of the small woman who had captured the B-52 pilot. When we got to the section about women in cages—the prisoners being held by the South Vietnamese government because of their political resistance—the discussion exploded in an angry denunciation of rape, torture, and the imprisonment of women all over the globe. At the conclusion of the slide show, the prisoners wrote letters to the political prisoners which Arlene planned to take with her on her upcoming trip to Viet Nam.[6]

We drove away from CIW grieving that we had to leave these new, precious friends behind bars. We comforted ourselves with the thought that we had somehow managed, for a few hours, to transcend the barriers that male powers had erected between oppressed women in different parts of the world.

On April 30, 1975 the puppet government of South Viet Nam surrendered and the Provisional Revolutionary Government (PRG) took power in South Viet Nam as a first transitional step towards reunification of the entire country. The U.S. had lost; Viet Nam had won. It was breathtaking to watch the victory unfold, to hear that Saigon had been renamed Ho Chi Minh City, and to recognize a new stage of history for the Vietnamese people.

Representatives of the Democratic Republic of North Viet Nam and the Provisional Revolutionary Government, including Women's Union officials, accepted an invitation to meet with anti-war activists in Vancouver, Canada. The purpose was to celebrate together and develop plans for future solidarity work focused on the critical needs of reconstruction. I was part of the planning committee for this meeting, which had to be organized within five days due to the scheduling requirements of the Vietnamese delegates.

Janice left early for Vancouver and I flew up with Sharon, another member of Women Arise. We arrived in the Vancouver airport just a few hours before the first session was scheduled to start. On the customs line, two immigration agents rifled through our bags which were filled with literature about political prisoners, the Bay Area Women's Union, the American Indian Movement, and Inez Garcia's case. All of a sudden, one agent beckoned to another and before

we knew it we were being marched off brusquely in separate directions. Once
I was in a closed room, two large men began assaulting me with a barrage of
questions that I was totally unprepared for: WHO WERE WE? WHAT WERE
WE DOING IN VANCOUVER? WHAT WERE OUR ORGANIZATIONAL
AFFILIATIONS? WHO WERE OUR CONTACTS? WHY WERE WE
ATTENDING A MEETING WITH THE VIETNAMESE IN VANCOU-
VER AND WHAT WAS THEIR CONNECTION TO ALL THE BLACK
POLITICAL PRISONERS IN OUR PAMPHLETS? I was totally taken off
guard by the questions. The war was over, we were attending a legal conference,
and I thought the Canadians were supposed to be liberals. I was confused, a
little scared, but mostly concerned that I wouldn't make it to the conference in
time for the opening session. Pragmatically, I tried to be conversational and told
the officials bits of information that I was sure they already knew, such as the
address of the conference center and the name of the Vietnamese representative who was the liaison for the conference in Vancouver, assuring them that
all of our work was totally legal. Finally I was told, without explanation, that I
could go. I was greatly relieved to see that Sharon was already waiting for me
in the hallway. But the knot in my stomach began tightening up again when
Sharon told me that she had refused to say anything to the agents, insisting that
she wanted to have a lawyer present. They had badgered her, but she hadn't
budged.

　　　　When we got to the conference and told Janice what had happened, she
was furious at me. To experienced activists, it was a non-negotiable principle to
refuse to talk to any government agent. She angrily explained that I could have
inadvertently provided these members of the state, whoever they were, with
information which could be used to put together a profile not only of my role
but that of other people I worked with. It was arrogant to believe that I could
figure out which information was harmless and which wasn't. I was mortified
and felt that I had broken not only Janice's trust but had potentially jeopardized
our entire relationship with the Vietnamese.

The memory of my mistake haunted me for years after. I worried that my naive and pragmatic cooperation was an indication of poor political instincts, and that left to my own devices I could make irreversible mistakes when the stakes were much higher.

Despite the pall the encounter placed on the beginning of the conference, the rest of the event was very inspiring. The women and men representing the Democratic Republic of the North and the Provisional Government of the South were extremely down-to-earth. They approached us as political allies and gave us a level of serious respect that I felt was way beyond the level of our contributions (particularly given my recent mistake). The Vietnamese pushed us to expand our material aid for reconstruction and we pledged to redouble our solidarity efforts in the future.

Our belief in the revolutionary model that Viet Nam offered went beyond political analysis and extended into a spirit space. On the wall above my bed was a poster with a drawing of Vietnamese peasants plowing their land. Written on the bottom were the words "Nothing can defeat the spirit of this land." That poster, which also hung in the homes and movement offices of many of my friends, encapsulated our belief that a victory in Viet Nam was inevitable and that their victory would be key in dismantling the power of the U.S. empire.

How could we have understood the capacity of imperialism to recoup from its defeat in Viet Nam before it had been demonstrated in subsequent decades? Could we have anticipated the difficulties the Vietnamese would confront in attempting to build an economically sound socialist society after their country had been devastated by decades of fighting and bombardment in an international economic arena still thoroughly dominated by world capitalism? The United States failed to aid in the reconstruction of the land it had strafed with B-52 bombers, napalm, agent orange, and countless other weapons of mass destruction, even though it was committed to providing aid by Article 21 of the Paris Peace Agreements. And although sectors of the solidarity movement initially had good intentions about contributing to reconstruction, material aid declined rapidly once the

*war was over. It was years before I, and others on the left, would fully understand
that winning state power was just the first monumental step necessary for social
liberation.*

—◈◈◈—

On September 11, 1973 I went to a showing of the Cuban film, *Lucia*,[7]
with Janice and a few others from Women Arise. The movie described the
changes in women's status in Cuba over three historical epochs, and it had provoked intense discussion within Cuban society about how far women's emancipation should really go. After the movie, we were arguing about whether the
changes depicted in the movie were merely tokenistic or genuine advances, when
a Latino acquaintance of Janice's pulled her aside. I watched as her face paled
and she started to look sick. When she rejoined our discussion a few minutes
later, she was shaking. A coup was taking place in Chile. President Salvador
Allende had been killed, his democratically elected government was under siege,
and people believed that the worst was yet to come.[8]

I knew little about Chile before that moment, but I learned a lot in the
next few weeks from Chileans who came together with North American supporters to share their horror about what was unfolding in their homeland. For
many around the world, Allende's election in 1970 held out the hope that it
was possible to achieve revolutionary social change through elections. But now
the U.S.-backed Chilean military, headed by General Augusto Pinochet, was
demonstrating the vulnerability of an elected socialist government that was hated
by the United States.

The Chilean Movimiento de Izquierda Revolucionaria (MIR) had
cautioned Allende's Popular Unity government about the liabilities of an
electoral strategy that wasn't backed by military power. But no one had anticipated the extremes of the coup or the virtual bloodbath that ensued, with 3,000
people killed in the first few months and tens of thousands disappeared and
imprisoned. Amidst the anguish and near-despair, a rippling reaction began to
crystallize among supporters of Chile in the Bay Area. The so-called "peaceful

path" was a utopian approach that was doomed to failure. With the U.S. armed-to-the-teeth and prepared to back counter-insurgency all around the world, any country that tried to build something new could only protect a fledgling social experiment if it were prepared to defend itself militarily.

A few weeks after the Chilean coup, on September 28, the Weather Underground Organization (WUO) bombed the Latin American headquarters of ITT in New York City because of this corporation's funding of Chilean right-wing activity in support of the coup.[9] I only knew a little about the Weather Underground, and in their early days as "Weatherman" I had been turned off by what I saw as their macho posturings. But when I read about the action against ITT in the pages of the *San Francisco Chronicle*, I felt a wave of gladness. I had not thought much about armed struggle in this country before. But at this moment, I began to appreciate the symbolic value of armed actions timed and targeted to resonate with the outrage of progressive people around the world.

———— ∞∞∞ ————

A few months later, on February 4, 1974, Patricia Hearst, daughter of California newspaper magnate William Randolph Hearst (who owned the *San Francisco Chronicle* and *Examiner*), was kidnapped by the Symbionese Liberation Army (SLA). Now the question of armed activities inside the United States began to take center stage for me and many others in the Bay Area.

The SLA was led by a Black former prisoner, Donald DeFreeze, who had escaped from Soledad prison and taken the name of Cinque in memory of the leader of the slave rebellion on the ship *Amistad*. Other SLA members included Vietnam veterans, lesbians, and Berkeley students. The SLA kidnapped Patricia Hearst in order to demand freedom for two of their members who were in prison as the result of a previous action.[10] As a first step, good faith gesture, they asked the Hearst family to begin a massive food give away to poor people in the Bay Area. Hearst tentatively agreed, and soon the People in Need program was set up. Despite many logistical problems with the food distribution apparatus, thousands of poor people, primarily Black and Brown, gathered at the distribution sites. Often they waited in long lines for hours to pick up bags of groceries that had been promised, only to discover in many cases that there weren't sufficient bags for everyone. Nationwide, the media was forced to report on the overwhelming number of families who did not have money for food and the children who didn't get enough to eat living in one of the richest areas of the country.

The audacity of the action and the concrete demand to feed the poor riveted the country, pushing a grudging discussion of the vast inequalities that existed in U.S. society, even while the majority of media and the left labeled the SLA as lunatics and agent provocateurs. Like many people around me, I was confused. I felt uneasy about the sexism involved in kidnapping a young woman who was being made to pay for her father's capitalist sins, and I distrusted many aspects of the SLA's political agenda. On the other hand, when I read their communiqués, they seemed to contain a positive vision:

> We are no longer willing to allow the enemy of all our
> people and children to murder, oppress, and exploit us nor
> define us by color and thereby maintain division among us, but
> rather have joined together under black and minority leader-
> ship in behalf of all our different races and people to build a
> better and new world for our children and people's future.[11]

The communiqués also exposed the vast nature of the Hearst empire—its ownership of multiple magazines, TV, and radio stations, its economic interest in Safeway, the California grocery giant, and in Exxon, the oil behemoth, as well as its ownership of vast areas of land in Mexico and other parts of Latin America. I also noted that the SLA talked specifically about the role of women:

> ...Other women are justifiably wary of the patronizing
> habit of many groups to rate sexism as an "honorable mention"
> oppression, last on the list of all the more important ones. The
> liberation of women is not secondary to anyone else's freedom.

We will never accept a tokenistic position in any organization
or party platform…Women must participate in the armed
struggle and be fighters. Fighting armed is not "macho"…
Armed struggle is an important and totally necessary element
of our revolutionary strategy.[12]

However, these aspects of the SLA's politics were ignored by most
parts of the left. Marxist-identified left groups denounced the SLA action as an
example of "left-wing infantilism" at its worst.[13] One group proclaimed: "To
carry out socialist revolution, it is necessary to drive out of the working class all
anti-revolutionary elements…The SLA represents just such an anti-revolutionary tendency." [14]

To me, their self-righteous denunciations didn't leave any room to assert the obvious propaganda value of the food giveaways or to affirm the anger
that Third World people on the long food lines were freely expressing to the
world about hunger, greed, racism, and the capitalist system.

A couple of weeks after Patty Hearst's kidnapping, the Weather Underground issued a communiqué about the SLA. The media had begun to call the
WUO "moderate" in comparison to the SLA and, in their message the WUO
pointed out this ironic example of the media's effort to "sow confusion" and
division. The WUO's message shifted the focus to examples of state violence:
the murder of a fourteen-year-old Black youth by three white policemen in
Emeryville, California; the 22,000 mainly Black and Brown prisoners who were
being held "hostage" in California prisons; and the terror bombing of millions in
Asia every day for years. It pointed out that most forms of militancy were historically denigrated as "premature"—from sit-ins, to draft-card burnings to urban
rebellions. "Don't do the enemy's work," the WUO cautioned."Movement
spokespeople who react to political crises by asserting their own moderation and
legitimacy are providing ammunition which will be used in the ruling class plans
to split and weaken us."[15] A couple of weeks later the WUO sent out a poem to
the SLA, written by a woman member. It began:

They call it terror
If you are few
And have no B-52's,
If you are not a head of state
With an army and police
If you have neither napalm
Nor tanks
Nor electronic battlefields.
Terror is if you are dispossessed
And have only your own two hands
And each other
And your rage.[16]

The communiqué, and even more the poem, spoke to me. A massive hunt for the SLA was underway by the police. Members of the SLA were clearly in great danger and the left condemnations simply mimicked the state's words and intentions.

Over the next months the drama and spectacle heightened. Patricia Hearst announced her conversion to revolutionary ideals, adopted the alias of "Tania," a woman who had fought and died by Che's side in Bolivia,[17] and she even joined a bank robbery of the Hibernia Bank in the middle of San Francisco to demonstrate her newly embraced politics. I was skeptical of Patty Hearst's conversion, wary of the theatrical quality of the SLA's actions, and questioned both their tactics and strategy; but, as the state's pursuit of the SLA intensified, I became convinced that it was important to express support for these women and men despite criticisms.

On May 17, 1974, following a tip from a landlord, the Los Angeles police surrounded a small house in the Black neighborhood of Compton. Over 500 officers, SWAT team members, and FBI agents converged on the area, pumping more than 5,000 rounds of ammunition and launching 83 tear gas canisters into the house. They let the ensuing fire burn out of control without calling the fire department, allowing those inside to surrender, or protecting

other houses on the block. All six members of the SLA were killed, some probably burned alive.

The massacre of these six people in broad daylight, covered exhaustive-
ly by TV cameras, was frightening, sickening, enraging. Of the six, there was one
Black man, Cinque, one white man, Willie Wolf, and four white women, Nancy
Ling Perry, Angela Atwood, Patricia Soltysik, and Camilla Hall. The state knew
that Patty Hearst wasn't inside the house and concluded that it had free reign
to murder people who had already been condemned by the media a thousand
times over. *"Terror is if you are dispossessed/And have only your own two hands."*
The words of the WUO's poem reverberated inside my head.

The small circle of people who had dared to express support for the
SLA was shaken. These radicals were familiar with the violence that the state
had unleashed against the Panthers, but here was a group that was primarily
white and their white skin had not offered any protection. The newspapers were
running banner headlines threatening life imprisonment for the remaining SLA
members and rumors were circulating that the government was planning on
rounding up people on suspicion of being SLA supporters.

In the wake of the massacre, Tom Hayden (a founder of SDS now involved in Democratic party politics) stepped forward to venture a controversial
opinion in the pages of the *L.A. Times*: "What is necessary for people to know is
that the SLA is an American phenomenon, growing out of the basic torments of
our society, and which cannot be exterminated by military force." Although he
didn't "condone" the SLA's methods, he argued that bloody confrontations like
the one that had occurred ten days before would only give rise to more groups
like the SLA. [18]

A memorial for the SLA was quickly pulled together by some Berkeley
SLA supporters. When I heard about it from Janice, I knew I needed to go, but
I also knew that I was scared and felt over my head in these dangerous political
waters. A few of Janice's friends had previously been called to testify at grand
juries investigating the Weather Underground. I felt that if I went to the memorial, I should be ready to defy grand juries or face whatever consequences there
might be. Yet I wasn't really sure I was ready. Janice always seemed very sure of

herself so I didn't feel like I could confess my fears to her, and there was no one else that I could confide in.

On the day of the memorial, the brilliant California sun seemed intent on irradiating the political horrors that were occurring under its watch. As we walked towards Ho Chi Minh park, christened in honor of the eminent Vietnamese leader by Berkeley radicals, I had a flash of incredulity that such a terrible massacre had really taken place a few hundred miles south of this Berkeley new world utopia. I also had a moment of disbelief that cynical Diana Block, in the past so skeptical of leftist lunacy, was now participating in a memorial for six self-identified guerrilla fighters who had been slaughtered by the police. But once the memorial began and people started talking about the people who had died, my detachment faded. Someone read a poem that was being circulated on a flyer through the crowd:

> *We cry, but keep on moving, building and loving!*
> *We cry in the night and go to see Ruchell in the morning!*
> *We cry one day and defy the grand jury the next!*
> *In the dark of the night we put our arms around our friends to comfort them,*
> *And in the dark of the night, we spraypaint with them!* [19]

The poem was corny and not that poetic to me, but it reflected the dedication and resolve circulating through the crowd. When people began to chant their anger against the government which was murdering in Viet Nam and murdering in Oakland and murdering in Compton, I didn't care anymore if the police agents who were in the crowd were watching me. I raised my fist and let the fury burst out of my mouth.

Twenty-five years later, in June 1999, Kathleen Soliah, one of the women who had spoken out at the memorial, was arrested in Minneapolis after being a fugitive for over two decades. She had been living under the name of Sara Jane Olson, was married to a doctor and had three daughters. She had been a performance artist and activist in the Twin Cities progressive community for many years. Twenty-five years later, she was being charged with placing two pipe bombs under police cars in 1975, allegedly in retaliation for the murder of one of the SLA members, Angela Atwood, in the Compton assault. The pipe bombs had been discovered before they detonated so no one had been injured. But, decades later, the state and the media were reviving this cold case to ramp up the war against "domestic terrorism." And in 1999, as in 1974, there still was little support in progressive circles for a woman whom the Hearst press was excoriating as the "SLA mastermind."

The state's institutional memory was shaped by political vindictiveness and an intentional strategy to resurface cold cases from the sixties and the seventies to disarm any radical propensities among a new generation of activists. Sara's activist friends from Minneapolis initiated a Defense Committee and others in California, including myself, put on educational events, raised money, and went to court to support her through this retrospective witch hunt.

Sara's trial took place shortly after September 11, and in the intensely anti-terrorist climate of that period, she decided to take the deal which the prosecution offered, despite her belief in her own innocence. During her subsequent incarceration at the Central California Women's Facility (CCWF), I was able to visit and correspond with her. Far from being an apathetic "soccer mom" or a representative of the "lunatic fringe," as the media had represented her, Sara remained an outspoken social activist. She could have chosen to do her time in prison quietly. Instead, she consistently exposed the terrible conditions inside prison and became a passionate advocate for others inside.

Cover of 1975 edition of *Sing a Battle Song: Poems by Women in the Weather Underground Organization*. The inside blurb explains that the cover represents a spirit mask "in celebration of our sister, Diana, who spent several years of her life in Guatemala." Reference is to Diana Oughton, killed in the 1970 Greenwich Village townhouse explosion.

A Single Spark....
Can Start a Prairie Fire

—Mao Tse Tung [1]

At this time, the unity and consolidation of anti-imperialist forces around a revolutionary program is an urgent and pressing strategic necessity. PRAIRIE FIRE is offered as a contribution to this unity of action and purpose. Now it is in your hands.

—Prairie Fire [2]

I WAS BUSY. MY LIFE WAS FULL. There was my job as a teacher's aide in San Francisco at a special school for recently arrived immigrant children and a newsletter I worked on to promote educational change in the public schools. And there was a women's study group that I was part of, which included Celine, Gina, and Jacqui from SF WAR, Karen and Jody, plus several other women. Here we studied political theory—Marx, Lenin, Mao, Sheila Rowbotham, Angela Davis, and others—and debated what a revolutionary strategy should look like.

This was a question that preoccupied me. All the various pieces of work that I was doing were good, up to a point. But there was no overarching vision to fit them all together, no set of principles and no organizational framework. And after the L.A.P.D. attack on the SLA, the need for a political collective that could serve as my base for thinking things through seemed more pressing than ever.

One day, Janice met me for dinner and I could see immediately from the expression on her face that the gloom that had enveloped her in the days following the SLA massacre had for some reason lifted. As soon as we had ordered our burritos, she opened her large bag and pulled out a small book with a red cover and gave it to me to look at, with the admonition not to get it dirty. The title—*Prairie Fire, Political Statement of the Weather Underground*—jumped out at me, and I felt a spark of excitement as I started to leaf through the pages and saw pictures of Che, a Vietnamese woman holding a hoe, and a demonstration of U.S. women with a banner that read "Women in Revolution, Sisters Unite." Part I was called "Arm the Spirit" and the chapters had intriguing titles such as "The Banner of Che" and "Turning Weakness into Strength." "Where did you get this?" I asked Janice, and as soon as the words had left my mouth I knew that this was one of those of questions that revealed how naïve I still really was. Janice put her finger over her lips and then went on to tell me in a whisper that the WUO had mailed the book out to a variety of public organizations and that she had been able to get one from a friend.

It was another couple of weeks before I was able to borrow *Prairie Fire* from Janice, and I had to swear that I would be very careful with it and not damage the pages with paper clips or coffee stains. That night, I stayed up and read it straight through. It wasn't very long, just under 200 pages, but there was so much to think about in each chapter. It wasn't dry and abstract like the phrase "political statement" implied. It was a passionate expression that seemed to come from the hearts as well as the minds of this group of young white revolutionaries. In the preface, they wrote that the book had been "chewed on and shaped in countless conversations, struggles and written pages. It has traveled around the country, growing…" and it was "written to all who will read, criticize and bring its content to life in practice."[3] Reading this, I felt like I was being drawn into a political process to grapple with the exact issues that I had been "chewing over" in my own mind up until now.

Much of the history the book covered was not new to me—the significance of the Vietnamese victory; the Native American genocide that was the basis for the settlement of what came to be known as the United States; the slave labor that was key to the economic development of the country; and the racism and white supremacy that continued into the present to define the political and economic structures of this society and formed the social basis for imperialist worldwide aggression in the second half of the twentieth century.

What was exhilarating was the way *Prairie Fire's* analysis did not hem and haw, but zeroed in on what white revolutionaries needed to do to join with the world's people against the common enemy, U.S. imperialism. The analysis was rooted in Third World Marxism as interpreted by the Vietnamese, the Cubans, and the West Africans.

"The unique and fundamental condition of this time is the decline of U.S. imperialism"[4] the book declared directly and unequivocally at the beginning. This decline had been instigated by the Vietnamese in their decisive liberation struggle, and would be led by the peoples of the oppressed nations around the world in Asia, Africa, Latin America, and the Middle East who, like the Vietnamese, were throwing off the shackles of colonialism through wars of national liberation.

But the national liberation struggles of oppressed nations were not just international phenomena. Within the current borders of the United States, borders that had been drawn through conquest, were Black, Native, Puerto Rican, and Chicano peoples who formed internal colonies, oppressed nations, that would lead the struggle against imperialism from inside the U.S. The responsibility of white people, who were part of an oppressor, settler nation was to support self-determination for those nations. We needed to work in solidarity with their struggles not only because it was morally right, but because these struggles were key to dismantling imperialism.

Within this general strategic framework, the WUO located its own specific role.

"We are a guerrilla organization…Our intention is to disrupt the empire, to incapacitate it, to put pressure on the cracks, to make it hard to carry out its bloody functioning against the people of the world, to join the world struggle, to attack from the inside."[5] This they did as an adjunct to and in alliance with the leading anti-imperialist forces of the Third World, who were defeating imperialism through revolutionary war. Armed struggle was by no means the only legitimate political activity (an argument the WUO had made in its early stages), but it was an absolutely necessary activity if people were serious about revolution. "Without mass struggle, there can be no revolution. Without armed struggle, there can be no victory."[6] They responded to the criticisms of armed struggle by those on the left with a critique of American exceptionalism—"the assumption that ... our revolutionary struggle is not subject to the same general conditions and the same general necessities as others."[7] They further explained, "It is an illusion that imperialism will decay peacefully. Imperialism has meant constant war...There is no reason to believe [the imperialists] will become humane or relinquish power....To not prepare the people for this struggle is to disarm them ideologically and physically and to perpetrate a cruel hoax."[8]

It all made sense to me. These were not the arguments of crazed, violence loving fanatics. Anyone who looked at the system without blinders could see that it would never simply evolve into socialism or that socialists could be voted into power. If you understood the depth of the problem, the rottenness of the system through and through (which *Prairie Fire* described in careful detail), the necessity for armed struggle seemed inescapable. The WUO wasn't claiming that they were capable of inflicting huge military defeats on the U.S. at this stage. Instead they saw this as an early stage that, in conjunction with other armed groups like the Black Liberation Army, would build a foundation and further awareness of the legitimacy of this aspect of struggle. Their actions were focused, specific and were complements to mass struggles—bombing police cars following the murder of Fred Hampton and Mark Clark in December 1969, targeting the Office of California Prisons in Sacramento after the murder of George Jackson in San Quentin in August 1971, and attacking the Pentagon after the mining of the harbors of North Vietnam in May 1972.

What the WUO was hoping for now, after four years of clandestine experience, was the conscious joining together of the mass anti-imperialist movement and the armed underground, "the unity and consolidation of anti-imperialist forces around a revolutionary program."

This was what I was looking for—a guide to action, a call for discussion, an organization of like-minded people to work, study, and build with. But when I suggested to my women's study group that we read *Prairie Fire* next, the polarization in the room was immediately palpable. Only Karen, who had been an early member of Weather, was enthusiastic. Others admitted they didn't know much about the WUO, but were suspicious of their arrogance, their male domination, their crazy, isolated actions like the Days of Rage, or disasters like the explosion of the townhouse in New York's Greenwich Village.[9] "Yes, they've made mistakes, but they've changed. The book shows this," I insisted. Finally we all agreed that we would stick with Mao's *On Contradiction* as our next reading but would read *Prairie Fire* after that.

I was close to all of the women in the group, but I realized that political differences among us were brewing. Jacqui and Celine were starting to study with a Marxist cadre group, Together in Struggle (TIS),[10] and I anticipated that its political perspective would influence their approach to *Prairie Fire*.

When we finally had the discussion, the tension was thick and every interchange charged. Some people had in fact liked the book and it had changed their impression of the WUO. But several others, including Celine and Jacqui, were more adamant than ever that Weather politics were a totally wrong direction for the movement. To them, the book confirmed that Weather was hopelessly anti-working class and anti-Marxist. *Prairie Fire*'s statement that "one of the defining characteristics of the U.S. working class is that it is composed of workers of both the oppressor and oppressed nations"[11] encapsulated the problem for them. They agreed that racism was a central, divisive force within the working class, but *Prairie Fire*'s analysis exacerbated the divisions. Celine pointed out that as an all-white formation, the WUO could talk about Third World leadership without having to be directly accountable to Third World people. Jacqui argued that the leadership of the WUO wasn't working class itself and thus they were conveniently able to blame the working class for their own limitations. I responded defensively, especially since my study of Marxist-Leninist theory was not extensive and I couldn't cite texts to substantiate my ideas. But, in my gut, I knew that the worldview laid out in *Prairie Fire* corresponded more closely to my experience of U.S. reality than any I had heard from the many M-L organizations in the Bay Area.

The charged discussion in the study group pushed me to think about why *Prairie Fire's* analysis of the working class made sense to me. Growing up in New York, I lived in a mixed, melting pot neighborhood of whites, Blacks, and Puerto Ricans. My family didn't have a lot of money and lived in a run down building which over the years was occupied increasingly by Puerto Ricans, Blacks, and Haitians. Yet, from the time I was little, my parents told me in hundreds of ways, verbal and non-verbal, that we were different from the people who lived next door. We lived in close proximity, but we inhabited different worlds.

My school was integrated, but it was tracked from first grade on, and the top academic classes my sister and I were in were almost entirely white. This separation only became more pronounced when I attended the academically competitive Hunter College High School. Only when I started tutoring kids in an after-school program did I actually spend time with students from another racial background during my high school years.

At the University of Chicago, which also had an overwhelmingly white student body, I again became involved in a tutoring program. Those of us who crossed The Midway, the boulevard which separated the insular campus world from the Black world of Woodlawn, were making a deliberate effort to do something about the poverty, violence, and racism that shaped the lives of the children we were tutoring. But it wasn't until I graduated from college and returned to New York to work in an experimental education program called Teachers Incorporated that I understood that genuine changes in a racist educational structure had to be based upon the self-organized empowerment of the communities themselves.

In 1968, New York City had finally responded to the demands of Black and Puerto Rican communities by developing a pilot project of community-controlled schools in three areas of the city. Community councils were elected in each of these areas, which had the power to reorganize the schools, hire new teachers and fire those who were not able to respectfully educate Black and Brown students.[12]

The goal of Teachers Incorporated was to recruit and train teachers to work in the new community control school districts. Over the summer, we attended formal classes to qualify for an emergency teaching credential, got a crash course in racism and education from a wide variety of community leaders, parents and educational professionals, and spent the summer living with a family in the neighborhood where we would be teaching. We all took very seriously the discussions about white privilege, the unlearning of racism, and the need for change in the attitudes of white teachers who genuinely wanted to be educators in these communities.

At the start of the school year, I was ready and eager to begin teaching kindergarten at a school in Harlem. Then the crisis hit. A small number of white teachers were asked to leave some of the community controlled schools and the United Federation of Teachers (UFT) went on strike to protest this supposed abuse of power by "rabid" community school boards. The Community Control Boards asked teachers who supported them to come to work and cross the picket line. The choice was straightforward to me. The union was not concerned with transforming a deeply flawed system. It was interested in maintaining the power and the interests of its overwhelmingly white membership over and above those of the Black and Brown children and parents. I couldn't defend "workers' rights" over community control, and so for ten weeks I walked through angry crowds of white teachers picketing as I made my way into the school each morning.

In the end, the union won the reinstatement of the teachers who had been fired, although the Community Control Districts retained a modified authority. The tensions between teachers who had supported the Community Control Boards and those who had been on strike remained sharp throughout the year. We sat at separate tables in the cafeteria and took opposing sides during teachers' meetings. In particular, the charges of anti-Semitism, which some of the teachers continued to level at the Community Control Boards, shocked and disturbed me. Many members of the union, including its president Albert Shanker,

were Jewish as were some of the teachers who had been fired, but to me the
charge of anti-Semitism was a smokescreen to avoid dealing with the legitimate
issues of racism that the communities were raising. Those of us in Teachers Inc.
who were of Jewish background carefully tried to explain to these veteran teachers why we didn't think the charges were true, but since we were young and were
already seen as pawns of the Community Control Boards, our opinions did not
carry much weight. However, when I heard the same allegations repeated by my
parents and their acquaintances, I lost my self-control and angrily retorted that
the charge was being used manipulatively to maintain white power in the cities'
schools.

I only spent a year teaching in Harlem, but the experience deeply
impacted my consciousness of race dynamics in the labor movement. From my
involvement in the women's movement, I understood that the "working class"
was further fractured by male supremacist privilege and power and that even
white radical women could be profoundly influenced by the material divisions of
race.

—————✺—————

I returned to our women's study group armed with arguments based on
my own experiences, but our disagreements about "class analysis" and other political positions only became more pronounced. Over the course of the next six
months, they came to dominate not only the study group but all of our relationships. When Jacqui and Celine had first started working with TIS, in many ways
I was sympathetic with their decision. From what I could see, the group was
very serious and analytical and prioritized the leadership of Third World people
in the organization. The cadre[13] I met seemed friendly, if a little stiff, and they
seemed to have a comprehensive political overview, which also was attractive.
But there were things that I couldn't put my finger on that kept me from wanting
to become involved with them.

When Jacqui decided to quit her part-time job as a clerical worker and
started a job at a downtown hotel in order to support a worker organizing effort

that TIS was involved in, it made sense to me, since I was involved in trying to organize teacher's aides, who were primarily Third World women, into our own union. But pretty soon Jacqui left SF Women Against Rape and also the Socialist Feminist Women's Union working group, and, although she explained that she simply didn't have time for those activities, I knew from reading TIS journals that their many criticisms of the women's movement probably also contributed to her departure.

Other differences emerged. TIS, like many other organizations in the New Communist movement, identified itself as Maoist, which meant that they considered the analysis of Mao and the Chinese Communist Party to be guiding world revolutionary strategy, and they supported China's position on international issues. In 1974, the national liberation struggle in Angola was at a critical juncture. The Marxist-led MPLA had defeated the Portuguese colonialists and was poised to assume the leadership of an independent Angola when the United States and South Africa dramatically increased their aid to two anti-Marxist groups, the FNLA and UNITA, in an attempt to boost their bid for power in post-colonial Angola. The Soviet Union, Cuba, and many independent leftist groups inside the United States supported the MPLA, but China threw its support to the FNLA and UNITA, denouncing the MPLA as a pawn of the social-imperialist Soviet Union. U.S. groups that followed China's politics, including TIS, echoed China's opposition to the MPLA.[14]

I admired many things about the Chinese revolution and could understand the reasons for China's critique of the Soviet Union and its revisionist politics,[15] but China's support of the FNLA and UNITA seemed motivated solely by its opposition to the Soviets which seemed like a destructive rationale to me. I was beginning to realize that there could be serious consequences when U.S. groups followed any other country's political line unconditionally.

None of us were experts on the region, so our tense fights about Angola simmered with displaced emotions, inexorably pulling our friendships apart. Part of me couldn't understand how this could be happening, why women to whom I had felt so close were now seeing the world in decisively different ways. Jacqui had been my lover and Celine had been my friend since seventh grade.

Sometimes while we were in the middle of a heated discussion, I would flash on the hours I had spent on the phone with Celine in high school—pouring out my anger at my father, dissecting the personalities and idiosyncracies of our friends and teachers, confiding in her my sense of diffuse but profound alienation with society. And now our closeness was being shredded because of a country on the other side of the world. It just didn't make sense.

But another part of me embraced the leftist logic of the time which insisted that it was impossible to maintain sincere friendships with people who held different political viewpoints, because these differences had real, critical ramifications on building a revolutionary movement.

We might have continued in this strained but indecisive mode indefinitely if I hadn't one afternoon picked up a paper that Celine had left on the kitchen table. It was a position paper outlining TIS's analysis of "homosexuality" and gay liberation. With scientific precision the organization laid out the reasons why homosexuals should have democratic rights in society, but could never be accepted as full revolutionary members into the organization because the homosexual lifestyle intrinsically involved pulls toward "petit-bourgeois individualism."[16]

I could feel my heart beating out of control as I read this document. I knew that several other so-called Marxist organizations barred openly gay members, but Together in Struggle had seemed too principled, too rational to adopt such a position. Besides, I couldn't imagine how Jacqui and Celine, both of whom had identified themselves as lesbians in the past, could be interested in a group with such a position.

Abandoning all of the restraint I had been trying to muster when dealing with our disagreements, I stormed into Celine's room. "What do you think of this?" I yelled, waving the position paper. "You can't possibly agree with this bullshit about *homosexuality*—it wipes out everything, everything we've been talking about and fighting for in the women's movement…" I continued to rant until I noticed the tense, closed look on Celine's face. "This is complicated," she answered in a stiff, angry voice. "Most Third World people don't even know what you mean by the women's movement, and white people's version of gay liberation is totally alien to working people's lives. You can't build real mass struggle by bulldozing your way through the contradictions as if they don't exist like you always try to do, Diana."

As she was speaking, I realized that something irreparable was happening between us. This wasn't like the disagreements about Angola or the working class. If Celine could read that paper and accept what it was saying on any level, then the chasm between us was too large to be bridged by reasoned debate. Women's liberation and gay liberation did not encompass my entire politics, but they were fundamental to me personally and to my vision of a different world. Besides, it was an absurd position, steeped in homophobia and hierarchy, to deny that gay people could be as full revolutionaries as straight women and men. A few months ago, Celine and I would have been hysterical, laughing at the contradictions in such politics, and now we were losing our friendship because of them.

Our women's study group dissolved. Celine moved out of the flat we shared and Roxie, a friend who was part of the Prairie Fire Distributing Committee, a group that had recently been formed to circulate the book, moved in as one of my roommates. The disagreements with Celine and Jacqui had pushed me further into the circle of people who were committed to the analytic framework and direction for action that *Prairie Fire* had proposed.

When I first read *Prairie Fire*, I felt that its sections on women's and gay liberation bordered on tokenism and this had concerned me. There was a short section, "The Rising of Women," which outlined how the subjugation of women was intrinsic to imperialism and decried the pervasive reality of male supremacy in all social institutions including the family and the work force. Even more briefly, it acknowledged lesbians in a section tepidly titled, "Women liking women" which asserted the right of everyone to live according to their sexual preferences without discrimination or reprisal.[17] To me, steeped as I was in women's movement theory and culture, and coming from the recent experiences

of homophobia within the movement, this section lacked the passion the rest
of the book contained, and I worried that the WUO, like so many other mixed
organizations, was merely giving lip service to women's liberation.

Then, the Weather Underground released a book of poems by women
in the organization called *Sing a Battle Song* in time for International Women's
Day, March 8, 1975. In the introduction, the women who had put the book
together explained:

> We have worked hard to build a women's commu-
> nity: developing programs around women's issues, growing as
> fighters, reclaiming the true history of the people, and develop-
> ing an ideology that integrates women's experience with that of
> the people as a whole...The voice/s of this book is one more
> way to share with you our thoughts and our growth.[18]

One evening in March, a group of women got together at my house.
We lit candles, burned sage and took turns going through the book, reading the
poems from *Sing a Battle Song*. The poems were about many things—Viet Nam,
Assata Shakur, being underground, being lovers, being friends. When my turn
came, I serendipitously read a poem called *Sisterhood is not Magic*.

> *Whatever did the witches do*
> *They must have quarreled beneath the stars*
> *about how to ease the pain of wounds*
> *With ergot,*
> *belladonna or*
> *nasturtium.*
> *And argued*
> *taking long moonlight walks arm in arm,*
> *About how to save the "devil's party,"*
> *where to meet most safely*
> *and best serve the peasants' needs.*

And when a sister went on trial, Jacoba for example,
Even lovers among witches
must have disagreed over what would be
her best defense.

Disturbing a quiet constellation
in a July sky.

To some
their magic
seemed easy

But we
who often walk
in their footsteps
know better. [19]

By the time I got to the end, tears were streaming down my face and I could hardly choke out the last lines. Janice reached over and took my hand and someone else put their arm around me. Whoever wrote the poem had grasped the confounding difficulties and the unanticipated obstacles to sisterhood that I had been experiencing over the last few months. But they hadn't thrown up their hands and pronounced sisterhood impossible. Instead they looked to history, to the persecuted women resisters, the witches, to reframe what was possible. I loved the image of the witches "taking long moonlight walks arm in arm" while they argued and plotted. I was getting clearer. I wanted to connect with women who had this type of vision, women who had committed their lives to fighting imperialism, to being underground, and yet still understood the need for women's magic and poetry.

―――∞∞∞―――

In the beginning of July 1975, I drove across country with Janice and Roxie to attend the first national Socialist Feminist conference in Antioch, Ohio, and the founding conference of the Prairie Fire Organizing Committee (PFOC) in Boston. The socialist feminist conference was attended by over 1500 women, with over 100 workshops on topics ranging from non-sexist teaching and women in prison, to women in Guinea Bissau and lesbian organizing. There were strategy sessions on workplace and community organizing and discussions about building a multi-racial women's movement. It was all interesting on a certain level, but somehow it didn't feel compelling to me. I wasn't sure whether it was the lack of a plan of action or the absence of militancy that kept me from being excited by the conference, but by the end I was more than ready to move on to Boston.

The Prairie Fire Conference, on the other hand, was a fascinating amalgam of political analysis and proposals for programmatic action. The plenary sessions were addressed by Black, Puerto Rican, Native, and Vietnamese leaders who exhorted the primarily white participants to work in solidarity with their struggles and rebuild an anti-imperialist movement committed to self-determination and the struggle against white supremacy.

The organizational model which was being proposed for Prairie Fire was based on the assumption that most Third World people within the U.S. wanted to organize among their own people as the best way to defeat colonialism and achieve genuine self-determination. Leading Third World organizations of the past decade had followed this path—the Panthers, The American Indian Movement, the Young Lords, the Brown Berets, CASA, and the Puerto Rican Socialist Party. The responsibility of white anti-imperialists was to build an organization that would take political leadership from Third World organizations, but focus on organizing other white people. Given this division of responsibilities, it was likely that most of the people in Prairie Fire would be white, although it was clearly stated that the organization was not exclusive.

All of this made sense to me. Most of the "multinational" organizations that I saw around me seemed to be majority white with some Third World people involved. I couldn't see how Third World people could overcome white power dynamics in such a situation to exert leadership and connect with their communities. Moreover, once the right of self-determination was recognized for each national movement, the peoples of that national grouping had to define their own path for revolutionary transformation for themselves and at this stage that wasn't a job for multinational organizations. Separate organizations might not be ideal, but they seemed like the most honest way of responding to the embedded racist structure that had been created by centuries of colonial conquest, slavery and white domination in the United States.

The strong lesbians who were already working with the Prairie Fire Distributing Committees on the East Coast also made a strong impression on me—Silvia Baraldini and Susan Rosenberg from New York, and Laura Whitehorn from Boston among others. They were outspoken and sharp about the need for Prairie Fire to commit itself to the fight against male supremacy and homophobia at the same time as they argued for the priority of solidarity with the Black liberation and Puerto Rican independence struggles. If I hadn't already been leaning towards joining Prairie Fire, my immediate attraction to these women and the political vision they expressed confirmed my decision.

It was only at the end of the three day conference when Janice, Roxie, and I attended the meeting of the newly established Bay Area chapter of Prairie Fire Organizing Committee, that I had a wave of anxiety as I looked around the local group, which was majority male, and wondered what I was getting myself into. A spark had been ignited, but what type of a prairie fire would we create?

Cover of *Osawatomie,* journal of the Weather Underground Organization, published shortly before the Hard Times Conference at the end of 1975.

VENCEREMOS

MEETINGS, MEETINGS, MEETINGS. *Meetings of every sort. Meetings to study political theory, meetings to plan and analyze our "mass" work, meetings to develop ourselves into cadre who could lead mass struggle; meetings of the chapter as a whole and meetings to orient new members, meetings of the Women's Caucus and meetings of childcare collectives; meetings to develop the organization's structure, meetings to evaluate past work and meetings to strategize for the future. To some of Prairie Fire's new members these myriad meetings were a tedious but necessary part of making a revolution. But I thrived on these collective gatherings where we could invent, debate and shape a program that reflected in reality the politics that we believed on paper. Better than classes, better than study groups, better than single-issue projects, our meetings aimed to translate a holistic vision of revolutionary anti-imperialism culled from movements around the world into an organizational practice. And more than with any other group of people, I felt that the women and men who joined Prairie Fire were my friends, a community with whom I could share politics, feelings, and love.*

Within a couple of months of having joined Prairie Fire, an election was held for Bay Area representatives to the national leadership, and to my surprise I found myself elected to this body. Perhaps it was my outspoken advocacy of women's leadership; perhaps it was my clear enthusiasm for the task of building the organization. Or perhaps I was simply a neutral candidate, someone with little history in this sector of the movement and therefore not yet identified with any particular leanings in the ongoing left debates—someone with no old

animosities dating back years, someone who could represent the new membership of a new organization.

In any case, I was elected to the National Committee, or NC, and in the
fall of 1975 I traveled to Vermont for an intense strategy session with PFOC's
newly elected leadership body. Most of the members were women and men
who had worked together in SDS and had sided with the Weatherman faction
when SDS split. I was excited to meet these long-time activists and engrossed
by the discussions even though they were filled with references to events and
political struggles unfamiliar to me. A major debate was flaring about the plan
for a nationwide Hard Times Conference, scheduled to take place in Chicago in
February 1976. I thought the slogan for the conference facile—*Hard Times Are
Fighting Times*— and I sensed that the arguments about the conference cloaked
nuances of political line that I couldn't grasp.

The conference aimed to bring together people from varied communities around the country who were impacted by the worst economic recession
since World War II. Most of the people at the NC meeting argued that this was
the right time to build a nationwide multinational coalition that could unite
working and oppressed people to fight the hard times. A few were concerned
that the conference program focused too much on the economic crisis and not
enough on support for self-determination for oppressed nations and the struggle
against white supremacy. However, everyone at the meeting agreed that the
sharp criticisms that had been raised by a Bay Area PFOC member, Clayton Van
Lydegraf (Van), were way off base and could potentially undermine the success
of Hard Times.

It was difficult for me to sort out semantics and personalities from concrete political differences, so I mostly listened and said very little at the meeting.
However, when I returned from Vermont, eager to mobilize the Bay Area chapter
around the preparatory work for Hard Times, I couldn't ignore the adamant opposition that was being expressed by several PFOC members. They were all men
and they were led by Van.

At sixty, Van was the only older leftist among us. He had been an activist since the 1930's, had held offices in the Communist Party (USA) and had

been an air force pilot in World War II. He left the Communist Party in the early sixties over political differences and joined the Progressive Labor Party (PL); but in the late sixties he left PL because of its opportunism, and began to work with SDS and other "New Left" activists in Seattle, Washington. He tried to take Marxist-Leninist theory, as he interpreted it, and apply it to contemporary developments. In 1967, he wrote a pamphlet called *The Object is to Win*, in which he articulated ideas that particularly influenced the emerging Weather faction of SDS:

> The most determined Black revolutionaries are taking
> up arms as the only way to win. No other section of the left
> has yet done this. These two facts express a definite differ-
> ence between Black activists and leaders and most of the white
> left...Political power from the barrel of a gun is not the issue
> exclusively for the oppressed nations and people of various
> other places and colors. It is a reality to be faced by whites in
> the U.S. also.[1]

In 1973, Van had refused to testify before a San Francisco grand jury investigating the WUO. He had worked with political prisoners at San Quentin since the early seventies, had helped to start the Bay Area Prairie Fire Distributing Committee, and now was a vocal and influential member of PFOC.

From Van's point of view, the Hard Times Conference represented an abandonment of the core politics that had been articulated in the book *Prairie Fire* and that had differentiated PFOC from the rest of the party-building left. According to Van, the Hard Times goal of building multinational working class struggle, led by PFOC, came dangerously close to "liquidating" (erasing) the leading role of national liberation forces, as well as women's autonomous struggle, and that would be a long step backward.

I was fascinated by Van, who made money working as a refrigerator mechanic and by picking apples in the Northwest every fall. He lived very simply, had few possessions, and his long, scraggly white beard made him look the very image of the aging revolutionary. His criticisms of the Hard Times politics sent warning signals buzzing through my brain, but his rhetoric seemed unnecessarily sweeping and his manner was inflammatory. He was eccentric and querulous and, in typical male fashion, he often took over the meetings. He definitely didn't like to be disagreed with. In Vermont, members of the NC had warned of his sexism, his obstinacy, and his divisive style. Most of his allies were men, including his roommate Phil who didn't talk a lot in meetings. But whenever he did, he took Van's side.

Van seemed to take a special interest in talking to me. At first I was worried that his interest might involve a sexual agenda, but he never approached me on that level. Soon I realized that he wanted to win me as an ally in the struggles with the rest of the National Committee. He also wanted to cultivate my political growth and leadership. I wanted to preserve my independence, but I also was eager to learn. And I did. Our conversations before, between, and after meetings deepened my understanding of theory and the realities of U.S. history.

Van passionately described how racism had held sway time and again within the white working class. Most white organizers saw racism as just a bad set of attitudes, but Van emphasized how racism, or white supremacy, was rooted in the real material privileges that even poor whites had in comparison to Native people and Black people throughout the history of this country.

For Van, the early days of the Communist Party in the U.S. were a high point of anti-racism, when the CP recognized the Black nation's right to self-determination and land in the "black-belt" South.[2] However, the CP's solidarity with Black struggle dissipated over time. At the point when Van left the CP, it was clear to him that its allegiance to the Soviet Union had totally corrupted its politics.

Van became emotional as he explained how a similar pattern had occurred with all other multinational left organizations whose commitment waned as their predominantly white leadership tried to reach out to broader sectors of the white working class by watering down their commitment to anti-racism. He could see the same pattern emerging in the WUO when he read their new political journal, *Osawatomie,* whose articles talked repeatedly about class struggle but little about racism.[3] He didn't want to see PFOC, which had so much potential, make the same mistakes.

After a conversation with Van, my mind would be teeming with ideas and I wouldn't be able to sleep. I appreciated Van's point of view, but I still thought that the Hard Times strategy was justifiable. Many Third World groups like the Puerto Rican Socialist Party (PSP), the American Indian Movement (AIM), the Republic of New Afrika, the United Black Workers, and the Chicano group, CASA, had joined the organizing committees for the conference in cities around the country. Sometimes I felt that Van was deliberately ignoring these facts in order to make his case. Plus, I was wary of being manipulated by a male leader's command of theory and history.

It was easier for me to be clear about the inadequacies of the Hard Times vision in the area of women's politics. Shortly before the Conference, the WUO printed an editorial in *Osawatomie* which immediately made me, Janice, and Roxie very angry. The article was titled "The Women's Question is a Class Question," and it focused entirely on the economic aspects of women's oppression. No mention was made of patriarchy, rape, violence against women, lesbian liberation, or the need for an autonomous women's movement. "This is terrible!" the three of us agreed, as did most others in our PFOC women's caucus. Van was eager to point out that this editorial was consistent with the overall program of the Hard Times Conference, and when we looked at the conference announcement and the workshops being planned, it was true. Jobs, equal pay, the right to unionize, and an end to racial discrimination were the only ways in which hard times for women were addressed.

As the conference grew closer, I was wrapped up in detailed preparations and had little time to focus on the larger political issues. I had never worked on a gathering of this magnitude, and since I was a newcomer, my primary responsibilities were in the logistical arena. In fact, my many tasks prevented me from attending much of the first day's sessions. Along with the other members of PFOC, I was very excited that more than 2,000 people had come to the conference, exceeding our expectations, and that such prominent authors as Toni Cade Bambara and Howard Zinn were present, as well as SNCC leader

Ella Baker and radical lawyer William Kunstler.[4] Clearly the extensive outreach
had paid off. However, I started to have premonitions of disaster when I heard
that the conference leadership had denied a request by the Black caucus, led by
the Republic of New Afrika (RNA)[5], to make a formal presentation at a plenary
session. "Why would they reject such a request?" I asked a man who was working with me at the registration table. "The program is so tightly scheduled it
would probably cut off a previously planned speaker," he offered tentatively. But
neither of us was convinced.

The Black caucus met anyway, joined by other Third World delegates,
and on the next day Third World leaders took the floor. Their demeanor was serious and respectful, but they clearly were angry. They criticized the conference
organizers for submerging the independent struggles of Third World nations
into a multinational working class struggle focused on economic issues, following the traditional pattern of the white-dominated U.S. left. They had expected
more from the organizers. The Third World caucus criticisms were followed by
a critique from the woman's caucus about the lack of prioritization of women's
and lesbian issues. There hadn't even been time set aside for a woman's caucus
until women had spontaneously insisted that it happen.

The criticisms hit me like a ton of bricks. It was one thing to hear Van
talking about the implications of the Hard Times political line and wonder
whether he was overstating the problems. It was quite another to hear these
same criticisms articulated by Third World leaders and realize that they had
looked to Prairie Fire as an organization that had broken with the white supremacy of the left, and now they had been gravely disappointed. On top of that,
there was the condemnation from the women's caucus which corresponded to
the problems many of us had identified beforehand but had pushed to the side
in our eagerness to proceed with the conference organizing.

The rest of the conference was inevitably shaped by the intervention of
the Third World caucus. While the final plenary session approved some ongoing
work projects, it seemed to me that this was just pro forma. To most people in
PFOC, the burning question was no longer what projects to vote on, but what
would be the political basis for our work as an organization in the future.

The months following the Hard Times Conference were consumed with an intense political process. Everyone in PFOC had been shaken by the criticisms of the conference and began to think about the reasons we each had gone along with the approach of Hard Times. For myself, I could see that I had glossed over my own reservations and had deferred to the other members of the NC, not just because they were more experienced than I, but because I was reacting to the charges of Celine, Jacqui, and many others that Prairie Fire's politics were anti-working class. The Hard Times Conference was our chance to prove them wrong. But look at what had happened!

Van, on the other hand, had been vindicated. As a seasoned leftist who had been through many organizational upheavals in the past, he quickly took the opportunity to assume leadership of the process to change the direction of the organization. He suggested that we call the process "rectification," a term adopted from the Chinese revolution, which involved a deep examination of a wrong political line and practice. With Van leading the way, we began to reexamine Lenin and Mao and to connect what we read to our individual politics. The greatest and harshest scrutiny was given the members of the National Committee who had developed the Hard Times strategy. Except, as we embarked on this examination, the truth of the hidden relationship between the WUO and Prairie Fire was revealed.

Most of the people on Prairie Fire's National Committee were secret above-ground members of the WUO, serving as double-duty leaders of both organizations. The Hard Times Conference had been developed by this joint leadership with a multi-purpose agenda. Some of the WUO leaders were questioning whether it made sense to remain underground now that the Viet Nam war was over and armed activity was less relevant. They proposed a strategy of "inversion" in which most of the WUO members would return to public political involvement. If successful, Hard Times could serve as a launching pad for inversion, allowing surfaced members to easily assume a leading role in the multinational party-building movement.[6]

Those of us who were inexperienced enough to have believed that there were two separate organizations were shocked and deeply disturbed by the exposure that Prairie Fire was linked with the WUO, not only politically but organizationally. I felt duped and betrayed. My personal sense of hurt and anger about the lack of transparency now fused with my concern about the politics of Hard Times. I became invested in helping to lead the rectification process which now shifted its focus to the problems with the leadership of the WUO and of PFOC.

As the layers of secrecy that had protected the WUO came unraveled, the leaders of the WUO (those underground and those who had functioned on Prairie Fire's NC) were called upon to account not only for the errors which had led to the conference, but also for a long list of mistakes involving arrogance, sexism, racism, and manipulative leadership practices. Those of us who had joined the PFOC leadership recently, without knowing its true structure, were mainly exempt from this avalanche of criticism, but the rest of the people in leadership were asked to write self-criticisms and tape statements. From underground, WUO members "spoke bitterness"[7] about their experiences and accusations spiraled. Prairie Fire went so far as to compile these statements and print them in a strident pamphlet called *The Split in the Weather Underground Organization: Struggling Against White and Male Supremacy.*[8]

Every so often, when I was at work teaching English as a Second Language to immigrant kids, I had a moment to step back from the frenzy of the process and I would wonder whether the WUO leadership really deserved this level of criticism. I would question whether this was the right approach to get comrades to understand their mistakes or the best way to develop our organization and practice going forward. But my own stake in the process was too large to take an eagle eye view for long.

What did we think we were doing? We were overturning the old, bringing in the new with the moral fervor of evangelists. We were trying to be serious, we were trying to take responsibility for the ugly, embedded history of racism and

sexism in the United States, we truly yearned to become the "new men and women"
Che Guevara had envisioned in his political writings, and we correctly understood
that this was not an easy process. We saw that, if such a process is to be undertaken
seriously in any society, it must involve introspection, reflection, and evaluation,
but we disregarded the need for an underlying spirit of mutual respect and love that
was absolutely necessary for individual and collective transformation to occur. We
had no perspective about the stage of struggle that we were in, and little kindness or
sympathy for each other or ourselves.

We were applying the process of cultural revolution that had taken place
as part of the Chinese revolution without a clear critique of the errors and brutal
excesses that had occurred. Translated to our tiny, fledgling organization in the
United States, these processes ironically ended up reproducing the self-aggrandiz-
ing, competitive, and denigrating models of leadership and authority that are
endemic to the capitalist system, even as we thought we were breaking with all that.
This problem was not unique to PFOC and the WUO within the U.S. left in this
period. Stories that have emerged from other parts of the new communist/party-
building movement indicate that political rigidity, top-down leadership, and a
harsh approach to criticism self-criticism were common contradictions in cadre
organizations committed to building "vanguard parties" on a democratic central-
ist model.

Despite the sharp demarcations we drew at the time, Prairie Fire evolved
from the legacy of the WUO and built on many of its strengths—its militant anti-
imperialism, its challenge to white supremacy and commitment to international
solidarity, and its assessment that a system based on violence will never be changed
through entirely peaceful means. And, like the WUO, it continuously wrestled with
how to put these beliefs into practice over the next two decades.

The rectification process led to the dissolution of the WUO and the
break-up of the complicated, functional clandestine networks the WUO had built
up over six years of practice. For some members of the WUO, the process caused
deep bitterness and alienation from all political work and organizing. Some members decided to remain underground to form a new clandestine organization,

The Revolutionary Committee, which pledged itself in its earliest communiqués to renew armed activity on an anti-imperialist basis. Other members decided to return to public life and some of those who surfaced decided to become part of Prairie Fire. This infusion of women and men who were strong anti-imperialists, who had gone through five or six years of living underground and were still committed to the process of building movement and organization, brought vital new energy and perspective to PFOC and helped move us from a period of internalized struggle into stronger, outward-looking practice. Many of these former Weather people were to become my best friends and political companions over the next years.

In November 1976, a national conference of PFOC was held in San Francisco. The conference was conceived as a means of bringing the organization together after the difficult process of rectification, a means of solidifying our politics and developing a unified program. Instead, the organization split antagonistically, with New York, Boston, and what was left of Chicago on one side and the Bay Area and L.A. on the other. We had debated the politics of women's oppression and women's liberation, the nature of revisionism in the Soviet Union, the correct perspective on armed struggle in the current period, and the structure and approach to leadership in the organization. At every workshop, in every caucus meeting, during every plenary, what might have been simple differences of opinion, developed into charged, angry, personalized fights. By the end of the three day conference, we couldn't even reach agreement on the definition of the differences and it became impossible to continue working together.

Once again, I was completely taken by surprise and caught off balance. Only a couple of months before, I had spent long evenings in New York, hanging out with the other women of the reconstituted National Committee, dancing at the local women's bars, talking late into the night about politics, relationships, personal dreams. I had shared many of their perceptions about the organization and differed with them about some things, but overall I had never felt greater

political and personal closeness than I did with these women. The rupture at the
conference was starker, more mysterious, and more painful to me than my break
with Celine or even the criticisms of the Hard Times Conference.

*To this day, if you ask people on different sides of PFOC what we split
about, we would come up with different versions. Opportunism, revisionism, chau-
vinism... We charged and counter-charged, all claiming the mantle of political
correctness and focusing on what separated each line and group from each other.
Such splits and antagonisms rippled through the movement and the result was a
fractious culture that ran counter to our stated goals of collective resistance.*

*For those of us who remained involved in the movement, it was the many
revolutions taking place around the globe that kept us inspired and committed.
We believed in the Cuban revolution's declaration,* Venceremos! *(we shall win).
As long as we didn't give up, we too could surmount the objective and subjective
problems which continually beset us. As long as we looked to the national liberation
movements around the world for political direction, victory was certainly possible.*

———— ⌇ ————

Shortly after the PFOC conference, I decided to go to Cuba with the
Venceremos Brigade which was preparing for its tenth brigade in the spring of
1977. Since 1969, volunteer brigades had gone at the invitation of the Cuban
government to participate in solidarity work in agriculture and construction and
also to challenge the U.S. ban on travel to Cuba.

I needed to be reenergized after all of the bitter fights of the previous
year. I wanted to experience a revolutionary society firsthand and gain perspective on what we were trying to do in the U.S. by involving myself in a struggle
that had actually won state power. I had read and heard enough to know that
Cuba was not a utopia. Racism and sexism had not been obliterated, the Cuban
relationship to the Soviet Union was an ongoing contradiction, there were many
questions about the limits on dissent imposed by the Cuban government. But
in the last year, I had seen firsthand, on a micro-scale, how difficult change was

to achieve, and so my questions about Cuba were framed by respect for their monumental accomplishments. Surely what I learned from my trip would help build our work here.

When I joined the Venceremos Brigade in January 1977 and began the preparatory work studying Spanish, learning about Cuban history, and fundraising for members' expenses, I expected to expand my political horizons and renew my energy. I didn't expect to fall in love with the leader of my Brigade section. In the midst of rectification, disenchanted with the entire process, Janice had left PFOC and we had broken up. I wasn't sure I was ready for a new round of emotional involvement when I first met Lola, but I was seduced by her physical warmth, her dramatic looks and personality, and by the fact that she wanted to be with me and to come out as a lesbian with me. Lola was fifteen years older— forty-three to my twenty-eight. She had been an actress in Chicago and part of the Weather support network from early on. She had four amazing children, three girls and one boy, ranging in age from seven to sixteen. When I first met her kids, in their run-down old Victorian in the Haight-Ashbury, with a view of the Golden Gate Bridge, I felt immediately that I wanted to be part of this family.

As 1977 unfolded, I was engrossed in learning about Cuba and enveloped in the excitement of this new multi-dimensional relationship. I savored the weekends when I would go to meetings where Lola would evocatively describe her trip to Cuba as part of the Brigade the year before. After our meetings, Lola and I would stop for a drink at Maude's bar on Cole St. before going back to her house to make dinner, help the kids with their homework, and untangle the squabbles that had arisen during the course of the day. Then we would smoke a couple of joints (which Lola always had ready) and spend the next hours making love and talking about our lives before we met each other.

Lola would tell me about her past life as an actress, about the joy of creating satire on stage, until she hooked up with the WUO and turned to "the theater of the political," as she described it with a laugh. With four small children in tow, she left the Midwest and her husband and moved to San Francisco to help build the support networks that were essential to Weather's survival. But now the WUO was gone and all the networks seemed to be dissolving. She understood, on one level, why this had happened, but she wasn't sure what all this meant for the complicated practice of clandestinity that she had so carefully nurtured. Lola had recently joined PFOC, agreeing with many of the criticisms of the WUO, hoping that she could contribute to building a different kind of organization, but there were questions, many questions... "It's the old baby and the bathwater conundrum," she would muse, and her eyes would get cloudy and her voice thick and she would roll another joint.

Lola's emotion-filled stories about the past seven years opened my eyes to another side of the history that I had been piecing together since I joined Prairie Fire—a side that Van's polemics could never adequately represent. Sometimes as I sat in meetings and listened to Van argue and argue about the importance of exposing the opportunism of other left groups, I would feel an eerie disconnect from this war of words, even as I was nodding in agreement. I would think of Lola's expression as she described the utter confusion she had felt when she first heard about the rectification process. "After all these years of struggle and effort, of trying to help Black and Brown comrades, wasn't rectification a little extreeeeeeme?" she would ask, dramatizing the last syllable to lighten the comment. But I knew that for her it wasn't light at all. Then there were her questions about Prairie Fire's new program and politics. "Are they really so different, so much better?" she would ask in a theatrically ingenuous way before quickly backtracking to acknowledge that, yes, she understood what we were trying to do, but at forty-three she had lived long enough to doubt everything. Cuba, I hoped, would somehow make it all clearer for me.

In fact, Cuba made it clearer and more confusing at the same time. From the moment we landed at Jose Marti airport, I felt the heart-pumping excitement of being on "liberated territory." The revolutionary reality was obvious all over— on the billboards that proudly trumpeted solidarity with the peoples of Angola, to the newspaper headlines denouncing the latest maneuvers of U.S. imperialism. As soon as I began to meet and talk with the young Cubans who were leading the

Brigade, I could see that this was not just a matter of billboards and slogans or a phenomenon imposed by an older generation of leaders. These young women and men defined themselves in relationship to the revolution. They were eager to show us its many successes and explain why they were committed to defending the revolution with their lives, if it came to that.

Over the next six weeks, I learned to lay bricks as part of the housing construction project our brigade was working on. I toured rural schools and health centers and listened to the enthusiastic descriptions of students, teachers, and health workers about the changes that had occurred since the revolution. I met representatives from Viet Nam, Mozambique, Angola, and Ethiopia, and participated in the May 1 International Worker's Day celebration in Havana, where Fidel addressed hundreds of thousands in a speech several hours long that summed up the accomplishments of the past year and emphasized the continuing importance of Cuban solidarity with Angola. Since 1975, Cuba had responded to Angola's request for military assistance by sending thousands of volunteer troops to help in the fight against the combined forces of South Africa and Zaire. Fidel praised the internationalism and self-sacrifice of these volunteers and held them up as a revolutionary standard for us all.

One day, we attended a meeting of one of the Committees in Defense of the Revolution (CDR) on the outskirts of Havana. The CDR's had been established toward the end of 1960, when acts of sabotage and terrorism against the revolution were escalating daily, culminating in the Bay of Pigs/Playa Girón attack in April 1961.[9] The Committees were originally organized on a block-by-block basis to consolidate resistance and neutralize the counter-revolutionaries. Since then, the CDR's had grown to become the organizational unit which discussed and facilitated everything from food distribution to vaccinations to the implementation of laws such as the new Family Code which had gone into effect in 1975.

Idela, the coordinator of the CDR we visited, ran the meeting with great efficiency. The agenda was very long and included hotly debated issues such as the necessity of fumigating a mosquito onslaught and allegations of unfair allocation of food rations. Almost everyone participated and had a loud, emphatic opinion. Idela calmly allowed the disagreements to be aired, but directed the meeting toward building a consensus. In the end, it seemed to me that people understood and accepted the compromises that were necessary in order to resolve problems.

After the meeting, the CDR hosted a party for the brigadistas, and I ended up at a table with Idela. As Idela drank a couple of glasses of rum and I sipped my first glass, she began telling me how important the passage of the new Family Code had been to her. It had been enacted after intensive debates throughout the country and was finally approved by over ninety-eight percent of all the participants. It mandated equal rights and responsibilities between men and women in regards to marriage, divorce, adoption, housework, and children. "It changed so much not only for me, but more importantly for my daughters," she exclaimed. She had had many struggles in her marriage over her desire for independence and her wish that her husband share housework and the care of their children. "And, of course, over love. The law can't change how men feel," she smiled with a note of resignation, "but it can give us women recognition and support for what is right."

The party went on into the early hours of the morning. Idela was a woman in her late forties and I was struck by her lack of self-consciousness as she lost herself in the Afro-Cuban rhythms that were enveloping the room. I also noticed how the people who had been shouting at each other earlier over some disagreement in the CDR meeting were now laughing and drinking together. I ruefully thought about how hard it was for us Americans to disagree but then come together in friendship.

Despite the fact that the Cubans continually encouraged us to put aside what they saw as sectarian differences in the interests of building unity, a strained dynamic operated among the brigadistas. Theoretically I wanted to build unity too, but practically I had already come up against disagreements with the Brigade leadership which was closely affiliated with the Communist Party of the U.S. (CP-USA). I had brought information to distribute about Assata Shakur, who had just been convicted of murder in March 1977 and sentenced to life plus thirty-three years by an all-white jury. In the early seventies, the CP-USA had worked with the Cubans to wage a massive international campaign in support of Angela

Davis when she had been charged as an accessory to murder in the Marin County courthouse uprising in August 1970.[10] Angela's name was so well known in Cuba that when Cubans saw my button with Assata's picture on it, they immediately assumed it was Angela. I thought the history of Cuban work around Angela could be a basis for building support for Assata, but Brigade leaders saw Assata as an extremist and discouraged any discussion of her case.

Then there was the issue of "sexual orientation." I had been open about the fact that I was a lesbian when I applied for the Brigade, even though I knew that among the Brigade leadership and in Cuban government circles there was little support for gay and lesbian liberation. While some of the other brigadistas supported gay liberation at home, they thought it was inappropriate to raise this issue when we were the guests of the Cubans. So this too became a point of tension. I had more success engaging the Cubans on our brigade in lively discussions about homosexuality, although we rarely saw eye to eye.

Toward the end of our six-week stay, we went to a party at Margaret Randall's house. Margaret was an American who had lived in Cuba since 1969, had written the early seminal work, *Cuban Women Now,* and traditionally hosted a gathering for each Brigade at her apartment in Havana. Listening to her talk about her life in Cuba and her work at the Cuban Book Institute, I was jealous of her immersion in the life of this country and her ability to work for a revolution which was already a reality. What would it be like, I wondered, to stay and work in Cuba, to learn from the people, to be personally transformed over time by exposure to such a different society.

Later, in a conversation with the leader of my sub-brigade section, I voiced some of my ambivalence about returning to the United States and all the daunting challenges of building revolutionary movement there. Lourdes, an Afro-Cuban woman with a no-nonsense approach to all of the myriad problems brigadistas brought to her, listened patiently but responded emphatically. "Deanna, please understand, we need you working in the United States! It is your country and you have to work to make others know what you have learned here, that's your responsibility as a conscious American." As soon as she said it, I knew she was right.

After that conversation, I allowed myself more time to think about Lola and her kids and how much I missed them. I started wondering whether the next issue of Prairie Fire's political journal, *Breakthrough*, would be coming out on schedule and how the work on our statement on women's liberation was going. The Cuban children started reminding me of the kids I worked with in San Francisco, to whom I had promised souvenirs of my trip. One thing had become clearer. For better or for worse, my own path was about struggling to make change inside the monster, the beast, the enemy country that I had been born into and which was my home.

"I send you Love and Revolutionary Greetings From Cuba, one of the largest, most resistant and most courageous palenques (maroon camps) that has ever existed on the Face of this Planet." Assata Shakur wrote these words in 1998, from her exile in Cuba. After escaping from prison in 1979, Assata was granted political asylum by the Cubans in 1984, infuriating the U.S. government and exacerbating the tensions between Cuba and the U.S. In 1998, the United States set a half million dollar award for Assata's capture (later increased to $1 million) and in response to the bounty placed on her head, Assata wrote an open letter to the world community:

"My name is Assata Shakur, and I am a twentieth-century escaped slave. Because of government persecution, I was left with no other choice than to flee from the political repression, racism, and violence that dominate the US government's policy towards people of color...

"All I represent is just another slave that they want to bring back to the plantation. Well, I might be a slave, but I will go to my grave a rebellious slave. I am and I feel like a maroon woman. I will never voluntarily accept the condition of slavery, whether it's de-facto or ipso-facto, official or unofficial."[11]

Venceremos *is not a future tense vow guaranteeing uncertain victories.* Venceremos *is the assurance of Cuba's revolutionary accomplishments over fifty years. It is Assata's pledge of uncompromising rebellion. It is our collective promise to carry on global resistance.*

INTERNATIONAL
WOMEN'S
YEAR

KLAN
KANT
STOP
US!

BUILD ON THE
VICTORIES
OF HOUSTON

Back cover of *Breakthrough*, Vol. II No. 1, Spring 1978. Photo of woman confronting right-wing counter-demonstration at International Women's Year Convention in Houston, November 1977, by *Breakthrough* photographer.

CLAIM NO EASY VICTORIES

Tell No Lies, Claim No Easy Victories
—Amilcar Cabral[1]

MY TRIP TO CUBA HAD REINVIGORATED ME on many levels and by the end I was happy to return to the Bay Area and jump back into my relationship with Lola and the varied political work Prairie Fire was engaged in. A group from PFOC had gone up to support the Klamath River Indians in their struggle to preserve control over their land and fishing rights. Black prisoners at San Quentin were being set up, attacked, and murdered by white supremacist prisoner organizations like the Aryan Brotherhood, the Nazis, and the Ku Klux Klan, with the active support of the San Quentin administration and the California Department of Corrections. The Black prisoners had called upon outside forces to plan a rally to challenge this aggression, and Prairie Fire had initiated the August 21st Coalition to respond to this request. And the second issue of our political journal, *Breakthrough*, was going to press just as I returned. I had begun to work on this issue before I went to Cuba and I was happy to see how it had turned out. I particularly liked the centerfold which prominently featured women political prisoners who Prairie Fire supported: Yvonne Wanrowe, Susan Saxe, Lolita Lebron, Marilyn Buck, and Assata Shakur.[2]

On another front, a fierce backlash was developing against the gay liberation movement and Prairie Fire had joined with gay and lesbian organizations to mobilize against these right-wing assaults. A former Miss America, Anita Bryant, was spearheading a national campaign, based in Miami, to "Save Our

Children" from the influence of the "homosexual lifestyle." Bryant's campaign coincided with a Supreme Court decision that upheld sodomy laws, local court decisions that removed children from their lesbian mothers, and the persecution of gay school workers. While President Jimmy Carter was expounding on the sanctity of the family from the White House pulpit, the government's AFDC (Aid to Families With Dependent Children) program was being severely cut back. Clearly, no one cared whether Third World women and their children were "saved" from poverty.

We quickly put together a leaflet called "The Meaning of Miami: Saving Women and Children for Imperialism,"[3] which we distributed at the San Francisco Gay Pride march in June. The state and the right-wing were determined to uphold the traditional, white, nuclear family model in order to stem the threat of gay liberation to the American social fabric. We argued that the gay liberation movement needed to link the defense of gay rights to anti-racist issues and the overall struggle against imperialism or it would end up being compromised and lose its potential to achieve fundamental change. We received mixed reactions as we walked through the crowds with our fliers. While some people welcomed a perspective that went beyond gay rights, others thought it was alienating to include a discussion about imperialism and Third World women in the middle of this gay liberation parade. Still, we felt that we had accomplished our goal of opening up these questions at the march, and we continued to promote our perspective as part of the ongoing coalition that was responding to the backlash.

At the same time, the upcoming International Women's Year Convention in Houston, Texas, was shaping up as another major battleground over the gains of the women's and gay movements. The United Nations had declared 1975 International Women's Year (IWY), and the U.S. government had used this impetus to develop a showcase national conference on women to be held in November 1977. Although we believed that the conference was a government effort to co-opt women's struggles, we also saw it as an opportunity for Prairie Fire to expand its work within the broader women's movement and put forward anti-racist politics on women's liberation.

The significance of the IWY Convention increased as preparatory conferences were held around the country to elect official delegates. The debates at many of these conferences centered on whether the delegates would support abortion, the ERA, and gay rights or denounce them. Several states elected delegations that were committed to a reactionary platform and were openly backed by the Klan, the Mormon Church, and Anita Bryant's Save Our Children. The right-wing was taking the offensive to redefine "women's movement" from a fundamentalist point of view. To us, it was absolutely necessary to present a strong rebuttal to these politics.

As the time for the convention neared, our energy was focused on preparing for Houston. I worked with other members of Prairie Fire's Women's Commission to produce a broadside called "SHOWDOWN AT HOUSTON" which included source material from right-wing groups that exposed more clearly than we could their perspective and plans. Phyllis Schlafly's anti-ERA grouping described the IWY pre-conferences as "a front to give media exposure and respectability to radicals, lesbians, and MSfits who want to agitate for their anti-family goals at the taxpayers' expense."[4] John Briggs, a California state senator and a Republican nominee for governor who was campaigning for the reinstatement of the death penalty, wrote in an *L.A. Times* op-ed piece: "Homosexuality is not simply the legitimate alternative life-style its advocates would have us believe. It is a direct assault on our most significant social institution, the family, and thus it becomes a public harm that legislatures have a right and duty to proscribe."[5] And we cited an article in the *Christian Science Monitor* describing the right-wing's plans to rent the Houston Astroarena for a huge counter-mobilization "a sort of picnic outing celebrating God, family, and country" where they would pass resolutions against "abortion, the Equal Rights Amendment, federal child care centers, and the legalization of homosexuality."[6]

We called upon women to unite on a very different basis: "As the attacks on women escalate, the choices before white women become clearer and harder. We can either fight for liberation against white supremacist, male supremacist roles... or we can try to preserve our individual privilege and security by jumping on the American bandwagon."

As the Convention came closer, the Klan escalated things even further
by announcing that they were going to Houston to protect their wives (who were
attending the Convention as part of anti-ERA delegations) from the "radicals
and the lesbians." Within the Prairie Fire leadership we began to have debates
about how we should respond to the right-wing threats. Some of us were wary
of accepting the bait of sensationalized media focus on the right-wing. We were
worried that we would end up putting too much energy into fighting the right
instead of using the opportunity to reach out to progressive women. But Van had
become riveted on the Klan and insisted that we needed to be ready to respond
defensively to any violence they might initiate.

Since the Hard Times Conference, I had worked closely with Van in
Prairie Fire's leadership collective. From time to time I had minor disagreements
with him, but for the most part I viewed him as my political mentor and agreed
with his opinions and proposals, which I considered original and strategic. His
sharp, argumentative, and critical style of leadership dovetailed with some of
my own personality tendencies, and so I easily adopted many of the same approaches as a leader of the organization. But in the work leading up to Houston,
my disagreements with him were becoming more disturbing. The Convention
was about the women's movement and its issues. To my thinking, Van's fixation
on the Klan skewed our work towards a power struggle between men.

A couple of times, Van approached me outside of our regular meetings
to discuss plans for possible self-defense actions. He told me he was working
with some people, including his former roommate Phil, on "another level," and
he thought I should come to one of the meetings of that group to help provide
"women's leadership." I was intrigued but also uneasy and finally I begged off.
I explained some of my hesitations to Van, but I wasn't sure enough of myself to
raise the disagreements to a boiling point.

One night, a week before the Convention, as we were debating our
different perspectives for the hundredth time, I got a phone call from my sister
in New York. My mother had just had a heart attack and was now in the hospital. Joyce wasn't sure how serious it was, but she thought I should probably fly
home. When I hung up the phone and returned to the meeting, my head was

spinning. For months my thoughts and energy had been focused on the IWY Convention. Karen and I were to lead the Prairie Fire delegation in rallies, presentations, and all the other convention activities. My mind couldn't have been further from my family and my mother.

When I explained to the group what was happening and expressed my confusion about what to do, Karen immediately said, "You should go home, Diana, we'll figure it out." So I booked a flight out the next morning, packed some clothes and the IWY convention schedule, and promised the others that I would be in regular contact.

—✥—

After a sleepless night, I dozed fitfully on and off throughout the six-hour plane ride to New York. Even though I spoke to my parents every week, I had lived away from home since I was sixteen. I had managed to get into college at an early age, desperate for independence from a household I found suffocating. Now at twenty-eight, I only saw my parents twice a year and usually tried to limit what they knew about my life, since our ongoing fights about values and politics never went anywhere.

As I thought about my mother, a stark, disturbing memory jolted me. I remembered how the calm set of her face distorted into suppressed fury when she learned that I was a lesbian on a cab ride to JFK airport a couple of years before. She had unexpectedly provoked the conversation when she abruptly asked me "Are you a queer?" with uncharacteristic stridency. When I said that I was and began to try and explain what my love for women meant to me, she cut me off. "All I ask is that you don't tell your father and we don't have to talk about *it* anymore," she hissed. Since I had long ago given up on an honest relationship with my parents, it wasn't difficult for me to nod my head and end the conversation. We hadn't talked about *it* since, though lately I had been contemplating introducing them to Lola. Even my father might be seduced by Lola's charm.

Toward the end of the plane ride I finally fell asleep. I was in the hospital visiting my mother when I realized that Anita Bryant was visiting the patient in the adjoining hospital bed. When I saw that Anita was coming over to our side of the room, I defiantly pulled the curtain around my mother's bed, but the gesture was useless because the scene quickly shifted and now I was in Houston in a loud, angry demonstration against the Klan. I noticed that across the street, my mother was wielding a picket sign declaring *Save Our Children!* I couldn't stop myself, I was going to break our rules of disciplined conduct and cross the street and confront her...

I woke with a guilty jolt. This scenario was unfair to my mother, who for most of my life was kind, gentle, and a constant, caring refuge from my father's belligerent idiosyncrasies. These were not the memories I wanted to be having when she was sick in the hospital. Maybe I was thinking about the hard times because I didn't want to remember the nights when I was seven, eight, and nine years old, when I would wait up for her when she was out late at the movies with a friend, and I was desperately worried that something bad would happen to her on the subway ride, or on the dark walk to our apartment, and then she would be gone and my sister and I would be left with my father, and I didn't know how things could go on if that happened. The tears began rolling down my face, and the man in the next seat glanced over and then quickly looked away in embarrassment. Fortunately, we were landing and this miserable flight was over.

I caught a cab and we slogged through rush hour traffic to my parents' apartment on 99th street on Manhattan's Upper West Side. When my sister opened the door, I could see the news wasn't good. Joyce's eyes were red and she looked dazed. "She died this afternoon," she choked out and we both started to cry. "They wanted to do a catheterization. They said it was necessary to prevent further attacks. They said the risks were very, very tiny. I was in the waiting room and they came out and told me she died during the procedure. I just can't believe it. She's only sixty-two. I shouldn't have let them do it, but it seemed to make sense. I didn't know what to do, and daddy said I should just handle it."

"It's okay, it's not your fault at all." I wanted to comfort Joyce, but I didn't know what to say because I couldn't believe it either, even though the possibility had been lurking behind my bad dreams. "What is daddy doing?"

I couldn't imagine how my father, who seemed to depend upon my mother for almost everything, would deal with this. "He's just watching TV. I think he's in shock, unable to express anything," Joyce whispered.

"So you just missed her." My father greeted me in a weirdly sarcastic manner when I entered the living room. "I came as fast as I could," I explained cautiously, and I put my arm around his skinny frame. "She was too good for this world," he said and stared at the TV for a few minutes accusingly. "What are we going to do next, when is the funeral going to be?" I asked, feeling that as a family we had no history, no background in death and dying that could help us figure out what to do in this situation. "I don't want a funeral, she didn't know anyone who would come to a funeral, it's just a waste of money," he declared in his usual contentious manner. Part of me wanted to scream, to argue that my mother was loved by many, that she had friends, and that money was a horrible, sick thing to be thinking about at this time. But I knew my father and I knew myself well enough to know that it would just turn into a shouting match that could escalate to encompass all our disputes. So I let it go, thinking that we would revisit it in a calmer moment. But we never did.

Instead, my sister and I arranged a simple burial a couple of days later. Joyce and I drove out with the mortuary limousine to the Jewish cemetery where my mother had wisely bought a plot a few years before, near to her own mother's grave. My father told us he couldn't handle watching her be put in the ground, so the two of us were the only witnesses when her coffin was lowered into the grave. It was wrong, but it was also fitting. An immigrant woman, who had moved to this country from Russia when she was ten, she had never seemed to expect much more than life gave her, and had made the best of what that was. As little girls, we had adored her. We made up pet names for her—moopy, mophead, momish—which we vested with all the love we couldn't figure out how to express in other ways. The names stuck for years and even when I began to resent her stoicism, her tolerance of society's injustices, and her acceptance of my father's rants and raves, for most of my life I took for granted her love for me and my underlying love for her. Now she was gone and my connections to family were frayed to the breaking point.

My father insisted on going out to dinner that night to the restaurant where he and my mother ate every weekend. Perhaps it was his way of remembering her, or, as my sister and I really thought, it was his way of forgetting. When we got there the waiter, who saw them every week, asked after my mother and my father quipped, "Here today, gone tomorrow—she died on Tuesday." The waiter looked stunned and rushed away to the kitchen. When he came back to take our orders, he said simply, "She was a beautiful, gracious woman. I will really miss her." When he left I angrily turned to my father. "He would have come to a funeral," I spat out. "You're crazy," my father spat back. My sister put her hand on my arm, and I swallowed my retort. We ate the rest of our dinner in silence.

The next day I made my reservation for Houston and that evening I flew out. I promised my sister and my father that I would come back over the Christmas holidays to help sort out my mother's things. Now the only closure I wanted was to get away. Karen, Lola, and the rest of the Prairie Fire delegation were scheduled to arrive in Houston the next morning and I had to be there with them to try and put my huge pain to some good use.

⸻

The next few days were a blur of caucus meetings, workshops, rallies, presentations, intense conversations and heated debates. Lola greeted me in Houston with open arms, and although I didn't give her a blow-by-blow description of what had happened in New York, having her there with her warmth, her affection and, yes, her motherliness, helped me in many unsaid ways. Everyone was very solicitous about how I was doing, but I made it clear that what I wanted at this point was to focus on the Convention and what we had come to Houston to accomplish. And we wasted no time in proceeding with our work.

Shortly after we arrived, there was a pre-Convention lesbian caucus of over 600 women. This had been planned to counter the right-wing's strategy to target lesbians and divide them off from the rest of the convention. Within the caucus, Third World women and anti-racist white women led a struggle to produce and adopt an anti-racist statement. It read in part:

As lesbians we cannot separate our struggle from the
struggles of all oppressed people. We recognize that the same
system that oppresses us as lesbians oppresses all people of
color. Therefore, the lesbian caucus of the IWY conference,
as a multiracial group, has as a basis of unity, a commitment
to eliminate racism within ourselves. We further pledge to
fight against the institution of racism in the United States and
internationally. In particular, we support the freedom fighters
of Southern Africa and all economic sanctions and boycotts of
South Africa and Rhodesia.[7]

Another significant struggle took place in the lesbian caucus. The
Justice Department offered to set up a formal liaison with the caucus in order to
"protect" lesbians from the right-wing at the Convention. The debate around
this proposal was very heated, but in the end it was defeated. The majority of the
caucus realized that this was an effort to use the threat of the right-wing to force
women into compromised positions with the state and to undermine our self-
reliance and collectivity.

The government formulated National Plan of Action was supposed to
be the centerpiece of the Convention. However, from the beginning it was clear
that the majority of delegates wanted to pass a platform that went way beyond
the government's tepid plans. Some of the progressive state delegations, including California, had raised money to assure that Third World and disabled wom-
en would be able to attend the conference which meant that the framework of
debate was much further to the left than the government had anticipated. Black
delegates led a struggle to unseat the all-white, KKK-affiliated delegates from
Mississippi, but were unable to get enough votes to accomplish this, because the
majority of delegates were unwilling to question the legitimacy of the electoral
process that had brought them to the convention. On the other hand, a caucus
of Third World women won passage of a resolution that denounced forced ster-
ilization of women and deportation of undocumented workers and supported

affirmative action, Native American sovereignty, and respect for all Native treaty rights. These victories, added to the resolutions supporting abortion, the ERA, and lesbian rights, represented a resounding rejection of the right-wing platform as well as the middle ground that the government sponsors had promoted.

Outside the convention hall, demonstrations responded to the right-wing on a much more militant level. A Chicana-led rally and picket protested arrests of undocumented workers by La Migra. A group of women physically blocked Christian Defense League members from marching into the conference exhibit hall. And a left-feminist caucus, in which Prairie Fire played an important role, held a demonstration that denounced the right-wing attacks and called for liberation and self-determination for Third World peoples.

At the end of the long third day of the convention, Karen and I were exhausted but exhilarated as we wandered around the vast Convention Center garage, looking for our rental car since we had forgotten to mark the parking space on our ticket. After fifteen minutes of haphazard looking, as we walked through the nearly empty floors of the garage, our conversation shifted to nervous jokes about a right-wing trap or the possibility that the state had decided to impound our car. At that very moment, just a few miles from the IWY convention, the right wing was holding their mass rally at the Houston Astro Arena and in the twilight zone setting of the dimly lit, cavernous garage, anything seemed possible.

Finally we found the car, and our relief turned to hilarity. Still giddy, we reached our motel room where the phone was ringing as we walked in. It was Jake, one of the three men who had come to the convention as part of the Prairie Fire delegation. "Where have you been?" His voice was sharp and tense. "Haven't you heard what's happened?" Before I could explain, his words spilled out. Van and two women, who the media was describing as members of the "Revolutionary Committee of the Weather Underground" had been arrested coming out of the right-wing rally at the Astro Arena. They were being charged with possession of explosives and conspiracy to use them against Senator Briggs of California. Two men, also allegedly from the Revolutionary Committee, had been simultaneously arrested in Los Angeles on the same charges.

My heart was pounding wildly. "Where are they?" I lamely asked unable to think of anything else to say. "In the Houston city jail, and the bail has been set at half a million dollars." By the time I hung up the phone my whole body was shaking and my voice cracked as I tried to repeat to Karen what Jake had told me. She quickly turned on the TV and within a few minutes we heard the sensationalistic headlines: "Terrorists disrupt Women's Year Convention... Nationwide conspiracy to attack the right-wing uncovered by the FBI." We looked with our dazed eyes on the blank faces of Van and the two women being escorted in handcuffs into the city jail and shook our heads in meaningless denial as we listened to what the newscasters were describing. What we were seeing went way beyond the realm of our paranoid fantasies at the garage. According to the reporters, this arrest was the result of a long, deep FBI infiltration into the "Prairie Fire Organizing Committee of the Weather Underground." And Van's former roommate Phil was an undercover agent who was behind it all.

Karen and I had known that Van was planning to go to the Astrodome rally which the Klan and other right-wing groups were holding. It made sense for our side to understand what was being discussed and proposed at this event, and Van was eager to take on the infiltration of the rally. Van had also alluded to the possibility that clandestine people were in the best position to "counter" the right-wing in Houston, and by now we understood that this was not just a theoretical proposition. But nothing we had discussed beforehand had involved Senator Briggs or augured major arrests. This was one thing we had not prepared for in all our meetings planning for Houston, but now we had no choice. We had to figure out what to do, and we had to do it without the benefit of Van's advice, which we had been relying on to guide us in major decisions for the past year and a half.

Adrenaline kept us going over the next few days. After lengthy phone conversations with other members back in the Bay Area, we quickly found two left-leaning lawyers in Houston who could temporarily represent Van and the two women who had been arrested. We convened an all night meeting in one of our motel suites and tried to answer people's questions as best we could without

sinking into a bog of fear, recrimination, or interpretation. The internal political
analysis would have to wait. Now the priority was to show support for Van and
the women, and to present an alternative perspective to the world about what
was transpiring. We came up with a plan about how to respond and the next
morning we got the word out about the arraignment to all the people we had
been working with at the convention. Despite the media's fear campaign and the
very short notice, the courtroom was packed.

At the arraignment we got to see the government's chief witness
transformed from the low key, nice guy we had known as Phil Gamache into the
aggressive, cunning agent, Richard Gianotti. Phil had been a quiet but consistent
part of Prairie Fire since 1975, when it was just a committee distributing the
book. He had presented himself as a Vietnam veteran who had been catalyzed
into political consciousness by the war, a common enough phenomenon in that
period when Vietnam Veterans Against the War (VVAW) was a thriving, radical
organization. Phil had been a member of Prairie Fire's childcare collectives and
our fundraising teams. He was a steady worker who kept his opinions to himself.
Now we heard him systematically lay out the details of his case against the five
people who were allegedly plotting to bomb the offices of California Senator
John Briggs. His voice chilled me, but even more enraged me. COINTELPRO
had targeted too many activists and destroyed too many organizations already.
We couldn't let them succeed with Prairie Fire.

Our anger helped shape our presentation at the press conference we
held immediately following the arraignment. The timing of these arrests, we
asserted, could only be understood as an effort to derail the IWY Convention, to
justify fears of lesbian and radical terrorism, and to take the heat off the right-
wing terrorists who were massed in force in Houston. The media was, of course,
slanted on the government's side, but we were pleased to see that we emerged
as articulate and militant women in the many TV, radio, and newspaper reports
that covered our press conference.

Once the press conference was over, our thoughts and conversations
inevitably shifted to Phil and the methods he had employed to try and undo

Prairie Fire. We knew the stories of agents who had infiltrated the Black Panthers and AIM, spreading disinformation, becoming bodyguards and confidantes, fanning internal divisions and escalating them into murderous connections. We understood that these types of operations were fundamental to the state's efforts to disrupt and neutralize Black and other oppressed movements. We even knew that one agent, Larry Grathwohl, had penetrated the Weather circles in the early days and had fed the FBI information for awhile before he was exposed. But that had been years ago. In Prairie Fire, we had implemented some basic security measures as an organization, but our unspoken, operational assumption was that as a legal organization of white people, we were not the ones who would be targeted.

Now all of our assumptions were blown wide open and we were faced with the harsh reality that Prairie Fire Bay Area had, since its founding, operated with an FBI agent in its midst. While Phil Gamache had never been a leader of PFOC, he had been trusted by Van and had been accepted by the rest of us. What did this say about our politics, about our methods of operation and about the nature of our interactions with each other? What did it say about the break up of the WUO, the split in Prairie Fire, the politics of rectification, the Revolutionary Committee and Van's leading role for the past year and a half?

My experience from the last couple of years made me reluctant to once again throw everything up for reinterpretation. But I also knew that we could not afford any more pretense, any more easy claims of the politically correct mantle. I listened guiltily to Lola's whispered accusatory questions in the middle of the night. "What were they thinking about doing at that rally? How could Van think he could get away with being a public leader at the same time as he was involved in clandestine work—isn't this one of the things which he criticized the WUO for? How is this better than the WUO? What do you, Diana, know about all this?"

I couldn't answer her. I didn't want to defend Van, because I too was very angry at him. And I didn't want to excuse myself because I had known that something was going on, although I hadn't known exactly what. I could no longer hide behind the cloak of a political ingénue. My deference to Van's

experience and wisdom was an accommodation to male supremacy, but it wasn't
an excuse. I was in fact a leader of the organization and I had to take responsibility for what had gone on at Houston, even if I didn't know exactly what had been
planned. I hadn't insisted to Van that his work on "another level" be accountable to the strategy our women's caucus had been hammering out for months.
I hadn't questioned the secrecy which put some women "in the know" and left
others out of the information loop, ultimately weakening our collective decision-
making process. I had managed to keep myself from being ensnared in this mess
partly because my instincts had kept me from meeting with Phil. I had used
women's intuition to protect me on an individual level when I should have been
asserting women's leadership to save everyone from this government trap.

—❦—

In the months that followed, Prairie Fire struggled to understand what
weaknesses had led to our current predicament, not only to move forward as
an organization but so that others in the movement could also learn from our
experience. The case of the LA5, as they came to be known, was being tried in
Los Angeles where the four members of the Revolutionary Committee had been
living underground. In order to provide the type of political and legal support
that would be necessary, we quickly decided to shore up our L.A. chapter by
sending half a dozen of our strongest members to live and work there. Everyone
understood the need for the move, yet it still represented a major upheaval for
people's lives, jobs, and relationships. And those of us who remained in the Bay
Area felt the added responsibility of continuing our work in a challenging time
with a weaker organizational core.

We needed to come to agreement with the five people on trial about
the correct legal strategy as well as a political evaluation of the mistakes which
had contributed to this situation. The amount of bail required for each of the
defendants was too large for us to raise, so all of our discussions had to take
place within the constrained framework of the L.A. county jail. A clearer picture
of the intensive FBI set-up began to emerge from courtroom testimony and

pre-trial discovery. For two-and-a-half years, pretty much since the founding of Prairie Fire, the FBI had managed to keep the organization under tight surveillance through the successful infiltration by Gianotti. His FBI instructions were "to locate and apprehend WUO fugitives" and Van had been a particular focus of the infiltration, since he was identified as a probable liaison with the WUO. Although Gianotti had made no progress towards locating and arresting WUO fugitives, the supposed purpose of his infiltration, he was able to provide the FBI with a wealth of information about the people in Prairie Fire and its operations. Over the course of time, as former WUO members surfaced without arrest and in some cases even joined Prairie Fire as public, legal members, Gianotti tried a new approach.

Gianotti/Gamache had presented himself as a veteran whose political consciousness had changed as a result of being in Viet Nam. As he became closer with Van, he offered his military background as a potential asset to the development of political/military clandestine work. Once it was clear that the WUO had split and that Prairie Fire in general and Van in particular were giving political support to the newly emerged Revolutionary Committee, Gianotti explained to Van that he no longer could be content with working on a public legal level with Prairie Fire. His heart lay in clandestine military work. In 1976, he introduced Van to a friend of his, William Reagan, whom he described as a Canadian fugitive, a member of the FLQ (Quebec Liberation Front), an armed clandestine organization fighting for the self-determination of Quebec. To establish Reagan's fugitive credentials, the FBI went so far as to stage a phony search for him in San Francisco, going door-to-door with his picture.[8] Phil appealed to Van to help his friend obtain false I.D. and a change of appearance. Reagan didn't simply want to disappear. Instead, Phil proposed to Van that he and Reagan could use their military background and clandestine experience to help the Revolutionary Committee develop armed activity.

With Van as intermediary, Gamache and Reagan were able to introduce themselves to the Revolutionary Committee, and despite some misgivings, the RC began to work with them. Gianotti pressured the RC to act decisively. With Gianotti and Reagan's guidance, they came up with a plan to bomb the offices of Senator John Briggs, a gubernatorial candidate whose anti-gay, pro-death penalty initiatives fit with the Revolutionary Committee's desire to target white and male supremacist forces. Then the state chose a high profile moment, when three of the RC members were coming out of the rally at Houston, to "expose" the plot against Briggs and also implicate them in plans to attack the Klan in Houston. Prairie Fire would also be linked, through Van and our public presence at IWY, to this violent plot against Briggs.

Looking back, it was easy for all of us to discern the ways he had manipulated the organization to arrive at his desired objectives. What was much more difficult to agree upon were the mistakes that Prairie Fire, Van, and the RC had made, which had allowed Gianotti to accomplish his goals. We couldn't even all agree that we *should* be examining these errors. Van in particular was reluctant to delve into our collective mistakes. While he agreed that more care was needed in evaluating the people we worked with, he cautioned against panic and a knee-jerk self-critical reaction. He did not want to apply a "rectification" process to the current set of mistakes.

For us in Prairie Fire, and to most of the other LA5 defendants, this was not sufficient. We looked back at the history and could see that Phil Gamache had been able to coast through almost every political struggle without putting his own opinions on the line because he, supposedly, had a working-class background, because he was willing to do lots of "support work" like childcare and leafleting, and because Van thought highly of him. Ultimately, it was this position, as Van's right hand, that shielded him from the struggles that were raging in the organization. Similarly, the RC accepted him because of his closeness to Van even though they were suspicious of his story, and even though their political discussions revealed many gaps in understanding and approach.

As we looked back, locating our vulnerabilities, analyzing more closely the dynamics which had been operating in the Bay Area over the past couple of years, we began to feel that, even while we thought we were leading a struggle against male supremacy within the WUO and within the left, in reality we were accommodating male dominance in our own organization on a level that was unacceptable. While the majority of the leadership collective was women, we had allowed Van to shape and guide most of the decisions of the organization in classically dependent ways. We didn't just blame him, we blamed ourselves. And the women of the LA5 blamed themselves. However, we women wanted to engage in a process of self-criticism and Van did not.

Many of Van's points were valid, as usual. He cautioned against playing into the hands of the state by blaming ourselves for all that they had caused. He argued that the five of them were now in the state's hands, behind bars, and that too much was at stake to engage in this type of self-criticism at the same time as the LA5 were preparing for trial. He accused us of a narrow, exceptionalist view which focused on our own weaknesses when every revolutionary movement in history has had its share of traitors and enemy infiltrators. We didn't expect him to agree with everything. We never intended to lay out all of these weaknesses before the world. But we wanted some sort of acknowledgement, beyond generalities and platitudes, that he had made some serious mistakes which had jeopardized others. Without that acknowledgement, the trust and respect we had given him for two years withered beyond repair.

Van wanted to mount a full scale political defense that would highlight the politics of revolutionary anti-imperialism and PFOC, but we disagreed. Given the testimony of Giannotti and Reagan, it was doubtful that the LA5 could build a strong legal case. Politically, we weren't all that sure we could defend the Revolutionary Committee's strategy. And there were already many Third World political prisoners whose cases required legal, political, and financial resources. A highly publicized political trial for the LA5 would only detract from them.

In the end, after much painful debate, the LA5 decided to accept a plea bargain which resulted in prison time for all of them, but much less than they would have faced if they had gone to trial and been convicted (which was the likeliest scenario). PFOC continued to support the five through their time in prison and once they came out. But we never mended our relationship with Van.

Van was sixty-two when he was arrested in Houston. From his point of view, his errors of judgment were small compared to the state's insidious assault on him and on revolutionary political practice over the decades. Women and men thirty-five years younger than him were telling him how he was supposed to approach this last major battle of his life, using the language of white supremacy and male supremacy against him, caving in to the state's campaign to distort and isolate someone who had been fighting all his life. He didn't want to listen.

Is it a fantasy of hindsight, of someone who is now approaching Van's age at the time of his arrest, to believe that we could have softened our fervid, stubborn, laudable insistence that Van be accountable to us and to the truth? Couldn't we have reached some better middle ground with this flawed but revolutionary elder? Or was our break with Van one more inevitable result of a style of leadership, a culture of criticism, polemic, and conflict exacerbation that Van, among many, had modeled?

Van died of cancer in 1992. During the final year of his life, some of his younger friends helped him through his difficult illness. If I hadn't been far away, underground at the time, I like to think that I would have been part of this effort.

Cover of *Breakthrough*, Vol. II No. 1, Spring 1978. Top—photo of Palestinian women freedom fighters by Liberation News Service. Bottom—photo of Southern African freedom fighters by Liberation Support Movement.

CHIMURENGA

WALKING AROUND NEW YORK'S STREETS during the holiday season, when I returned to visit my father after my mother's death, the words to a Holly Near song kept circling again and again through my head: "*It could have been me, but instead it was you, so I'll keep doing the things you were doing as if I were two.*"[1] When I first heard Holly sing the song shortly after the Chilean coup, I was inspired by its insistence that we in the United States shared commitments and risks with people struggling all over the world. Given the arrests that had just occurred in Houston and L.A., the words had a different, more frightening immediacy.

I had worked almost every day for two years with Van, and I had nearly gone to a meeting with Richard Giannotti which could have inexorably involved me in the so-called conspiracy…it could have been me spending this holiday behind bars. Yet here I was in New York, passing by the opulently lavish holiday displays at Tiffany's, taking in the new art exhibit at the Museum of Modern Art, mingling with the crowds of oblivious people while Van and four others were spending their first holiday of many in jail. I wasn't inspired, I was scared. I knew that I wanted to keep struggling for what I believed in, but I wasn't sure what level of sacrifice I was prepared to make.

Of course, I didn't talk about any of this with my father or my sister. The events in Houston could have taken place on another planet as far as they were concerned. Even though the *New York Times* had run an article about the case, "FBI Agents Describe Bizarre Years With Militants,"[2] Prairie Fire's name was never mentioned. Neither of them had any idea that so much had transpired in my life in the month since my mother's death.

Only I realized that the tears that welled up when I spoke with my sister about my mother were being shed for more than her. I had never really trusted my parents' judgment or advice, and I had no other close relationships with older people of their generation that I could remember. My reliance on Van and my affection for him had always been guarded, but part of what I appreciated about him was the fact that he had experience I could learn from and that his advice usually seemed worth listening to.

As I went through my mother's things with my sister, I became lost in a heavy nostalgia. There were clothes in her walk-in closet that she had owned since we were little girls, costume jewelry in an assortment of decorated boxes, and photographs stored in dozens of disorganized manila envelopes. She had been an emotionally contained person, but her belongings overran their containers and defied organizing labels. As we went through the drawers and boxes and envelopes, Joyce and I both agreed that in many ways she *was* a mystery to us. What we knew about the facts of her life could probably be written in one or two pages, and despite all the times each of us had urged her to tell us more, she would always just give a dismissive smile and say, "there's nothing to tell." We, being complicated, analytical young women, could not accept that there wasn't more story to excavate. But our digging had never been successful, and now we could only hypothesize and embellish the few facts we had.

"There were her 'days off,'" I reminded my sister. From the time I was seven and Joyce was five, my mother would leave us with my father every other Saturday and go off to shop, see a movie, and have dinner with a friend. Although in most ways she accepted the traditional, deferent wife's role, she had negotiated this space from my father. "It shows what a strong, independent core she had," I insisted.

"She never converted even though *he* wanted her to," my sister reminded me, referring to the fact that my father had converted to Christianity a couple of years before he met my mother. "I was desperate, I was suicidal," he had explained to us dramatically many times. "I needed spiritual salvation and Judaism offered nothing!" He never mentioned the fact that his conversion took place during the Holocaust, when millions of Jewish people were being carted off to ovens, and it wasn't until many years later that either of us realized this telling connection. We grew up attending Riverside Church, knowing that our heritage was Jewish but unable to explain to all of our Jewish friends in school why we had another religion. My mother had attended church with us, reasoning that, "God is God no matter what religion you believe in," but she had never formally converted. In the past ten years, she had begun sending money to plant trees in Israel, a quiet assertion of her identity apart from my father. "I know what I'm going to do," Joyce announced, brightening. "I'm going to send money for a tree in Israel in her name."

We had been feeling close, sitting in the bedroom we had shared growing up, going through my mother's things, disclosing memories. But as soon as Joyce mentioned trees and Israel, I stiffened. I knew that this is what my mother would have wanted, but to me the tree-planting campaign was an insidious way to get Jews around the world to participate in colonizing Palestine—symbolically planting roots in a land they had never seen, from thousands of miles away. From the time I had started reading about the history of Zionism, I had seethed at the perverse logic that saw the occupation of Palestine as a just response to the Holocaust. It seemed like one of the cruelest tricks of imperialism that a people who had suffered so much bigotry and intolerance over the centuries, a people who had nurtured anti-capitalist, revolutionary thinkers and activists such as Marx and Emma Goldman could turn around and found a state based explicitly on racist religious exclusivity, occupation, and genocide. "It might make mommy happy, but it certainly wouldn't make any Palestinians appreciate her legacy," I muttered, but quickly changed the subject as I saw the pained look on Joyce's face. The chasm which more often than not existed between us was once again a yawning presence in our childhood bedroom.

My father, meanwhile, seemed to have reestablished his daily routine much better than we'd expected. As long as he could go down to the corner store to get the *New York Times* in the morning, have his nap in the afternoon, and eat a baked potato and piece of steak for dinner, he seemed to be okay. He regaled me with stories about his youth, as he always had, and barely mentioned my mother. His emotional energy and passion had been spent early in life, before he met her.

He only got angry with me once when I got home a half an hour late for dinner one evening. "Where were you?" he yelled as I walked in the door, confronting me just as he had countless times when I was a teenager. And just like I had then, I made up a sequence of logistical mishaps which accounted for my dereliction and promised I wouldn't do it again. The anger I'd felt toward him after my mother's death had faded, and now I just hoped that at seventy-two he could bury his loneliness in his memories and neurotic routines.

By the end of my two-week stay, I remembered everything which had driven me to leave New York. I looked out of our fourth floor apartment window at the burnt façade of the tenement building across the street. After years of sirens screaming every other night and barely averted disasters, a fire had consumed most of that building shortly after I moved to the Bay Area. And nothing had been done to fix it since. This was the vacant and desperate view that greeted my father each day when he rolled up the blinds. This was the view I had to escape before it threatened to engulf my belief in possibility and change.

⊷∞⊶

One of the immediate decisions facing me when I returned to the Bay Area was where I was going to live. The household I had shared for the past year and a half was breaking up because a couple of my roommates were moving to Los Angeles as part of Prairie Fire's reorganization. What I wanted was to move in with Lola and her kids. They lived in a large house with a couple of other women, but there was an extra bedroom available. The events of the past few months made me want more emotional anchoring and security in a family structure. To me it made perfect sense. But Lola was hesitant. "It's been so much fun the way things are between us," she explained. Did I really want to see up close what it was like to be forty-four years old with practically no income, a teenage daughter who often wasn't speaking to her, a teenage son who wanted his father, and two little girls who never stopped bickering? "You may not want to stick around," she concluded with a tense laugh. "I'll help you, I'll support you, I want to be there for you and the kids," I protested. Finally she gave in.

I already helped take responsibility for Lola's kids as part of her child-care team, so I knew many of the ins and outs of their lives. Prairie Fire had started the childcare teams in response to the needs of women in the Bay Area chapter who couldn't participate in the work of the organization unless they had consistent support with their children. Very soon, we became committed to the teams as a way to alleviate the contradictions of the traditional nuclear family. The childcare teams also reflected our desire to nurture a radical political framework for the new generation. Over time, the team responsibilities evolved from just taking care of kids when their parents weren't around to a weekly commitment on the part of each person to take a shift which included cooking, cleaning, and chauffering the children where they needed to go. Each team had monthly meetings where we discussed what was going on with the children and tried to help the mother, or parent, deal with whatever issues were coming up.

The teams were liberating; they nurtured our vision of alternative family structures, and they helped us coalesce as an organization with deep interconnections. But they could also be interventionist, over-controlling, and judgmental. Those of us who were not parents, and did not have the final responsibility for the children, were eager to give authoritative advice. Lola left many meetings in tears as team members tried to instruct her on accepting her daughter's anger as natural when Marla hadn't spoken a civil word to her for weeks.

Lola's kids were still adjusting to the major shift in their lives since the WUO had broken up and Lola had joined Prairie Fire. Along with Lola, they had been immersed in semi-clandestine networks in which they had different underground names, learned to keep secrets, and had close relationships with people in that other world. Now they were no longer connected to any of that, but no one had ever seriously tried to explain to them what had happened. We spent many hours at our childcare team meetings trying to figure out the various problems the kids were having, but we never directly talked about this critical piece of the puzzle. We avoided this discussion partly in the name of security because we couldn't expose Lola's role or endanger people who were still underground, and partly because we hadn't sorted it all out ourselves. Instead we chose, like many parents do, to focus on the more superficial aspects of each child's personality and situation. Marla was an academic whiz whose structured personality seemed to be the polar opposite of Lola's. At sixteen she seemed to want to put as much distance between herself and Lola's free form style as possible. Keith was a sports fanatic who most resented Lola's decision to leave her husband, his father. As the only boy, he fought to figure out a place in a family of women and looked to Lola as his emotional bedrock. Dolores at ten was wise-beyond-her-years and wrote moving poetry about Viet Nam, and Lola looked to her for emotional anchoring. Lorraine was an ethereal child who painted magic pictures and seemed removed from most of the family drama that took place every day. And there was constant drama—over chores, over school work, over Lola's attention and, once I moved in, over my new role and relationship to all of the above. Within a month, I recognized that Lola was right—living with this intense family was very different from being Lola's lover. But I loved them all and, despite the constant bedlam in that Haight street house, it still was a refuge from the even fiercer political upheavals raging in PFOC and in our work in the world.

—⊶∞⊷—

When we returned from Houston, we began to reevaluate not only our organizational dependence on Van and the dynamics that led to the arrest of the LA5, but also our decision to put great emphasis and resources into the International Women's Year Convention. Some of the Third World groups we worked with and the May 19th Communist Organization (formed by the chapters that had split from Prairie Fire) argued that despite the anti-racist stands taken in Houston, ultimately the government had succeeded in using the Convention as a wedge between Third World women and men. They insisted that this was part of the state's strategy to co-opt Third World women into identifying with the white-dominated women's movement and divert them from defining their liberation in the framework of national struggles for self-determination.

I couldn't easily accept this perspective. At Houston, I witnessed Third World women defining their own struggles and insisting that white women support them on an anti-racist basis. True, most of the programs that had been approved at the Convention were reforms, but it seemed to me that there was a place in the movement for these types of incremental advances. Although I agreed that the state wanted to pit Third World women and men against each other, and was trying to use the women's movement to accomplish this goal, it seemed too narrow and arrogant to insist that all Third World women's struggles had to occur within the framework of national liberation movements, especially when we knew from our discussions with women within those movements that they had to deal with many internal problems of sexism.

Other women in Prairie Fire countered that aspects of IWY might have been progressive, but we didn't have the capacity to deal with the complicated dynamics of the U.S. women's movement at this stage. I was torn. Part of what had attracted me to Prairie Fire from the beginning was its commitment to women's liberation. Now, like many left groups before us, we were talking about putting it on the back burner. Rape, childcare, welfare, reproductive rights, domestic violence, lesbian liberation, and the family were all critical issues for women of different communities and different nationalities. I wanted to believe that there was a way to work with Third World women to address these problems without being interventionist or divisive, but maybe I was naïve to think this was possible.

After awhile, I compromised and agreed that since Prairie Fire was a small organization, and had just suffered a major setback, we should focus our efforts on program areas where we could more easily work with Third World leaders on programs that supported self-determination. We didn't want to throw out our commitment to women's liberation. We just needed to redirect it for the time being. So for the next few years, PFOC kept its commitment to women's liberation active through our solidarity with international women's struggles in Zimbabwe, Palestine, the Phillipines, Iran, and Central America.

It would have pushed our thinking and process of debate if we had studied A Black Feminist Statement, *which was written in 1977 by the Combahee River*

Collective.[3] *"As Black women, we see Black feminism as the logical political move-*
ment to combat the manifold and simultaneous oppressions that all women of color
face."[4] *The perspective of the Combahee Collective grew out of their experiences of*
racism in the women's movement and sexism in the Black liberation movement.
"The reaction of Black men to feminism has been notoriously negative...Accusa-
tions that Black feminism divides the Black struggle are powerful deterrents to the
growth of an autonomous Black women's movement."[5]

   It would have been better if we could have listened to the insights of the
burgeoning Third World feminist movement and applied them to our solidarity
work. But we weren't able to make that leap. It wasn't until the eighties that Prai-
rie Fire again took up work in the U.S. women's movement and began to develop it
on a different basis.[6]

⸺⸺◦⧟⧟◦⸺⸺

Once Prairie Fire decided to shift its focus from U.S. women's struggles,
I joined our growing Zimbabwe solidarity work. Zimbabwe's fight to overturn
Ian Smith's white settler regime was, at the time, one of the most advanced
anti-colonial struggles in Southern Africa. I was eager to work with the Bay
Area members of the Zimbabwean African National Union (ZANU), who had
impressed me with their friendliness and their desire to work closely with North
Americans who were committed to doing practical solidarity. As I got to know
them, I discovered that they were brilliant, dedicated people who loved to debate
theory and its applications to practice.

   I became closest with Leonard whose vast knowledge base and incisive
analytic mind epitomized revolutionary thinking to me. Leonard was a co-
founder of ZANU, a Marxist-Leninist organization which, in our opinion, was
the leading group in the Zimbabwean national liberation movement. Leonard
was currently ZANU's Director of Publicity for the Western hemisphere. Sitting
in his living room in San Francisco's Fillmore district, I became immersed in the
history of his country. "The whole world has its attention focused on Africa,"
Leonard expounded. "Africa is cardinal to the policy choices of world imperial-

ism. And due to the strategic location of Zimbabwe the outcome is critically important...Because they, the imperialists, want a Zimbabwe that is merely nominally ruled by Black people but that in essence is still not Zimbabwe at all. They want to create a buffer for South Africa."[7]

Leonard was scathingly critical of the so-called "peaceful solutions" that the U.S. and British had repeatedly tried to impose upon Zimbabwe. ZANU's founding slogan, "We are our own liberators," had challenged the view that independence could be granted by the colonizing powers, or be achieved through peaceful means. "If they were so much interested in achieving a bloodless settlement," Leonard argued, "they could have done it three, four, five years ago, when the Africans were not armed, when they were not seriously fighting."[8]

When Leonard talked about *chimurenga*, the Zimbabwean word for people's war, his eyes lit up and he became even more eloquent than usual. Chimurenga was a political, a military, a moral, and a spiritual force. It was only through chimurenga that Zimbabweans, including women, could be unequivocally liberated on every level.

It was the only force capable of achieving victory over imperialism, proven in the mountains of the Sierra Maestra, in the rice fields of Viet Nam and in the plains of Mozambique. Listening to Leonard, I wished I could be part of such a unifying and transformative exercise of collective power.

However, I knew that the priority for our solidarity work with Zimbabwe was political education and material aid. To achieve these goals, Prairie Fire worked with Campuses United Against Apartheid (CUAA) which was campaigning for the University of California to divest itself of investments in those countries of Southern Africa which practiced apartheid and racism. We opposed the recruitment of American mercenaries who were part of a secret international apparatus, fighting on the side of the Rhodesian government. And we sponsored many fundraising events that sent significant amounts of money to support the Patriotic Front.

In May of 1979, ZANU held a historic seminar in Mozambique focused on the role of women in the national liberation struggle. A ZANU woman who lived in the U.S., Naomi Nhiwatiwa, was designated to explain the significance of the seminar to progressive forces in this country. In each of her presentations, Naomi always started with the fact that one-third of ZANU's armed forces, ZANLA, were women, a fact rarely mentioned in the mainstream media. Naomi explained that traditional patriarchy had been made much worse by settler colonialism. So, when ZANU was founded in the sixties, women quickly began to play an active role in the armed struggle to overturn both systems of oppression, and their numbers and responsibilities had increased throughout the seventies. During the seminar, Naomi had been struck by the level of satisfaction that women in ZANU expressed, despite all of the hardships they were enduring. "I saw women who were determined to liberate themselves and determined to liberate Zimbabwe, and they did not envy my position. In fact they felt sorry for me. They felt sorry for me because I was not in the process, I wasn't terribly active."[9]

Naomi concluded that participation in chimurenga was key to the transformation of Zimbabwean women's situation and key to guaranteeing that the gains made during the struggle would not be lost once victory was won. When American women pressed her about how the process of women's liberation would be safeguarded once a political/military victory was won, Naomi answered honestly "The only thing I'm really betting on is the women in the ZANLA forces… These are women who are used to giving commands, who are used to leading;…if anything should happen, I am just hoping that the experience they have and the life they lead will make it difficult for them to go back to the status quo."[10]

I loved discussing complicated political questions with Naomi, Leonard, and the other ZANU members. How would the contradictions within ZANU play out once victory was achieved? How would ZANU manage to deal with the lack of technical skills among Black Zimbabweans if most of the whites fled the country after an independent state was established, as had happened in Mozambique and Angola? Was ZANU's current focus on women opportunist, driven by the need to assure women's involvement in the armed struggle at this critical stage? Having built a strong political relationship with ZANU, we could open up a full range of questions without being considered interlopers. Rather,

ZANU members approached us as comrade revolutionaries with whom they
wanted to discuss questions of ideology and strategy.

Our discussions also addressed the raging debates within the U.S. left:
was party-building the appropriate strategy when there seemed to be so little
evidence of mass movement in the country? Where did the fight for lesbian
and gay liberation fit within an overall revolutionary struggle and would it
be important within the context of Zimbabwe's reality? And could the Black
struggle in the U.S. be described as an anti-colonial struggle? This question in
particular was the subject of many hours of conversation, since Leonard, like
many Marxist-Leninist revolutionaries from other countries, saw Blacks as an
oppressed minority within the U.S. working class and believed that the arguments about domestic colonialism were a well-intentioned but incorrect effort
to impose a national liberationist framework on a class struggle. We were unable
to convince each other on this point, but being able to discuss such questions
openly and with mutual respect gave me encouragement at a time when our efforts to build solidarity with the Black movement in this country were filled with
many, complicated challenges.

Lolita Lebron at an event in San Francisco in 1980 welcoming her after her release from prison in September 1979, by *Breakthrough* photographer.

REPRESSION BREEDS
RESISTANCE

HOT SUMMER SOUNDS DRIFTED UP FROM THE STREET *four stories below where groups of women and men were hanging out on the stoops drinking, arguing, singing a cappella "Nothing you can do can make me untrue to My Guy." I lay in my bed, windows wide open, absorbing the music that enveloped my body, my mind, my dreams. "Turn that jungle music down!" my father would yell when he came home from work early and stumbled upon me dancing feverishly to "Baby I Need Your Lovin, Gotta Have All Your Lovin." I would yell back indignantly that it was insulting to call it jungle music, it was Motown and even Ed Sullivan had the Four Tops on his TV show.*

With "Heat Wave" sizzling in my ears, I read the searing letter James Baldwin wrote to his nephew in The Fire Next Time.

"This innocent country set you down in a ghetto in which, in fact, it intended that you should perish... You were born where you were born and faced the future that you faced because you were black and for no other reason... You were born into a society which spelled out with brutal clarity, and in as many ways as possible, that you were a worthless human being...

"...And this is the crime of which I accuse my country and my countrymen, and for which neither I nor time nor history will ever forgive them, that they have destroyed and are destroying hundreds of thousands of lives and do not know it and do not want to know it."[1]

I knew in my gut that Baldwin was right. I could see it for myself on the TV news, watching as ferocious dogs mauled Black children in the South who dared to drink at whites-only fountains or use whites-only bathrooms. I could see it when I looked across the street from our apartment building at the crumbling facades of the tenements and saw the desperate, angry looks on the faces of the men and women who leaned out of the cracked windows and yelled to each other at all hours of the day and night. My country was destroying Black lives and most white people seemed to be like my father and mother—they didn't want to know and they didn't want to care.

How did it all fit together? There was a glaring, crooked, ruthless disjunction between the liberating, mind-altering, brilliant impact that Black musicians, authors, and performers were having on the culture and thinking of American society, and the suffocated, tracked, segregated, demeaning conditions which most Black people were subjected to. On some inchoate level, I sensed all of this in my teenage years, but I had no idea how to express it or do anything to change it.

As I evolved, politics for me had to be about support for Black Liberation, just as it had to involve women's liberation if it were to mean anything real. Prairie Fire's analysis that the Black Liberation Movement was the strategic lynchpin for revolutionary movement in the United States coincided with my experience. But in the late 1970's, in the wake of COINTELPRO's devastating government attacks on the Black movement, it was a complicated process to figure out the best ways of putting solidarity into practice. Prairie Fire's relationship with the Zimbabwean struggle was based on a recognition of ZANU as the clear leadership of that movement; consequently we could easily accept direction for our work from them. But this model did not translate into our relations with the Black movement inside the U.S. Organizations like the Afrikan Peoples Party (APP), the African Peoples Socialist Party (APSP) and the Republic of New Afrika (RNA)[2] were all struggling to redefine political strategy within the Black nationalist sector of the movement, but the process was fraught with internal debates. The situation was further complicated by the fact that many of the leaders of the Black movement who hadn't been killed by the state were now in prison. By the late seventies, prisons had become a key site for Black/New Afrikan ideological debate and struggle.

In June 1978, prisoners at San Quentin, led by Tony Bottom (aka Jalil Muntaqim), began to publish a revolutionary prisoners' newsletter called *Arm the Spirit,* which Prairie Fire produced on the outside and helped to distribute around the country. A quote from George Jackson formed its banner headline: "Settle your quarrels, come together, understand the reality of our situation, understand that fascism is already here, that people are already dying who could be saved, that generations more will die or live poor, butchered half-lives if you fail to act."

Its objectives were to report on prison struggles around the country, to serve as a voice from behind the walls to guide the work on the outside, and to provide a platform to link domestic and international movements. Each issue of *Arm The Spirit* was the product of intense, reciprocal interchanges among prisoners, and between them and the people who worked with them on the outside.

Notes From an Afrikan P.O.W. Journal (Notes) was published by the Stateville Prisoner Organization in Illinois, and Prairie Fire was in touch with its founding editor and principle writer, Yaki, who wrote under the name of Atiba Shanna. The writers of *Arm the Spirit* and *Notes* were nationalist-oriented and were also steeped in Third World Marxist-Leninist and Maoist theory. They were committed to developing from *inside* prison a strategic analysis of how to rebuild the Black liberation movement, utilizing the potential for prisons to become political cadre training centers. They called for a national Afrikan prisoner organization or "NAPO" to be created and led by the prisoners themselves. *Notes,* Book One, asserted: "The relationship existing between the "prison movement" and the overall struggle… has been and will continue to be a dialectical relationship… 'Control' or 'Direction' [by] the outside forces has been more or less the norm….We believe that we're approaching another phase where the influence flows from the inside to the outside."[3]

Prairie Fire agreed with the concept of a NAPO led by prisoners and supported by coalitions on the outside. We also recognized that this position was the subject of sharp debate, and we attempted to work with groups with varying points of view. But inevitably we got caught between the different forces and the escalating disagreements. One Black group began to publish articles accusing us of interventionism. They claimed that our support of prisoner self-organization was coming from our desire to preserve white control of prison support work and that it undermined their efforts to build a national prison program.

We were very shaken by these charges, but after carefully examining our history we couldn't accept what was being said. PFOC's prison work had been guided from the beginning by the prisoners and had been developing for several years. We couldn't back down on our accountability to those inside now, just when their efforts were beginning to take off.

The situation was wrenching for me. When Lola and I went to Maud's to unwind after a long meeting, I would keep searching for an explanation and a way out of this predicament. "How could the disagreements have become so charged? How can we ever figure out building solidarity with the Black movement when we're being labeled as a racist group of controlling white people?" Lola listened to my churnings but would try to bring me some perspective. "Honey, you're never gonna find a yellow brick road out of this Amerikan racist mess! All we can do is try and find enough brains, courage, and heart to keep going... and keep our ruby red dancing shoes ready for action... We definitely need our ruby dancing shoes!" Then she would drag me out on to the dance floor, and within a few minutes we would both be shaking and singing along with everyone else on the dance floor, pouring ourselves into Gloria Gaynor's throbbing declaration, "I will survive, I will survive!"

We weathered that storm, we trusted our principles, and in the end Prairie Fire was able to strengthen its relationships with the organizations in the Black movement with which we had the most political unity. We were committed to taking leadership from Third World movements, we believed that this was strategically and morally necessary, but we learned and relearned that this was a general political mandate—not a mechanical concept which could be applied to our political work with cookie-cutter precision. There was no magic blueprint for untangling the five hundred year morass of white power and privilege and reconfiguring a just and equitable framework for relationships between Black and white people in this country. But we had to keep working at it.

On March 4, 1978, I attended a rally in Chicago sponsored by the National Committee Against Grand Jury Repression (National Committee), an organization convened by Puerto Ricans and Chicano/Mejicanos. The demonstration marked the 24th anniversary of the March 1, 1954 attack on Congress by four Puerto Rican Nationalists, Lolita Lebron, Rafael Cancel Miranda, Andres Figueroa Cordero, and Irving Flores, demanding independence for their colonized nation.[4]

During their subsequent two decades of imprisonment, the Nationalists had never renounced their goals, and now a new generation of independentistas was demanding their release. The campaign was being waged on multiple levels. On October 26, 1974 the Fuerzas Armadas de Liberación Nacional (FALN) had announced its existence by bombing five major New York City banks. In its communiqué, the FALN had explained:

"We have opened two fronts, one in Puerto Rico, the other in the United States, both nourished by the Puerto Rican people... These bombings... accent the seriousness of our demands for the release of the five Puerto Rican political prisoners, the longest held political prisoners in the hemisphere."[5]

Over the course of the next four years, the FALN carried out over sixty bombings on a variety of targets, exposing the colonial stranglehold that the U.S. had over Puerto Rico and consistently demanding the release of the Nationalists. In response, the U.S. government launched a series of sweeping grand juries to investigate the FALN and thirteen Puerto Rican and Chicano/Mexicano activists were jailed for their refusal to testify. The grand jury resisters argued that the grand juries were convened as a political witch hunt and that their larger purpose was to disorganize and suppress the growing political movement in support of Puerto Rican independence and Chicano/Mejicano liberation. Just before the Chicago, March 4 rally, several grand jury resisters had recently been released after spending many months in prison.

I knew little about the Puerto Rican struggle before I read the book
Prairie Fire. Growing up, I was acquainted with some of our Puerto Rican
neighbors. I loved the savory smells that wafted from their apartments, and I
made polite conversation with them when I met them in the elevator, but I didn't
have any connection to them beyond these superficial interchanges. Unlike the
major Black presence in newspapers, TV, and radio, there were few public reference points for the Puerto Rican experience in the fifties and sixties.

Years later, when I read the section about Puerto Rico in *Prairie Fire*,
many things clicked into place. *Prairie Fire* explained how Puerto Rico had become a colony of the United States in 1898 as a result of the Spanish-American
War and described its unique strategic significance as a market for U.S. goods
and a military center for the U.S. in the Caribbean. The Puerto Rican people
had always militantly resisted this destructive colonial relationship and therefore
posed a particular threat to the entire nexus of U.S. imperial domination.

After reading about Puerto Rico, I remembered how my father often
complained that Puerto Ricans were taking over the neighborhood. Now, I could
connect this influx to Operation Bootstrap, the U.S. scheme to industrialize
Puerto Rico that resulted in the forced displacement of hundreds of thousands
of Puerto Ricans to cities in the United States. Nearly half of the Puerto Rican
population was now living on the U.S. mainland.

Since its formation, PFOC had been active in the Puerto Rican
solidarity movement. As I learned more about the Puerto Rican struggle and
met Puerto Rican activists, my respect for their politics and practice rapidly
grew. "Repression breeds resistance" was their rallying cry, and the March 4th
mobilizations, which the National Committee held in several cities around the
country, seemed to prove their point. Courageous adherence to principles had
built support rather than scared it away as the government had intended. It was
wonderful to see grand jury resisters, Jose Lopez, Maria Cueto, Raisa Nemikin,
Roberto Caldero, and Ricardo Romero out on the streets again. They pledged
to continue the fight to free the other jailed resisters and the Nationalists, despite
the threat of more grand juries.

The keynote speaker at the Chicago rally was Angel Rodriguez Cristobal, a member of the central committee of La Liga Socialista Puertoriqueña, which had been founded in 1962 in Puerto Rico by Juan Antonio Corretjer. Angel spoke of the growing, militant struggle on the Puerto Rican island of Vieques. In the 1940's, the U.S. Navy had expropriated three quarters of Vieques in order to turn it into a naval base and testing ground for military operations, squeezing the local population and threatening the livelihood of the Vieques fishing community. On February 6, 1978, a month before the Chicago rally, a flotilla of fishing boats had physically blocked NATO warships from conducting maneuvers that had been organized by the U.S. Angel explained : "There is a popular imperialist saying that goes, 'The big fish will swallow the little fish.' But the reality is another thing. The big fish will swallow the little fish if the little one is not organized and only if the little fish allows the big fish to choose where and when to confront each other."[6]

But Angel had sharp words of criticism for the U.S. left: "It is unbelievable that in 1978, even after the experience of Viet Nam, and after the terrible experience of Nazi Germany, the North American left can still sleep peacefully and remain peaceful while Vieques is being used night and day by the Marines as a target practice area." [7]

I knew that Angel was addressing his remarks to those in the left who were only willing to support a sanitized, peaceful version of Puerto Rican independence. In 1974, 20,000 people had rallied at New York's Madison Square Garden in a massive, unified show of support for Puerto Rican independence. Since then, however, the solidarity movement had become sharply divided over the question of support for the armed clandestine activity, reflecting divisions in the Puerto Rican movement itself.

The Movimiento de Liberación Nacional (MLN), which had emerged on the U.S. mainland as a key proponent of armed resistance to colonialism, was formed in 1977 by Puerto Ricans and Chicano/Mejicanos.[8] It was committed to building a joint struggle for the independence of Puerto Rico and the reunification of Mexico with a socialist vision for both. The relationship between PFOC and the MLN was growing because of our agreement with the MLN's principled

stand of non-collaboration with the grand juries and their outspoken support of
armed resistance. We also admired its ability to combine theoretical work with
grassroots organizing, and appreciated the MLN's commitment to working with
North American allies.

We studied Lenin's *The State and Revolution* with the MLN, developing a new understanding of how the bourgeois capitalist state deliberately fos-
tered the illusion of democracy when true democratic rights were only enjoyed
by a tiny minority of the population. The illusions of democracy were enshrined
in the electoral process where people were seduced into believing they could
vote in real change when elections only offered a choice between representatives
of the ruling class. Since Puerto Ricans didn't even have a vote in the government of their colonial master,[9] participation in any aspect of the electoral process
only trapped them in a meaningless political exercise.

The MLN also helped us to understand imperialism's strategy for
manipulating "democracy" in the wake of the upheavals of the sixties and seventies. We studied a report from the Trilateral Commission[10] with them called
The Crisis of Democracy.[11] According to the report, the central problem facing
the capitalist countries was "excess democracy" and the solution was a "greater
degree of moderation in democracy." The greatest threat to governability came
from the "previously passive or unorganized groups in the population." The
preservation of an orderly governmental process was contingent upon forcing
these "newly mobilized strata to return to a measure of passivity and defeatism"
through implementation of strategies of "marginalization."

One of these marginalization strategies involved massive urban reloca-
tion of Third World populations out of the major city centers and into the literal
geographic margins to reduce the potential threat to the city centers when these
groups became enraged and engaged. In public policies like "urban renewal"
and "gentrification," which displaced Third World people to the suburban
peripheries, we could see clear evidence of Trilateral strategies being put into
action. COINTELPRO's strong arm methods worked hand-in-hand with the
Trilateral Commission's more gradual, insidious efforts to insure permanent
fracturing of the internal colonies into disempowered, disappeared, fragmented

minorities. Based on our new found understanding, PFOC began to actively organize against gentrification policies and the misleading calls for "neighborhood
safety" that mobilized white residents to participate in Third World displacement.[12]

⸺⸺⸺

The pace of Puerto Rican resistance and government repression
intensified throughout 1978 and 1979. On July 4, 1978, two Puerto Ricans,
Nydia Cuevas and Pablo Marcano, seized the Chilean consulate in San Juan to
protest the July 4th celebrations. They called for independence for Puerto Rico
and freedom for the Nationalists. Three weeks later, on July 25, Puerto Rican
police, under the direction of the FBI, ambushed and killed two young Puerto
Rican independentistas, Carlos Soto Arrivi and Arnaldo Dario Rosado on Cerro
Maravilla mountain in Puerto Rico.[13]

Meanwhile in New York City, the FBI arrested William Guillermo
Morales on July 12, 1978, claiming that they had captured a member of the
FALN. Morales was caught shortly after an explosion in which he lost most of
the fingers on each of his hands. Since Morales was the first alleged member of
the FALN to be arrested, his capture was heralded with great fanfare by the government and the media. In April 1979, Morales was convicted of possession of
explosives and sentenced to eighty-nine years in prison. But then a month later,
on May 21, Morales escaped through a window of the prison ward of Bellevue
hospital, where he was being fitted for prosthetic hands.[14] William Morales' daring, almost miraculous escape given his limited use of his hands, was a landmark
event. In the words of the MLN's political journal, *Libertad:* "The escape of
William Guillermo Morales is the escape of every Puerto Rican and oppressed
person from the claws of those who would enslave us...Were he here today, compañero Morales would say *Hasta la Victormia Siempre!*"[15]

To us, Morales' escape not only demonstrated his individual audacity
and daring; it validated the capacity of the armed movement on the U.S. mainland.

A few months later, on September 6, 1979, President Jimmy Carter granted executive clemency to the four nationalists who were still in prison.[16] From our perspective, it was the FALN's campaign combined with the mass movement in Puerto Rico and Latin America that had achieved the release of the Nationalists. When we learned that the negotiations for the Nationalists' release also involved a prisoner exchange with the Cubans,[17] this only added to the geopolitical significance of the victory. Of course, Carter did not talk about any of this in his explanation of the clemency. He asserted that the release was a humanitarian gesture because of the age and poor health of the Nationalists. He was careful to state that his decision had nothing to do with the FALN which, he reemphasized, was a terrorist organization.

On November 11, 1979, a year and a half after I heard Angel Rodriguez's speech in Chicago, he was found hanging in his cell in a U.S. prison in Tallahassee, Florida. Angel had been arrested with a group of fishermen who tried to obstruct a Naval exercise on Vieques. At his trial, Angel declared himself a prisoner of war, following in the footsteps of the Puerto Rican Nationalists who disclaimed the jurisdiction of the United States judicial system over them. He received a six month sentence for trespassing on "Navy" land and was sent to prison in Tallahassee, Florida. The day before his death he had been visited by a delegation that included Juan Antonio Corretjer, and he showed no sign of demoralization or anxiety.

The U.S. tried to represent Angel's death as a suicide, but no one in the independence movement believed this for a minute. Everyone knew it was an assassination meant to silence his significant political role. In response, the FALN exploded a bomb in a Naval recruiting office at a shopping center in Chicago on November 26. And, on December 3, 1979, Los Macheteros and two other Puerto Rican clandestine organizations jointly attacked a US Navy bus in Sabana Seca, Puerto Rico. Two U.S. sailors were killed and eight others were wounded.

The MLN had another slogan—*Esta Lucha Va Llegar a la Guerra Popular!* (This struggle will become a peoples' war). The events of 1979 convinced us in PFOC that the Puerto Rican struggle was steadily moving towards the development of a peoples' war and that this struggle was providing strategic leadership for anti-imperialist movement in the United States.

———∞∞∞———

While I was immersed in the dramatic developments of the Puerto Rican movement and the frenetic demands of solidarity work, my relationship with Lola was unraveling. May 16, 1979 was my thirtieth birthday, and I could hardly keep the tears from streaming down my face at the birthday dinner Lola had surprised me with. As I looked around at the kids making silly jokes and waiting expectantly as I opened their presents, a sticky melodrama was playing out inside my head.

Lola and I had started out so sweet and right but gradually, incrementally, the sweetness had become cloying and the rightness had become a superficial frame. Friends would tell me we seemed like the perfect family and I would cringe inside. What made it impossibly worse was that Lola now seemed to want the relationship more than ever. I was paralyzed by the discrepancy.

It wasn't as if she hadn't warned me. When I had wanted to move in with her, she had told me as clearly as she could that the smoke and mirrors of romance would inevitably be altered if I plopped myself down in the middle of her family. When I first moved in, I was glad to find that she was wrong because I loved so many things about this new living situation. I especially savored the mornings when we had breakfast all together in the sunny nook off the garden— Marla gulping down her juice before she dashed to the bus, Keith devouring a huge bowl of sugary cereal, Dolores eating a different kind of granola each week, and Lorraine slurping a soft boiled egg, which I found particularly endearing even though it made me slightly nauseous. I had my routine English muffin and Lola had a croissant from the Tassajara bakery down the block and both of us washed it down with a cup of strong espresso. Then we each took off on our separate ways, but to me the shared moment in the breakfast nook had secured an inviolable connection which stayed with us throughout the day.

For the first few months, I also enjoyed how Lola often decided to clean the house at 11:00 at night, after the kids were in their rooms and she could turn on her own mood music and get high while she scrubbed and dusted and I obligingly scrubbed and dusted by her side. And it made me feel grounded in concrete practicalities when we sat down each month to look over the vast array of her bills and together tried to figure out which ones could be paid, which ones could wait, and how much money she would need to pay for food, clothes, movies, and events for the month. Until we started to bicker about how often she wanted to clean at night instead of go out for a drink, or go to bed early to give us a chance to make love. Or I would want to continue dissecting the political debate that occurred at a meeting earlier in the evening, while Lola wanted to kick back and listen to Coltrane or Gato Barbieri. After a while, the bill questions could not be contained in one problem-solving session each month, as the unpaid piles kept getting larger. I was full of thrifty suggestions, but the sad and resentful look on her face made me realize that such suggestions were easy for me to make since I had no real responsibilities for anyone but myself. (The little bit of money I contributed to Lola each month from my part-time job as a teacher's aide hardly counted).

After years of having to juggle and maneuver, Lola yearned to buy the special athletic shoes Keith was begging for, or the elaborate magic wand that tantalized Lorraine from the store window she passed each day on her way to school. Often, I would find that those "extras" made it into the house by the end of the month, even though they had been crossed off the list Lola and I had laboriously made together. I would bite my tongue because I could see that there really was no way for Lola to keep her head above the quagmire of bills on the limited income of her part-time jobs as an acting teacher. Sometimes splurging was the only way to forget the insoluble situation.

As I ran down the day-to-day problems with our relationship in my head, it didn't seem like each of them individually, or even the sum of them together, was responsible for my changing feelings. Rather, it was our inability to talk about anything straight on or to even make time to get to the bottom of what was happening between us. The smoke and mirrors that had glued our romance together in the beginning had morphed into an opaque barrier we didn't seem able to deconstruct.

I also knew that part of the problem was a predicament that I could hardly admit to myself, let alone to Lola: I was falling in love with someone else. The first time Lola saw me dancing with Kyle at a party, she pulled me aside and jibed with a mixture of stoned clarity and jealous bitterness, "Some day you and Kyle are going to be together, I can feel it." I vehemently denied it, but she persisted. "Your youth, the way you dance so in synch, your karmic energy together, it just has to be."

That had been over a year before, and for awhile I had consciously avoided Kyle in order to insure that Lola's premonition would not come true. But recently I had started working with her on designing a poster to raise material aid for Zimbabwe, and the two of us had found ourselves working late into the night together. Kyle was a visual artist who culled symbols from her dreams and the deep recesses of her imagination, using them to create imaginative political art and posters. In our work sessions, I would watch the pictures flow from her head into her hands and on to the paper. Then I would figure out the words to complement the picture that was taking shape.

One night, Kyle gave me a poem she had written for me. All the things I had been surreptitiously feeling about what was happening between us as we created this mix of art and politics were laid bare in the emotionally crafted words of this poem. Reading it made me dizzy with guilt and desire, and I spent an hour looking for a place in my room where I could hide the poem so that Lola could never find it.

"This is all wrong, it makes no sense," I would repeat to myself every time my thoughts strayed to Kyle. I was scripting a soap opera which went against all my values, one that would be hurtful not only to Lola, whom I still loved in many, many ways, but also to the kids. I resolved again to avoid Kyle and to focus on all the things that were strong and positive in my relationship with Lola. But on the night of my birthday, the logic of my principles was unable to contain my tears as we all sat together in what was supposed to be a wonderful celebration of my thirty year turning point. Finally, I had to cut the dinner short and go for a walk, saying that I had to sort out the many emotions which inevitably marked this new stage of life.

In fact, turning thirty was part of why I burst into hysterical weeping as soon as I left the house. I walked up and down the hills, crying as the fog wafted in from the ocean. Relentlessly, the fog crept over Golden Gate Park and proceeded to totally enshroud some of the houses on the block while inexplicably leaving others uncloaked, standing out in stark relief. As I pondered the irrational, unpredictability of the fog's behavior, something shifted inside of me. It wasn't right that I was losing patience with Lola. It wasn't right that my dreams were filled with someone else's hands. It wasn't right that I was considering leaving this family that had captured my heart and embodied my ideals. But at thirty, I had to face the fact that my passions didn't always match my ideals. As a twentieth-century lesbian feminist, there was no excuse for trapping myself in the conundrums of a nineteenth-century tragic romance. To do so would only prolong everyone's pain.

A few days later, I told Lola that I wanted to move, that I needed "space." Of course, I still wanted to be part of her life and part of the lives of the kids and I was so, so sorry that it wasn't working out. She said she understood, she had anticipated this, it made sense given our different life stages, it was okay. Together we devised an explanation for the kids, which didn't explain anything. Since, in their short lives, they had already heard many such pseudo-explanations from adults, they didn't press for anything more.

I found a place to live with some friends who had a refurbished, livable shed in a garden in back of their apartment, and within two weeks I left, almost a year to the day after I had moved in with Lola. It wasn't until a few months later that Lola and I had a grief-ridden, rage-filled confrontation where all of our long-suppressed feelings exploded in bursts of uncensored accusations that alternated with wracking self-blame. The scene was necessary, but it made it impossible to continue being cordial friends. We both assumed that over time we would be able to reconfigure our feelings and build some type of friendship, but it didn't turn out that way.

Cover of pamphlet by the May 19th Communist Organization, circa 1978.
Illustration by the Madame Binh Graphics Collective.

THIS IS THE TIME

This is the time
we were all waiting for.
Our guns are light in our hands
the reasons and aims
of the struggle
clear in our minds…

Ahead of us we see bitter hardships.
But we see also
our children running free
our country plundered no more.

This is the time to be ready
and firm.
The time to give ourselves
to the Revolution.

—Josina Machel[1]

I WAITED FOR A MONTH AFTER MOVING OUT OF LOLA'S HOUSE before I brought Kyle over to my new place. It was a perfect hideaway, removed from the house in front of it, tucked under trees and vines, beside a blooming flower garden. I had windows on three sides which invited the sun, fog, and moon

to become part of the landscape inside. Kyle built me a desk that extended
the length of one entire wall, where I could write and she could draw. And we
moved the bed into the center of the room where we could get the best view
of our favorite tree as we lay there, sometimes for hours on end. We absorbed
the sound of the rustling leaves into our lovemaking and into our sleep, and on
some weekends we would even skip meetings and events and just spend the day
touching and talking—about our dreams and our childhoods, and about desires
I had hardly realized were mine.

It was slow, it was heady, and its rhythm felt wonderfully different from
that of any relationship I had had before. As we listened to Nina Simone, over
and over, one song from her newest album, *Baltimore*, would replay all week
inside my head. "A little love, that slowly grows and grows, not one that comes
and goes, that's all I want from you. A sunny day with hopes up to the skies, not
a day that comes and dies, that's all I want from you."[2] It was simple and trite,
not laced with the passions and convictions that complicated my life. Throughout that summer and into the fall, I suspended disbelief, I released myself from
worry and guilt, and I embraced the feeling that a little love and hopes up to the
skies were what I wanted most at this moment.

But outside of the protected space of the shed, events continued at a
rapid pace and then accelerated dramatically. On November 2, 1979, Assata
Shakur was liberated from the maximum-security wing of Clinton Correctional
Institution for Women in New Jersey. According to the *New York Times*, three
Black men had come to the prison as visitors and once inside had demanded
Assata's release at gunpoint. At the prison gates, they had been met by a white
woman and all of them were able to quickly drive away. When I heard the news,
my heart started to pound uncontrollably. After years of writing and chanting—
FREE ASSATA!— some people had, amazingly, figured out how to make the
slogan real. And, from the accounts, at least one white woman had shown what
solidarity could really mean by taking part in the action.

Assata's escape had been precisely timed to take place just before
a large Black Solidarity Day rally in New York, which had been planned for
months. 5,000 Black people and allies had participated in a five-mile march from

THIS IS THE TIME

Harlem to the United Nations demanding education, housing, health care, land, reparations, self-determination, and freedom for all Black political prisoners and prisoners-of-war. International representatives from Zimbabwe's Patriotic Front, the Southwest African People's Organization (SWAPO), the Palestine Liberation Organization (PLO), and the Pan African Congress of South Africa joined the marchers. At the rally in front of the U.N., a statement Assata had written before her escape was read:

> November 1979 and crosses burn the face of Amerika... I've been in prison six-and-a-half years and I can feel what's coming in the air. Prisons are becoming more brutal and repressive. Behavior Modification Programs are booming. People are receiving longer sentences with fewer chances of being paroled. Thirteen-year-old children are being sentenced to life in prison... We've got to build a strong Human Rights Movement. We've got to build a strong Prison Movement. We've got to build a strong Black Liberation Movement and we've got to struggle for liberation. [3]

A few days after the march, on November 8, the Black Liberation Army (BLA) issued a communiqué claiming responsibility for Assata's liberation.

> The existence of Black Political Prisoners and scores of B.L.A. prisoners of domestic war in the united states is the result of brutal suppression of Black People's National and Human Rights. Recent history of the Black Movement in the u.s. is cold testimony to this political and social repression carried forward under the auspices of "criminal law enforcement." Comrade-Sister Assata Shakur was freed from racist captivity in anticipation of Black Solidarity Day, November 5th, and in order to express to the world the need to Free All Black Political Prisoners in the u.s. [4]

In the next weeks, we were riveted on reports of the massive woman hunt, the surveillance, the interrogatory knocks on the doors of her possible contacts all over the East Coast. In defiance, people produced a poster, to be hung in supporters' windows and confound the FBI search, declaring ASSATA IS WELCOME HERE!

As the months passed, and the police didn't seem any closer to finding Assata, we started to believe that the impossible had really been accomplished and Assata would remain free. As we analyzed and discussed the significance of her liberation, a group of us decided that we could no longer put off our own accountability to Third World forces that were committed to developing an armed clandestine capacity. The words to Josina Machel's poem rippled through my head: "This is the time we were all waiting for…This is the time to be ready and firm."

So we began to plan to go underground. We weren't an impulsive group, and we were well aware of the dangers of a precipitous exit. We knew that building clandestine infrastructure, which included networks, safe houses, storage facilities, and ID generation, was an important role we could potentially play. Beyond that, we had more questions than answers about what our role as a small group of white people could be.

We were critical of the "foco" theory which French radical Regis Debray articulated, drawing from the experience of the Cuban revolution.[5] Foquismo asserted that a small group of armed guerrillas could become the focal point or catalyst to build popular support for a more generalized, popularly supported armed struggle. We thought that the foco approach relied too heavily on the force of moral example and underplayed the integral connection between armed struggle and mass struggle. It led to isolation and defeat as had happened with Che Guevara's guerrilla force in the mountains of Bolivia. On the other hand, we knew that most of the radical changes in the United States had started with small numbers of people militantly insisting that a different reality was possible, from abolition to unions to women's rights. If we developed our work in conjunction with Third World strategies of mass-based people's war, we could potentially use the skills and resources we had access to as white people to aid the development of clandestine infrastructure. At the same time, we might be able to assist in actions that had a clear political message and would concretely advance the goal of liberation, like Assata's escape had done.

     This was our general perspective, but each of us had questions, doubts, and gnawing fears about our capacity, our ability to sustain ourselves politically and materially, the character and logistics of our relationships with Third World forces, and the personal sacrifices we would have to make. Sometimes we voiced these questions in our group discussions, but more often they erupted in whispered non-committal speculations during late night car rides, or they were displaced in tearful arguments in the privacy of our bedrooms.

     I hadn't yet talked to Kyle about what was going on. As I lay in bed next to her, staring at the moon through the window, I couldn't fathom how I would be able to take this leap. There were so many known and unknown sacrifices involved—ranging from the likelihood of never having children to the probability of going to prison. But the loss I was most focused on was the loss of Kyle because it wasn't just part of the long list of shadowy, eventual possibilities. It was hard for me to imagine Kyle coming underground with us, no matter that she shared so many of our convictions, no matter how much she loved me. She was an artist, a dreamer, and it made little sense to me or anyone else for Kyle to become part of our precarious, fledgling experiment, which was driven by a dream, but required the most down-to-earth, practical mind-set. "Maybe a few years down the road when we are more established and know what we are doing," I would say at the meetings which we had begun to hold in restaurants in obscure outreaches of the city. Everyone would nod yes in agreement, but inside me I knew that this was even more of a fantasy than the rest of our fantastic project.

———∞———

     It was the middle of March, 1980, and Kyle and I had rented a cabin for a week by the beach just south of Santa Cruz. I had decided beforehand that sometime during that week I would talk to her about what was going on in the other part of my life, but I kept putting it off. Our "little love" was growing and I couldn't bear to disrupt its motion. In between our walks on the beach, our conversations, our reading and lovemaking, Kyle was teaching me to draw, or as she put it—she was helping me to access the part of me that was able to translate perceptions into visual representations if I would only try. And I, who had given up making any effort in this realm after first grade, was discovering to my delight that if I concentrated not on the picture that I was creating but on what I wanted to create, something expressive did emerge.

One night, I stayed up late reading *Burger's Daughter*, a recent novel by Nadine Gordimer, which had been banned in South Africa when it was first published.[6] It was the story of a young white woman, Rosa Burger (named for Rosa Luxembourg), whose parents were communists and part of the Black African-led revolutionary movement fighting against apartheid. In the book, Rosa's father has just died in prison and Rosa is at a turning point in her life, questioning whether there is a purpose to the all-consuming political struggle. Maybe, as other acquaintances argued, the struggle was really a misplaced dream, an endless futile effort fueled by self-righteous slogans and dogmatic political lines, that could only result in loss and sacrifice of personal happiness.

I was trying to muffle the sobs that the book provoked when Kyle, who had been half asleep in the other room, came in and quietly put her arms around me. I explained the intensity of the book's subject matter to her, but I still couldn't tell her that my tears were being spilled not only for Rosa's dilemma but for my own.

The next day, we received an unexpected phone call from San Francisco. PFOC had been invited by ZANU members to send a representative to Zimbabwe's Independence Day celebrations which were to occur on April 18. Based on my role in the work (and Leonard's suggestion), it made sense for me to be the representative.

I was overjoyed. Over the past four months, I had been in close, almost daily contact with Leonard about the developments in Zimbabwe. In December 1979, the Patriotic Front had signed an agreement with the Rhodesian government, brokered by the British at Lancaster House in London. The Lancaster

Agreement set out terms and a process for establishing political independence for Zimbabwe, including elections for a new government to be held in February 1980.

The settlement was laden with compromising clauses which should have been unacceptable from the perspective of many of the ZANU representatives in the U.S. The compromises included the principle of separate representation for whites through twenty reserved seats in the new governing body; and strict provisions regarding the acquisition and compensation for land, enabling whites to retain control of this most important resource.

In the period leading up to the elections, even the inadequate terms of the agreement were continually violated by the Rhodesians and their allies. Despite the obstacles, ZANU won a resounding victory and Robert Mugabe, ZANU's candidate, had been elected as prime minister. The results of the elections had been announced in early March, and we had celebrated at Leonard's house when we heard the news. Even though the celebration was mixed with debates about the prospects for the future, we all agreed that this was a tremendous step forward in the fight to overturn white settler colonialism in Southern Africa.

I was thrilled at the prospect of visiting Zimbabwe and being able to participate directly in this historic occasion. This was also the reinforcement I needed for the choices I was making in my life. Later that day, as Kyle and I sat on the porch in Santa Cruz looking out at the ocean, I told her about my other plans. She was less surprised than I expected and didn't offer any arguments against the plans. I could tell that she was trying to swallow her feelings in order to be politically supportive of my decision, yet she didn't pretend that she was eager to go underground with me. "Somehow, we'll figure it out," we kept assuring each other.

Before we left the cabin the next day, I hurriedly finished *Burger's Daughter*. Rosa decides to leave South Africa and lives in Europe for a time. But the detachment and lack of social commitment that she experiences there push her to go back to South Africa. Upon her return she writes, "It's strange to live in a country where there are still heroes. Like anyone else, I do what I can."[7] She rejoins the struggle and is arrested in the aftermath of the Soweto uprising.[8] At the end of the book, she is in prison, her future is uncertain, but she is all right. She is surrounded by people who, like her, are doing what they can to change an intolerable system.

Re-reading Burger's Daughter *more than twenty-five years later feels eerily like reading a journal from my own past. The words are not mine, but the thoughts, the struggles, even the complicated, contradictory relationships resonate for me as if I had lived through them. I wonder, as I read, whether anyone picking up* Burger's Daughter *today for the first time, in the era of post-apartheid South Africa, would see Rosa's life questions as relevant or compelling.*

In 1979, reading Burger's Daughter *made me feel like the difficult process I was going through deciding my future was not a self-invented mental crisis. While I realized that the conditions for revolution in South Africa were quite different from those in the United States, the political and moral choices for white people were not that distinct. I had to do what I could do. For me that meant going underground.*

∽∞∽

I spent the next couple of weeks preparing for my trip to Zimbabwe— getting vacation time from my teacher's aide job and consulting with Leonard, who was getting ready for his trip back as well. I collected pencils, pens, and paper which I could give as gestures of friendship and material support along with copies of *Breakthrough* and our pamphlet on Zimbabwean women. On April 4, 1980, I walked through the door of my shed after work and the phone was ringing. As soon as Roxie exclaimed, *"Diana!"* I knew something was wrong. Eleven Puerto Ricans had been captured in a suburb of Chicago, accused of being part of the FALN. [9] Roxie began rattling off a list of their names, and while I didn't recognize most of them two jumped out at me—Dylcia Pagán and Elizam Escobar.

A year and a half before, in 1978, Dylcia and Elizam had traveled to the West Coast as part of a national tour to build support for the Puerto Rican Nationalists who at that time were still in prison. While they were in San Francisco, I had a chance to hang out with them and learn something about their background. Elizam had grown up in Puerto Rico, where he went to school and became involved in the Liga Socialista which was being led by Juan Antonio Corretjer. He moved to New York in the early seventies, where he developed his work as a visual artist and taught at the Art School of El Museo del Barrio. Dylcia grew up in East Harlem and had been involved with the civil rights movement and community activism since she was a teenager. In the early seventies, she began to work as a TV producer and writer dedicated to creating positive images of Puerto Ricans on television at the same time as she was the English editor of the bilingual daily paper, *El Tiempo*.

What I remembered most about Dylcia was her baby son, Guillermo, who was her constant companion on this trip. Guillermo was a beautiful, active, chubby baby whose crawling explorations of our homes knew no limits. Guillermo was also the son of William Morales who, at the time of Dylcia's trip, was in a New York prison awaiting trial. It was remarkable to me that Dylcia could be so engaged while her compañero was in prison. It was also remarkable that little Guillermo seemed so happy and carefree, so untouched by the whirlwind of politics around him. I remembered watching Dylcia bounce Guillermo on her lap as he giggled. Dylcia laughed back at him, mirroring his glee. What would happen to Guillermo now? [10]

As I boarded the plane for Zimbabwe ten days later, I tried to put aside the haunting image of Dylcia and Guillermo. From the moment the FALN 11 (as they became known) were captured, they made clear their stance of non-partic-ipation with the U.S. government's legal charade. They were freedom fighters in the Puerto Rican struggle against colonialism and consequently they rejected all criminal charges that the U.S. leveled at them. Instead, they demanded to be treated as Prisoners of War, POW's, in accordance with the Geneva Conventions. The clarity of their position made complete sense to me, even though I knew it might be difficult for most people in the United States to comprehend. In 1972, the United Nations Committee on Decolonization had called for the decolonization of Puerto Rico and the recognition of Puerto Rico's right to

self-determination and independence. As colonial subjects, Puerto Ricans had a
right to fight for independence according to international law, just like Algerians
had a right to fight the French and Zimbabweans had a right to fight the white
Rhodesian settlers.

I was inspired by the steadfastness of the FALN 11, but their heroism
reawakened doubts about my own courage. I hoped that participating in Zimbabwe's momentous victory would cement my resolve once and for all.

People were converging on Zimbabwe from all over the world, and
the planes we were traveling in became venues for intense debate about what
the future really held. Few among us could ignore the problematic aspects
of the Lancaster House settlement and the many unanswered questions that
were facing the new government. I had barely stepped out on to African soil at
Salisbury's[11] international airport before I was bombarded by the contradictions
that were playing out on all levels of Zimbabwean society. The airport was filled
with Black and white officials and police, but it was the white ones who were
barking out the orders and were taking charge of the process of our entry. Their
Black counterparts were standing to the side looking tense and unsure of what
their role was supposed be. As we wandered through the city the day before the
Independence celebration, we were hard put to find many signs of the imminent
change in state power. From the hotels where the white managers reprimanded
Black domestic workers, to the stores and restaurants where sales people and
consumers were predominantly white, the power and privilege of the settler
order seemed completely entrenched. I wasn't sure what I had expected, but all
of us guests were anxiously looking to see some signposts that the hated system
of white rule was really, finally, coming to an end.

However, the next day once we got off the bus in Mbare, the African
township where the celebration was to take place, the evidence of impending
change was everywhere. Black Zimbabweans thronged the streets, running with
ZANU signs in their hands, their songs and chants filling the air, and although
I couldn't understand most of the words, the repetition of the words ZANU
and ZANLA was impossible to mistake. As we walked from the bus to Rufaro
stadium, we passed by tents where people displaced by the war were living and

felt hostile stares. One young man shouted, "Just remember, this is our Independence Day!" His shout made me realize how strange it must be for the Black people who lived in Mbare to see dozens of white people, who had never come into this area before, walking through their township with a sense of entitlement, as if it were the most natural thing in the world to celebrate the Black overthrow of white rule. Even more disconcerting than the outburst of resentment, was the sight of hundreds of police in the area—a mixed white and Black force clearly bent on maintaining control of the crowd whose enthusiasm for independence might become uncontrollable.[12]

We arrived at the stadium around 8:00 PM and were seated in the general public section. Looking around at the thousands of people—mothers, babies, children, grandparents—waving the new green, gold, red, and black Zimbabwean flag, I started to realize that this occasion was more momentous, more joyous, more transforming, not only for Zimbabweans but for Africans all over the globe, than I could ever fathom from my distant vantage point in the Bay Area. For the first couple of hours there were various cultural performances ranging from bagpipes to African traditional dancers and guerrilla singers. There were cheers and applause, but people told me that that they would not be really happy until they saw Mugabe with their own eyes. For the past couple of weeks, rumors of assassination plots were rampant and everyone knew that he had been sleeping in a different house every night to keep the Rhodesian/South African plotters from having their desired success. Even now, nothing about this independence was guaranteed.

Then Bob Marley and the Wailers were announced and the crowd's pent up energy exploded. Marley came on to the stage chanting Viva Zimbabwe! and then began singing "Positive Vibration." People started dancing and singing in a massive outpouring of euphoria. Then Marley started to sing "I Shot the Sheriff," and the dancing became infused with militant energy, with a throng of fists waving in the air.

Suddenly, the police ran on to the field and surrounded Marley as if they thought that someone might actually shoot the sheriff. And, simultaneously, outside the stadium gates, the police decided to release clouds of tear gas to dis-

perse the thousands who could not fit in the overflowing stadium, but were also
dancing and singing to the uncontainable music.

Near pandemonium erupted as tear gas wafted through the stadium
and people started gasping, coughing, and grabbing handkerchiefs and scarves
to cover their eyes and noses. My eyes began to sting, but I was more furious
than panicked. How dare the police try and derail this celebration? Did the
Rhodesians think they could stop the transfer of power with a few bursts of tear
gas after Zimbabweans had been fighting for decades? Or was it just vengeance,
a ploy to defuse the joy? Around me people were cursing the police with a fury
beyond words. Then ZANLA forces appeared on the field and began marching
through the stadium with fists clenched, calling for calm and order. The crowd
responded with shouts of "ZANLA, ZANLA!" and "Pamberi ne Chimurenga!"
Marley struck up the song "War," followed by "Africans a liberate Zimbabwe."
At that point, every woman, man and child present stood up to sing this song
that expressed the hope Zimbabwe represented to Africans around the globe:

> *No more internal power struggle*
> *We come together to overcome the little trouble*
> *Soon we will find out who are the real revolutionaries*
> *Cause I do not want my people to be tricked by mercenaries*
> *Mash it up in a Zimbabwe, Natty trash it in Zimbabwe*
> *Africans a liberate Zimbabwe.*[13]

As we sang, tears of anger, joy, and residual teargas streamed down my
face. Never had I felt the potency of masses of people as I did at that moment.
And never had the life and death terms of the conflict seemed clearer to me.

Finally, just before midnight, Mugabe arrived in a car encircled by eight
ZANLA guerrillas, and the frenetic energy of the crowd surged again. Before he
and the new president, Canaan Banana, were sworn into office, the British flag
was lowered exactly at midnight. Alongside the Zimbabweans that I had come to
know in the course of the evening, I gazed in awe as the new flag was hoisted to
its sovereign position at the top of the pole.

Over the next ten days of my trip, I visited villages in the countryside and met with some of the brand new government officials who, up until a few weeks ago, had been guerrilla commanders and fighters. Everywhere I went, I heard people voice an elated hope laced with well-founded anxiety. These women and men knew everything about fighting guerrilla war, but they were only just starting to prepare for the huge challenge of assuming government responsibilities in a volatile situation where no one knew what the white population would do next.

A couple of evenings before I was supposed to leave Zimbabwe, I was returning to my hotel when a group of young Zimbabwean boys jerked my bag from my arm and quickly ran off. More surprised than scared, I started running after the kids shouting "Just return the passport, keep the camera, please I only need the passport!" Later that evening, as I was telling the story to friends, we all laughed at the absurdity of my good faith plea for such a reasonable solution to this random theft. "Only an American could make such a sincere appeal for her passport," one of my Irish acquaintances joked.

The next morning I went down to the police station to file a report because I knew I couldn't expect to replace the passport unless I dealt with the authorities, and my plane was leaving the next day. The scene at the station was barely controlled bedlam. Hundreds of Black people lined a large room, waiting for their turn to talk to the police about whatever problem had forced them to come to this most mistrusted agency. Waiting in line for several hours, I was surrounded by tense and tired people who had come to recover lost items, complain about excessive government charges, or in the case of the woman I happened to stand next to, file charges against her husband for domestic abuse. I could hardly see a glimmer of the new Zimbabwe that had been ushered in a couple of weeks before. When I finally got to speak with the white officer who was responsible for missing items, he barely suppressed a snicker when I told him what had happened. He became more hostile when I was adamant that it would be impossible for me to identify any of the young people who had grabbed my bag. He rudely shoved the stamped police report into my hands. "Eh, now you see why civilized people want to get out of this country! I'm not sure your embassy will be that anxious to help someone like you, a friend of Mugabe's," he sneered.

I was exhausted and unsure of my next step, and wanted to consult with my friends before heading for the American embassy. When I stopped at the hotel desk to see if I had any messages, the clerk greeted me. "Miss Block, we found this on the front steps of the hotel a few hours ago." Amazingly, it was my passport. "One of those kids heard my plea," I immediately thought. Admittedly, there might be some other, less romantic explanation for its miraculous appearance, but I preferred to believe that my appeal for the one piece of personal property that mattered to me and could not benefit anyone else had reached the ears of at least one of the youths, and at some risk they had figured out a way to get it back to me.

When I returned to the United States and began showing my slides and telling the story of my trip, I always concluded with this small story about my passport. To me it expressed something important about the complicated dynamics of the new generation of Zimbabweans upon which the future of the nation hinged.

It is extremely painful to think back on the promise that Zimbabwe's independence seemed to hold given the drastic reversals that have occurred in the ensuing decades. What went wrong in Zimbabwe? The answers (and continuing questions) fill many books. There was the carry over of white power and privilege from the settler colonial state into the economic and political structures of the post-independence era. There was the neoliberal agenda of the IMF and World Bank which enforced severe structural adjustment programs that further imploded the shaky Zimbabwean economy. And there has been Mugabe and ZANU-PF's hegemonic policies, internal corruption, and anti-democratic practice that have culminated in violent repression against rising mass opposition.

One thought provoking perspective is offered by Horace Campbell in his book Reclaiming Zimbabwe.[14] *Campbell holds the "patriarchal model of liberation" responsible for the "decomposition of the liberation platform of the Zimbabwean political leadership."[15] According to this critique, first developed by*

Zimbabwean feminists struggling to rebuild a grassroots women's movement in the nineties, the new Zimbabwean state took over the militaristic and patriarchal organization of the colonial state instead of overthrowing it. In order to reconsolidate the patriarchal order after independence, given women's advances during the national liberation struggle, ZANU adopted policies to "redomesticate" women.[16] The women's section of ZANU was enlisted to help enforce reactionary campaigns to reinstitute "traditional African cultural values" that "defined how respectable African women should behave." Virulent homophobia was added to the arsenal of government repression as Zimbabwean feminists linked with gay and lesbians as well as other grassroots activists to oppose policies of structural adjustment.

African feminist scholar, Patricia McFadden, expresses the renewed commitment of the Zimbabwean women's movement to work towards true emancipation when she writes:

"Let me warn you... the backlash will be real and difficult to withstand. It is vicious and ever-present: patriarchy can be so hegemonic and overwhelming...the isolation, the threats, the violence, in some cases the murder of feminists...the Otherness and the marginalization. But we have to take it as it comes, and make the Women's Movement a political movement, redefining ourselves as political agents, strengthening and using the Movement to take this continent to a new place."[17]

When I returned from Zimbabwe, superficially my life proceeded as before—meetings, organizing, events, debates and, more and more rarely, times when Kyle and I would retreat into the world of our bodies and our dreams. But it was becoming clearer that my overground life was a temporary phenomenon, and each day it was yielding space to my underground life that was soon to become my only life. I was learning to juggle different modalities of daily communication, language, and clothing. I was learning how to invent a story that could serve as a bridge between the two worlds. It was complicated and challenging, like placing pieces in a very intricate, abstract puzzle. But there was no picture

on the package to help guide us, and it wasn't clear what type of picture would
emerge if we succeeded in putting all these tiny pieces in their proper places.
Only Kyle and a few other people beyond our group knew what we were up to.
For everyone else, we were creating a fictional narrative that we hoped would
allow us to slip away without attracting too much attention.

"It's going to be very challenging. I'll be working in small rural Mexican
villages teaching literacy skills and working with community organizations. It
will build on some of my experience in the San Francisco public schools… It's a
five-year project that will allow me enough time to get to know the communities
I'm living in." I was sitting in the living room of my sister's Washington Heights
apartment, explaining why it would be difficult for me to be in touch with her on
a regular basis. "It sounds interesting," Joyce responded carefully, as she might
with one of her therapy patients who had just come up with a new scheme to
change her life.

As the words came out of my mouth, the story sounded totally implau-
sible to me, and I didn't know what I would do if my sister began to delve into
my unexpected decision to leave my previously fulfilling life in San Francisco.
For whatever reasons, she didn't ask any questions. The night before, I had told
the story to my father who had reacted with his usual rancor. "Another one of
your meshuggeneh plans. You might as well be going to fight with the gorillas in
Nicaragua." He dropped his protests after I agreed that I would try, as much as
possible, to keep calling him once a week, which was the mollifying routine I had
stuck to since leaving home at sixteen.

As I sat with Joyce in her tasteful living room, which offered a glimpse
of the Hudson River in the day and the glimmering lights of New Jersey at
night, I felt the urge to enhance the credibility of my story, to make up details
that would convince her that it wasn't only logical, it was enviably exciting; but I
knew this would be inviting trouble, so I bit my tongue and changed the subject.
"What's it like teaching at City College?" I asked her boyfriend, and we spent
the rest of the evening discussing the contradictions of being a low-paid English
instructor without tenure in the academic hierarchy, and then moved on to the

enormous obstacles confronting my sister in trying to start a private therapy practice in New York City, which probably had more licensed clinical psychologists per square mile than anywhere on the planet.

When I was leaving, Joyce squeezed my arm and whispered, "Please be safe, Diana." I could hear layers of subliminal messaging in those four words and focused on steadying my voice as it began to choke up. "Of course, I will," I managed to reassure her. "Take care of daddy," I added, not to advise her on a duty that I knew she had already accepted, but to let her know that I recognized I was leaving the responsibility for our aging, cantankerous father in her hands.

The world moved on. Reagan took the reins as president and immediately began rolling back all social welfare programs, instituted registration for the draft, and accelerated aggressive strategies against Nicaragua and the Soviet Union. The FALN 11 were convicted of seditious conspiracy and each received sentences ranging from fifty-five to ninety years in prison. In response to her sentence of ninety years in February, 1981, Carmen Valentín stated: "Revolution doesn't get accomplished by mere thought. Action must lead the way, and that is what the FALN is. The FALN is action on behalf of the millions of Puerto Ricans who have been victims of colonialism and exploitation. This action has to take place because without it our territory will not be free."[18]

In Puerto Rico, the Macheteros blew up nine Air National Guard planes, which were sitting on the runway in the military-only area of the San Juan airport, causing $45 million in damage. The planes were part of the U.S. military commitment to help the Salvadoran government fight the FMLN rebels.[19] The Macheteros sent a videotape of their preparation for this action which was played repeatedly in Puerto Rico on the news.

An attempted expropriation of $1.6 million from an armored Brink's truck in upstate New York by members of the Black Liberation Army and white allies went terribly wrong, leading to a shootout in which a Brink's guard and two police officers were killed, as well as one member of the BLA. [20]

We knew we needed to take all of these developments into account, to analyze the lessons they offered and learn from the serious mistakes that had been made. However, at this stage we were too busy with our own preparations and determined not to be deflected from our timetable. There would be plenty of time for discussion and debate once we reached our underground destination.

After months of emotional turmoil—aching scenes in which Kyle and I would talk and cry and weave fables about the future—we had reached a strange, almost mystic equilibrium that allowed us to focus on the pleasure of the moment and nothing beyond. I carefully went through all my belongings, sending most of what I owned to Goodwill and leaving a few boxes of books and clothes in Kyle's basement to make it clear to anyone who might investigate that I was planning to return, someday, from my "trip to Mexico." A couple of large duffle bags and one box contained the items I insisted were necessary to assure my safe passage to the other world—a blue batik embossed with the faces of Zimbabwean women that Kyle had made for me; a flowered ceramic lamp that my sister had given me on my twnty-first birthday; a copy of *Burger's Daughter*; a few Nina Simone albums; and my collection of earrings—amethyst, turquoise, malachite—accumulated over the years. The earrings all fit into a pouch embroidered with dragons that Kyle gave me a few days before I left. I loaded my things in a rented car and drove away on a brilliantly sunny day, without a hint of fog, leaving San Francisco behind.

PART TWO

WITH EYES
NOT YET BORN

FBI's wanted picture of Claude.

AMERICA'S MOST WANTED

THE RAIN WAS STILL COMING DOWN IN PITTSBURGH as I finished unpacking the belongings we had accumulated since our escape from L.A. two years ago. I was glad for the sound of Tony talking to his toy trucks and cars in the next room, giving me a foothold in the present. Over the years, I had adjusted to the stark differences between my public movement life and the lives we had created for ourselves underground. Now that I allowed myself to look back, I remembered again how sharp the disjunction had been and what an uneasy mixture of challenge and pain I had felt in the early days.

There had been the satisfaction of arriving at our new underground house in L.A. We had accomplished the first, dramatic step, and as we sat together in the furnished living room, which was surprisingly comfortable and even had a fire place, we looked at each other and happily acknowledged: *We are here, we are underground*—even though we had merely driven a few hundred miles to another location in the same state.

Then there was the excitement of inventing new lives: our names, our birth certificates, our social security numbers, our hairdos, our family histories, and our job resumes. We rented mail boxes for communications we didn't want going to our home addresses and constructed hidden compartments in closets and drawers for documents we didn't want to have visible in our houses. It was unexpectedly easy to find jobs in daycare centers, hospitals, and restaurants, and to begin establishing the outlines of our new personas. Stepping outside the framework of our "movement bubble" was in many ways exhilarating. In Prairie Fire, our interlocking lives had been a source of community and a base of support for all our daily activities. But once we were away, we could see how our constant meetings, political events, debates over political line, and political struggle with one another had kept us internalized and removed from the realities of most people's lives. Now the protective left insulation was gone and we would have to plumb our inner resources to find the political compass for our activities. Ironically, as we were embarking on this most "radical" undertaking, we were getting to know people from more conventional backgrounds and perspectives. Hopefully, we could eventually organize some of them as progressive supporters.

One of my first acquaintances was with a quirky, outspoken nurse in my new job as a unit clerk at a hospital. Belinda lived with her mother and five dogs. She often came to work with her hair askew and traces of dog fur on her white uniform. Our connection began when I overheard her berating one of the doctors for neglecting to give an elderly Black man enough pain meds to keep him comfortable after his back surgery. "This is not about manipulative behavior," she declared to the young male doctor who was looking very uncomfortable. "This man's pain is real and it's our responsibility to help him with it!" Afterwards, I told her it was good she had stood up to the doctor and asked her whether she was worried about offending him. She gave a caustic chuckle and said "Oh it's okay. If they fire me, I'll just go back to being a waitress. Almost as much money and less stress."

We began to get together now and then after work, grabbing a bite to eat at Denny's, a restaurant I had never eaten at before then, and taking her dogs for a walk in a nearby park. After a couple of months of getting to know each other, I suggested that we go to see the new movie *Missing* about the Chilean coup.[1] I was anxious to see the movie and I thought that going with Belinda would be a good way to open up more political discussion between us. The plot was a slightly fictionalized version of a true story about an American investigative journalist working in Chile, Charles Horman, who disappeared shortly after the coup in 1973. As the journalist's wife and his politically conservative father begin to search for him, they are confronted with the multiple lies of the new regime, plus the refusal of the U.S. embassy diplomats to help with the search.

As I watched, unexpected memories began to flit through my head: Janice's stricken face when she first heard the news of the coup; the tense, pain-laden debates among our Chilean acquaintances as the stories of disappearances, torture, and murder got worse and worse; my first time experiencing the weight of a political defeat in another part of the world deep in the pit of my gut. It was uncanny to be sitting in this movie theater in Los Angeles, watching the truth about the coup unfold on a movie screen before hundreds of people who had barely registered the news ten years before, when it had first happened. How could I explain any of what I was feeling without divulging what I shouldn't to Belinda, who was intently watching as Jack Lemmon came to the realization that the U.S. government was deliberately covering up what had happened to his son? I had never hyper-ventilated before, but I was having a hard time breathing. I told Belinda that I had to go to the bathroom and by the time I returned I had somehow gulped down my memories and was able to watch the rest of the movie with a more detached eye.

I was glad that the movie made Belinda angry. "How can they keep this kind of thing from the public?" she asked accusingly as we left the movie theater. "That's why I never even read the paper anymore," she continued, "cause you can't believe anything they say!" I started to tell Belinda about other hidden examples of U.S. treacherous foreign policy in Latin America, but after listening for a few minutes she wrinkled her nose in disgust and declared, "Humans are too deceitful, animals are much more honest!" Before I could respond, she continued, "Take my mother…" and I felt a twinge of disappointment that the conversation about politics was not going any further. But it was also a relief to listen to Belinda's hilarious comparison of her mother's personality traits and those of her oldest, dearest dog. I was starting to see that there were different ways to make political connections, and hammering at people wasn't necessarily the most effective way.

It took another couple of months before Belinda and I came out as lesbians to each other. This presented a new set of complications when I realized that Belinda might be interested in getting involved with me. This was definitely not the direction I wanted our relationship to go in, and I panicked because I didn't want to lose her friendship over this. After consulting with Jody, I concocted a story that Jody was my girlfriend and the next time I asked Belinda to the movies, Jody came as well. The ruse worked and I was able to continue my friendship with Belinda, but I felt guilty about the lie, which would only con- firm Belinda's opinion of human deceit if she ever found out about it. I was also concerned that living underground had unlocked my ethical gate against casual fibbing, and now it seemed like I was in danger of lying whenever it was conve- nient, or even for enjoyment.

When was a lie necessary to protect our situation and when did it transgress principles of honesty in communication? How could we tell tactical lies without subverting the authentic content of our relationships? With Belinda, I tried hard to strike a balance and eventually she agreed to store some papers for us after I told her that I was involved in some political activities I didn't want the government to know about. Luckily, I only gave her some inconsequential docu- ments as a test of her reliability, because shortly after I did we were surrounded by the FBI and had to leave L.A. When we left L.A. and decided that it was too dangerous for us to try to preserve any links with our friends there, Belinda was the person I missed the most. I never found out if the FBI came to talk with her during their investigation of our whereabouts after we left, or how she ultimately tallied the balance between lies and truths in our friendship.

It was also challenging in that first period to undertake work around clandestine methodology and infrastructure. Never call each other's houses from our home phones, never take a direct route from one person's house to the other, never give our real home addresses to our jobs or friends at our jobs, always watch the rear view mirror to keep track of cars that could be following us—our rules proliferated and became internalized as part of our daily life routine. And, in some peculiar manner, the rules helped to erect a mental buffer against the longing for the lives we had left behind.

In those first months, as I drove home from work every day, there would inevitably be a moment when I would see the signs beckoning "San Francisco, North" and I would imagine myself continuing past my exit on the freeway, putting the car on cruise control and gliding effortlessly northward towards San Francisco to the Army Street exit and Kyle's house on Guerrero. There was no objective force keeping me from doing this. There would be no legal consequences at this stage if I were to show up and slip into bed beside her. There was nothing except my political convictions and the dozens of rules that I was still assimilating, some of which I was already breaking, since, in my imaginary flight, I had forgotten to watch the cars behind me.

One day at a time, I would instruct myself, and gradually the temptations became more infrequent and the signs for San Francisco took on less of a personally charged aura. About a year after I left, I found out that Kyle had started a relationship with another woman in Prairie Fire. By then I was convinced that it would never make sense to try and bring Kyle into the constraining framework of our underground lives, and I accepted this new girlfriend as a good thing for her. Yet, night after night, I found myself sometimes driving, sometimes taking the bus, sometimes walking up and down San Francisco's laborious hills, winding around its crooked streets, seemingly lost except that the street names were intimately familiar and hopelessly foreign at the same time—Eugenia, Army, Potrero, Mission, Valencia, Treat, Elizabeth, Guerrero— I was trying to get somewhere and to get a hold of someone, but I never knew who until after I woke up.

After a while, I became impatient with the irremediable nostalgia and the lost dreams. I realized that there were some possibilities brewing in the here and now, if I would only open my eyes. Claude and I often went out for dessert after a meeting or to a movie on the weekends. Our conversations were becoming more personal and more honest. Claude had also left a lover behind when he came underground, and as time passed we were able to open up and talk about the impact of these losses on each of us. I found myself glancing at him during a meeting, noticing that his makeover underground look—with beard and closely cropped hair—was more attractive to me than his former tousled hippie style. I liked the sound of his voice and the way he expressed his opinions quietly without running over the women in the group. The fantasies about him began to creep into my sleep, until I realized that the main thing holding me back from approaching him was my commitment to a lesbian identity, which now seemed to be morphing along with all other aspects of my underground persona. I was reluctant to reverse the process of coming out, which had been so complicated and protracted, and I didn't want the lack of potential women lovers to drive me back into the arms of heterosexuality. However, deep inside me, I realized that my current desire to sleep with Claude was not really a rejection of my sexuality, but an acknowledgement that it had always included attractions to people of both genders. I explained all of this tentatively to the other women in our collective, and they cautiously agreed that it made sense. Then I talked to Claude. He was a little surprised, but interested, so we decided to go ahead and try it out.

Despite the formal, overly cerebral start to the relationship, it quickly shifted into a powerful physical and emotional connection. We were political comrades sharing the difficult work we had both chosen to do, and we were also in love!

Now, several years later, we were a fugitive nuclear family setting up house in America's most livable city, and I needed to figure out how to make it our home for now. After looking at various bulletin boards, we found a daycare home for Tony with a family in the nearby Homewood neighborhood. The Wallaces were very loving and attentive to Tony, and although he was the only white child in their care, the only unusual aspect for him was the fact that the family didn't celebrate birthdays or any other holidays because they were Jehovah's Witnesses.

We proceeded to get social security cards, praying that our new set of numbers would have more longevity than our last ones. I found a job as a secretary at the University of Pittsburgh and Claude got work as a clerk at a film production company. Salaries in Pittsburgh's still depressed economy were about half of what we had been making in Minneapolis, but rent was cheap and we had some savings accumulated from our two stable years.

Once it stopped raining, we discovered that there were four different playgrounds within five minutes of our home and, if we drove a little further, there were beautiful walks along Pittsburgh's three rivers whose tree-lined banks were saturated with the dazzling reds, oranges, and yellows of falling autumn leaves. We located the city's three art movie theaters, checked out the museums, and scoped out the best thrift stores for additional furniture and clothes for Tony's quickly growing body. With each passing week, the turmoil of the last couple of months in Minneapolis receded further to the background, and there were days when I forgot to brood on the significance of our names on *The Ten Most Wanted* list. But no sooner had I dropped my mental guard than we were blindsided by a new ominous threat.

We saw the trailer one night as we were watching TV after Tony had gone to bed: "YOU CAN HELP CAPTURE AMERICA'S MOST WANTED!" Viewers were encouraged to tune in on Saturday nights at 9 PM to be part of a groundbreaking new show designed to track down the country's most notorious fugitives. I looked over at Claude and could see from the tension tracks creasing his face that for him, like me, our lives were once again spinning out of control. Next day in the local paper's TV section, we read how Fox TV had contacted John Walsh, a leader in the victims' rights movement since his son's abduction and murder a number of years before, to host this new innovative "reality" show. The show would feature reenactments of brutal crimes and profiles of known fugitives with the goal of enlisting national audience support in their capture.

FBI lists and post office pictures were one thing, but now we were facing the inevitability that our names, our faces, our pictures, and whatever sensationalized facsimile of our story the FBI wanted to invent, would be on prime TV, potentially co-opting neighbors, landlords, co-workers, and acquaintances into a process of spying, identification, and notification of the police. What should we do? What *could* we do?

We anxiously awaited the premiere of the show. The ads in the paper indicated that the first fugitives featured would be a serial rapist, a murderer, and a child molester. We didn't think that the FBI could twist our story into any of those categories. But maybe the advertisements were purposely misleading and we would appear in place of one of the other infamous fugitives. On the other hand, it seemed likely that Fox would want to initiate the series with the most socially abhorrent characters in order to gain sympathy for this new media endeavor and avoid any questions about its larger political agenda.

That first Saturday, we were riveted to our TV's. And what we saw was deeply disturbing, even though we ourselves were not mentioned. Introduced by lurid and insinuating music, we watched in horror as the featured rapist lured women into his den and, with the utmost callous pleasure, proceeded to violate them. After the first reenactment, host John Walsh appeared, commenting in a fatherly tone about the crime we had just witnessed, displaying mug shots of the alleged perpetrator and repeatedly beaming the anonymous hotline number that viewers could call if they thought they knew something, anything that could lead to the fugitive. "You don't have to be certain," Walsh reassured would-be tipsters. "Anything you have noticed out of the ordinary might help." Then more music and on to the next scenario where similar hapless victims were stalked and murdered in cold blood before our unbelieving eyes.

America's Most Wanted was sucking its viewers into a voyeuristic world of sex and violence while bestowing upon them the mantle of superhero in the righteous battle against the scourge of criminals who were taking over America. The crime reenactments carried a disclaimer of "fiction," but they were present-ed as factual and true, effectively dispensing with the concept of innocent until proven guilty. If the fugitive were caught, it was difficult to imagine how a jury could objectively weigh the true facts, if they had first been exposed to *America's Most Wanted's* accusatory narrative.

Years before, I had worked on an article in *Breakthrough* about the Federal Law Enforcement Agency's development of the Neighborhood Watch program in the seventies. In the name of fighting crime and protecting neighbor-hood safety, ordinary people (first in white communities, but later also in Third World ones) became spies, secret witnesses, and, in some cases, vigilantes for the police, crafting the ideological and organizational building blocks for a police state apparatus. Through *America's Most Wanted*, Fox TV was taking the im-petus behind Neighborhood Watch to a new level, harnessing the power of the mass media in the service of law and order and breeding a nationwide culture of suspicion, mistrust, and snitching. The show was debuting at the same time as new nationwide drug laws were offering legal incentives for those arrested to turn against each other. Although *America's Most Wanted* was careful to begin the series with white fugitives, it seemed to us that the primary impact of this new level of mass community involvement with law enforcement would be felt by Third World people who were increasingly being locked up in prisons across the country.

We had no doubt that sooner or later our story would be featured on THE SHOW, as we generically named it. Over the next couple of months, we argued and debated how we could best respond to the inevitable airing of our story. Should we be prepared to leave our current homes where people saw us every day and would be most intimately familiar with our faces? Should Donna and Claude, the most vulnerable members of the group, find jobs where only a couple of people could see them on a day-to-day basis, thus limiting their exposure? What made the situation even worse was that we had no idea what types of pictures and other identifying material the FBI actually had on us. Eventually, Rob spotted one of the FBI's *Ten Most Wanted* posters at a neighborhood post office, and we each stopped by to sneak a quick look. The pictures of Donna and Claude seemed to have been taken from afar with a telephoto lens during their trip to Louisiana. Both of them were wearing hats and dark glasses which made them barely recognizable even to us. Seeing these pictures offered us some relief, yet it was hard not to worry that THE SHOW would come up with something more damaging.

After all the debates, we decided that our best defense remained our normalcy. How we presented ourselves in the world with neighbors, coworkers, and friends contested the terrorist stereotype, and as we continued to build relationships we hoped they would never make the leap between us and the scary, wanted fugitives on the TV screen.

THE SHOW took over our Saturday nights. In the beginning we decided that all of us needed to be at home, glued to the TV each Saturday at 9 PM when it aired. We couldn't afford to be caught by surprise if THE SHOW broke with its usual planned format and aired a surprise story about us. Moreover, we needed to insure that Tony was in bed by 9 PM each Saturday to avoid any questions he might have about a show which was so different from the PBS fare that we usually watched. Over the years, the curfew became harder to justify and eventually we had to tell him that this was an adult program which was only appropriate for grown-ups to watch.

——⦿——

The daily fabric of our lives was assuming a new degree of stability. I transferred to a better administrative position in the University Student Health Services, where I got to work with staff who were involved with HIV prevention and education. Claude had been promoted to management of his company's video production department, Rob was working in the library of Carnegie Mellon University, and Donna was a medical assistant in a doctor's office. We moved Tony from the Wallace's daycare home, which he had outgrown, into a preschool/childcare center. He quickly developed a new persona as the class jokester, while eagerly absorbing all the new books and building toys that the school had to offer.

We made friends with a family we met at Gymkhana, where we had enrolled Tony in a preschool acrobatics class. Beth and Michael were both professors at the University of Pittsburgh where he taught physics and she taught philosophy. Their daughter, Katie, was adorable and very coordinated, gliding effortlessly across the balance beams. Soon, we were going to each other's houses for dinner, discussing the Iran-Contra scandal and the new revelations of CIA involvement in cocaine trafficking that was helping to support the deadly activities of the Contra army against Nicaragua.

One Saturday morning, when Claude and Tony were leaving the building where Gymkhana had its gym, they passed someone in the lobby who looked uncannily like a man we had done political work with in San Francisco. The man was holding a child's hand and didn't seem to notice Claude, who grabbed Tony and pulled him quickly into the parking lot. Still giggling from his somersault workout, Tony thought this was a new *"pullgame"* that Claude was playing with him, and he gleefully described it to me when he got home amidst gales of laughter.

Claude wasn't laughing as he whispered to me whom he had seen.
My first response was to dismiss it as paranoia. Why in the world would Clark
Dymitri, who had been active in Bay Area Southern Africa solidarity work, turn
up at Gymkhana in Pittsburgh, Pennsylvania? It was probably just someone who
looked like him. But Claude prided himself on his memory for faces and insisted
that it was undoubtedly Clark. We pulled out a local phone book and there was
Clark's name, in black and white, staring up at us on the page with an address in
a Pittsburgh suburb. "Maybe it's someone else," I offered weakly, knowing that
the uncommon spelling of Dymitri made this very unlikely. I already knew that
this was another one of those periodic crises which would require meetings and
phone calls to decide our course of action.

By now our crisis-driven discussions had become somewhat rote. The
drastic alternatives were limited and we knew it. Clark had been an uneven
friend in the Southern Africa campaign work. Sometimes we would work together very well, but at other times he would decide that Prairie Fire was too controlling and ultra-leftist, and would join with others to accuse us of grandstanding
and hegemonic practices. Donna remembered that she had heard through the
grapevine that Clark had become politically disaffected and had decided to
leave the Bay Area and move back to the Midwest. Although it was unlikely that
he would actually turn us in to the police if we ever bumped into him again, it
wasn't entirely impossible given the flip-flops in his history. On the other hand,
if we decided that Clark's presence in the greater Pittsburgh area was too great
a risk, the only solution was to pick up stakes once again and try to find a part of
the country where we could never bump into anyone we had ever known. Or we
could agree to a risk-reduction approach and simply avoid Gymkhana, where
it was likely that we would collide with Clark again. I could feel the familiar turmoil in my stomach at the idea of taking Tony out of Gymkhana just as we had
taken him out of the daycare center in Minneapolis. But this time the threat was
much more concrete and specific, and I quickly agreed that the easiest solution
was to make Gymkhana off limits.

The harder part this time was explaining the decision to Tony and to
our new friends, Beth and Michael. We told Tony that acrobatics was just too

expensive right now for our budget (at least a partial truth), and that in kindergarten next year he could start soccer which wouldn't cost as much. Tony was
not that attached to acrobatics, so the thought of playing soccer was an adequate
diversion. Beth and Michael were sympathetic to our financial dilemma and we
all agreed that we would make sure that Tony and Katie would continue to have
regular play dates even though they would no longer see each other every week
at Gymkhana.

Meanwhile, every Sunday when we opened the paper, we ritualistically
turned first to the weekly TV section, flipping the pages to Saturday night to
see which bloodthirsty fugitives the next week's *America's Most Wanted* promised to feature. Finally, one Sunday when we turned to the TV section there it
was—sandwiched between a child molester and a convenience store shooting—a
blurb describing Claude and Donna as top ten fugitives belonging to the Puerto
Rican terrorist group, the FALN. We should have anticipated that the FBI would
not bother with subtle distinctions and would make them into members of the
FALN, either because they believed this was true or because they thought it
would be more sensational. What other surprises were in store for us on next
week's SHOW? What fictional reenactments would they concoct? In a series of
coded pay phone calls with Karen and Jody, we decided that we should all pack
a few belongings to be ready to leave if absolutely necessary.

By the time Saturday evening rolled around, every part of my body was
on hyperactive alert. We made sure that Tony had a lot of exercise that day in
order to make sure that he was ready for bed before 9 PM. With a sense of dread,
Claude and I sat down in front of the TV and waited for the sickeningly familiar
musical prelude. The episode opened with the same poor mug shots of Donna
and Claude we had already seen on the post office wall. It went on to give a
summary of FALN armed attacks on the U.S. mainland in the seventies, identifying the group's goals as independence for Puerto Rico and linking the FALN to
other clandestine groups that operated on the island. It was eerie hearing this
chronology of events and groups, which we knew well, presented like a history
lesson on national television.

Then the story switched abruptly to New Orleans in 1985 and a video taken surreptitiously from far away. An indecipherable figure, which THE SHOW identified as Claude, was allegedly giving money to two FBI agents in exchange for phony explosives. The narrator explained authoritatively that the exchange was part of a sophisticated effort to break an FALN terrorist out of prison, an effort which the FBI had successfully infiltrated. They mentioned in passing that Donna and Claude had somehow escaped from the FBI's elaborate net and went on to display pictures of various Puerto Rican political prisoners. They concluded the episode with footage of Bay Area demonstrations in support of Puerto Rican independence and the FALN 11, which brought tears to my eyes. At the very end, they flashed pictures from Donna and Claude's high school year books which resembled them even less than the mug shots did. Host John Walsh wrapped-up with his usual plea for hotline callers, sounding much flatter than usual; this politicized narrative did not lend itself to his emotional manipulations in the same way as the gory episodes did. There was a commercial break, and *America's Most Wanted* moved on to it usual round-up of suspects.

Claude and I looked at each other in relief. No reenactments, no group photo montages, no hints as to our geographic whereabouts. Instead, we had just watched a story about clandestine groups fighting for Puerto Rican independence and their white allies. While Claude and Donna were depicted as extremists, it was clear that their motivation was political and rooted in their commitment to Puerto Rican independence and freedom for political prisoners. Our story had forced radical politics into a show that was dedicated to reducing all social conflict in this country to good vs. evil and cops vs. criminals.

It was hard not to feel a glow of satisfaction in the following days, even though we cautioned each other not to be lulled into complacency or a false sense of security. In fact, we reminded ourselves, the story had now been broadcast to millions. We knew that each show produced hundreds of called-in tips, including many false leads, but even the false leads could potentially have a ripple effect that might impact us eventually. We needed to preserve our vigilance and our security rules, which we were slacking off on as time passed.

Over the next few years, before we returned above ground, the same
version of our story aired two times more. We tried to figure out if there was any
rhyme or reason to the timing of the aired episodes—was there a lead they were
following, a political point they wanted to make, or simply a dearth of other hot
material that caused them to show the episode when they did? We never figured
this out, just as we never could fully understand why they framed our case
with as much political context as they did. Inevitably, as the years of Saturdays
passed, we eased up on our rules, deciding that it was enough for one household
to be stuck in front of THE SHOW each week as long as the others were within
reachable contact. The last time that they featured our episode we didn't even
pack our bags in advance.

*In June 1999, almost five years after we returned to public life and
stopped paying any attention to THE SHOW, Sarah Jane Olson, aka Kathleen
Soliah, a Bay Area radical associated with the SLA,[2] was arrested near her home
in St. Paul, Minnesota after twenty-four years of living underground. Initially,
it was rumored in the papers that her arrest was made as a result of a tip received
after a segment about her aired on* America's Most Wanted. *As I read the description of her arrest in the paper, all the old fears swept over me. This is what I had
been anticipating all those years of Saturday nights locked in front of the TV: the
sudden, cataclysmic disruption which would shred in minutes all the trappings
of normal life which we had so painstakingly constructed. Reading about Sara's
grace under pressure, her daughters' grief in the courtroom, and her neighbors'
shocked disbelief, strangely felt like déjà vu to me.*

*The scenario of capture is embedded in the nerve endings under my skin,
in the chronic aches in the sinews of my muscles, and in the gnarly knots that
coil inside my stomach whenever I hear about the arrest of a political activist in
a decades-old case, reminding me that the state is relentlessly unforgetting and
unforgiving of those who resist.*

Left—Diana at nine with father, Austen, taken in an instant photo booth.
Right top— Sister, Joyce, seven, and Diana, ten. Right bottom—Diana, eight
with mother Luba and Joyce, five.

RISKING A SOMERSAULT
IN THE AIR

I WAS READING MARGARET RANDALL'S BOOK, *Risking a Somersault in the Air: Conversations with Nicaraguan Writers.* "The idea that a poet is necessary to society, and the dignity and strength such necessity carries with it, is a concept as hard to come by in twentieth-century U.S. life as it is complex and difficult to explore, even in a country like Nicaragua."[1] Through a series of interviews, Randall's book explored the revered role of writers in the Nicaraguan revolution and the enormous challenges they faced as revolutionaries, guerrillas and, eventually, government officials. The title was suggested by one of the Nicaraguan writers, Michele Najlis, who described her decision to take up writing in the midst of her responsibilities as part of the Sandinista government: "Well, I'm going to take the leap and see if I can be a writer or not. It's a bit like risking a somersault in the air, and not knowing if you're going to land on your feet or break your neck."[2] To me, the metaphor had multiple applications, and the book was personally motivating.

In high school and throughout college, I had written journals and occasional short stories and poems, but once I became involved in politics these intensely personal explorations no longer had a place in my life. The Third World critique of the Western canon and the privileging of European writers within U.S. society spilled over into questioning the role of white artistic expression in general, especially if that art focused on personal rather than political narratives. In Prairie Fire, we might agree with the Nicaraguans about the necessity of

art in *their* society, but we found it difficult to figure out a role for it in our own
political work.

When I went underground, the terrain shifted in this area, like in so
many others. In L.A., I joined a women's writing group as a way of meeting
progressive people and also to experiment with different ways of expressing my
politics beyond the polemical fliers and articles that I had written in *Prairie Fire*.
The women in the group liked my poems and I began to send some of them
out to women's magazines under the pen name of Renee Pierce. I was delighted
when the feminist magazine *Sinister Wisdom* published my poem called "Stress
Management," which I had written after reading an article in the paper describing the uncontrollable screaming which sometimes broke out among the women
in the semi-conductor industry in Indonesia. The poem began:

> *The stress management classes in Silicon Valley*
> *could not describe*
> *the appropriate exercises*
> *to manage the screams*
> *of women upon row*
> *of women conducting semi-lives.*
> *1000 bonded chip leads a day .*
> *equals three dollars and fifty cents*
> *equals six days a week*
> *and not money left for the seventh,*
> *equals headaches, eye strain, exhaustion –*
> *stress that defies*
> *the measures devised*
> *for civilized levels of silicon tension.*[3]

Another women's journal, *Off Our Backs*, published a poem I wrote
about the anti-abortion movement called, "Silent Scream." Clandestinity was
enabling me to surface a creativity that had been hibernating for many years.

Since we left L.A., my writing impulse had been forced underground again by my increased fear of exposure of any kind. I was reluctant to record my thoughts even on the pad of paper that I kept in drawer of the night table by my bed. Yet, I was boiling over. *Risking a Somersault* reignited my determination to write although I realized that I would need to walk a tightrope between what was admissible and inadmissible on paper and invent an acrobatic language that captured the essence of what I was experiencing, if not the specific details.

Elaborate metaphors aside, I proceeded to check out the course list at the University of Pittsburgh and enrolled in Creative Writing 101. My first assignment was to write a poem about a childhood house that I remembered. As soon as the instructor announced the topic, I could feel my resistance rising. I had decided to take this class in order to figure out how to express my political thoughts and feelings, not to write about sentimental memories of my childhood. I vented my frustration to Donna, but she thought I should try to use the assignment to locate the roots of who I was now in my early experiences. Besides, this could be a way of getting beyond the didactic qualities in my writing style.

So I sat down to write my house poem and, as soon I began, images of the apartment on 99th street where I grew up formed and the words for my poem took shape. I could feel the claustrophobia, the urge to get out of a house that represented the center of my father's existence but hardly of mine:

> *The outside was better*
> *than the inside*
> *even though my father proclaimed*
> *our four rooms large, even huge*
> *with a hallway big enough*
> *to put furniture in,*
> *a palatial living room,*
> *walk-in closets,*
> *a laundry right in the basement,*
> *and 2 genuine balconies*
> *with a river view*

that he would stare and stare at,
trying not to look
four far stories down
at the cracking sidewalks
or the loaded garbage cans
or the differently colored people
lining the streets.

My father would proclaim, over and over again, what a great deal our apartment was—its size, its Upper West Side location, its rent-controlled price. For him, all of this boasting wasn't a case of the glass being half full rather than half empty. Rather, it was his effort to set himself above the world outside. Beyond the walls of our apartment, everything was inferior, everybody was suspect, starting with the tenement hotels across the street and the people of color who were moving in to fill up the neighborhood. His contempt extended to his city civil service job where the work was mindless paper pushing, his coworkers were morons, and his boss was a bitch who was out to get him. Still, he needed the job since he had given up on being a lawyer almost as soon as he had graduated from Columbia law school. "I'm just a weakling," he would declare, partially referring to his skinny physique and his chronic stomach problems, and partly alluding to his mental attitude. "I was never cut out for the cut-throat competition of the legal world," he would complain in a tone of mixed self-mockery and jealousy. "But *you,*" he would say, turning to me and deliberately excluding my sister, "we named you *Diana* for the Greek Goddess of the hunt and you are strong like her and can make it in this world."

I knew I couldn't use this house poem to explain how my father's confused turmoil and his skewed vicarious ambitions for me made me want to scream until our relationship became one long shouting match during my final years at home. I couldn't describe how I had to get out of that house sooner rather than later and cashed in on my high grades to graduate high school at sixteen. I went away to the University of Chicago even though my father threatened to cut me off unless I went to school in New York, but it didn't matter to me because Chicago had given me almost a full scholarship. Besides, my mother had let me know, quietly, that she would send me a check every month from her own bank account, where she kept her salary from her job as a manicurist. I could say little of all this in my poem, but I could say some of it and imply some more.

No the inside was not better
than the outside.
It could have been large
if it hadn't been shrunk small
by couches and chairs, hassocks and lamps,
drapes, carpets, wallpaper, knickknacks
and the lumpy sofabed
which my mother unfolded
and slept in by herself
each night.

How could the inside be better
than the outside
when the balconies were tight and narrow
and only my father
dared perch his skinny frame
on a folding chair balanced carefully
against the wrought iron railing
which leaned against nothing but thin air.
So much better
to be four stories down
with solid street under your feet
and not just a view
but real trees, grass and river
at the end of the block.

As this poem took shape on the page, I began to feel oddly liberated. I could refer to the truth about my parent's dysfunctional relationship without having to mince words. I could freely paint the eccentric details of my childhood because these truths were not verboten and would not, in this cloaked poetic form, tie Pat Hoffman to Diana Block. What's more, the topic gave me permission to look back to my early history, when my later choices were perhaps already being shaped, but were not yet determined.

When the instructor gave us our next assignment to write a poem about an early favorite color, I was eager to take it on. There was no question as to what color that would be. In Prairie Fire it had been a standing joke that if there ever was an opportunity to choose a color—for a poster or a banner—I would always want green, long before the color had come to be associated with any kind of political/environmental agenda. I had a collection of green earrings and, when I went thrift store shopping, I always came home with another green top or pair of green pants. When we went underground, "no green" was one of the first non-negotiable clothing rules for me.

I had never probed my attraction to green, but now I needed to say something serious about my passion for this color. Surprisingly, the memory answers appeared effortlessly. It wasn't just any shade of green that I loved—it was forest green, the particularly dark and mysterious shade of green in the glossy pictures inside my huge *Tales of Robin Hood* book, which I read and reread starting when I was seven or eight years old. When I watched the *Adventures of Robin Hood* on our black and white TV each week, I could easily imagine his forest green tights and tunic and Maid Marian's long, flowing velvet green gown, which she traded for green tights and tunic whenever she was participating in one of their legendary expropriations. My poem, "Sherwood Green," emerged:

> *Robin Hood was the first*
> *green thing*
> *that touched my heart....*
> *it wasn't really the smell of venison, roasting over fire,*
> *or the gallop of steeds flaunting the wind,*

not even

the deep wooded peace of oak and violet

that made me long

for Sherwood green.

But, here was a gang

who shared their merry.

Here were hoods

who knew how to help –

whose light feathered arrows

had not only point

but purpose:

using free air

to fly against

stone-hearted wealth,

they spread the rich green,

in a generous arc,

to those who lived

on the wrong side

of the tracks.

"Rob the rich to give to the poor —that's the way it should be," my father would pronounce after we had watched an episode of *Robin Hood* together. "But don't think for a minute that's the way it is in real life. It's a dog-eat-dog world and there are no Robin Hoods any more!" But the intended lesson somersaulted in my head. Instead of a mandate for resignation, it became a challenge to figure out how to change this dog-eat-dog world.

Did the Robin Hood legend actually feed the seeds of my social consciousness? Was it literally Sherwood Forest that gave rise to my love of green? Probably not, but it didn't matter because my memory gave it that meaning, and the poem that I wrote said true things about me, about my history and about what I believed. I was able to share all of this with my teacher and the students in my class at a time when exposing anything about myself was preciously rare.

To them it was a metaphoric statement that captured a childhood vision of right and wrong. Never in their wildest imaginings could they have guessed that Pat Hoffman, who worked as a secretary at the University of Pittsburgh and took creative writing 101 in her spare time, was an outlaw who wanted, like Robin Hood, to put her philosophic commitment to the poor and oppressed into actual practice.

How had my childhood and youth led me to the choices that I later made? I couldn't put all of it on to paper, but I could think about it and transform what I discovered into poems and stories in a way that was meaningful to others yet would not make us vulnerable. And so, over the next couple of years, I wrote about my experiences growing up on the Upper West Side of Manhattan. I wrote about my friend in third grade, Denice, who was Black and lived in the projects on Amsterdam Avenue, a few blocks from my house. We sat next to each other in school and whispered jokes to each other when the teacher wasn't looking, but because of some invisible wall we left our friendship in the classroom and never tried to have play dates after school. When I was tracked into the "gifted class" in fourth grade and Denice wasn't, we would wave to each other in the hallways, but never really talked again.

I wrote about my best friend in fifth and sixth grade, Ginger, whose mother had "dates" with men for money in the hotel apartment on Broadway where they lived, and, when she did, Ginger couldn't go home and so she would come over to my house. Ginger was brazen and sharp and tough in ways I wasn't, and when we touched at night during our sleepover dates it was the most exciting thing I had ever felt. When I went to Hunter, a competitive academic school, and Ginger went to Joan of Arc, the local junior high, we vowed to stay friends. But by eighth grade, she was doing heavy drugs and sleeping with men twice her age, and, when we got together, after the first few minutes we had nothing to say to each other. In ninth grade, I heard that she had been sent to a reform school and I never saw her again, though for years afterwards she would reappear in my dreams, and I would hug her in happy relief that she was still alive.

I wrote about the conflicting feelings I had as my body changed and I was greeted by catcalls and dirty whispered comments from the men who stood on the corner. I wrote about our various Puerto Rican neighbors whom my father practiced his Spanish with and my mother became friends with, exchanging tips on beauty products and recipes in their own invented form of Spanglish. I even wrote a fantasy-laden story about my mother in which I discovered that she had been secretly in love with her best friend, Eva, for all the years that I was growing up. In the story, this revelation explained so much about my mother—her long, almost nightly calls to Eva, the weekly "day off" she would take to go shopping and to the movies with Eva and other friends, the sofa bed in the living room where she slept by herself for as long as I could remember. Her secrecy about her sexuality might have even been the key to why she refused to tell us any details about her life before she married my father, and it might even account for her fury when she learned that *I* was sleeping with women.

Portraying my mother as a closet lesbian provided a clarifying, satisfying lens through which I could retrospectively view our relationship, and I was glad I could write this version of history in a context where absolutely no one would ever associate the story with the real Luba Block. But, even though I wanted this story to be true, I knew that it was fiction. The more I wrote poems and stories that probed my personal history and the roots of my political choices, the more I realized how I was conforming the narrative to the goals of cause and effect reasoning. While each piece I wrote had truth to it and represented a part of who I was, the sum was not at all sufficient to explain who I had become.

At one point during this twisting memory process, I learned through the circuitous routes that we had established for such communication that my father had died. My sister had called one of my friends with the information, and although the friend told my sister that she didn't know where I was, the message had been passed on through various hands until I received it in a payphone call with a lawyer who we were in touch with at the time. Standing in an ice cold phone booth, I assimilated the news in the instantaneously numbing fashion that I had learned to use when processing all new, unexpected information during these phone conversations. There was no point in asking for details—the person on the other end had no access to information about the circumstances of my father's death. There was no time to break down and sob in response, because, if I let myself go, I would forget to ask the other questions that had been the purpose of the phone call. And so I thanked the voice on the other end for getting me this significant message, registered the fact that I would never have another phone call with my father, and finished the conversation. It wasn't until I was back home, had tucked Tony into bed, and was alone with Claude that I could let myself go as I told him the news.

What do you do when your father dies and the distance that separates you cannot be measured in miles or even by degrees of emotional estrangement? When you cannot ask your sister, who forwarded the news, the simplest of questions—the when's, where's and how's of his passing? When I could not even share with her, the only other person who was likely to grieve his death, the messed up mix of sorrow, bitterness, and love that I was feeling? What could I do to assuage the guilt that I had held at bay for the years since I had stopped speaking to him, but now inexorably came seeping through my carefully erected defenses?

When we first went underground, I had tried to call my father every couple of weeks, alternating times and location from which I called to hopefully confuse those who might be listening in. But he demanded that I conform to the rigid, weekly schedule that I had followed in all the previous years since leaving home, and when I told him that this wouldn't work for me any longer he told me to stop calling all together. I complied and never spoke to him again. I could have tried to reopen the terms of communication at some point, but I gave up. At the time, it seemed easier to simply shut off all contact than wend my way through the emotional and logistical minefields of our relationship. Now he was dead and all I could do was write a poem to him. It started with sorrow and bitterness and, in the process, excavated from my memory some of the more tender aspects of who he was.

To Daddy-Father-Sir

Lonely.
Lonely life, lonely death,
stalking the four rooms
that made up home
for thirty odd years.
Berating the walls, the windows, the ceilings
for what was there
no more.
Listening, listening
to echoes of fights, complaints, harangues –
the boom the rant the rave
of your voice, towering above the others.
Your voice, the strongest thing always
in your hundred pound frame.

Daddy, father-sir
how did it happen
when that death
which seemed ready to take you
for decades
finally arrived?
did it sneak up and mug you
sleeping on a park bench,
your long skinny legs
drawn up beneath
your used Saks Fifth Avenue overcoat?

Or did the life squeeze from your bowels
in one of those exhausting, exhaustive bouts
of running from bathroom to bed to bathroom,

cursing your stomach, the butcher, the cook (your wife)?
except now it was only you
cooking for yourself
and blames and curses
with nowhere to go
could only add bile to bile.

Was it a long winter cold
that lasted through summer?
The gnawing worry that
fires, airplane crashes or hurricanes
would bring you to a premature end?
Or did you just wear out
one long, sleepless night
beseiged by pictures and dreams
of betrayal and loss –
dead wife, deserting daughter –
replayed one time too many?

But maybe, just maybe
I like to dream,
death came upon you singing –
sitting by the window, rocking
like all the years you sang and sang
helping us children find sleep each night,
your voice booming out strong,
towering above the street noise
of shattering glass and drunken brawls,
shaping sound stories of gentler times.
Your voice making the night friendly,
safe for dreams,
building a harmonious bridge for us

between waking and sleep.

Maybe, maybe
you were singing
and your voice sailed out
of your tired mind, tired body
and you were gone.

Years later, when I returned and was able to talk to my sister, she told
me the real story of the end of my father's life. She told me how one day the space
heater which he often used in the winter to warm his frail body tipped over and
started a fire and he was too dazed to do anything about it. The neighbors smelled
the smoke and called the fire department and were able to rescue him before he was
hurt or too much damage was done, but after that everything seemed to go down-
hill. She told me how his mind started to slip and the doctors weren't sure whether
it was Alzheimer's or silent strokes, but he, whose main power in life lay in his
voice, became speechless. "I don't know what to say," he would repeat over and over
to my sister in a monotone, unable to find the will to struggle with this final inca-
pacitation. And Joyce told me how he never mentioned me at all since he had hung
up the phone on me several years before. Except once when she came to the house
and he stated calmly and authoritatively, "Diana is here," and then subsided into
silence leaving her wondering whether this was his imagination or hers at work.

When he died, the doctors called it "complications from pneumonia."
She described his lonely cremation and her sadness that no one who cared for him
was there to share it with her. She didn't tell me this story with accusation at my
absence but laid it out simply as she remembered it. And as I listened, I was struck
not only by the consistency of my father's death with his life. I was struck by the
way in which my sister had put aside her resentment at the scorn my father had
heaped upon her for years as we were growing up. She had stepped beyond her
justifiable alienation and anger to become his caretaker and steadfast companion
in his final days.

I kept the poem about my father buried among my papers. It was probably the best poem I had written about my childhood, but it was too raw and too true for me to share it in a writing class. After I wrote it, I became impatient with looking backwards and probing my past. There was too much happening in my present world that needed to be written about. When we got an assignment to write about some childhood incident where we had been afraid, it was Tony's fear that I decided to write about.

Tony's sleep was becoming punctuated with nightmares. His screams would jolt me awake and, after comforting him back to sleep, I would sit in the dark of the living room, wondering how much of this was normal childhood imagination and fantasy fed by TV shows that we couldn't entirely limit to *Sesame Street*, and how much was a byproduct of *our* fears transmitted to him through the daily tension of our body language, the whispers of our living room conversations after he went to bed, and the ominous sound of the music from *America's Most Wanted*?

When I was three, I had seen a witch in a play about Rapunzel and had run screaming from the theater while all the other children sat placidly in their seats, enjoying the witch's scariness. Was fear a genetically transmitted sensitivity? When we had recently taken Tony to our local greenhouse in the park, transformed into a haunted house for Halloween, he had become impossibly spooked and we had to leave. I could protect him against gratuitous fear, but how could we, who were constantly fighting to manage our own anxieties, pretend that we could eradicate fear from his life? This subject was infinitely complicated to me, but I wanted to communicate some of my thoughts. I called the poem "The ABC's of Fear."

> *The fronds waved wild*
> *oscillating shadows*
> *of tortured light.*
> *Breaking out from the walls*

bounding across the ground
becoming every wild thing
conjured in his head,
every bad thing living
in the world.
He arched his back
and clung to me.

How to explain
that the monster house
was only a greenhouse by day,
transformed by night,
and some fears
were made to be fun.

How to instruct
on the species of fear?
Expose the ones that need to be
exorcised –
like the childhood scream
still echoing in my chest
from my first three-year-old fright,
watching a simple witch
my funny fear bone struck
unable to watch
one second longer.
Distinguish the ones that must be
disproved –
like the fear
that fear itself
is passed in mother's milk.
And claim the ones that must be

conquered
like the siren jolt
that wakes my body,
every nerve naked,
at the very first crescendo note
of his nightmare scream.

How to explain
the difference?
That the shooting men
ripping apart his sleep
are not that
but just a dream,
but the shooting men
upon shooting men
looming, zooming
across the TV news screen
are just that
and not a dream.

When asked
– Will the shooting men get me? –
how to reassure –
No, no –
and still explain
some fear is not fun
but is serious and sane.
That children in South Africa,
for one,
learn early that fear
cannot be taken lightly
should not be exorcised

> *will not be disproved*
> *but must be conquered*
> *and turned*
> *inside out.*

Interestingly, this poem provoked one of the most intense discussions in my class. People forgot to talk about the language and the style, and instead plunged into a debate about what causes fear in children and how to deal with it. A couple of the other students had young children and were also grappling with their night terrors. One student felt that the reference to South Africa was extraneous and made no sense. A chorus of people disagreed with him, arguing that it was an interesting way of introducing a political comparison with the conditions for children in a country whose political turmoil was making its way onto the pages of the *Pittsburgh Post-Gazette* almost every day. The conversation then evolved into a more general discussion of how and why to introduce politics and world events into poetry.

That night, I went back and reread portions of *Risking a Somersault in the Air*. This time I was struck by a passage from Randall's interview with Tomás Borge, a founding member of the Sandinistas, the Minister of the Interior in the revolutionary government, and a poet. "The role of the writer in the revolution is, first of all, to write well... *To write in such a way that people feel like reading what has been written...* In this respect, form and content must be in a dialectical relationship that the writer, in my opinion, should have engraved in indelible letters on his brow, on his fingertips, in his heart."[4]

What made people want to read something that wasn't familiar or comfortable, something that challenged their socially constructed notions of right and wrong, something that pushed them to perform a mental somersault of their own? Living underground had sharpened my writing skills because I had a greater stake in reaching other people with what I wrote. I had also discovered great personal satisfaction in crafting words that could approximate the nuances of lived experience. Whatever happened in my unpredictable future, I wanted to cultivate this exacting joy.

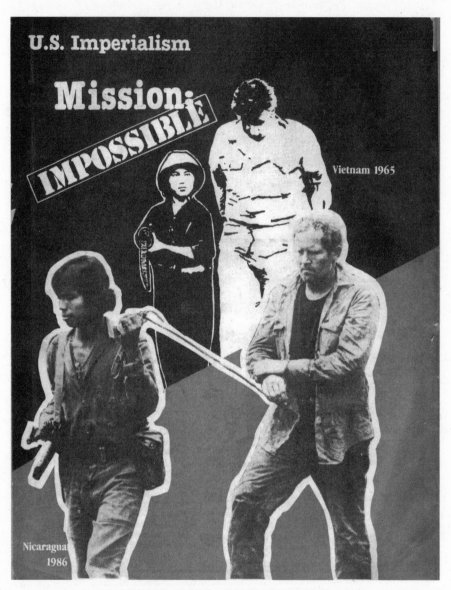

Back cover of *Breakthrough*, Vol XI, No.1, Winter/Spring 1987. Photo collage showing Vietnamese woman with captured B-52 pilot (top) and Nicaraguan government fighter with captured CIA mercenary who was shot down delivering supplies to the Contras.

No Hay Camino

Caminante   *Walker*

No hay camino   *There is no road*

Se hace camino   *The road is made*

Al andar.   *By walking*

—Antonio Machado[1]

WHILE I WAS FOCUSED ON MY PERSONAL NARRATIVE, documenting my road toward social change and revolution, a metanarrative was taking shape on a global scale, which was reversing the path of the monumental social revolution of the twentieth century. *Perestroika* and *glasnost,* Russian words heretofore unknown and unspoken by Americans, had become popular currency, not only on the left and among academics, but also for talk-show hosts and newspaper columnists.

Perestroika referred to the process of economic restructuring and the introduction of market-driven reforms that Mikhail Gorbachev initiated in the Soviet Union after he became the General Secretary of the Soviet Communist Party in 1985. Perestroika's reforms included limited private ownership of businesses, an elimination of the monopoly of the Soviet government on trade operations, and the opening up of foreign investment in the form of joint ventures with other countries. Spurred by the nuclear disaster at Chernobyl in the Ukraine in 1986, and the government cover-up of the extent of the damage and the gross mismanagement which had caused the accident, Gorbachev's policy of glasnost (openness) was taken up on all levels of Soviet society. The relaxation of censorship, the opening of political debate, and the greater tolerance of criticism and dissent unleashed a social torrent that eventually questioned every aspect of Soviet society and history.

Perestroika and glasnost radiated an aura of change and excitement. For years the anti-revisionist left, of which I considered myself a part, had scathingly critiqued the path that the Soviet Union had taken since the thirties—the stagnant, bureaucratically planned economy, the brutal purges, the police state apparatus, the gulags, the invasions of Czechoslavakia, Hungary, Afghanistan. There were endless, fierce arguments as to whether the Soviet Union was merely revisionist—having long ago departed from the revolutionary socialist vision of Marx and Lenin that had guided its birth—or whether it was in fact "social imperialist" and posed a greater threat to the world's people than U.S. imperialism itself, an analysis that had been developed by the Chinese communist party. But there was little disagreement within the anti-imperialist left that the Soviet Union required fundamental change.

Still, there was something chilling to me about the seeming universal embrace of perestroika and glasnost by capitalists and leftists alike in the United States. Obviously some type of restructuring was needed. Certainly openness and true democratization were critical. But were capitalist market reforms the key? How could anyone trust the term *democracy* when it was it being molded and shaped like silly putty by a Soviet leader who was being pushed and shoved by Ronald Reagan, who had vowed from the beginning of his tenure to defeat communism everywhere around the world? Even more worrisome, what would perestroika mean for the nations of the Third World like Cuba and Viet Nam which relied heavily on the economic and political support of the Soviets? Could a revolutionary vision of socialism be retained or would it be an inevitable casualty of the maelstrom of rapidly moving, unpredictable changes? The six of us debated these issues among ourselves, but we desperately wanted to discuss the situation with other people who shared an anti-imperialist perspective.

I had begun to take a Spanish literature class to improve my Spanish and to delve into a new area of literature. My teacher, Isabella, intrigued me with her breadth of knowledge which extended from classic Spanish writers to modern Latin American ones. She was vibrant, attractive, and about my age. Unlike my English writing teachers who preferred to glean political insights from personal narratives, Isabella grounded her discussion of each poem and short story in the history and politics of the era in which the work was produced. I loved her approach and the engaged manner in which she conducted our classroom discussions, although I was frustrated by the limitations of my Spanish which hampered my ability to express all I thought about these thought-provoking works of literature. One day Isabella told the class a little about her Ph.D. thesis, which was focused on the development of Afro-Cuban literature. With the pretext of wanting to hear more about the thesis, I asked her to have a cup of coffee after class. She quickly agreed, indicating that she also had been wanting to make this more personal connection. Luckily, she decided that we could conduct our out-of-class conversations in English, which immediately opened up the boundaries of our communication, since her English was worlds better than my Spanish.

Isabella explained that she had felt a deep affinity with the Cuban revolution from the time she had first heard about it from her father, a Spanish leftist who had fought against Franco in the thirties. Isabella was studying in Paris at the Sorbonne in 1968 and took part in the student rebellion that shut down the city for weeks. She considered herself a leftist first, a teacher second, and an academic parenthetically. She had traveled to Cuba several times and had become enthralled intellectually and emotionally with the resurgent popularity of Afro-Cuban literature and art in the eighties. After teaching literature in a secondary school in Barcelona for years, she decided that she wanted to pursue her Ph.D. in Afro-Cuban literature. The University of Pittsburgh had an excellent program in Cuban literature and was able to offer her a generous fellowship to pursue her degree there. "This is one of the great, intractable ironies of our times," she said to me in a voice laden with bitterness. "America offers academic expertise and opportunity even in specialized disciplines focusing on the Third World. Many of us who cannot find this advanced study in our own countries are drawn to study and teach here, despite ourselves. At what price is yet to be seen, at least in my individual case…"

As she talked, my mind was exploding. It had been so long since I had had a conversation of this depth on these sorts of subjects with anyone besides the six of us. Despite the limitations of my classroom Spanish, despite the constraining structure of our student-teacher relationship, Isabella had identified me as a like-minded person, a person she could talk to, and this made me feel very good. I wanted to tell her that I too was passionate about Cuba, had gone there with the Venceremos Brigade and had talked at length with the Afro-Cuban leader of my brigade about the contradictions of life for Black Cubans. But I knew that I could not simply apply glasnost to this situation, so instead I constructed a story about a "good friend" who had spent a lot of time in Cuba as the basis for my side of the conversation.

Isabella listened closely and when I was finished with my narrative (which I made up as I went along), she looked at me intently and said, "It is good to meet an American who understands things like you do, Patricia. I began to know this when I listened to you in class, but sitting with you now, I feel it even more." I could feel the tears coming into my eyes which I didn't want Isabella to see, so I quickly made a light disclaimer about what that must say about the other Americans she had met.

Over the next year and a half, while Isabella worked to complete her thesis, she became the person I could talk to about perestroika and glasnost; someone who could sympathize with my worries about what the disintegration of the Soviet Union would mean for Cuba and for international dreams of socialism and change. She identified as a Marxist, but her mistrust of the Soviet Union ran deep, fed by her awareness of the ways that Eastern Europe suffered under the Soviets. On the other hand, her experience living and studying in the United States and her analysis of the U.S. as the key world imperialist power kept her from greeting the era of perestroika with much optimism.

In the fall of 1989, we watched with a mixture of hope and worry as Poland, Czechoslavakia, Hungary, Bulgaria, and Romania overthrew their Communist governments through a combination of mass upsurges, elections, and, in the case of Romania, an armed takeover. Along with the rest of the world, we were glued to our TV's in November of 1989 as the Berlin wall, the international

symbol of the "iron curtain," was symbolically dismantled by cheering throngs
of East and West Berliners who were finally able to move freely between the two
parts of their city after twenty-eight years of forced separation. Who could argue
against this liberatory action, an inevitable response to an authoritarian, repressive policy which eliminated freedom of movement for East Germans? Yet, long
before the official dismantling of the Soviet Union in 1991, it was clear to us that
an unstoppable process had begun that would have a serious, irreversible impact
on the balance of power in the world.

As Isabella and I got together for tea after class to discuss a short story
by exiled Uruguayan writer Cristina Peri Rossi or a poem by the Guatemalan revolutionary poet Otto René Castillo, our conversation would wind its way forward
to the present, to what was happening to the Soviet Union and the long term
ramifications of the disintegration of Soviet power. How would Cuba fare in this
new era? The Soviet Union had provided critical economic assistance to Cuba
since the sixties. If the Soviet Union was no longer, if its economy was unraveling
at the rate that the newscasters claimed, how would Cuba sustain itself, ninety
short miles away from what was rapidly becoming the world's only superpower?

Isabella knew that I cared deeply about the future of Cuba and the other
Third World socialist countries from the viewpoint of a committed bystander.
She didn't realize, of course, how much my own hopes and possibilities for the
future seemed to be tied up with the situation of the socialist countries. Since we
had arrived in Pittsburgh, we had accelerated our search for options for the seven
of us beyond the borders of the United States. The long term prospects for life
inside this country looked very bleak indeed. Isolated as we were, we didn't see
how we could rebuild an active clandestine capacity. And making security our
exclusive priority was politically useless and personally debilitating. In the past,
political fugitives from the U.S. had found asylum in Cuba, in other parts of Latin
America, in Africa, China, and even in the Middle East. While political exile had
its own set of contradictions, we all agreed that it was preferable to indefinite
clandestinity or protracted incarceration.

For two years we tried to figure out how to make this option a reality.
We had multiple calls with various lawyers. We went over and over the pos-

sible destinations. We plotted scenarios which might allow us to get out of the country quietly. Many nights, I would jolt awake, filled with worry about the danger of our proposed travel trajectories and the prospect of restructuring our lives in another country—learning a new language, finding jobs, redefining another country as home—all of the difficult challenges that immigrants all over the world faced. I comforted myself with the hope that Tony would grow up in a place where he might, from an early age, be part of a collective effort to forge a different social reality.

After several false starts, it seemed like we were moving closer to an actual plan for departure. I began to make lists in my head of precious things to take with me. I wanted to avoid the mistakes I had made in L.A. and put some forethought into paring down our belongings. But, just as it seemed as if a final decision was in the works, everything stopped. Our lawyer intermediaries were at a loss to explain, but we all knew that this was not a fluke or a temporary set-back. In this global tempest of confusing change, how could we expect any country to risk an international incident over seven white Americans on the FBI's most wanted list? I stopped making my mental lists of the pictures and books I wanted to bring with me into exile. I tried to accept, once again, that for now we were stuck in a life of internal exile.

Isabella talked a lot about exile. She had known many Chileans who were living in Spain and France since the 1973 coup. In Cuba, she had met Nicaraguan, Salvadorean, Palestinian, and African revolutionaries who were living in exile because it was too unsafe for them to continue the struggle inside their own countries. And, in Pittsburgh, she was part of a community of international scholars who joked about their own forced academic exile, resulting from a lack of academic positions in their own countries. I knew that Isabella was in deep conflict about whether she would accept one of the teaching positions in the United States that had already been offered to her, once her dissertation was complete. If instead she returned to Spain, it was questionable that she could ever find a University-level position teaching the subjects she loved. "This is the era of exile," she told me one day with a characteristically melancholy sigh. "Political exiles, refugees, immigrants; one way or another, we have all been

forced on the road by imperialism, doomed to a life of yearning for our home-
lands." She laughed caustically. "Perhaps I am being over-dramatic, since I am a
privileged exile who has a choice. But so many people don't have a choice. Ay, I
do not yet know which path I will choose."

As Isabella talked, confiding in me as someone who was sympathetic
but removed from this reality, I wanted to scream, "I too am living in exile! I too
dream every night about the people I left behind and the city I cannot enter.
When people at work talk about going to San Francisco for a conference or a vacation, I become absurdly overwhelmed with envy because they are able to visit
and enjoy that city that they don't know at all, while I, who have so many friends,
so many memories, so many ties to it, cannot go back, even for a weekend. I want
to leave this country that everyone else is trying to come to, but even that is no
longer a possibility. Instead I am consigned to an invisible exile, masked as a normal, rooted American life." Of course, I didn't say any of this, not only because
of the enormous security breach it would have been, but also because I would
have felt ridiculous comparing my longing for San Francisco with a Palestinian's
longing for the land that had been viciously stolen from them, or a Chilean's
longing for a country whose socialist experiment had been slashed into bloody
shreds. The existential yearning for an unobtainable place might have similar
qualities, but the geopolitical circumstances of their exile and mine were vastly
different. Still, Isabella's reflections on exile helped me, as well as her, identify
some of the pain we were each feeling, living in Pittsburgh, far away from much
of what we held dear.

*"The contemporary world is a place of exile and refugees; the displaced
run like rivers through myriad countries, flowing towards the seas... The exile
loses her life in an instant. That moment in which one steps over a threshold,
across a border, to disappear, life as it was vanishes. Like trees, human beings find
it difficult to be wrenched up, our roots torn away."[2]*

*Political prisoner Marilyn Buck wrote this haunting description of exile
in the introduction to her translation of Cristina Peri Rossi's book of poems,* State

of Exile, *published in 2008. Marilyn explains the great affinity she felt for Rossi's poems:*

> *"This is where I begin, the translator in exile of a translator of exile. My point of view as a political prisoner in internal exile is not so different from Peri Rossi's after she fled the military dictatorship of Uruguay. She went into external exile, while I, a political militant, did not choose external exile in time and was captured. I became a U.S. political prisoner and was sentenced to internal exile, where I remain after more than twenty years."[3]*

> *My discussions about exile with Marilyn helped me to better understand aspects of my own experience and my drive to write about it. Rossi says in her prologue "If exile were not a terrible human experience, it would be a literary genre. Or both things at the same time."[4]*

> *Arguably,* Arm the Spirit, *is part of that unnamed literary genre of exile.*

⸎

Neither Isabella or I yet realized, in 1989, that our yearning was not only for a place but also for an era that was rapidly disappearing, a period when leftists around the world still believed that socialist revolution was not only an obtainable goal but also a sustainable reality. With the dismantling of the Soviet Union came the deconstruction of socialism as a potentially positive reconstruction of the world's economic order. Fed by commentators and pundits who proclaimed "the death of socialism" and conflated the problems that had plagued the world's first self-identified socialist revolution with the concept of socialism itself, doubt and deep confusion became rampant among leftists of all persuasions. Then the nadir came. In February 1990, the Sandinistas lost the elections in Nicaragua and the struggle that had served as a revolutionary compass and a guiding centerpiece for U.S. activists throughout the eighties suffered a crushing blow that disoriented and demobilized the U.S. left for years to come.

When I first heard about the Sandinista defeat, watching the evening news with Claude, I felt like someone had punched me in the stomach. My immediate reaction was that this couldn't be true, it had to be just one more propaganda ploy of the Bush administration, which had supported Violeta Chammorro's winning, anti-Sandinista UNO party.

How could we have been so out of it, sitting here in our Pittsburgh bubble, piecing things together as best we could through the leftist news sources that we had available, but failing to see the handwriting on the wall as soon as the Sandinistas agreed to hold the elections a year early under pressure from the U.S.? In the weeks that followed their electoral defeat, we understood that we were not alone. Progressive supporters all over the world had believed what the Sandinistas themselves believed—that it might be a hard fight, but in the end their optimistic campaign slogan "*Todo será mejor, everything will be better,*" would prevail.[5]

For days, I couldn't take my mind off the defeat. I remembered the elation in the Mission district in San Francisco after the Sandinistas rode triumphantly into Managua on July 19, 1979. San Francisco was filled with thousands of Nicaraguan exiles who had supported the FSLN,[6] and after the victory they renamed the 24th St. BART station, *Plaza Sandino,* and many went home to assume positions in the new Sandinista government. Soon stories came back about amazing changes that were going on: a national literacy campaign, the takeover of land and houses from the wealthy who had fled, the overhaul of the media, the establishment of health clinics all rural Nicaragua, and the many reforms that began to take place for women. Hundreds of Americans went to live and work in Nicaragua, imbued with a renewed hope that revolution in this hemisphere was possible, and that there was a role for them in this whirlwind of change. Just before I went underground, I had lunch with a friend who was packing up to move to Nicaragua for a year. "You should think about doing this too, Diana," she encouraged me, and I nodded in agreement, wondering what it would be like to be preparing for a year working with the Sandinistas instead of getting ready for an underground life inside the United States.

From underground, we studied Sandinista history and we followed, as much as we could, their political struggles as they responded to the Reagan administration's stated commitment to destroy the revolution. We watched as the U.S.-orchestrated Contra war escalated. Over time, some of the lies and corruption which fueled the war were exposed by the Contragate scandal,[7] but the war went on anyway. Over the course of the decade, the Contra war had succeeded in sapping Nicaragua's resources, eventually killing over 50,000 out of a population of 3.5 million, and gradually, intransigently it eroded the capacity of this new social experiment to fulfill the changes it had promised in the beginning. We read about the growth of the U.S. solidarity movement, the thousands of people who traveled to Nicaragua to offer material help, the Pledge of Resistance which was signed by thousands more who promised to take to the streets in massive civil disobedience if Reagan dared to make good on his threat to invade Nicaragua. But in the end, the Reagan/Bush strategy succeeded without an invasion. It wore down the people, threatened their future well-being, provided the specter of endless low-level war, endless shortages of goods, endless poverty until they could stand it no longer and 54% deserted the Sandinistas at the polls, enough for Chamorro to proclaim a resounding victory.

Stepping back, it was easy to rationally understand why the Sandinistas had been defeated in the elections. In fact, it was hard to fathom how we had been so sure that they would win. We had hung our hopes on the revolutionary will of the Nicaraguan people, their memory of the atrocities of the Somoza dictatorship and their collective capacity to continue to risk a somersault in the air when they had no assurance that they would ever land on their feet again. Easier for poets to do than for a people battered by a U.S. proxy army. Now, fundamental political questions loomed. If Nicaragua wasn't able to sustain its revolution, what country would be able to? What was to keep the United States from undermining and destroying every revolution, every progressive movement now that it was the only superpower in the world? How could anyone anywhere preserve revolutionary optimism or the will to carry on, when every victory seemed only transitory? Could we sustain a commitment to resistance on a purely existential basis simply because it is human to resist tyranny and injustice?

"What is going to happen to El Salvador and Guatemala? What is going to happen to socialist revolution?" I cried to Isabella after the Sandinistas
lost. And Isabella, whose face had begun to assume a permanent melancholy
cast, sighed, "At times like these, we can only remember the words of Antonio
Machado, *'No hay camino, se hace camino al andar.'*[8] We will keep up our walking, Diana, and we will figure out a new path, somehow."

Over the next years, I read various analyses which pointed out the in-
ternal weaknesses of the Sandinistas that contributed to their defeat in the 1990
elections. Their early mistakes in suppressing the indigenous Miskitu people's
desire for autonomy and self-determination were skillfully exploited by the U.S.
to organize the Miskitu into the Contra army.[9] *The hierarchical structure of the*
FSLN and the lack of internal democracy kept power and decision-making in the
hands of a few leaders and made it very difficult to have full debate about strate-
gic priorities for the revolution in the face of the U.S. multi-faceted assaults. And
endemic problems of male supremacy kept women from exerting their leadership
potential and de-prioritized women's programs as more and more resources were
diverted to fight the Contra war.

In 1992, Margaret Randall published Gathering Rage, *based on ex-*
tensive interviews with Nicaraguan women in the post-Sandinista era and her
own experience of living and working in Cuba and Nicaragua for almost three
decades. In the book, she argued that the failure to integrate a feminist vision into
the center of the revolution was the critical problem not only for Nicaragua but
for all socialist revolutions to date. "If revolution incorporates feminism it will
transform itself,"Randall insisted.[10] *On the one hand, Randall believed that the*
Sandinista revolution had "opened a vast economic, social, political, and cultural
space for women, empowering them with a strong sense of their personal and
collective identities. In no previous victorious revolution have women played such
an essential role as in the Nicaraguan struggle."[11] *Yet, as the pressures from the*
U.S. accelerated and the revolution fought to survive, Randall believed that male
supremacy reasserted itself, women's autonomous leadership was undermined,
and women's issues were relegated to a secondary place. The lack of attention to

women undermined the connection between masses of women and the revolution,
making them more susceptible to manipulation by U.S. propaganda and the UNO
party. [12]

Reading Gathering Rage, *I had to agree that women's liberation,*
women's empowerment, had been attacked or contested in every revolutionary
struggle once state power was achieved. My own experience in the left reflected
the inexorable pull away from "women's issues" and the difficulty of integrating
feminist consciousness and program into a left agenda. Aspects of Randall's faith
in feminism's transformative potential seemed over- simplified to me: she glossed
over many important contradictions within feminist movement and ideology. But
I was convinced, more than ever, that it was critical for women to have genuine
power within any process of social transformation and the program for women's
liberation needed to be a priority on every level, at every stage of a revolutionary
process.

If at some point I were able to resume public organizing, I wanted to
apply these hard-won global lessons and once again put women's struggles at the
center of my own political work.

In the summer of 1990, Isabella finished her Ph.D. and decided to return to Spain to look for a job there. "Nicaragua made up my mind for me," she
explained. "I just could not stay any longer in this country which was responsible for fracturing that dream." When Isabella left, she gave me a poster. It had
simple line drawings of the sun, the moon, and a blue bird. Beneath the drawings were Antonio Machado's words:

> *Caminante*
> *No Hay Camino*
> *Se Hace Camino*
> *Al Andar*

The poster has hung in a prominent place on the wall of each house I
have lived in ever since then.

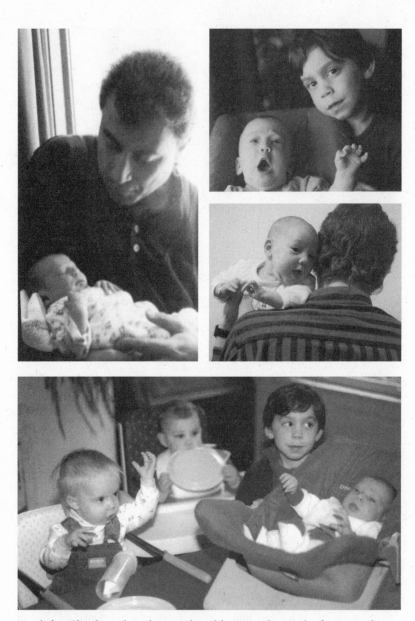

Top left—Claude with Leila, one day old. Top right –Leila, four months and Tony, six years. Middle right—Ericka, three months and back of Karen's head. Bottom (from left to right) Zoe, one year; Ericka, twenty-two months; Tony, six years; Leila, one month.

WITH EYES NOT YET BORN

But it's beautiful to love the world
with eyes
that have not yet
been born

And splendid
to know yourself victorious
when all around you
it's all still so cold,
so dark.

—Otto Rene Castillo[1]

WHEN WE THOUGHT THAT WE MIGHT BE CLOSE to leaving the country, Rob gave me a blank journal so that I would be able to, at long last, record all my thoughts and feelings once we had arrived safely in a new land. After our exit plans fell through, I decided to use the journal to record some of Tony's musings which struck me as particularly poetic or funny or childishly wise.

"I want to be a red leaf, so I can fly and fall down," Tony announced, looking out the window at the autumn leaves outside our front porch.

As he was eating a carrot for a snack, he exclaimed: "I want to wish on this carrot. I want to wish that we go to a far, far away city, or on a dancing barge to Japan."

After watching a PBS documentary about Martin Luther King, Tony had a lot to say. "Martin Luther King was very angry when he was alive. He said *freedom* like this—" He pursed his lips and mustered all the anger and adamancy he could in his five-year-old voice to declare, *"FREEDOM! FREEDOM! FREEDOM! FREEDOM!"* until I stopped his chanting to explain that Martin Luther King was angry because of the way Black children in the South were not allowed to drink out of the same fountains as white children or even use the same bathrooms. Tony got very quiet, and I could see him turning this around in his head. "I wish I could be alive when Martin Luther King was alive," he said. "Then I could be his friend."

Overhearing a news story about the U.S. invasion of Panama in December 1989,[2] Tony turned to me and said earnestly, "Panama, Panama...that's a nice name. If I have a little brother or a little sister, could we call him Panama? But no, I think it's a better name for a little sister."

"This is why children are so important," I wrote in the journal, including my own thoughts for once after his interesting comment, "in order to turn the invasion of Panama into a vision about babies and hope."

Tony's segue between Panama and babies was less random than it seemed. Since the six of us had realized that there was no present hope of leaving the United States, the issue of having more children was on everyone's mind. When Claude and I had decided to have Tony back in Los Angeles five years before, we had all expected that he would be followed quickly by the other children Karen and Jody, and Donna and Rob would have. The FBI encirclement, our escape from L.A., and our fugitive status inevitably put those plans on hold. Yet we began discussing the possibility of having more children soon after arriving in Minneapolis. We all agreed, at least in principle, that this should happen, it *had* to happen. The only question was when.

Why have children while we were underground? Were we oblivious to the danger, cavalier about the impact on the children, selfish in our desires, or were we just stubborn about our determination to be parents and indomitably hopeful that somehow it would all work out? These are the kinds of questions people have asked

*since we have returned, and it is hard to explain without sounding trite or ro-
mantic. We wanted to have children in order to create new life, to carry ourselves
forward into another generation, to experience the joy of having a child, to see
the world through different eyes, to insist on hope for the future—common enough
reasons, the same ones that motivate people around the world to have children in
situations far more ominous, difficult, and hopeless than ours. If we allowed fear
to stop us, we would have accepted defeat.*

Although we all wanted more children, over the years the question of
timing became an increasing source of tension among us as we struggled to get
our bearings, moved from city to city, and grappled with the weekly uncertainties
presented by *America's Most Wanted*. Given our situation, there would always be
"reasons" to put the decision off, and the delays obviously impacted Karen, Jody,
Donna and Rob more than they did Claude and me, who were lucky enough to
have one child already. Having children needed to happen sooner rather than
later, before it became physically impossible for women who were rapidly approaching the end of their childbearing age.

And so, in a flood burst of new-life affirmation, we decided that this
dark period of history was the right time. Karen and Jody asked Claude to
become the donor for their child and decided that Karen would be the biologi-
cal mother. Claude and I were both happy to agree to the request and for a
few harrowing months, Claude and Karen alternated making the trip between
Pittsburgh and St. Louis, dispensing with our usual rules about limited contact
between the cities. Ericka was born in February 1990 to everyone's delight,
including Tony's. Tony had grown up believing that Karen and Jody were his
aunts, a benign lie which we had told him to explain our special relationship
with them. Although Tony didn't learn about the blood ties between him and
Ericka until he was older, he knew that this baby was an intimate, exciting new
part of his family and he was very eager to get to know her.

Nine months later, we were thrilled when Zoe was born in November
1990. Donna and Rob were "cousins" to Tony, and now he had a little cousin
close by to play with and help take care of right in Pittsburgh.

Claude and I also wanted a second child. I wanted another child to affirm my forty-year-old creative capacity after so many disappointments, and to be able to plunge my unused energies into a new baby. I also wished for a girl-child on levels that were deep and hard to fully rationalize. I wanted a girl to share and explore my own identity as a woman. I wanted a girl to defy the biases which for centuries had privileged male children and driven parents around the world to throw baby girls into rivers or sell them off as soon as they could. I wanted to raise a girl who could become part of the global momentum for women's liberation. But I also mistrusted these reasons, which were too much about me and my yearnings. When people at work asked me whether I wanted a girl or boy, I simply explained that a girl would be nice because I already had a boy.

After anticipating that I might have more problems getting pregnant at forty than I had at thirty-five, I got pregnant the first time we tried and that made me glad. Right before my appointment to see a midwife, at eight weeks pregnant, I began to bleed. The midwife confirmed that this was an early stage miscarriage, a sad but common occurrence that didn't have major implications for my capacity to have another baby. Claude was supportive and optimistic, so as soon as the medically advised three-month waiting period was over we tried again and within a couple of months I was pregnant.

This time my happiness was tinged with anxiety. All the advice I had received confirmed that the best thing for me and the baby was to keep my thoughts positive, but often while I was typing at work or taking the bus to pick Tony up after school, I would find myself worrying that all the difficult events that had occurred since my pregnancy with Tony had left an indelible, damaging mark on my body and on my mind.

The night before I was to have my CVS test to check whether the baby was healthy, I woke up shaking from a nightmare in which a doctor was coldly informing me that my baby's heart had just one ventricle. The CVS test went smoothly and, once I got the normal results and began to feel the baby's first fluttering movements, I started to let go of my worries and focus instead on the little person inside of me. But a few weeks later, on a routine check-up at seventeen weeks, the midwife was unable to find the baby's heartbeat and rushed me to the hospital. Once I was hooked up to the ultrasound, I followed with agonizing precision the doctor's futile efforts to find the beat in a heart which had clearly stopped.

Numbness, denial, grief, guilt, more guilt... the midwife reassured me that all of the feelings I was experiencing were normal, reasonable, part of the grieving process. I couldn't tell her how everything I had yearned to create had warped into a morass of stagnation and lifelessness. I couldn't explain that deep inside of me I felt that I had killed this baby by allowing the list of fears, tensions, frustrations, and disappointments to permeate my body and suck the life from my belly.

I had to wait for several days before they could induce the labor and delivery which was necessary for this second trimester miscarriage. Claude suggested that we get away for a few days, and so the three of us went up to Erie, a low key town with bike riding trails and beaches. In between digging caves and fashioning sand castles, Tony kept darting over to the blanket where I was trying to focus on a book. "We'll just make another baby, right mommy?" he kept repeating in a half reassuring and half questioning voice. Every time he came over, he pulled me out of the pit I was sliding into and made me sit up and answer in a reasonably optimistic tone, "We'll try, tony-baloney, we'll certainly try..."

During the four days that I had to live with this no-longer-alive baby inside of me, I found myself thinking about death. In the past, I had been wracked by distant deaths in Viet Nam, Attica, and Philadelphia, but I had managed to keep personal knowledge of death at arm's length, until now. I had missed my mother's death by a day and had aborted any grieving process by rushing to Houston, back into the political whirlwind. I hadn't found out about my father's death until a year after it was over, neatly avoiding the heartache associated with his life's ending by being underground, leaving that painful process for my sister. Was it *karmic* vengeance that accounted for my present situation, since neither politics or science could adequately explain why I now had a baby dead in my womb? To keep from tripping further, I wrote a poem, "Miscarriage Juju":

Only one ventricle –
the heart has
just one.
The words
split my ears,
tear at what is inside me
growing,
hurl me awake, clutching
my stomach, my stomach.
Then slowly stroking,
patting my skin already stretching,
I try to smooth away belief.

Days later
we watched
this tiny person
swish around;
the life miracle
projected as a gray blob
slipsliding on the screen.
The one clear movement
pulsing adamant in the center,
the live, beating heart
offered the scientific proof
not to worry.

Yet weeks later,
Where is it? Where is the beat?
Searching, hunting,
listening to every inch
of stomach.

Moving back and forth
carefully, so carefully
not to miss it.
Straining to hear, to see.

Where
Is
It?
Where did it go?
No longer heard –
(silence = …)
No longer seen –
the still, unmoving
blank, gray screen.
Dropped off what edge?
Held hostage by what prophetic dream?
Where the reasons?
Where the answers?
Not in the chromosomes all neatly counted.
Not in the spine all closed and straight.
Not in the tissue uninfected.
Not in the blood.
Not in anything tested
or objective.

Then what juju brought this on?
Some earrings lost?
A near death missed?
The stars?
The moon?
An unknown totem wronged?

All the signs that hover
on the backside of my mind
waiting
to claim their due
when reason fails.

When I woke up in the dusky light the evening after my induced labor, Claude was sitting next to my bed, staring out of the hospital window. Since my frenzied call to tell him of our loss several days before, he had been there for me, trying to offer what support he could. Being a man, he was one step removed from experiencing the loss of life inside his body, but I never doubted that this miscarriage was a sharp, painful thing for him as well. Now, the resigned, sad set of his face staring out the window reminded me of his ache, even though he didn't articulate it like I did. Watching him in the almost-dark, I realized that we both had to seize this time to move decisively outside of ourselves or we would sink. While the loss counselors at the hospital advised us to bury the baby, find a support group and take time to focus on our grief, we both knew this wasn't *our* path. Within a few weeks, Claude threw himself into a video project he had just begun about a local graffiti artist. And I decided to join the Pittsburgh AIDS Task Force.

Among the deaths that we had all missed experiencing first hand, were those of our friends in the Bay Area who had died of AIDS since we had gone underground. AIDS was a startling and newly emerging disease when we left the Bay Area. It had not yet touched any of the gay men that I worked with closely in Prairie Fire. Over the course of the eighties, inevitably, some of these men were among the tens of thousands in the United States who were infected early with the HIV virus, when it was being denounced as "the gay plague." Word of their deaths drifted to us through our convoluted message chains, bringing home the personal dimensions of this massive epidemic. Once we tried holding our own small memorial for a man who had been deeply involved in Puerto Rico solidarity work with us, but our mourning felt isolated and removed. All across the country, gay and lesbian communities were assuaging their grief collectively. They were turning outrage and mourning into an outpouring of creative art and activism. We wanted to connect in some way to this passionate political response to the epidemic.

As the epidemic evolved, we began to understand that the most devastating impact of AIDS was occurring in the Third World, especially in Africa, and that in the United States AIDS was rapidly expanding beyond the gay male community. Increasingly the people being infected were Blacks, Latinos, and women. Many of our friends from the Bay Area and Prairie Fire had become involved in AIDS organizing and in many instances had become activists in ACT UP.[3] It was exciting to read about the sit-ins at the offices of Burroughs-Wellcome and the FDA (Federal Drug Administration), and the blocking of traffic on the Golden Gate Bridge to demand more government funding for AIDS research.

We obviously couldn't join ACT UP, but Karen and Jody argued vehemently that it was worth the minimal security risk to become involved in local AIDS work in St. Louis, and recently Donna had joined the AIDS Task Force in Pittsburgh. I held myself back from doing AIDS work even though I thought it was a crucial effort. Underlying my hesitation was my fear that once I reentered the realm of political organizing, I would not be able to limit myself to the safe boundaries that security dictated.

My miscarriage propelled me beyond this internal debate. "Silence = Death"[4] had taken on new meaning for me. There was a global crisis of sickness, prejudice, and discrimination right at our doorsteps and I needed to be part of the collective response. I had recently read the book, *Women, AIDS & Activism* put together by women in New York ACT UP.[5] It focused on the invisibility of women within the epidemic, even though the incidence of AIDS among women, particularly women of color, was dangerously on the rise. When I joined the AIDS Task Force, I decided to become part of the fledgling women's organizing committee, and I quickly forgot my personal concerns as I was drawn into the raging debates about the relationship between the dominantly white gay male organizational leadership and the changing racial and gender character of the epidemic. The women's committee had been formed shortly before I joined, and, although there was lip service support for the group in the Task Force, in reality its work was marginalized and invisible just like the women it was trying to represent. Although I consciously wanted to avoid the mistakes of past political struggles where every disagreement turned into a super charged battle, I encouraged the women's committee to bring these problems to the attention of the rest of the organization. I had planned to keep a low profile in the Task Force, but when the other women in the group asked me to be one of the speakers at the committee's first educational presentation about women, I only hesitated a few minutes before agreeing. I didn't see what reason I could give for refusing, and besides I really wanted to speak.

Public speaking was one of the things I had most enjoyed about political work before I went underground. The night before the presentation, I had one of my recurrent nightmares. I was speaking in front of a crowded audience, enjoying the rush of communication, when an FBI agent whipped out his badge. The group dispersed in panic and I stood paralyzed, choking on my words.

Despite my anxiety, once I began my presentation to the Task Force meeting the next evening, I was able to focus on persuading the seventy-five people gathered in the room that they needed to put more resources into outreach to HIV-positive women. By the end of the evening, it seemed like our women's committee had sparked a new level of interest in expanding this work. Afterwards, my spirit was soaring. I hadn't realized how much of my old, suppressed identity was linked to speaking out and publically debating ideas. In the future, I would have to evaluate every request to speak on a case by case basis, but I was glad that I had taken this step forward in reasserting who I really was.

My biggest joy in the AIDS work was working with the women who were HIV-positive. After our first presentation, we got enough support from the Task Force to begin an outreach project, and soon we had connected with a number of positive women in the area. We couldn't turn our small group into

a mini-social service agency, but we could offer the women a space to come
together with their kids to relax, share battle stories, and collectively strategize
about how to survive with their dignity intact. One of the women I got to know
best was Tina, a Black woman and former drug user who had been diagnosed
with AIDS only after one of her twin daughters had become very ill. Tina had
then discovered that the fatigue and constant, incurable yeast infections she had
been experiencing for years were really symptoms of HIV, which the doctors
had missed since they weren't the common symptoms that most men had. Now
Tina had no tolerance for doctors and little patience with the case managers who
were supposedly trying to help her and the twins. In the beginning she was very
suspicious of our committee of primarily white middle-class women, but as we
got to know her and supported her in dealing with Marissa's downward health
spiral, we began to build some trust.

Marissa was seven and had full symptomatic AIDS when we met her.
She was very small, disturbingly quiet, and constantly in and out of the hospital.
Her sister, Morena, was asymptomatic, full of energy, and very protective of Marissa. While Tina sat with the other women, eating and talking, Morena would
patiently push Marissa on the swing for what seemed like hours on end. Every
time the swing would reach the high point of its arc, Marissa would explode in
giggles of delight which would gradually fade to her usual quiet as the swing
headed back down. I imagined that it was those lilting, carefree giggles that kept
Morena pushing, even though Marissa never demanded it of her. Every once in
a while, Tina would glance their way and give a wave and a smile, then go back
to venting about the doctor who had coldly reminded her (as if she didn't know
better than anyone, thank you) that while Morena might not have symptoms
now, within the next couple of years she too would start to get sick. Tina's bitter
stories made me marvel again and again at the level of ignorance and insensitiv-
ity that people in the "helping" professions could display when dealing with a
woman with AIDS.

Often I would bring Tony along and he would take a turn swinging Marissa, although he much preferred getting on the swing next to her and making
funny faces as he pumped excitedly back and forth at twice her speed. He looked

forward to these gatherings, except when they interfered with his weekly soccer games. Sometimes he would ask me questions about Marissa, Morena and the other kids who came with their moms. He especially wanted to understand why Marissa was so sick and small while Morena was so lively and fun to play with. I explained that this was a question that scientists were still trying to figure out.

One day in the car, after we had dropped Tina, Marissa, and Morena off at their small apartment on Pittsburgh's north side, Tony asked me if the baby that had been in my tummy had died of AIDS. I gulped and pulled the car over to the side of the street. When the miscarriage happened, Claude and I had tried to explain to Tony as much as we understood about what had happened. But how could we expect him to accept a vague, inconclusive explanation which amounted to "the baby had a sickness"? Like me, he was searching for something concrete and definite, something that made sense. I had never told him why I had started to do AIDS work immediately after I lost the baby, so it was only logical that he should make a literal connection between the baby's sickness and AIDS. Now I tried to reassure him that the baby couldn't have AIDS because Claude and I knew for sure that neither of us had the HIV virus and therefore the baby couldn't have it either. We were trying to make another baby, I added, and hopefully this one would not get sick.

———— ∞ ————

What I didn't tell Tony that afternoon was that I was pregnant again. Claude and I had decided not to tell him until the first trimester was over and the results of the CVS test came back. We had waited four months after the miscarriage and we both had gone through a course of antibiotics which the doctor recommended. I took the pills as if they were a magic potion, one of the few things I could do to lessen the odds of another mysterious demise. I began taking my temperature to map out my ovulation schedule, in what had now become the routine precursor to my repeated efforts to have another baby. Then on January 17, 1991, Operation Desert Storm began its massive bombardment of Iraq and I lost interest in my temperature and became totally preoccupied with the cyclone of death and destruction unleashed by the United States in the Middle East.

In August 1990, Iraq had invaded Kuwait and immediately the U.S. had sent 400,000 troops to Saudi Arabia. While the Iraqi invasion of Kuwait seemed wrong, I knew that the U.S. response was part of a larger, strategic game plan meant to definitively consolidate the U.S./Israeli position in the Middle East and demonstrate that, in the "New World Order," the U.S. could flex its military muscle wherever and whenever it wanted now that it was the world's only superpower.

Iraq was given a deadline of January 15 to withdraw from Kuwait, which it didn't comply with. Within two days, smart bombs, cluster bombs, and cruise missiles rained down on the people of Iraq—the most technologically advanced weapons of mass destruction in the world. I was tens of thousands of miles away, but even though I avoided the TV and couldn't even make myself read through the articles in the newspaper, the shatter of explosions and the wail of Iraqi mothers shrilled inside my head. At work, I could hardly contain my outrage. When people asked "how are you this morning," I would respond with the grim statistics. "How well could I be with 25,000 Iraqis dead, 100,000 wounded and for what?" Many of the people I worked with were against the war too, but they didn't want it to invade our daily work lives. Pretty soon I could tell that they were becoming tired of my recital of war crimes.

But what could I do besides rant and rave? We couldn't go to anti-war rallies because they were sure to be filled with government agents who would be all too happy to stumble upon most-wanted fugitives in the course of their routine spying on anti-war protesters. I was suffocating and didn't know how much longer I could live this way, shackled by self-protection and self-censorship.

After Desert Storm began, I couldn't make myself take my temperature for awhile, and by the time I started again we had missed my ovulation peak. When my period didn't come, I had a hard time believing that I was really pregnant. Yet within a couple of weeks, I began to feel nauseous and all the familiar patterns of the first trimester began again for the third time in a year.

The Gulf War was over by the end of February, when Iraq withdrew from Kuwait and the Coalition forces declared an unconditional victory. I had a baby in my tummy and this time I was determined not to let my mind linger in the dark recesses of past failures or current global catastrophes. I needed to draw some boundaries if I wanted to nurture the life inside of me. After work, after my weekly AIDS meeting, after Tony had gone to bed, I would sit quietly in the living room, hands on my stomach, and try to envision this new person emerging whole, healthy and astoundingly alive.

There were times during the first months when I was convinced that I had lost the battle and another miscarriage was happening. At the seventeen week point, right around the time when I had lost my last baby, I thought the kicking had stopped and rushed to the midwife dreading the worst. As soon as she put the stethoscope to my belly, she smiled and gave me the earpiece to listen to the wonderful, wild, galloping sound of my baby's heartbeat.

As time went on, the kicks became stronger and more consistent. When we told Tony that I was pregnant again, his first reaction was cautious. "When will we know if the baby is okay?" he worried. We explained that every day, the chances that this baby would be all right were getting better and better, but we wouldn't know for sure until the baby actually arrived sometime in the beginning of November. I put his hand on my stomach and immediately the baby began to kick which startled him, but then made him laugh. Tony started careening around the room singing, "We're going to have a baby THIS TIME! We're going to have a baby THIS TIME!"

A month before the baby was due, I asked the midwife to tell us what the gender of the child was. I hadn't wanted to find out when the CVS test was first done because it would have made it harder for me to handle if something had gone wrong again. Now, I was ready. I had convinced myself that I didn't care about the gender as long as the baby was healthy, but I when learned that I had a girl inside of me, I was very happy. We hadn't yet figured out a name for a boy, but we had picked out the name Leila for a girl.

During Desert Storm, I had reread a book that I first read years before, *My People Shall Live*, by Leila Khaled. Leila Khaled was a Palestinian revolutionary best known for her role in hijacking two airplanes in 1969 and 1970. On the first page of her book she explains, "I expropriated an imperialist plane and returned to Palestine to pay homage to our occupied country and to show that we had not abandoned our homeland."[6] Leila had an iconic stature within the international anti-imperialist movement because she had broken through the barriers of sexism within Arab political movement to participate in the Palestinian armed struggle. Her commitment was rooted in revolutionary optimism: "We shall recover Palestine and make it a human paradise for Arabs and Jews and all lovers of freedom."[7]

Reading *My People Shall Live* reminded me that neither Israel nor the U.S. had been able to contain the Palestinian *intifada*, the popular uprising against Israeli occupation which began in 1987 and was still going strong in 1991. The war against Iraq had to be understood in this framework, and even the defeats of the Gulf War had not stopped the upsurge in Palestine. Naming our daughter Leila would be a tribute to that spirit of resistance. But after we had chosen her name, I was stricken with doubt. Was it fair to name children for *our* heroes (especially since we could not openly recognize and celebrate these heroes as long as we were underground)? How could children ever live up to such larger-than-life characters, or why should they even want to? "Every parent gives their children a name that has meaning to them," Claude argued. "Of course, she will be who she will be and she'll make her own meaning for her name. Besides," he teased, "what would we name her instead, *Petunia?*" I stopped debating the name, but I did look Leila up in a name book to discover what other possible meanings it held. I was fascinated to discover that *Leila* meant "from the night" in both Arabic and Hebrew, an appropriate enough description of this child who had emerged from a veritable night of catastrophes. A couple of weeks before her birth, I wrote our Leila a poem:

To Leila, looking forward to her birth

Leila, little woman,
conceived in a dark time

when the winds of change
are cycloning blindly
in a backwards direction,
come head first, strong
tunneling through
with the generous eyes
of the not-yet-born,
searching for the light.

Not to burden you
with too much history,
too many heroes;
not to weigh you down
with wars lost, wars undone
wars yet to be won.

Yet and still, yet and still
you will need hope and hands
from many lands
to learn to live
boldly,
enthusiastically,
head strong against the wind.

Leila was born on a record cold November 4. The evening before her birth, Tony began jumping up and down chanting, "Have the baby tonight, mom! Have the baby tonight!" I didn't really think that this would be the night since it was still five days before my due date. But I woke at 2 AM with gas pains that quickly turned into the intense contractions I remembered from my labor with Tony. By the time I got to the birthing center, my contractions were coming every five minutes and I could hardly make it to the Jacuzzi tub, which was one of the great attractions of the center. My pain wasn't relieved by the Jacuzzi or

the special pillow tower that I was supposed to try leaning over. I kept trying
new positions, dimly aware that Tony was patting my hand gently, but everything
just kept getting worse. I had only been in labor three hours and it was feeling
unbearable. "I need Cathy! Get the midwife!" I groaned and Tony, Donna, and
Claude all dashed out of the room to find her. In agony, I was trying to turn from
my side to sit up when suddenly, amazingly, I saw the baby's head start to crest. I
began yelling for the midwife in earnest, "My baby's coming, my baby's coming," scared that this miracle of speed meant that something was wrong. They
all rushed in and with one push Leila was there—her head, her shoulders, her
whole complete self and her beautiful newborn baby cry, the baby that we had
tried three times to have.

I slept for a little while, Leila slept, Claude dozed, but Tony couldn't
sleep. When he saw me open my eyes, he came over to where I was resting with
Leila on my tummy. "Can I read quietly to you and Leila?" he asked, and I nodded drowsily. For some reason, Tony had picked out the picture book, *Follow
the Drinking Gourd*,[8] and in a soft voice he began to read the tale of the escaped
slaves who had followed the constellation of the Big Dipper, known as the *drinking gourd*, north in order to reach freedom. I tried to hold my tears, thinking
Tony wouldn't understand them, but my heart was overflowing. Together we
had managed to create this perfect moment.

I wanted the moment to be there indefinitely, but of course life went on.
In the next couple of months, I experienced the challenges of having a newborn
and all the preoccupying ups-and-downs of the first few weeks. Our escape from
L.A. had cut short the normal process of adjustment—the attention to feedings,
sleeping, the gradual process of getting to know the unique, evolving chemistry
of a new baby. Now I had the chance to see this period through in the standard
way, and I realized that it was not a stage of motherhood that I particularly enjoyed. I loved holding and feeding Leila (when she would let me) for a couple of
hours at a time, but the long uninterrupted days together were difficult. The two
of us seemed to disagree about feeding, sleeping, rocking—almost everything.

When Leila was a month old, we began to look at daycare possibilities for when I would return to work after eight weeks of maternity leave. We looked at daycare homes and daycare centers, debating the pros and cons of each. The day I brought her to the St. Ignatius daycare center, Leila had been crying furiously since I had bundled her into her car seat, and there was no way I could get her to stop. As I walked in the door with this wailing baby, I imagined that no one would want to take such an irritable infant. The infant room was organized and peaceful. Some babies were asleep in their cribs, others were on their tummies or beginning to crawl, undisturbed by Leila's continued wailing. Linda, who was the lead teacher in the room gave us a glowing smile and then asked if she could hold Leila. "Of course," I said, and handed her into Linda's arms. Almost instantaneously, Leila stopped crying as Linda rocked her back and forth. I saw Leila gazing up at Linda's face, entranced, and all my questions about the philosophy of the center flew out of my head. This was the place for Leila.

Over the next year, every time Leila entered Linda's infant room she would magically shed the fussy, demanding personality that she often displayed at home. She happily joined the other babies in the calm but stimulating daily routine that Linda and her two assistants used to guide these new little people as they started to find their precarious way in this startling world.

Top left—Tony, Claude and Leila. Top right—Leila and Diana. Middle right—Tony and Diana. Bottom— Claude and Diana's feet. This picture, taken by Tony, made us think that he had unconsciously absorbed our unspoken rule to avoid taking pictures of the adult faces in his family. Over time, we relaxed about this rule and began to take a limited number of family snapshots.

INTERROGATING SURRENDER

It's this way:
being captured is beside the point,
the point is not to surrender.

—Nazim Hikmet[1]

ONE DAY, TONY CAME HOME WITH AN ASSIGNMENT from school to draw his family tree. "Mommy, you need to help me," he insisted enthusiastically. "What were the names of my grandmas and grandpas? Did they have brothers and sisters? What about their moms and dads? Aren't any of them alive any more?" I winced at the hint of accusation I heard in Tony's voice. He must have been the only child in his class who did not have ready answers to such simple questions. What kind of family keeps the names of its ancestors under a veil of security? We had never presented Tony with his genealogy before because he had never asked, and our rule of thumb was to come up with answers only when there was a need. But now he had come to me, demanding a complicated, rooted history. We couldn't safely tell him the real names and origins of our parents—Austen George Block, my father, who had grown up on New York's Upper West Side or Luba Simon, my mother, who had emigrated from Russia when she was a child. And we certainly couldn't tell the revealing story of Claude's father, Murray Makovski (aka Marks), whose family had barely escaped the Nazis by emigrating to Argentina, or Hennie Bienstock, who had been hidden in orphanages across Europe before managing to be rejoined with her family in Argentina, where she met Murray and gave birth to Claude.

So, on the spot, I invented a family fable. Although I left in some logical gaps, which could easily be explainable by emigration and distance such
as the names of great grandparents, Tony appeared satisfied with the result.
We had created a tangible tree on paper that he could present with pride to
his class. The only part of the story that upset him was that all of his grandparents appeared to be dead. "Everyone in my class has at least one grandma or
grandpa," he complained. In fact, this was the least fictional part of the entire
fairy tale. Of our four parents, only Claude's father was still alive. Declaring
Murray dead was the part of this benevolent lie that made me feel most guilty.
Some day, I vowed, we would figure out a way for Tony to meet his only living
grandparent.

Relying on a bedrock of emotional honesty in a web of factual fabrica-
tion could not suffice forever with our children. Once they were older the fibs,
which seemed benign when they were toddlers, would morph into festering
lies. The alternative was to tell them the truth and expect them to lie about this
information to the rest of the world. It was an unsolvable conundrum within the
nexus of our current world. And so our children, who helped to ground and
center us in our fugitive life, also became a prod to search for a way to leave it.

When we first went underground, the principles that guided those who
had undertaken armed resistance seemed clear and immutable. The goal was
never to surrender—physically, legally, politically, or spiritually. This stance took
the form of definitive non-participation when it came to the legal arena. The
FALN 11 had refused to participate in their trial in any way, declaring themselves prisoners of war in an anti-colonial struggle whose actions were protected by international law.[2] White revolutionaries such as David Gilbert, captured
in the Brinks expropriation,[3] had also refused to participate in courtroom trials
on any level. They had received the maximum sentences possible. But gradually, as increasing numbers of clandestine activists were arrested, new positions
began to evolve. When the Macheteros[4] were arrested in 1985, they decided as
a group to pursue a political/legal strategy, using the courtroom as a forum to
argue that the U.S. constitution prohibited colonialism and therefore the U.S.
had no legitimate jurisdiction over Puerto Ricans who were part of a colony.

The terms of the debate opened up and people in a variety of political cases began to reconsider the tactical wisdom of dealing with the courts and the legal system. This tactic would allow the possibility of shorter sentences. However, the bottom line remained a refusal to cooperate with the state to give any information about others. And tactical legal decisions should not mean renouncing a revolutionary political vision.

In this shifting context, was it wrong for us to consider a legally mediated surrender? The question began to jump out at us at every turn. As far as we could tell, the Third World forces we had wanted to support had been decimated and we didn't have any connection to whatever small groups might still exist. What good were we doing living silently and invisibly underground if we were unable to transform our silence into action, if we were unable to use our invisibility for clandestine movement building? Even if we refused to surrender physically, weren't we still surrendering our capacity to act if we continued to live as we had been, constantly shackled by security? Yet even if we resolved the issues of political principle on the side of physical surrender, how could we get to the other side of that ephemeral but oh so pronounced divide between underground and overground without all of us landing in prison forever? Being political prisoners for the rest of our lives would not be a satisfactory resolution to our desire for political efficacy, nor would it be a fulfilling answer to our children's need to know the truth about their families

The film *Through the Wire* gave us a chilling sense of the state's game plan for political prisoners. We were able to see this documentary in 1990 on our local PBS station. It was directed by Nina Rosenblum, narrated by actress Susan Sarandon, and told the story of the experiment in sensory deprivation torture that Alejandrina Torres, Susan Rosenberg, and Silvia Baraldini were subjected to from 1986 to 1988 at the High Security Control Unit at Lexington Federal Prison in Kentucky. [5] While we were busy setting up our underground lives in Minneapolis, these three women were secreted in a literal underground basement cell where they were kept under twenty-four-hour surveillance in a bare white-walled room under intense, bright lights. They were awakened several times a night and were continually strip searched and interrogated.

I had known Susan and Silvia since the founding conference of Prairie Fire in 1975, and I met Alejandrina, who was the stepmother of Carlos Alberto Torres, in one of my trips to Chicago to support the case of the FALN-11. By depositing them at Lexington, the government had put their commitments to the test of torture, experimenting to see if such conditions could break women who considered themselves revolutionaries. Alejandrina, Silvia and Susan had risen to the challenge.

The faces that I saw on the TV screen were gaunt and harried, their voices were laden with tension, but they spoke unrepentantly about their political beliefs and the reasons they became involved in the movement. They were also unified and fierce in condemning the government strategy to make them an object lesson to other activists about the price of resistance. Instead of being broken by this experiment in sensory deprivation and isolation, they had turned the tables on the government by rallying the support of international human rights groups, prisoner support committees, and radical parts of the women's movement in a battle to shut the Lexington Control Unit down. In 1988, the unit was closed based on an initial ruling in a lawsuit Susan and Silvia had filed against the U.S. government. The lawsuit argued that their political beliefs and associations, rather than their behavior, had been used as the basis for their transfer to Lexington, and this violated their first amendment rights.[6]

Through the Wire haunted me about the drastic possibilities that might await us, but it also pushed me towards return. Many people I had worked with and cared about were now behind bars, but they were not surrendering their spirits or their capacity to resist. We couldn't let fear of prison keep us from trying to find a way back to public political life. But we needed to figure out how to use whatever advantages we had in our current situation to minimize the prison time that we collectively would face. The main thing working in our favor was that the FBI had not been able to find us after all these years, despite the *Ten Most Wanted* list, post office mug shots, cheap crime magazine stories, and reruns of *America's Most Wanted.* Another major plus on our side was our new lawyer, Michael Deutsch, who agreed to help us negotiate with the government. Michael had defended the Attica Brothers since the uprising and subse-

quent massacre in 1971. He had helped litigate the shut down of the Lexington
Control Unit, and he had represented Puerto Rican prisoners of war ever since
he met Rafael Cancel Miranda in the infamous Control Unit at the federal prison
at Marion. In the recent period, he had successfully negotiated plea bargains for
other radical activists. Michael understood where we were coming from politically, and we could trust him not to compromise our non-negotiable principle—
not to provide any information regarding others.

So in 1992, after twelve years of Republican hegemony, when Clinton
was elected president, we decided that the time was right to investigate our options with the government. While we knew that the Democrats would not alter
anything basic about the U.S. system, we hoped that a Democrat-led judicial
department would be a little more open to negotiations around political activists.
In 1978, the Puerto Rican movement had achieved the release of the Nationalist
prisoners with Jimmy Carter, the last President who had been a Democrat. Perhaps the changing of the guard in the Attorney General's office would have some
type of trickle down effect to the U.S. Attorney in Chicago who was responsible
for our case and would allow us some wiggle room to return.

Once we decided to approach the government, we wanted it to happen quickly. We were worried that opening up this process would make us more
vulnerable to arrest than ever. The complicated logistics that we developed for
our infrequent contacts with Michael added an overlay of tension to our nerve-
wracking conversations about this highly charged subject matter. From the
beginning, Michael counseled patience in what he expected to be a drawn out,
convoluted process, but we were incurably anxious. First, we had to wait while
the new Democratic appointments to the Justice Department were made, since
we certainly didn't want to begin negotiations with Republican officials who
were on their way out. Month after month, Michael had no news for us, and we
began to feel that our hope for return was a pipe dream, doomed not only by
the political climate but by the indecipherable bureaucratic machinations of the
government. Then, on a cold, snowy afternoon in February 1994, just when we
were becoming accustomed to the lack of forward motion, Michael reported that
he had positive news. He had held an initial set of conversations with the U.S.

Attorney's office and the government was open to a negotiated return. The only current charges were against Donna and Claude and the state would agree beforehand to a cap on their sentences, although it was not yet clear what the cap would be. Finally, if we all came back, they wouldn't press any charges against the rest of us.

When I hung up the payphone after this conversation, I was reeling. This was our best case scenario and my heart was ricocheting madly between excitement and anxiety. Now that the phantasm of return had become a concrete, stated possibility, the stark reality of the choices before us were more difficult and painful than ever. Because it was Donna and Claude who would be doing the time, going to prison, and separating from the kids, while the rest of us would, presumably, get to resume our lives. Was this fair? Or if fairness wasn't the issue, was it a decision that we could all collectively agree upon without causing lasting bitterness, guilt, and rifts among us? My mind whirled through dozens of fractious scenarios as I drove home through the flailing snowflakes.

In the weeks that followed, we got together among ourselves in every possible combination to reexamine our options, discuss the potential ramifications on our lives, on our children, and on the movements to which we were politically accountable. We dissected, we cried, we fantasized, we relived all the errors we had made in the past that had brought us to this irrevocable choice. We combed the news for signals about the general political climate in the country that might help us make a decision. All indications were that a law and order agenda was gaining greater sway legislatively and socially. In November, 1993 California voters had approved three strikes legislation, which made a third felony conviction, regardless of the specific nature of the offense, grounds for a life sentence. While this law didn't directly impact our case, it was a chilling indication of the prevailing wind. If we didn't take the deal the government was offering and then were caught, what kind of time would each of us be facing in this repressive environment?

One night, I woke up from a nightmare in which I had disastrously dropped my pocketbook, spilling all our false ID's in front of a plain clothes police officer. Still shaking from the dream scene, I looked over at Claude and saw that he was wide awake, staring up at the ceiling. "We don't have to do this. We could just go on as we are," I whispered to him, and in that dark night moment I meant it. But he pulled himself back from the chasm that he was looking into and repeated what he had said from the moment I told him about the government's offer. "This is as good as it's going to get! There are no other options." And I knew that I agreed with him.

We waited until Michael had a concrete proposal before making a final decision. More months passed before he had the details. The government agreed that all charges against Donna and Claude would be dropped except the conspiracy to transport explosives. Claude would face a maximum of ten years and Donna a maximum of five because they considered her role as more peripheral. Michael thought both of them would probably end up with lesser sentences. We would give the FBI a list of all the aliases and social security numbers we had used, most of which they probably already had. No other persons or organizations would be implicated. Together we decided to go ahead with the deal.

By then it was summer of 1994 and Michael thought the surrender could be finalized by the end of the year. 1994 had started on an auspicious note when the Zapatistas announced their existence to the world on January 1 from the jungles of Chiapas, Mexico, ushering in a new paradigm for revolutionary struggle. A few months later, in April 1994, Nelson Mandela had been inaugurated as the first Black president of South Africa, ending decades of apartheid and colonial rule. We held on to these inspiring global signposts as we waited to hear when our surrender would actually occur.

As soon as we had communicated our decision to Michael, our fears shifted to new terrain. How could we trust the Government to keep its word about this deal when its history was filled with broken promises and lies? Yet, we also knew that there were exceptions to every rule. We needed to trust Michael's experience and judgment; we had no choice. At some point, I stopped thinking about catastrophic possibilities and focused on shaping a plan to get through this grueling period with our minds and relationships intact.

Claude and I decided we needed to get married. We had never seriously thought about marriage before. From my early feminist beginnings, I had been politically opposed to the institution of marriage, and hadn't seen any reason to change my approach once Claude and I got together. Besides, what could it possibly mean to have the state "legalize" our relationship when every other aspect of our lives was illegal? But now, anticipating that Claude would be under direct government control in prison, we wanted to avail ourselves of every protection possible to maintain maximum contact during our pending separation. So we gathered together the necessary documents and made a date with a local Justice of the Peace.

We told Donna and Rob and Karen and Jody about our appointment, but we didn't tell the kids or anyone else. How could we explain why we were getting married on a weekday in September with no party or celebration, wearing the same clothes that we wore to work each day? This was a marriage of necessity and I thought that I was ready for this official procedure. Yet in the middle of this ever-so-terse ceremony, when the chubby faced government official asked me if I would take this man to love, cherish, and obey, I started to laugh. Once I started I couldn't stop. I was laughing so hard I was crying and my stomach was hurting. I saw Claude's quizzical look and I heard the concerned voice of the chirpy assistant, who was serving as the witness to our marriage, counseling me not to be so nervous about this important event, and her concern only sent me into deeper gales of hysteria. Like women who report that they detach from their bodies during sex and watch the whole event from some remote point in the ceiling, I was observing this wedding from a recessed corner of my mind's eye and every aspect of it oozed absurdity—our names, the canned patriarchal vows, the pretense of free choice when, in fact, it was a shotgun marriage and the state was holding both the shotgun and the marriage license at the same time. I was veering out of control, and only Claude's increasing pressure on my hand brought me back and reminded me that there was a good reason for this irony-cloaked ritual. I croaked out an apology and made an appropriately feminine excuse about getting the jitters because I was so happy and excited, patting Claude's arm energetically to emphasize the point. I managed to get through the rest of the ceremony, except as I took out the ring to slip on Claude's finger, I dropped it and Claude had to go foraging in the dust underneath the table to find it. Finally, it was over and Claude and I could leave. I was concerned that Claude would feel bad, despite knowing the context for my hysteria. But he didn't take it personally. "I hope you don't get another laughing jag when we turn ourselves in," he teased.

It was October and all the legal papers were signed, but we still didn't know when we would be returning. In my mind, I began to question once more whether this whole plan was a phantom hope that would fall through at the last minute, just as our other plans had failed in the past. I was writing more in my journal, not just about the children, but about myself and what I was feeling, skirting around the edges of what could safely be committed to paper. As my journal entries became more literal, striking symbols began to surface in my dreams. In one dream someone asked me my address and I began to say it "4026 Guer..." I choked on the name, *Guerrero*, the street I had lived on for four years in San Francisco, which means warrior in Spanish. As I choked, I began to spit up yard upon yards of dental floss, coiled deep inside me, something that was meant to be cleansing, but had become corroded and rotten inside my stomach.

In another dream, Tony and I were walking along a narrow beach, holding hands, as we often had on our vacations in Erie and Delaware, when many giant, curious sea creatures appeared before us. While we were looking at them with naïve interest, one of the creatures picked Tony up in his jaws and dangled him over a steep, rocky cliff, like those I had often gazed at with awe during trips up the Northern California coastline. An inner voice whispered, "something so horrible can't happen." When I looked down again, Tony was drifting gently among calm, aquamarine waves—released, saved.

I tried to savor the happy ending of the dream once I woke up, but my tension was winding tighter and tighter because I knew that soon we would have to tell Tony the truth about who we were. In August, right before the start of the school year, we had told him that we might be moving to Chicago sometime be-

cause Claude's job was transferring him. The story was a compromise between
telling him nothing about the cataclysmic changes that were about to occur in his
nine-year-old life, and divulging the real story before we knew for sure when we
would be leaving. Tony had not taken the news about our prospective move to
Chicago well. He started to cry hysterically, an uncommon response for him, and
it was hours before he was calm enough to listen to some of the possible advantages of life in Chicago. His initial response made me dread the day when we
would have the conversation about what this move was really all about and what
it would entail for him.

It was even harder to figure out how to prepare Leila, who was just
about to turn three, for what was going to happen. I read an article in the paper
about a recent study proving that three years was the most sensitively critical age
for childhood experience of loss and trauma. At two, children were too young to
really be aware of the loss and, once they were older they had more tools to be
able to assimilate and understand. Like many research studies, it pointed out a
problem, but didn't present any solutions. In our case, we couldn't tell the government to hold off on the deal till Leila was four and better able to handle her
father going to prison. It just aggravated my brooding.

In the beginning of November, we had Leila's three-year birthday party
in the Pittsburgh Children's Museum. I watched her scamper around joyously
with her friends, playing with the life size doll house, exploring the tunnels and
play structures, and patiently holding still while Claude painted a delicate flower
on one cheek and a vibrant rainbow across her forehead. Tears started trickling
down my face, and I hurriedly made my way to the bathroom, lecturing myself
on emotional discipline.

The day after Leila's party, we got the word from Michael. The date was
set! Donna and Claude were to surrender in Chicago on December 6. If they
wanted to see their families in Chicago for a couple of days immediately before
their surrender, the Government would not interfere. Since there were no outstanding charges against Jody and Karen, they could surface at any time.

We had less than a month to wrap up our lives in Pittsburgh. After
seven years of an achingly slow, drip-drop rate of change, we were now pro-

pelled into a frenzy of activity. The rapid pace of this leave-taking felt almost as frenetic as our whirlwind departure from Los Angeles. We had to pack, we had to figure out storage for our stuff, we had to give notice on our apartments and at our jobs—all the ordinary machinations associated with moving. But the most important and difficult job was telling people why we really were leaving and who, in truth, we were.

We had to start with Tony. We could not put it off any longer. We picked a weekend afternoon and set up a play date at a friend's house for Leila. We told Rob and Donna to stand by, just in case he (or we) needed their support. We sat down in our living room, facing the African wall hanging with the bright yellow batiked lion that had been a favorite of Tony's since Karen and Jody gave it to our family when we first moved to Pittsburgh. Tony fidgeted on the sofa, filled with tension as soon as we told him that we had something we wanted to talk to him about.

"Remember the book, *Living in Secret*,[7] that we read last year?" I started carefully with the words I had been mentally rehearsing for months. Tony nodded. "Of course, mom!" He was impatient because he knew it was a rhetorical question. *Living in Secret* was about a girl whose mother comes out as a lesbian and then goes through a tumultuous divorce. When the father gains legal custody of the girl, she goes underground with her mother to keep the father from finding them. The book was a powerful story about lesbians, homophobia, and the complicated demands of "living in secret." Tony and I had read it together out loud and discussed it thoroughly, including the intricacies of their underground lives. Now Claude and I hoped that this book would be a comprehensible segue for Tony into the mysteries of *our* secret lives.

I took a deep breath. "Well, all of us... Jo, Tim, Kate, and Marty (Donna, Rob, Jody, and Karen)... we've all been living in secret, living underground since just after you were born." Once I started, I wanted to keep going until I had spit it all out. "You see, we were trying to help a Puerto Rican prisoner who was in prison because he was fighting for Puerto Rico's freedom, just like Nelson Mandela fought and went to prison in South Africa. Dad and Jo were helping with part of the plan. The Government found out about it and wanted to put Dad and Jo and the rest of us in prison, so we all went underground so that they couldn't find us." My words were tripping out over each other. The story I was telling was vastly oversimplified, but we needed to tell Tony something that he could grasp, something that would correlate with the stories that he would inevitably see on TV or read in the papers. There would be time to explain the complexities later. I looked over at him to see if he wanted to interrupt or question, but he seemed transfixed by the tale, so I went on.

"You were only two weeks old when we left Los Angeles, which is where you were actually born. We went to Minneapolis and when you were two we moved to Pittsburgh, which of course you already know. We've been safe for these years and happy that we could all be here with you and Ericka, Zoe and Leila, but we don't want to keep living like this. If we did, we would have to keep secrets from you and everybody forever. And we would always have to keep being scared that someone would find out who we really are—just like the girl in the book was scared. If the Government found out who we were by accident, it would be much, much worse. And you would never be able to get to know your grandfather, who really is alive and I know you want to be able to meet him! So we are going to go to Chicago in the beginning of December, and Dad and Jo are going to turn themselves in to the government…and they will have to go to prison for a while." When I paused for breath, Tony turned to Claude and asked quietly, "How long are you going to have to go to prison for, Dad?" Claude took Tony's hand. "We're not sure yet, a number of years probably. But you'll visit me all the time. Only me and Jo will go to prison. Everyone else will be around to take care of you and make sure that you are safe." I could see Tony's eyes starting to tear up, but instead of breaking down like I expected he asked, "What's my grandfather's name? When can I see him?" "Murray, Murray Marks, and you'll see him when we get to Chicago," Claude answered.

Then Tony showered us with questions. What were our real names? Why wasn't Puerto Rico free already? How often could we visit Dad in prison? Could he also visit Jo? He was trying to wrap his mind around this earthshaking news in the most reasonable, logical way a child could. We answered his questions for another hour, and then he and Claude went off to buy a walkman for him to listen to on the trip to Chicago. Part of me felt that the talk had been too easy, too rational, without the disorientation, outbursts, or accusations that we had expected. But another part of me accepted that all our talks with Tony about history and the freedom struggles around the world had prepared him for this day. It was likely that he would react more dramatically in the future, but for now a huge weight had been lifted off our shoulders. We had begun the protracted process of telling Tony the truth, and it felt like everything else would fall into place.

We had also been telling our friends that we might be moving to Chicago because of Claude's job transfer. Now we wanted to tell some of them what was really happening. Each of us had developed relationships that we wanted to be able to continue in the future. We didn't want these friends to learn who we really were from a newspaper article or a knock on the door from the FBI, investigating our lives retrospectively after we reemerged. But would they still be our friends when they found out that instead of the progressive, non-violent people they thought they knew, we were fugitives wanted in a prison escape conspiracy?

Before our goodbye dinner with Beth and Roger, I was almost as nervous as I had been before our conversation with Tony. How should we frame our story, where should we start, should we apologize for being dishonest with them all these years? Claude and I debated our approach for hours. Finally we decided to just jump in and see how the conversation went. And after a glass of wine, that's what we did. Amazingly, as with Tony, once they had registered the news, they were more interested in talking about our history and the reasons for our political choices than in berating us for our lies or our connections to illegal activity. After another glass of wine, I asked them, "Now that you know who we are, do we seem like entirely different people than the Pat and Greg you've been friends with for the past six years?" Roger was quick to answer: "Of course we didn't know the exact kinds of activities you'd been involved in, but from the time we met you we liked you because you were the most radical thinking people we knew. Why else do you think we had you over to dinner so frequently? Certainly not to discuss your scholarly publications!" At the end of the evening, before we said goodnight, Beth took my hand and said, "Anything

you need, Pat, please let us know. If you want us to take the kids when you first
go to Chicago, or anything else…" I could tell that she meant it.

Everyone we told our story to reacted in similar fashion. Rob and
Donna got offers of media help from their friends at the *Pittsburgh Post-Gazette*;
a friend I worked with in the Pittsburgh AIDS Task Force gave me names of
people we could stay with in Chicago; still others offered money to tide us over.
Each telling of the story not only released layers of secrecy but also affirmed
that, despite my trite name, my dyed-blond hair, and my muted political expression, more of the real *Diana* had emerged over the years than I had imagined.
How exhilarating to be out as *Diana* all the way again!

Finally, we called our families. Neither Claude nor I could deal emotionally with making the calls directly. So, using one last pretense, I called
Claude's brother and explained that I was a legal assistant working on Claude's
case. I told him that Claude would be surrendering soon and we needed his
help in contacting Claude's father and sister to arrange to meet the family in
Chicago. His brother's understandable first response was disbelief and caution,
after years of no-contact and intermittent harassing phone calls and visits from
the FBI. But as I gave him more details about the plan and provided Michael's
number to call for verification, he began to warm up and agreed to contact Murray and the rest of the family.

A couple of days later, I was standing nervously outside the phone
booth as Claude called what we hoped was my sister's home number. I had
lost track of Joyce after her name stopped appearing on the pages of the New
York City phone book a couple of years before. Searching the rosters of the
American Psychological Association, I had found a Joyce Block with a clinical practice in South Bend Indiana. It seemed like a long shot. Standing at the
edge of the phone booth, I listened anxiously as Claude inquired whether this
was the home of Joyce Block, the sister of Diana Block. When the person on the
other end apparently answered affirmatively, I began to cry. Claude went on to
explain that he was a legal assistant who was working with Diana to facilitate her
return. I could tell that Joyce was eager to talk and ask questions because Claude
had to tell her politely several times that he couldn't talk about all that now. He

reassured her that there would be time to get into all the details in Chicago on December 6.

We were speeding away in the car, according to our rules for these calls which were still in the mega-risk zone, before Claude was able to tell me what Joyce had said. "I thought Diana was dead," was Joyce's first response. The tears I had been managing to contain poured out once more. "What else? Didn't she tell you anything about herself?" After not allowing myself to wonder about my sister's life for so many years, all of a sudden I felt desperate to know something about her. "You have two nieces. One is just turning nine and the other is two and a half." The rest of the way home, I could only think about this stunning news. Despite our profound distance over the last decade, my sister and I had managed to give birth at almost the exact same times, six and a half years apart. Now our children were almost the same ages. I was not a believer in *blessings*, but now I could find no other word to describe this serendipitous connection. In a few weeks time, not only would I get to meet my two nieces, but Tony and Leila would discover two cousins they never knew they had.

─────

While our newly opened communications with friends and family were exceeding our best expectations, the relationships among the four of us (Donna, Rob, Claude and myself) were shredding. Every conversation about where to store our things or which hotels to reserve for our separate family reunions in Chicago seemed to end in a fight that internally spiraled into unspoken hurts and fears. Claude's growing silence was becoming insufferable to me, and my nagging tone put him on edge the moment I opened my mouth. At night, when I would try to fall asleep, my imagination would run roughshod over all the rationality of my daytime plans for our return. How would I ever support myself and the kids while Claude was in prison? How could we expect political comrades we hadn't seen in over a decade to support us politically or materially when the world had somersaulted 360 degrees to the right since we last had spoken to them? Could I preserve my relationship with Claude over years of absence?

What would it be like to see Kyle again when I reemerged with two kids and a husband? How would I re-process my sexual identity once the constrictions of our clandestine lives were no longer operating?

I was sitting on a milk crate the day before we were to leave for Chicago, surrounded by boxes, suitcases, and plastic bags—the mixed accumulation of our seven years in Pittsburgh. I had lived in this house on Sherbrook Street longer than I had ever lived anywhere except my parents' apartment in New York City. Tony had only a dim memory of our last house in Minneapolis and Leila had always lived here. We had filled two storage spaces with the furniture that Rob and I would come back to claim once we knew where we were going to move. I had sent Tony and Leila to play with the next-door neighbor kids for one last time when their bickering began to get too much on my nerves. Claude was downstairs cleaning the basement. I had reminded him that we didn't really need to clean it that thoroughly, but as soon as the words were out of my mouth I realized that there wasn't much else left for him to do before tomorrow. It was still much too early to try and catch some frayed sleep on the foam pads which we had left out for our last night in Pittsburgh.

I was too tired to do anything more, too tired to focus on my list of anxieties, too tired to even feel the excitement that bubbled beneath the surface of my worry. In twenty-four hours, I would start again to use *Diana* as my name. Goddess of the Hunt, familiar of the moon, feminist deity—there was a time when I had appreciated my name and its many mythic associations. But ever since we went underground, I had worked hard to estrange myself from its sound so that I would never involuntarily jump when I heard it called or erroneously answer with those syllables when someone asked me the simple, every day question, "What's your name?" When we told Tony what my real name was, he had burst out laughing. "That's a silly name for you, Mom, it doesn't fit you at all!"

Tomorrow I would have to reverse the disassociation process in one huge leap and embrace the forbidden name once more. I rolled the syllables around in my head—*Di-an-a, Di-an-a, Di-an-a, Di-an-a*—trying to reclaim them as mine.

Top—Leila (right) and friend on a float at the
Puerto Rican Day parade in Chicago, June 1995.
Middle—Tony (far right) on a float at the same
parade. Bottom—Our group, "the ten most wanted,"
in Chicago, December 1994. Back row—(left to
right) Donna, Karen, Jody, Diana; Middle row—Tony
(covering his face), Ericka, Leila, Zoe; Front row—Rob
and Claude.

RETURN

RETURN. *It was the stuff of dreams, fantasy, fiction, memory, vision, and stone cold wrenching reality. It was the ironic culmination of all our years of earnest clandestine effort and our proud affirmation that we had survived with our political souls intact. It was the eerie conjunction of the new family we had created and the old family we had left behind, the sometimes awkward meeting of the relationships we had forged in the shadows of underground and the relationships we had abandoned in the shade of the past. It was a stunning reentry to cities that we had gazed upon for years across invisible walls, and a reclaiming of identities that no longer fit us as seamlessly as they had thirteen years before. It bore similarities to the process which hundreds of thousands of people have experienced in the twentieth century—returning from forced exile or coming out of prison— but it was distinct because we had never been removed from the language, culture, geography, or the governing jurisdiction of the country we grew up in. And prison was not a shackling structure we were leaving behind. Instead it loomed gargantuan and foreboding before us, threatening to suffocate the gladness of our return.*

    Tony and Leila were crammed in the back seat next to excess bags and boxes that we couldn't squeeze into the trunk of our small red Toyota for the four-hundred-mile ride from Pittsburgh to Chicago. The gray clouds threatened snow and we couldn't escape the Christmas music on the radio or the endless commentaries warning us that we only had twenty-five days left to shop. I wasn't sure whether it was more upsetting to hear Leila's repeated questions about how Santa Claus would find us on Christmas, or to realize that Tony had not once pressed us about Christmas presents or school plans since we had told him we needed to leave for Chicago in the middle of fourth grade. When he asked, a couple of hours into the trip, whether I had ever lived in Chicago before, I was relieved to talk about something concrete and manageable, although it took me a few seconds to sort through my memories for the ones that made most sense to share. I told him that I had gone to college at the University of Chicago. I told him about my fond memories of the Art Institute and the Academy of Sciences on the edge of Lake Michigan, which were both very near the hotel where we would be staying once we reached Chicago. I described Hyde Park, the University neighborhood with its tree lined streets, small shops, and large apartments that I had rented with roommates after my first year living in the dorms. I explained how I had graduated from U of C after only three years at the age of 19. I had skipped a couple of years in elementary and high school and then I took a slew of tests at Chicago that exempted me from the first year of classes. I was eager to leave school because I was tired of studying and I wanted to get out into the real world. I also described how two or three times a week I crossed the huge grassy expanse of the Midway, which separated the University from the Black community of Woodlawn, to tutor reading and math to elementary school children. This always seemed like one of the most important things I had done while I was at the University. I graduated in June 1968, a couple of months after Martin Luther King Jr. was assassinated, escalating tensions between the Black people in Woodlawn and the white, insulated University community. I was more than ready at that point to move on.

I didn't tell Tony about the alienation that had clouded my time at the University of Chicago. In a period when campus activism was spreading like a prairie fire across the country, I was unable to put my personal turmoil aside and become involved with student organizing. The SDS men I dated were snobbish and arrogant, and the cliquishness of campus leftists made me feel excluded and estranged. Later, once the women's movement had opened me up and helped me step outside of my private sphere, I regretted having closed myself off from the radical student energy of that era. Was it some type of poetic justice that now had me eagerly approaching Chicago as the site of our reentry into public life, upending the forced privacy of our lives for the past years?

My musings abruptly ended when Claude began to curse. "The goddam car is overheating! We 're going to have to pull over," he hissed. We were an hour and a half outside of Chicago, soon it would be dark, and we were supposed to meet up with Claude's family early the next morning. We were also driving under false ID's that we were planning to abandon as soon as we reached the city. There was no way we could afford a breakdown and possible interactions with tow trucks and highway patrol. Leila, who had been lulled into a nap in her car seat by my stories of student life in Chicago, woke up and began to scream. Tony looked miserable. Claude pulled over at the nearest gas station and the three of us waited in suspense inside the cold car while he located a torn hose and rigged up a patch sufficient to get us to Chicago. We drove the last leg of the trip in an unnatural, tension-filled silence. My attention was so fixated on the heat gauge that I hardly registered that we had reached the city until we pulled into the garage of the hotel where we were planning to spend our last few nights together.

The next morning, we met Claude's father, sister and stepmother in the hotel lobby. To the onlooking hotel staff, we must have seemed like a typical family reuniting after a casual separation. After quick embraces and introductions, Tony and Leila happily became the focus of all attention. With his German accent, white hair and beard, and friendly conversation, Grandpa Murray seemed to meet Tony's expectations of what a grandfather should be. And Leila was immediately beguiled by her new aunt Iris's beautifully manicured long red fingernails. We all proceeded up to our hotel room where we quickly summarized the legal aspects of our return and Claude's impending court appearances, which no one wanted to dwell on. Then the children were presented with presents which happily preoccupied everyone.

These were my new in-laws, whom I had never met before. Although Claude was not one to focus on personal memories, I knew that he had been estranged from his father since he was a teenager and started to grow long hair, smoke dope, and, most significantly, demonstrate his radical political viewpoints.

Although Murray had been peripherally involved in left politics in Argentina, once they moved to the United States to escape the repression of the Peronist regime when Claude was five, Murray had opted for assimilation. Claude was closer to his mother, Hennie, but her identification with his father's viewpoints led him to separate from her as well. Hennie had died just before Claude went underground, after a long fight with metastasized breast cancer. Claude had been anxious about this reunion, anticipating the anger and recriminations which too often had characterized his relationship with his father in the past. But either Murray had mellowed, or he was swallowing his feelings given the extremely sensitive nature of the meeting.

We went to the science museum and the aquarium, strolled along the lakefront, and on Tony's urging we went up to the top of the Sears Tower. We took family pictures in front of Chicago landmarks, and for the most part I became caught up in the rhythm of pretense that this was simply a long awaited family gathering. On the second night, as we were waiting for our dinner entrees at a Chinese restaurant, Murray mentioned that the FBI had watched him and Claude's stepmother, Catherine, eat many dinners in their Colorado home, since it was under surveillance for many years. "They thought they were being so clever," Murray said, "changing the color of their car every week, but we knew what they were up to, and of course we had nothing to hide since I hadn't heard anything, not one thing, from Claude for all those years." His resentment was palpable and Claude began to apologize defensively. For a minute it seemed like all the old hurts that had been marinating throughout these sunny two days would come seeping out. But Leila interrupted with an apparent non-sequitur about our red car, our dinner arrived, and the moment passed.

We put Murray, Iris, and Catherine in a cab to the airport that night, reassuring them that there really was no need to stay around for Claude's surrender. They had given us a pleasant family respite for a couple of days. Help with the complicated, painful changes of the next few weeks would have to come from other people.

The next morning, the four of us reconnected with Donna, Rob, and Zoe before a meeting with our lawyers. The three of them had had a very emotional but supportive visit with Donna's family. As we mounted the stairs to the People's Law Office, we strained to make small talk before the onslaught of serious discussion. Jan Susler, whom we had never met before, greeted us with a burst of warmth which immediately eased some of the tension. Jan was part of the People's Law Office collective and had represented the Puerto Rican political prisoners for years. She immediately endeared herself to all of us by making Zoe, Leila, and Tony comfortable with books and toys in an area close by the conference room where we would be meeting with her and Michael. Then we adults settled down to hash through our plans. We had many difficult issues to discuss, but at least we were finally all together in the same room. No more hunched telephone booth calls or hurried gatherings in hotel rooms. The presence of our lawyers shifted the ossified dynamics among us and allowed us each to voice our concerns more honestly than we had been able to do for months among ourselves.

The next morning Donna and Claude would surrender. The formal indictment would be the following day and then a bail hearing would occur, probably the next week. Michael and Jan cautioned that we should not get our hopes up about bail. The prosecutor's office and the Chicago newspapers had a long history of vilifying the Puerto Rican Independence forces, the FALN, and all who were associated with them. They were sure to paint Donna and Claude as dangerous terrorists, and it would be difficult for the Judge to justify releasing them. Still, we needed to fight for what we wanted every step of the way. "Fight politely," Jan emphasized, and the four of us laughed nervously. I left the meeting feeling reassured and cautiously hopeful. After all, we had the best possible lawyers to guide us through the pernicious channels of courtrooms and prisons.

The rest of that day and evening, Claude and I focused on keeping the kids busy. There was nothing more we could plan and little more we could say to each other that hadn't been said dozens of times before. Shortly before we left Pittsburgh, I had given Claude a poem. I knew he wouldn't be able to take it into prison with him, but I hoped it could accompany him somehow.

To Claude, To Take Inside

If I could, I would
put together for you
some very special thing –
weighty
but weightless,
brilliant
but invisible –
for you to keep
safe and true
hidden in your mind's eye:

splices of all the best
scenes from all the
thousand-odd movies
we've watched together;
a patchwork of all the
rooms and routes, spaces and places
we've been through together;
an earring in the shape of the ocean,
a candle reflecting touch and heat,
a virtual reality album of child births,
growths and forever changes.

But before this weighty, weightless thing
got too laden down,
too baggaged up
to do you any traveling good at all,
I'd wrap it –
clumsily, of course (as always)

with the corners pointed
and the paper crinkled,
tape everywhere
so you'd be laughing
as you opened it up
and we'd both know
you would be able
to keep it
close but light
tucked inside
your heart.

I had watched him read it, seen his eyes momentarily tear up before he characteristically tucked his emotions inside his heart. Now, I couldn't think about his leaving anymore. Instead, I spent the night tossing and turning, trying not to disturb Tony and Leila's sleep or Claude's fitful snoring. Once we all walked into the Federal Building the next morning, once Claude and Donna surrendered and we were in their domain, would they dispense with all the legal niceties that had been agreed to in the negotiations? Would Rob and I end up spending tomorrow night in jail too, torn from the kids without any preparation?

Those were the last hours I spent in solitary worry for the next several weeks. Once the alarm clock went off, we barely had enough time to shower and pack up before the expected knock came. We opened the door and there were Roxie and Nancy, our old Prairie Fire friends, plus several young people who were now part of the Chicago chapter of PFOC. For a few minutes, we hugged and registered how we all looked the same except for added wrinkles and gray streaks in our hair, but then we had to say goodbye to the kids and leave for the Federal Building. Tony was looking morose, but Leila was excited by all the activity and the toys that Nancy and Roxie had wisely brought. Then Claude and I were whisked away in a friend's car.

We stepped out of the car into a crowd of federal marshals and TV cameras. The government had said they would keep our surrender quiet, but it was a media circus. After thirteen years of suppressing my public self, the voice I had used during demonstrations, acts of civil disobedience, and press conferences reemerged. We were restrained but adamant. Claude, Donna, Rob, and I had nothing to say to the media. Michael and Jan would take their questions, but they should stop crowding us and let us get on with the planned business of the day.

As we entered the building and the doors closed behind us, my stomach sank as Claude and Donna were separated from Rob and me. I watched as the marshals handcuffed each of them, twisting their hands behind their backs. Then they walked slowly away, down the halls to the unknown entrails of the building, with Jan and Michael by their sides. Rob and I were left standing in this twilight zone space, surrounded by the FBI agents we had been running from for all these years. There was no wall of subterfuge to protect me and I couldn't even raise a symbolic fist in the air. Somehow we managed to walk calmly and steadily through the crowd, instead of bolting frantically as we wanted to do.

I was hugely happy to see Nancy waiting for me outside, and I could tell that she was relieved to see me too. Claude and I had each worked closely with Nancy in the seventies. She had moved to Chicago as part of Prairie Fire to work in solidarity with the Puerto Rican forces in Chicago who were spearheading the campaign to free the FALN 11. Nancy was no longer a part of Prairie Fire, but she continued her solidarity work with the Puerto Rican movement. Now Nancy told me that she and her partner Steve wanted me and the kids to stay with them for the next several months. Her daughter Rosa, whom Claude had cared for when she was a baby, was away at college, so her room was empty. Her son, Michael, was in high school and had generously offered his study as an extra space for us. Howie, another old friend of ours, had invited Rob and Zoe to stay with him. I struggled to keep myself from bursting into tears when I heard about these bighearted invitations. Instead, I told Nancy about the tumult of feelings I had watching Claude and Donna walk away in handcuffs. It was uncannily natural and easy to talk with her after all this time, and we only cut off the conversation so that we could go back to her house and check on the kids.

When we got there, Tony was absorbed in a new computer game and Leila was restlessly watching a video which she abandoned to jump into my arms. "Is Daddy in jail now?" she demanded, and though the question was painfully direct, I was glad that she understood enough of what was happening to ask. The rest of the day was filled with old friends, talk, stories, and plans. Everyone had ideas about what type of job I might get while we were in Chicago, where Tony could go to school, and how we might find daycare for Leila and Zoe. I was completely exhausted by the time I tucked Leila in and said good night to Tony. I lay down in the adjoining room and the last thing I was conscious of was the sound of the El train rumbling a couple of blocks from the house. The noise was strangely anchoring. *This isn't a dream, I really am back,* I registered before I fell asleep.

—∞∞∞—

Claude and Donna were arraigned the next day. Although this was a pro forma event, the courtroom was crowded with supporters. I was particularly moved to see how many people from the Puerto Rican community were present. Donna and Claude were brought in surrounded by guards, and I could see the strain in their faces from spending their first night in jail. What had they been going through for the last twenty-four hours, while I had been talking and eating and playing with the kids? A cloud of worry and guilt began to settle over me. But then Donna looked out across the courtroom and Claude did the same, and their faces transformed in glad recognition of so many dear faces from the past assembled on the benches. Michael and Jan asked that a bail hearing be held, and the Judge set a date for ten days later. I watched helplessly as they were shackled and escorted out of the courtroom. I needed to switch gears, because now I had to rush and meet my sister at a nearby hotel coffee shop.

It was pouring rain and, even though the coffee shop was just a few blocks away, I was soaking wet by the time I got there. How should I greet my sister after thirteen years, when for most of those years she thought I was dead? How could I start to explain what had transpired during all that time? Knowing my sister, I imagined that she would be as nervous as I was. I walked into the coffee shop and spotted her at a corner table. She looked a little thinner, but otherwise the same. I walked over, she stood up, we embraced, and I could feel that her clothes were also damp from the rain. Both of us began to cry. "You're drenched!" "You're soaked too!" we each spurted out simultaneously. "It was pouring the whole drive from South Bend," Joyce explained. "You learned how to drive!" I exclaimed.

For the next few hours, the words poured out. We started with our children and went on to everything else. Her husband had gotten a tenure-track position in South Bend a few years before. It had been difficult for her to adjust to the huge difference between life in New York and life in Indiana, but she was starting to appreciate the slower rhythm of a smaller city. She had also been able to start a solo private practice as a clinical therapist, something she had not been able to do in New York.

Joyce listened with concern as I summarized our case, the negotiated deal, and the many unresolved issues that still lay before us. I asked her to tell me about our father's death and listened to her difficult description of the last year of his life as he became more disoriented due to Alzheimer's disease. "I'm so sorry," was all I could find to say. "It's really all right," she said and squeezed my hand. When we finally looked at our watches, four hours had passed and Joyce still had to drive back to South Bend. We arranged that Tony, Leila, and I would take the train down to see her and her family the next weekend. Just before we parted, Joyce handed me a book. It was called *Family Myths* and Joyce was the author. "I dedicated this book to you," she said.

That night, after Tony and Leila were in bed, I began to read Joyce's book. The dedication, "To my elusive but beloved sister, whose life inspired these reflections," sent shivers down my spine. [1] Little did Joyce know when she wrote those words that her elusive sister was living just a few states away in Pennsylvania. And I would never have guessed that while I was busy avoiding the FBI, my sister had etched my disappearance on to the frontispiece of her book.

The book explored how the myths that parents construct about their children mold the children's expectations of themselves. In a section about me,

Joyce delved into the ways in which my father had used the myth of *Diana,* the Roman goddess of the hunt, to construct a larger-than-life, heroic persona for me. In turn, Joyce wrote, my life choices to become a revolutionary unwittingly fulfilled the lofty expectations my father had for me, even though he had not wanted them to be implemented in the ways I chose. As I read, a rant began to seethe in my head. How could Joyce presume to know what had motivated me? How could she reduce my political choices to the family dynamics in our childhood home?

Then I stopped myself. How could I expect her to understand who I was? I had been away for so long, and in the past I had never had the patience to try and bridge the misunderstandings between us. I had chosen remoteness even before security considerations had demanded our complete separation. I hadn't returned to repeat the dynamics of the past—politically or personally. Of course, my sister and I had differing interpretations of our family's myths. But could we finally give up the skewed images we had of each other and build something new?

The next day I looked through a plexiglass wall at Claude, who was clothed in an orange jump suit with a chain around his waist. As we tried to make conversation through the visitor phone line that was listened to by the guards, I realized how much the terms of this relationship would also need to be reshaped in this new era. Our lives had been sewn together over the past thirteen years—from our shared visions of change, to the caretaking of our children, to our weekly Saturday night dates watching *Americas Most Wanted* together. Now, phones in hand, we watched each other for subtle facial expressions. Claude joked about the concrete slab bed and thin mattress which made our old bed in Pittsburgh seem like posturpedic heaven. We discussed the plans for the bail appeal and the different day care possibilities for Leila. I had just begun to tell him about my visit with my sister when the guard came by to announce that our thirty minutes were up.

We had tried to connect beneath the stilted string of words, but this was our first attempt and it was very hard. After I left him, after we matched hands on either side of the glass in a dismembered version of a parting hug, it began to sink in how much we would have to stretch, maneuver, invent and fight in order to create a different language and a meaningful subtext in order to communicate in such a warped setting.

―――◦◦◦◦―――

That night, Nancy drove Rob, Zoe, Leila, Tony and I to the Puerto Rican Cultural Center (PRCC) for a welcome dinner. After Claude and Donna's court hearing, José Lopez, the Director of the PRCC, with whom I had worked before going underground, invited us to this community event. "It is very important for us to have this welcome to honor you and your family and what you have done for our movement," he said firmly before I could express any hesitation. José was the brother of Oscar Lopez Rivera, one of the Puerto Rican prisoners-of-war, and a leader of the campaign to free the FALN 11 from the moment they were arrested in 1980. He was a professor at Northeastern University, executive director of the Puerto Rican Cultural Center, and he had also played a major role in developing Puerto Rican political strategy on the mainland since the seventies. It wasn't easy to argue with José, even though the idea of an honoring dinner, especially in Claude and Donna's absence, made me uncomfortable.

As we approached the PRCC building, I forgot my anxiety, as I caught sight of the dramatic murals depicting the heroes of the Puerto Rican Independence movement emblazoned on the side of the building. "There is Juan Antonio Corretjer. This Center is named for him, just like you are," I excitedly told Tony who had learned the true origin of his name only a few weeks before. Tony took a few minutes to study Juan Antonio's face before a group of youth from the Center steered us inside to take a tour of the building. The PRCC had been founded in 1973 and, though I had heard about its growth from afar, being inside the Center was another experience entirely. We toured the gallery area where posters and pictures from the past three decades were displayed. I started to cry when I saw a photo of Lolita Lebron at the victory event we had held for her at the Mission Cultural Center in San Francisco in 1979, shortly after her release from prison.

I would have liked to dwell on the pictures, but Leila was pulling me excitedly towards the childcare area, the Centro Infantil, named after Juan Antonio's wife, Consuelo Lee Correjter. Both of Nancy's kids had attended the Centro when they were young, and she had many moving and funny stories to tell about their experiences as some of the only Anglo children at the center. Leila wanted to stay and play in this bright space filled with books and toys, but we were being asked to move on to see the classrooms of the Pedro Albizu Campos High School, founded in 1972, which offered students a focus on Puerto Rican and Latino history in addition to traditional academic classes. Then we got in line for the feast which José, in his role as Puerto Rican chef, had cooked with the help of other community members.

After we were all stuffed full of delicious pollo, arroz, platanos, y frijoles, José got up and began the formal welcome of the evening. He talked about the history of the independence movement, the sacrifices that had been made by Puerto Ricans from Mariana Bracetti, Albizu Campos, and Lolita Lebron to the current political prisoners.[2] He situated our acts of solidarity as North Americans in this continuum, and he recognized how these sacrifices impacted our families. This level of solidarity was something the Puerto Rican movement would not forget, he concluded, and he pledged the support of the entire community to Claude and Donna and our families in the coming period. After he finished, other members of the community rose and talked about how they saw the importance of what we had done.

As each one spoke, my perception of our history shifted. During the years after our escape from L.A., we had all struggled to maintain our mental sense of purpose and connectedness to the Puerto Rican movement. But, in our isolation, our awareness of the continuity of Puerto Rican movement had inevitably diminished, and this impacted our understanding of our own history as well. In this crowded room, surrounded by smiling faces, I began to appreciate why this formal acknowledgement was important, not only for us but for the Puerto Rican community also. We were North Americans who had defied the proscribed limits on solidarity. We had been willing to act because of our belief in the right to Puerto Rican self-determination and because we saw this struggle

as integrally connected with the fight against imperialism as a whole. We might
be personally wracked by our shortcomings and eager to critique how things
might have been done differently and better, but our history and our practice
still contained lessons that were important for current and future generations.
I looked over at Tony and I could see his mind working to assimilate what José
and the other Puerto Ricans were saying about his family. I knew that this public
affirmation of who we were would help him, as well as Leila and Zoe on a more
subliminal level, get through the months ahead.

⟶⟨∞⟩

      Ten days later, we jammed into the courtroom for Donna and Claude's
bail hearing. Jan and Michael had been right—the Chicago press had done its
best to frame Claude and Donna as terrorists. However, the *Pittsburgh Post-
Gazette* and other papers had run more sympathetic stories. The *New York
Times* article was ironically titled "Neighbors Anyone Would Want, And Most
Wanted by F.B.I., Too."[3] The story went on: "Neighbors on two quiet middle
class streets of Squirrel Hill have been stunned by the news that the people they
knew as doting parents, helpful friends, and community volunteers had turned
themselves in on Tuesday to the Federal authorities in Chicago after nearly a
year of negotiations, hoping to win reduced sentences." It reported that, after
we surfaced, the FBI had gone door-to-door through our neighborhoods asking
provocative questions about us. But no one had taken the bait. What emerged
instead was a picture of dedicated parents who were involved in the AIDS Task
Force, in gardening, in little league baseball, and in videotaping an inner-city
literacy project. The article noted the scores of letters that had poured in urging
Judge Hart to grant clemency to Donna and Claude. A letter for Donna was
quoted, "Considering her situation, she might well have kept to herself all this
time. Instead she reached out to families in crisis and gave them support and
hope where no one else could or would." And one neighbor said of Claude,
"There are some people you meet in life and you truly feel that it is a lifetime
friendship. Greg Peters is one of those people to me."

The hearing was filled with emotional testimony from many Pittsburgh friends who had flown in to testify on their behalf. With my sister on one side of me, Nancy on the other, José in the row behind, and our friend Roger from Pittsburgh in front of me, the confluence of different parts of my life contributed to the dizzying sensation I felt as I tried to second-guess what the Judge was really thinking. We had all tried to tamp down our expectations, and I hadn't even told Tony and Leila that it was possible that Claude and Donna might be able to get out of jail for awhile. So when the judge rejected the prosecution's arguments that Claude and Donna were a danger to the citizens of Chicago, and pronounced that under the circumstances—the defendants had after all voluntarily surrendered and the holiday season was coming up—he would grant bail of $250,000 each for a month's time, I could hardly believe it. A spontaneous cheer spread across the room which was only silenced by the pounding gavel. A month was a limited amount of time—the judge could have let them out until their sentencing later in the spring—but it was a significant and welcome gesture. $500,000 was a sizeable bail, but we had already lined up a few people who were generously willing to put up their homes as collateral, so we were confident that we could get them out.

As I left the courtroom, surrounded by the crowd of people from diverse communities who had stepped forward to speak out, and even put up their property on our behalf, I promised myself that I would make it a priority to do the same for others, if the need should ever arise, in the future.

Cover of *Libertad*, the magazine of the National Committee to Free Puerto Rican Prisoners of War and Political Prisoners, Fall 1995, with pictures of fifteen incarcerated Puerto Ricans.

Light Will Always
Be Showing

THE MONTH OF RELEASE WAS A GIFT, but it also was a pressure cooker for our simmering emotions. The kids were supposed to enjoy the time with Claude, while knowing that soon he was going away for a long time. Claude was supposed to reconnect with dozens of old friends, when he knew that these reunions would soon be severed again. I was supposed to enjoy the month, while registering Tony for school, finding daycare for Leila, and obtaining my real birth certificate, a new driver's license, and a job. Claude and I were supposed to put aside the tensions between us, the fears about what the coming years would mean for our relationship, and savor our last few weeks together. It was an impossible scenario and there were fights and tears and sleepless nights. But there were also some precious moments that made me very glad for this month of life together in this new sphere.

Claude's birthday was December 31. While we were underground, we couldn't celebrate our real birthdays with the kids. Now the taboo had been lifted, so when Nancy proposed hosting a party for Claude on New Year's Eve, we agreed. Karen, Jody, and Ericka had flown in for the holidays from San Francisco, where they had returned to live a month before. Old friends from both coasts flew in to welcome us back. Our Chicago compañeros showed up in force, and José cooked another magnificent meal at Nancy's house to celebrate. Wine, food, music, talk, and lots of kids running every which way—we couldn't help but be absorbed in the elation of the present moment.

The mood grew more reflective when Nancy gave Claude a scrapbook filled with pictures from the seventies that she had kept hidden in a basement box while we were away. José presented him with a plaque from the Museo de Historia y Cultura Puertoriqueña and thanked him and Donna, in person this time, for the sacrifices they and their families had made for the Puerto Rican people. Claude seemed overwhelmed by all of the attention. After thanking everyone for making this birthday celebration possible, he went on to talk about something that had struck him as he read the newspaper in his MCC jail cell.

"The day after we surrendered, the papers were filled with stories about how dangerous we were, our links to the FALN and international terrorism. The FBI held a press conference, displayed various things they had found in our house in L.A. and spread them out on a table for the media's benefit as evidence of our violent history. There were a few rifles, some ammunition reloading equipment, books by Fanon, Regis Debray, Mao, and Marx. Among all these items was a small tin plaque given to me as a gift when I was in Cuba as part of the Venceremos Brigade by a family who was about to ritually burn their one-room, palm-roofed *bohio* before moving into a modern new apartment.[1] This *Playa Girón* plaque memorialized the family's participation in the defense of Cuba during the U.S.-led Bay of Pigs invasion in 1961, and it caught my eye since it was mounted at the *bohio*'s entrance. It was one of the few political mementos that I brought with me underground, and I had really been sorry to leave it behind when we left L.A. so quickly. Sitting in my cell, it made me laugh to think that this plaque was being touted by the FBI as a symbol of our involvement in an international terrorist conspiracy. It also made me realize, once again, what a powerful threat Cuba has been to the rulers of the world."

It had been a long time since I had heard Claude speak like that. In fact, when I thought about it, I didn't think I had ever heard Claude "make a speech" before. In his role as newscaster on KPFA, Claude had been the interviewer, not the one to tell the stories.[2] And in Prairie Fire, Claude had usually deferred to others when it came to public speaking. This new situation was already changing him, pushing him to articulate thoughts that at other times he might have kept to himself. Everyone started to clap and Claude turned red.

A friend who had been asked to take photos of the gathering insisted that we assemble our underground group for a picture to mark our return. For a second, I hesitated—after so many years of refusing to be photographed, was it really all right? But people had already brought Leila, Zoe, and Ericka from upstairs where they had been playing and pulled Tony away from the computer. We squeezed in next to each other on the maroon velveteen couch in the living room, the kids sitting on our laps, Claude and Rob on the floor in front. For some reason, the girls started to count us in unison: "One, two, three"—Donna, Rob, Claude,—four, five, six, seven, eight, nine, ten—Jody, Karen, Zoe, Leila, Ericka, Tony, Diana." "Why it's the *"ten most wanted,"*—an onlooker declared, and we all started laughing giddily, even though the kids probably didn't have any idea about the meaning of the joke. When they got older, I thought, we would be able to show them the picture and explain how funny and freeing it had been for all of us to sit together, take a simple picture, and make light of the chilling phrase, *"the ten most wanted."*

A month had seemed like a long, unexpected span when the judge announced the period of release in court. But after Claude's birthday party, the days evaporated, and soon it was the night before the mandated second surrender. In some ways, this surrender was harder than the first. Before, the word "jail" had been abstract. Now Leila and Tony had seen the foreboding Chicago Metropolitan Correction Center, they had both visited Claude in jail, and they knew what it was like to have to walk away and leave him behind. This time the whirlwind of return had subsided and we were already constructing new routines in Chicago that would be ruptured by Claude's departure.

Claude and I sat numbly in front of the TV, listening to Leila talking to her stuffed animals in the next room. "Daddy needs to go back to jail because the bad guards want him to be there. You won't be able to visit him, but I will," she explained to her seal, her bears, her puppies, and her monkey, remembering the rule that nothing except money could be brought inside on prison visits. Tony came into the room with a picture he had just drawn and gave it to Claude. It showed a bright sun with red rays shining through black barbed wire.

He had written a title across the top: "Light Will Always Be Showing." It was a
declaration and a pact. Claude couldn't take any belongings into jail, so the next
day, after he left, we mailed it to him. "I hung the picture Tony drew right next
to my bed," Claude wrote in his first letter from the Metropolitan Correctional
Center.

———— ⌀⌀⌀ ————

      Through a network of friends, we found a wonderful daycare setting
for Leila and Zoe in the home of a woman who had cared for the children of
other political prisoners, first in New York and now in Chicago. BJ opened her
arms and her heart to our girls. She found picture books about children whose
parents were prisoners, she encouraged the girls to tell stories and draw pictures
about their visits with Donna and Claude, and she integrated their experiences
into the stimulating preschool curriculum that she had developed for the eight
children she cared for. She had a bright yellow house and a big back yard in
which the children played every day unless the temperature fell below zero.
Often, the most joyful part of my day was seeing Leila bound out of the car up
the steps to BJ's, eager to join her new friends and the day's activities ahead.
      Our friend Howie taught at a public school close to Nancy's house.
The school featured a Spanish immersion program, and although Tony was
nervous about being plunged into fourth grade Spanish, he liked Howie and
already had met children of our friends who went to Inter-American. The
principal and teachers were sensitive to his difficult situation, which we openly
discussed with them before enrolling him at the school. Tony walked to school
in the morning and attended an after-school program in a nearby church. He
started picking up Spanish and joined the chess club. He didn't complain
much, but I knew he badly missed his friends, his teachers and his uncompli-
cated life in Pittsburgh. One day he showed me a poem he had written:

The Statue

The statue
is staring
at me.
Copper Green
out on an island
out on the Hudson
staring at me and you.
I wish its name would be different
because it's not true
to the place where it sits
in New York City, NY, USA.
I don't even know why some people say
"Everyone in america is FREE."
Now I look at that statue looking at me
and I turn around.

"That's a heavy poem," I said. "I can understand why it's a different feeling from when we visited the statue in New York."

When Tony was seven I had taken him to New York City to show him the city of my birth. He had wanted to visit the Statue of Liberty, so even though it was hardly the side of New York I wanted to share with him, we had gone. I held my tongue during the tour, among the swarming crowds, climbing up into Liberty's torch, listening to the guide's glowing descriptions of the symbolic meaning of Miss Liberty to immigrants from all over the world. I quickly forgot this part of our trip, but now I could see that the tour of Miss Liberty had hibernated inside of Tony for the past two years. But when I tried to talk about what the poem meant to him, he told me had homework to do.

A couple of weeks later I looked over Tony's shoulder at the computer game that he was playing and asked him about it. Since we had come to Chicago, he had become engrossed in Sim City which gave the players tools to construct

their own simulated cities. Tony proudly pointed out the different parts of his
city to me and commented, "There aren't any prisons in this city." It was only
then I noticed the name he had given this particular simulation. It was called
"fuck prisins."

The next evening, I went to a coffee house during one of my weekly
nights out. These precious evenings away from the kids were made possible by a
specially organized Prairie Fire childcare team, and I could use them for anything I wanted—to go swimming, see a movie, or get together with a friend. Most
often I found myself writing. The poem "Now I Can Tell You" (at the beginning
of this book) flowed from me on my first evening out. Sometimes I wrote in my
journal, sometimes I wrote letters to Claude, and other times, without planning,
another poem would take shape. This time I wrote a poem/letter to Claude.

> *Tony sims a city,*
> *calls it* fuck prisins.
> *Puts in homes, businesses, skyscrapers,*
> *water, bridges, pollution, homeless,*
> *even high crime areas.*
> *But no prisons.*
>
> *You walk the wired roof*
> *once a week.*
> *A tease, you say –*
> *Sears and John Hancock*
> *flaunting their steeled accomplishments;*
> *the lake*
> *a limitless blue*
> *enticement.*
>
> *Tony dreams you jump off*
> *the tallest building in Chicago,*
> *wakes up crying.*

I dream
a bedazzled, dark
ocean sky,
the one we've been longing to see
for 10 years,
but you cannot see it, smell it,
grasp for it.
The night comes sinking down,
an enveloping steel gauze.
I wake up crying,
but in the light-bound day
how not to forget?

Tony draws a picture
calls it "light will always be showing."
We send it in.
You hang it where it fits,
rebuking your locked door.

After I wrote this poem, I reread it every few days for a couple of weeks. Occasionally I tweaked a word here or there, but mainly the rereading gave me a chance to sit and reflect. The separation from Claude and foreboding about the future crystallized most sharply in my restless nights. During my waking hours, the feeling of liberation from clandestinity overrode most everything else.

When I mentioned to my sister how important writing had been to me when I was underground, she suggested that I think about writing a memoir. The idea was attractive but I was hesitant. I wrote in my journal:

"The idea of undertaking such an individual project immediately makes me feel nervous and guilty. How can I presume to write about our collective experience? How could this be possible while Donna and Claude are away in prison? ... I am dubious that it can ever happen, or at least not for years. Besides, it seems likely that politics will likely take over any spare time I might have for written self-expression."

Already, political activity was taking over most of my spare time. Shortly after Claude and Donna returned to jail to await sentencing, I started a job as a program coordinator with Vida/SIDA, an AIDS education and prevention project based in the Puerto Rican community. I had been asking around about possible jobs and one of the people I spoke to was Viola Salgado, the director of Vida/SIDA. Viola had been at the Puerto Rican Cultural Center the night of our return celebration. When I sent her my newly put together resume which included the work I had done as part of the Pittsburgh AIDS Task Force, she called me to come in for an interview at their storefront office in the heart of the Humboldt Park community.

The windows of the storefront were covered with posters in Spanish and English promoting AIDS prevention and advertising various community activities, including an event in support of Puerto Rican political prisoners. The busy front area was filled with young people talking on the phone and working on computers. Viola's office towards the back was a little bit quieter. Viola explained that Vida/SIDA was started in 1988 as an all-volunteer effort by the Pedro Albizu Campos High School, which was housed in the Puerto Rican Cultural Center. The students and staff had begun to see that the HIV epidemic was spreading in the Puerto Rican/Latino community, but no one was talking about it. Vida/SIDA was initiated with a door-to-door campaign distributing condoms and educational materials, and it soon grew as a peer-to-peer advocacy program. In 1993, it received its first government funding which had recently been renewed.

The work had enormous challenges, Viola continued, because it was impossible to fulfill Vida/SIDA's mission to empower the community to respond to HIV without educating about all of the colonial, racist realities that Puerto Rican people faced on a daily basis. Given gentrification, mis-education, discrimination, and incarceration—Vida/SIDA saw its focus on AIDS work as necessarily connected with the breadth of the PRCC's many other activities. Together, they provided the political basis for community empowerment. This perspective made perfect sense to me. It was very exciting to see a radical model for AIDS work being put into practice.

At the end of our meeting, Viola offered me a job as a program/grants coordinator. I realized that the job offer was primarily a demonstration of political support for me and our family, especially since I had made it clear to Viola that I would be moving to the Bay Area in June, after Claude and Donna's sentencing. But I hoped that I would be able to bring some useful skills and experience to the work while I was there.

I was rapidly drawn into the whirlwind of work at Vida/SIDA. At first, I was nervous about figuring out what my role as a white person in this mainly Puerto Rican organization should be, but it soon became clear that my experience writing a few grants back in Pittsburgh, as well as my background developing an HIV education curriculum for women, were welcome resources. Once I relaxed, I began to get to know the other program coordinators, who were mostly half my age, and we worked together to develop new curriculum for high school youth. Grant writing, curriculum development, meetings with high school administrators to introduce our program filled the weekdays. The Puerto Rican organizers worked non-stop and pretty soon I was bringing Tony and Leila along to weekend community events and distributing educational fliers in the neighborhood. To the kids it was a natural extension of the gatherings with HIV-connected families that we had organized in Pittsburgh. To me, it was wonderful to be part of organizing efforts about HIV that were led by Puerto Ricans who had a far-reaching vision and had been rooted in this community for over twenty years.

To the government, the dedicated politics and successful work of the PRCC were a continuing threat that needed to be contained. Shortly after I began working at Vida/SIDA, an anonymous newsletter named *El Pito* began appearing in stores and community centers around Humboldt Park.[3] *El Pito* cleverly posed as an alternative voice within the Puerto Rican community and put forward a so-called "leftist" critique of the direction of the PRCC politics. The unnamed editors criticized the PRCC for abandoning revolutionary politics and support for the Puerto Rican political prisoners in favor of petit-bourgeois entrepreneurship and electoral politics. But everything I had witnessed since our return spoke of a different reality. The campaign to free the prisoners was integrated into all aspects of the PRCC's work. To me, the breadth of the PRCC programs and the alliances they had built with Puerto Rican elected officials was a sign of their political growth and sophistication. It was the capacity to combine grassroots community building with commitment to Puerto Rican independence and political prisoner solidarity that I respected most in the PRCC's evolution.

April 4, 1995 was the fifteenth anniversary of the capture of the FALN 11 in Chicago. The 11 were still in prison, plus half a dozen other Puerto Ricans who had been arrested in the following years. The PRCC was planning an event to mark fifteen years of imprisonment and we had all spent the past few weekends helping to prepare. The day of the event, a new issue of *El Pito* appeared mysteriously in stores around Humboldt Park and even on tables and window sills in the lobby of the auditorium where the event was to be held. As before, it was filled with satiric cartoons and innuendoes. It had become clear that *El Pito* exploited honest disagreements that existed within the Puerto Rican community in order to undermine the PRCC's work. The timing of this new issue was specifically intended to disrupt the expanding campaign to free the political prisoners.

Despite *El Pito*, the commemoration took place without a hitch. The many moving cultural performances and speeches were a testament to the politics and spirit of the prisoners, the PRCC, and all the participants. But there was no longer any question that the PRCC and its constituency were under a frontal COINTELPRO-type attack. The personal darts and the spotlighting of interpersonal conflicts, which were *El Pito's* hallmark, succeeded in sowing doubts and fanning divisions. In addition to all the work the PRCC was already doing, now it had to make time to address insidious slanders without even being able to identify the slanderers. It made me furious that vicious agents were still trying to destroy a grouping that had managed to preserve its fundamental political orientation throughout the tumults of the past two decades. It also strengthened my commitment to this community that had opened its collective arms to us upon our return.

It wasn't until two years later, in 1997, that the agent behind El Pito, *Rafael Marrero, was publically identified after he became the star witness in the prosecution of a professor from the University of Puerto Rico, José Solís. Solís was arrested in Puerto Rico and brought back to Chicago to be tried on charges of conspiring to bomb a military recruiting station on Chicago's Westside in 1992, when he had been teaching at DePaul University. When he was arrested, Solís was offered immunity if he agreed to become an informer and testify against José Lopez and other independentistas. When he refused, the FBI punished him by pressing charges in the bombing incident. Solís maintained his innocence throughout the trial, while Marrero admitted that he himself had actually carried out the bombing (which had been timed to coincide with a PRCC march in support of freedom for the political prisoners), but claimed that Solís had been involved in the conspiracy. During questioning, Marrero also admitted his association with* El Pito.

José Solís was convicted and paid for his principles with the loss of freedom for three years, yet another instance of the continuing U.S. counterinsurgency war against the Puerto Rican independence movement.

∞∞∞

A few weeks before Claude and Donna were scheduled to be sentenced, on April 19, 1995, the Federal Building in Oklahoma City was bombed. Although it was soon clear that the bombing was connected to the right-wing militia movement and motivated by a fundamentalist, racist ideology, the attack was rapidly spun by the media and the government into one huge broiling terrorist plot with repressive implications for the left as well as the right. Within four days, with public outrage at its height, Clinton introduced the sweeping "Counter-Terrorism" bill which gave the President tremendous arbitrary power to declare who is a domestic or overseas "terrorist" and authorized secret trials for citizens and immigrants who were accused of lending any type of support to domestic or international "terrorist" organizations.

We girded ourselves for the worst. Although the negotiated deal had put the cap on Claude's sentence at ten years, in this climate it seemed like any

sentence might be possible. On the day of the sentencing, when we heard Judge
Hart pronounce six years for Claude and four for Donna, Tony squeezed my
hand excitedly and whispered, "It's not ten years!" Hart was the same judge
who, in 1988, had sentenced the Puerto Rican codefendants in this case to five
and three years each. He had stuck to the same standard he used in those cases
and had given Donna and Claude analogous sentences. Under the applicable legal guidelines, Donna would be eligible for release within two years and Claude
within four. We now had a target date that we could look toward, a horizon that
wasn't close, but was within sight.

The next month was spent preparing for our moves to the West Coast.
Donna requested to be sent to FCI Dublin, which was the closest women's prison to San Francisco, and after some research Claude put in a request to be sent
to FCI Sheridan in Oregon, about a hundred miles outside of Portland. Both
requests were agreed upon by the Federal Bureau of Prisons. Rob and I began to
pack our accumulated possessions from the past six months and made a plan to
move our stored items from Pittsburgh. Meanwhile, Donna and Claude geared
themselves for their trip, whose exact date would remain unknown until a couple
of hours before they had to leave. They had heard grim stories about how high
security prisoners were transported with their hands "blackboxed." In addition
to the usual handcuffs and waist chains, their hands would be almost completely
immobilized inside a painful restraining device. They would be powerless to respond to any of the vicissitudes of climate or human turbulence that might occur
while they hurtled thousands of miles through the air.

Claude was moved before we expected. It was hard for me to tell the
kids that he was no longer at the downtown MCC jail. Up until then, he had
been physically close to us, we could visit him twice a week, and he was still a
regular part of our lives. Now he was gone, out of sight and out of touch, though
definitely not out of our minds. After I told Leila that Claude had been moved
and we couldn't visit him for at least another month, she tossed and kicked and
moaned next to me in my bed, which she crawled into every night. Over the past
few months, I had become accustomed to the sound of the El rumbling nearby.

Now the noise started to warp my sleep. One night, I got up and wrote a poem to try and keep the nightmares at bay.

Night Lock

Leila knows you're being moved –
shunted invisibly across the country
in the cuffed June heat.
She can't see it, can't say it
but her sleep is shackled by it –
twisting and turning,
struggling to break
free of the blackboxed dreams
that leave us both sleepless,
swollen and wasted,
aching for the first sane light;
while you are wardened blindly
across this dreamless country
from locked hub to locked hub.

After a week, Claude finally called from Sheridan. He had survived the ordeal, although his hands still ached from being blackboxed, and he was settling in to his new environment. Hearing his voice again, we all began to feel a little better.

The weekend before we left Chicago, we marched in the annual Puerto Rican Day Parade with the PRCC contingent. Through the streets of Humboldt Park, through a virtual sea of waving Puerto Rican flags, Tony and Leila rode a float with dozens of other kids who were all enthusiastically waving their flags and holding up pictures of the political prisoners, including one of Donna and Claude.

Losing myself in the music, chants, dancing, and the smells of Puerto Rican food, I realized that the last six months had given me an opportunity to discover a side of Chicago that I had never experienced during my time attending the University in its Hyde Park enclave. Part of me wanted to stay here, bringing Leila to BJ's bright childcare home every morning, living in Nancy and Steve's cozy, supportive home, working productively for Vida/SIDA and the Puerto Rican movement, building on the threads of stability that we had begun to establish in these months. But more of me wanted to move on/move back to the city I had been yearning for all these years. I needed to reverse the geographic direction that we had taken ten years ago when we left Portland for Minneapolis in order for my return to be complete.

Pictures taken with Claude in prison at FCI
Sheridan. Top (left to right)—Karen, Tony,
Claude, Leila, Ericka, Diana. Middle—Tony,
Claude, Leila, Diana, Joyce. Bottom—Claude
and Diana.

RECONSTRUCTING MEMORY

I'm 46 years old and
I crest an ordinary San Francisco corner
and come face to face with fog
so dense, so translucent
it shrouds the ground,
 releases the hilltops,
and forces me to stop –
look back.
46 years old and
 I turn a corner and am struck
by a street whose shape, whose name
wound endlessly through my dreams –
now miraculously concrete,
here to be walked on.
Struck by faces and voices
disappeared and exiled for so long,
lost to sight and sound for so long,
but now so casually present,
so themselves again,
that they threaten to bury
the ten year weight of yearning
that I have promised not to forget.

I FIRST RETURNED TO SAN FRANCISCO with the kids during their spring break in March. We left sleet and snow in Chicago and stepped out of the airport into the brilliance of San Francisco sun, enhanced by traces of a recent rain shower and white cloud collages in a deep blue sky. On our way into the city, I couldn't stop myself from exclaiming at every familiar, mundane landmark that we passed, although the kids clearly didn't understand what all the fuss was about.

The next week saw a constant stream of reunions with old comrades and friends. I managed to squeeze in a couple of trips with the kids to the Golden Gate Bridge and Fisherman's Wharf between brunches, dinners, coffees, and teas. There was even a special welcoming event for us, hosted by Prairie Fire, in a new storefront women's art gallery near Dolores Park.

While I had traversed the country from Los Angeles to Pittsburgh, many of my friends were still living in the Mission district, Noe Valley, Duboce Park, and the Inner Sunset—the neighborhoods where we had all lived in ever-fluid, collective households, mixing and matching apartments, roommates and lovers years ago. Of course, they had all evolved and aged in one way or another. Some owned houses, many had professional jobs, most had settled into families—lesbian, gay, and straight. As I sat and talked with friends, navigating through the years of distance, there were moments when I couldn't help but notice how comfortable and even staid many of them seemed. Here I was at forty-six just beginning my life again with no home, little money, and a partner in prison because of the political commitments we had all shared in the past. While many of my friends were still politically involved, the pace of their activity had mellowed and the routine of their lives had stabilized. I cautioned myself against resentment, knowing that if I had made a different choice years ago, my life would most probably have assumed a similar shape to theirs. Besides, we were now benefiting from their relative privilege, since they were able to pledge generous support to help our families through the next difficult period.

Whenever I felt myself slipping into bitterness, I would focus on the new generation—the children of people I had last known as impulsive, twenty-something activists. Four of my friends had children who were three and four years old, within six months age of Leila. They had recently started a weekend playgroup for the kids, and now Leila could become part of the group. As in Chicago, doors were opening to us in many unexpected ways.

The hardest reconnection was with Kyle, but not in the ways I expected it to be. I had anticipated tears, pain, and huge happiness—an updated remix of the scenes that had preceded my departure thirteen years before. Instead, it was more like one of my repetitive dreams in which I snuck back to San Francisco and ran directly to Kyle's house, but she was too busy to see me and I was unnerved by the absence of connection. In real life, Kyle was not too busy. We took Tony to the Academy of Science and Leila to the Children's Playground in Golden Gate Park. We walked and talked some more about the high and low points of life over the past years and some of the changes that had transpired— her art, my writing, what we expected for our children in the years to come. We skirted over the last time we had seen each other—our vows to stay close whatever happened, our tears, our last embrace. We barely registered the fact that now we each had long term partners, I was no longer living as a lesbian, and the trajectories of our lives had become inalterably separate. I hadn't expected to resume our same relationship, but I had imagined that some surge of passion would reverberate from the fiery intensity that we had shared in that other era. The lack of surge disoriented me and, for a moment, made me question all of my memories, all of my longings. Perhaps, over time, outside of the pressures of a reunion, more connection would return.

By the time we left San Francisco at the end of the spring break, I had found a place to live in a household of younger lesbian women which was right around the corner from Buena Vista, the school that Tony would attend in the fall. I had also reserved a space for Leila in the same daycare center that two of the other playgroup girls attended. The outlines of our new life in San Francisco were taking shape.

Between our visit in March and our move in July, when I thought about
San Francisco I focused on the scarlet bougainvilleas and the purple Mexican
sages. I pictured the constant surprise of hillside precipices and the crooked
streets with their sharp turns that opened unexpectedly on a breathtaking crest.
I remembered the deceptively peaceful expanse of ocean beach that was secretly
plagued with precarious riptides at the furthest Western edge of the city and
the continent. Despite the warm welcome we had received, I knew that our
return would be filled with its own share of precipices and riptides. I needed to
anchor my plan to move back in the predictable variations of the San Francisco
landscape which I still loved.

The first few months were hard. This was no longer a transitional
stage. This was the life I had yearned for, and now I had to figure out how to
make it conform to some of the expectations I had nurtured all these years.
Beneath the signposts of San Francisco familiarity, there were striking, dis-
quieting differences. There were people panhandling on corners and freeway
off ramps; sleeping under park benches and tucked under raggedy blankets in
doorways; rattling their shopping carts homes through the streets and parks of
every neighborhood. They were a constant, present reminder of the abyss that
lay between the brightly painted Victorian house facades and the vast reality of
homelessness that had taken up residence in San Francisco and many other urban centers between the seventies and the nineties. They were a constant goad
to my political conscience. Now I had another chance to figure out how I could
best contribute to making change in a desperately worsening environment. I
wanted to be deliberate about my choices.

When I walked around the streets of the Mission, I could still feel
the insistent presence of progressive politics. Signs of events, demonstrations,
walk-a-thons, concerts, and plays about San Francisco Women Against Rape,
Mumia-Abu Jamal, ACT-UP, police brutality, the Zapatistas, and so much more
were plastered on doorways, windows, and lampposts. But they were sandwiched between "For Sale" signs for houses, condos, and tenancies-in-common
which were emptying out rental flats and apartments in a rush of evictions
calculated to gentrify the Mission. There were dozens of political groups—anti-

racist, feminist, queer, environmentalist, globalist. Yet, as I began to investigate their programs and activities, it seemed that each one operated separately from the others, pursuing projects and goals that I supported, but without the breadth of vision or ideological orientation that was necessary to build a more unified political movement. In fact, the burgeoning non-profit industrial complex seemed, in many ways, to have taken over the spirit and structure of the left.[1]

The positive missions and programs of the non-profits were distorted by the competitive drive for funds and a marketable agenda, which too often seemed to mirror rather than challenge corporate templates. In the seventies, we had funded our political activities through salaries from "straight" jobs, a multitude of benefit events, and individual donors who supported our goals. Sometimes Prairie Fire members were given financial support by the organization to do specific projects for a limited period of time. But our expectation was that each of us would need to work not only for our own survival, but to help support our collective goals. Now the situation had flipped and young progressive people searched for jobs with non-profit organizations that could fulfill their desire to do meaningful, social change work. But jobs were tied to funding and funding was tied to the thousands of foundations that had mushroomed in the past twenty years, efficiently modeling the corporate mentality for the well-intentioned non-profit sector. Instead of working together, each non-profit was fragmented on its own track, scurrying competitively to procure grants and recruit the youthful, passionate, hardworking personnel who would assure its survival. I couldn't prove it, but it seemed like a deliberate, systematic plan to co-opt and disorganize the left under the guise of working for social justice.

Or was what I felt just the bitter nostalgia of every aging radical who longed for the good old days of revolutionary fervor and idealism? I could see that many young progressive people were struggling to figure out how to implement their dreams of change in the context of a very different social climate than that of the sixties and seventies. I couldn't pretend that the methodologies of the past could simply be applied to the current reality. I didn't want to be a sour political dinosaur.

Where did my personal reality fit in this contradictory environment? How could I reconcile being forty-six years old and a single parent with my desire to recreate the time when politics had shaped my daily existence? How could I find political work that made sense to me, while accepting the fact that I was not available for meetings every night of the week and acknowledging that I craved some space for writing and reflection?

To begin with, I had to focus on our survival and assuring a livable, functional environment for the kids. I spent several months applying to non-profit organizations for jobs where I had background knowledge and relevant skills. After dozens of applications, a few first and some second interviews, I realized that I couldn't compete with the hundreds of young people who wanted careers in the non-profit arena and were willing to work sixty hours a week. Besides, I couldn't support the kids and Claude on an entry-level, non-profit job. While hunting for something permanent, I was working at a temporary administrative job at a hospital, a couple of blocks away from our new home. When a permanent job with an adequate starting salary and good benefits opened up, I took it with mixed relief. It wasn't what I had envisioned, but it offered security, a decent working environment, and I could walk over to Buena Vista and get to know the kids' teachers during my lunch break. Maybe after working in San Francisco awhile, I would be in a better position to land a non-profit job in an area I was interested in. Or maybe I would go back to school for my master's in social work or public health, which would make me more marketable. In the meantime, I had found a job that paid the bills.

～∞～

Of my many priorities in those first few months, visiting Claude was at the top. Karen came with us for our first trip to Sheridan in the middle of July. By the end of the first day, I was very glad that she was there. A plane trip that should have taken an hour dragged out into four. Sheridan was about an hour and a half from the Portland airport, and we sped along the freeway in our rental car, knowing that visiting ended at 5:00. We would have the whole next day to spend with Claude, but Leila's plaintive pleas of "I want my daddy" propelled us forward to try and see him that afternoon.

We pulled through the gates of Sheridan just before 4:00 PM, but then it took us ten minutes of searching through the maze of prison buildings before we found the right one. We tore out of the car and breathlessly presented ourselves to the guards at the front desk only to be told that we were five minutes past the time when visitors could be processed. No amount of reasoning or impassioned explaining that we had come over seven hundred miles could budge the staff. They had heard despondent crying from children like Leila hundreds of times before. It meant nothing to them. As we were to learn time and time again, the rules were meant to discipline visitors, as well as prisoners, into submission. When we realized that we were getting nowhere with the guards, Karen and I hurried to get the kids off the grounds and away from the scene of disappointment and humiliation. In the future, we would learn the letter of their law so that we could maximize our sense of control over visits.

The next morning, we were among the first in line when the processing began. Even so, the procedure was long and tedious. A single guard slowly checked to make sure each adult visitor's name was on the approved list, reviewed ID cards, and finally made everyone, including the tiniest children, go through the metal detector—stripping jewelry, shoes, and belts off until the detector no long beeped ominously at the hidden penny in a pocket or an ankle bracelet that a visitor had innocently forgotten. Luckily, the line was filled with children of all ages, and while Tony preferred to observe every detail of the absurd routine, Leila began to play a clever version of standstill hide-and-seek with the other kids, which allowed them to play without losing their place in line. *She's already begun to learn the rules of this place*, I thought ruefully.

Our learning process was just beginning. Once we were inside the visiting room, we waited for what seemed like an interminable amount of time for Claude to appear. "Is daddy ever coming?" Leila complained again and again until I was on the verge of screaming at her, just like mothers around the visiting room were doing, trying to assert some control over their kids in a location where they virtually had none. Finally, there was Claude, walking out of

the doorway in the corner. Leila ran and threw herself into his arms, before the
guards could blast a cautionary message over the loudspeaker: "NO RUNNING
AT ANY TIME! PARENTS MUST CONTROL THEIR CHILDREN!"

So began the first of many visits at which we strove to make a connection in this deformed environment, where the chairs and tables were bolted to
the floor, the glaring fluorescent lights concealed cameras that watched our every
move, and the only toys and story books were kept in a children's playroom
where prisoners were not allowed to go. A child was forced to choose between
being with her father in the toyless, sterile visiting room, or going off to the playroom without him. The only other outlet was the food machines, which featured
a massive variety of junk food at inflated prices. Every time Leila became tired of
sitting on Claude's lap and playing with his hair, or Tony grew bored with the
constricted adult conversation, they requested more quarters for the machines
and we helplessly gave in. Eventually, they agreed to check out the playroom,
much to our relief, and we finally had a breathing space for some uninterrupted
conversation. Claude seemed okay, but he admitted that the visit was harder than
he had anticipated. Our strain was mirrored in the faces of all the visitors around
us. It was echoed in the tantrums of the children struggling to come to grips with
their fractured relationships with fathers, uncles, cousins, or brothers. "This is
how tens of thousands of families spend their weekends," I said to Karen and
Claude. "When they're lucky enough to be able to visit," Karen commented, and
we all nodded in dull agreement, unable to feel very happy about our relative
privilege in this sphere.

The worst moment was, of course, the leave taking. What should have
been privately experienced grief became the public property of everyone in the
room. It was all very well for me to resolve that I would not break down in front
of all these burly, surly guards, but I couldn't tell Leila not to wail "daddy, daddy,
daddy," or urge Tony to finish the endless, wordless hug he was giving Claude.
Then I realized that it hardly mattered what the guards thought of these wrenching family scenes that were being recapitulated in prison visiting rooms across
the country. This outpouring of grief was the only collective acknowledgement
of our suffering, and in some way sharing it helped alleviate the isolation of each

family's daily routine of loss. But I could see that this goodbye was breaking Claude's heart.

When we left the prison, we drove to the Oregon coast, about an hour west of Sheridan, where Karen's cousin David and his girlfriend, Virginia, had a cabin. The minute we opened the door, the kids flew out of the car, out of the world of cages and wires and senseless rules into the welcoming calm of fir trees, green grasses, ocean views, and caring, generous people who didn't know the three of us, but made us feel welcome in every way possible. I was struck dumb by the juxtaposition, unable to fathom how this place of such natural, free beauty could coexist with that institution of locks and human pain, unable to justify how I could be here, resting in the rose light of sunset and the peaceful quiet of the space, while over at Sheridan it was forever artificial glare and the mind-numbing noise of iron gates, metal doors, and people whose lives were chained.

After that first emotionally jagged visit, we developed a routine for these trips that masked their lack of normalcy. We came to know other prisoners who were friends with Claude, and other children whom Leila and sometimes Tony played with. We learned which guards were reasonable and still had some human compassion, and which ones were hawk-eyed, authority-crazed machines who delighted in targeting the tiniest infringement of the endless rules.

In between the visits, we spoke to Claude on the phone a couple of times a week. The kids sent him projects they had worked on in school and at childcare, and Claude sent each of them scrapbooks of pictures from magazines and cards he thought they would like. Each of us tried to focus in our own way on building our new lives. Tony was seemingly immersed in baseball, schoolwork, and the new friends he was making at Buena Vista, but whenever people asked him how he liked San Francisco, he would growl that he didn't like it at all and that he really missed Pittsburgh. When I tried to get him to explain more he refused, adamant that it should be obvious why Pittsburgh was a better place in every respect than San Francisco.

When I dropped her off at her childcare center, Leila always eagerly ran off to play with her new friends. When I picked her up, I could hardly tear

her away from whatever she was involved in. But her high energy was punctuated by outbursts of sorrow that slapped me with hurricane force and threatened
my own precarious equilibrium. "I miss Daddy and Donna everywhere—in the
car, in school, in the playground, in the climbing structure… and I don't miss
anyone else, just Daddy and Donna!" She talked to her stuffed animals about her
loss and she reinvented stories in her picture books with the theme of prison at
their center. But what hit me the hardest were her plans for what she was going
to do "when daddy gets out of prison." They always involved sharing some present, in-the-moment joy with him as if it would have the same glow three years in
the future, as if she would be the same four-year-old girl when he finally got out,
when she was seven.

      I hadn't had time to write much poetry since I arrived in San Francisco,
but one day after we went shopping and Leila announced that she was going
to wear the new pair of socks that we had just bought "when daddy gets out of
prison," I wrote a poem.

> *She makes her four year old plans –*
> *the bought-today pair of socks*
> *she will wear then;*
> *the now-in-her-hand package of candy*
> *that she will share that day;*
> *the way you will hoist*
> *her who-knows-how-great-weight*
> *on your shoulders*
> *so you can both take in together*
> *the wide open air,*
> *three years from now*
> *when you are free.*
>
> *She rants*
> *in her brashest voice*
> You governors you,

you give me back my dad!
you give me back my dad!*
again and again.
But already she knows
that the "governors" are more deliberate
and more cruel than monkeys.
So she retreats to her plans –
the breakfast we will eat,
the car we will drive,
the road we will take
on that day.

She reads the book
specially bought for her,
My Daddy's in Prison,
but invents her own refrain –
This is his bed
where he will sleep
but he can't get out
cause he's in prison.
this is the place
where he will eat,
but he can't get out
cause he's in prison.
This is the room
where he can meet
but he can't get out
cause he's in prison.

She dreams the governorguards
let you out
for 100 days

but after one day
they say it was a joke
and make you go back
until she is seven.
More cruel and deliberate than monkeys,
they have their own plans,
heedless of hers.

*In the children's story *Caps for Sale,* the peddler
repeatedly yells at the monkeys who have stolen his
caps—*You monkeys you, you give me back my caps!*

I had pledged to visit Claude with the kids every couple of months, a
daunting challenge given our financial circumstances. Fortunately, we received
exceptional help which made these whirlwind trips possible. Various friends
alternated making the trips with us, providing emotional and logistical support,
caring for the kids for part of each weekend so that I could visit Claude by myself
for some desperately needed time "alone" in the crowded visiting room. David
and Virginia offered their apartment in Portland and their cabin at the ocean for
us to stay in and supplemented that with cooking, conversation, and games to
help us make it through the difficult evenings in between our scheduled visiting
times. And the incredible Rosenberg Fund for Children granted us money to
pay for three trips a year.

When Karen first told me about the Rosenberg Fund, I couldn't believe
that a resource existed that would help the children of radical activists like us.
She explained that it had been started by Robby Meeropol, the son of Ethel
and Julius Rosenberg. In the most infamous case of anti-communist furor in the
early cold war era, the Rosenbergs were wrongfully executed on June 19, 1953
for supposedly stealing the secret of the atomic bomb, a crime they did not
commit. Robby was three and his brother, Michael, was five when their parents
were killed and their last names were changed to that of their adoptive parents,

the Meeropols, a few years after the execution.[2] Karen, whose parents had been affiliated with the U.S. Communist Party for a period of time, had met Robby when she was a kid at a lefty summer camp, and had been friends with him for many years afterwards. In 1990, he had fulfilled a lifelong dream by starting a fund to support the children of activists who were the targets of government repression. Some of the first recipients of the Rosenberg Fund's assistance were the children of Puerto Rican and Black political prisoners. Now, Tony, Leila, and Zoe were able to receive assistance with visits to their parents in prison as well as money for summer camp, which we couldn't otherwise afford. As a beneficiary of the Rosenberg Fund, I saw the burgeoning non-profit world from another angle. Robby Meeropol had found a means to use the tools of the current era to support the current and potential future generation of radicals.

In 2001, Tony participated in a summer gathering sponsored by the Rosenberg Fund. He was part of a poetry workshop led by the Puerto Rican poet, Martín Espada, in which he wrote a poem about his experience of visiting Claude in prison. Until I read the poem, I had very little sense of how Tony remembered these difficult visits.

Prison Visit

Stress not known to be there
like quicksand, it pulled me under
so that when I tried to speak to him,
nothing came out.
I was choking on reality
sitting in that room, among men soon to be shackled.
No one was really there,
just people in dog suits thrown a bone so that we
could pretend we were human.

We were the man's best friends
for we always obeyed.
We sat in straight lines
fed his machines quarters and dimes,
we didn't embrace for too long.
They were playing chess and moved us like pawns.

It was hard to speak truth with the father I loved.
They didn't only imprison his being,
they imprisoned our minds.
Together but separate
howling inside like mutts for reasons
hard to find.

———— ⊗⊗⊗ ————

I made a visit to another type of institution in the early fall of my return.
Lola, whose physical radiance still periodically burst into my dreams, had been
diagnosed with multiple sclerosis shortly after we went underground. Her
condition had deteriorated to the point that she was now living in a nursing
home. The team from Prairie Fire, which had helped Lola deal with her accelerating disease and her four kids, had fallen apart over time. Now, only one or two
people from the old group even visited her in the nursing home.

Some said that Lola bristled at any advice and was defensive about
efforts to help. Others explained that once her mother moved to the Bay Area
and took over caring for Lola, it was difficult for them to know how to plug in.
I could imagine how hard it must have been for her to cope with a debilitating
illness and at the same time deal with those who wanted to help her cope. Lola,
who saw her body as a means of liberatory self-expression, who celebrated the
pleasures of all the senses even when her comrades were counseling restraint;
Lola, who refused to face head-on life's minor, daily pains—either disdaining
them altogether or elevating them to the level of tragic, fatal flaws.

Everyone looked guilty when I asked them about the kids. Despite their efforts to assure me that the kids were all doing fine—at college, or working in various parts of the country—I couldn't believe the level of disassociation from Lola's kids. After all the love and energy our child care team had put into caring for these children, after our stated commitment to collective forms of parenting and responsibility, how could so many people have walked away? Except, like I had walked away. Each of us had individual reasons that served as justifications, but masked a larger collective failure all the same.

I was determined to see Lola, but it still took me two months after I returned to make the trip to her nursing home on the outskirts of Oakland. I went with Bonnie, the one person who had been visiting Lola every weekend. Bonnie warned me that she was much changed. The multiple sclerosis had begun to affect her brain and Lola went "in and out" of recognizing people. I was braced, but when I entered the room and saw her pale, bloated face staring up vacantly amidst the tangle of IV wires and stiff white bedding, my heart sank. Yet as soon as I said, "Hello," Lola lifted her head to look at me and excitedly exclaimed, "Diana!" For the next fifteen minutes our words commingled in a rush of memory. We talked about her kids, I told her about my kids, we summoned up anecdotes about Lorraine's magic experiments and Keith's hoop dreams.

I deliberately avoided any mention of the path my life had taken since I last saw her, but then suddenly out of some unpredictable recess, Lola spoke: "You turned out to be much more of an actress in the underground theater than even I was, Diana." Her familiar wry inflection immediately catapulted me into an era when we were constantly skirmishing over our distinct roles in the political arena. As in the past, I couldn't fathom whether her observation was made in admiration or resentment, or a messy mix of both. I turned away for an instant to reach for a glass of water before responding, and when I turned back she was lost. Her focus was gone and her eyes were closing. Bonnie, who had been sitting quietly in the room the whole time, suggested that her medication had probably knocked her out and it would be best if we left. She tried to comfort me. "It was amazing how much she remembered when she saw you," but it only made me feel more guilty for having been away for so long.

Lola died seven months later. Her funeral was held in New York where most of her relatives lived, but Bonnie and Lola's mother, Lillian, pulled together a memorial in a Berkeley park for friends in the Bay Area. People who had not seen Lola for several years came to the gathering, as well as two of her children who lived on the West coast. We went around in a circle, sharing memories, conjuring her presence through pictures and poems and anecdotes that said as much about each of us as they did about her. The amiability of the gathering was shattered when it came time for Lillian to speak. "Where were all of you fine friends when she was lying in the nursing home? Where were you when thirteen- year-old Lorraine was having to do the shopping, the cleaning, and the caretaking every day? It's all well and good that you are here now that she's gone, talking about your grand left politics, telling cute stories about my daughter, but where were you then?"

Some of us tried half-heartedly to answer her, to take responsibility, to apologize. Others silently dismissed her comments as grief-driven jibes. I was glad that Lillian had spit out the tension that had been hovering beneath the surface of the memorial, even if the truth of the matter was more complicated than her blunt denunciations. Perhaps this was a small failure in the framework of global revolutionary failure. But it pointed to contradictions that needed to be named and claimed. Our visions of revolutionary collectivity had been just, and we had tried many creative ways to embody those visions in our daily interactions and relationships. In some ways, we had made breakthroughs, but in many respects we had fallen dismally short. Unless we made an effort to examine and reflect on our failures, how could we honestly hand down our positive legacy? How could we ever look Lola's children in the eyes and hope to become their friends once again?

After the memorial, some of us were able to open up conversations with Lola's children about our shared history. It had been impossibly confusing and painful for them when the adults they had relied on had drifted away, one after the other. It was difficult not to label us as hypocrites, and for awhile they blamed our political fervor, which seemed to supersede our personal responsibilities. Yet now, as young adults who were balancing their own personal and political commitments, they no longer wanted to deny their good memories of the childcare team. They didn't want to negate with cynicism the revolutionary ideals their mother had nurtured in them. Our willingness to be accountable unfroze some of their resentments and allowed us to begin constructing new relationships on a different basis.

I still carry in my mind's eye a photo I took of the five of them playing in the garden behind the ramshackle house in the Haight. Sometimes, I can forget all that ensued and simply remember how happy it made me to share breakfast in the nook each morning for the year I lived with them. But the present has trumped nostalgic yearnings. Over the years, it has been a better joy to witness the growth of these children who now are writers, filmmakers, historians and actors, all trying to engage the complexities of the current world through their creative political expression. I recognize Lola's spirit living in each of them.

California Coalition for Women Prisoners collage. Top—Ericka and Zoe with CCWP banner at a demonstration in front of FCI Dublin. Bottom—CCWP logo.

THE FIRE INSIDE

Last time I walked these streets,
I could have picked up the phone
and called any one of you –
whether I did or not,
I could have
without knowing
if I was on your phone list,
without worrying when
the fifteen minute phone limit
would click your voices shut.
I could have sat with you
in a San Francisco, New York, or Chicago
coffee house and planned
freedom for all political prisoners
and I wouldn't have been talking
about you in the third person...

—Poem to the sisters inside FCI Dublin,

December 1995

DONNA WAS IN FCI DUBLIN, forty minutes away from San Francisco. The kids and I began to visit her shortly after our first visit with Claude. Walking into the Dublin visiting room was like entering a vault filled with icons. The faces I had kept in a secret album in my head for years kept popping up at various tables across the room. In July 1995, Dublin held eight women political prisoners, the largest aggregation of political prisoners in one location in the United States. Dylcia Pagán, Carmen Valentín, Alicia Rodriguez, and Lucy Rodriguez were all part of the original FALN 11 whose 15 year of incarceration we had just marked in Chicago. Linda Evans, Marilyn Buck and Laura Whitehorn were all codefendants in the Resistance Conspiracy case in which they, along with Susan Rosenberg, Tim Blunk, Silvia Baraldini, and Alan Berkman, had been charged with targeting various government and military installations, including the bombing of the U.S. Capitol in 1983 to protest the U.S. invasion of Grenada.

Of course, I knew that all of these women were at Dublin before we went to visit Donna, but I hadn't expected to see so many of these sisters at once, in such close proximity within the small prison visiting room. I hadn't expected to be able to touch each one in the brief hugs of greeting that we were momentarily permitted before they were interrupted by the bark of one of the guards. I hadn't anticipated the palpable aura of their collective presence that rose above the physical separation between tables and subverted the prison rules which forbade "cross- visiting." I hadn't imagined how close I would immediately feel to each woman, even though I hardly knew any of them on a personal level.

After that first visit to Dublin, I knew that I needed to connect on a deeper basis with some of these women whose histories were so intricately linked to my own. I started by visiting Laura Whitehorn.[1] I had known and worked with Laura in the past. She was in Boston at the founding conference of Prairie Fire, part of the group of women who vehemently proclaimed the importance of lesbian visibility and leadership within the organization. She was in Vermont at the first struggle-filled meeting of the PFOC National Committee, and she was in Chicago for the upheavals of the Hard Times Conference. I saw her briefly in New York City during the anger-laden period of rectification and the break up of the Weather Underground. She had later gone underground herself and, in May 1985, I was badly shaken when I read the news of her arrest, sitting in the kitchen of our house in Los Angeles. I lost track of her case in the frenzied period after our escape and only intermittently got scraps of information about her.

In 1992, in the stacks of the University of Pittsburgh library, I found a copy of the book *Hauling Up the Morning,* which contained writings and art by U.S. political prisoners.[2] Looking through the book, I began to cry when I came upon a picture that Laura had drawn in prison. It showed a woman in a black and white patterned keffiyah patiently stitching a Palestinian flag. It was titled "Scene from the Intifada." This was the hidden, woman's side of the Intifada that was rarely depicted on TV or in the newspapers. It also reflected a different side of Laura than the one I had known in our harried meetings together.

My relationship with Laura had never been particularly personal. We had intersected in the framework of meetings and debates and scenarios, where we had little chance or even desire to relate specifically to each other. But now Laura was living in a caged space within easy driving distance of my house in San Francisco. There was no excuse for not connecting this time around.

Our first visit wasn't easy. While we didn't have very much personal history to review, we had reams of shared political history to pick apart. We had often been on opposite sides of fierce political debates, and for an hour or two it seemed like we might sink back into the quagmire of those old divisions. But at some unmarked moment, our energy shifted. Maybe it was the child of another prisoner sitting at the table next to ours who tripped and fell as she was running over to the vending machines. Both of us simultaneously rushed to help. Maybe it was the stories that Laura then began to tell me about the dozens of women friends she had made inside over the past ten years. She talked about their pain at grappling with loss of their kids; the terrible, stigmatized treatment they suffered if they were living with HIV and AIDS; the unremitting racist treatment that Black and Brown women were subjected to. Then I began to talk to her about Tony and Leila and how hard it was to deal with their confused grief about their father in prison. I told her how mixed up I felt about the current political landscape which seemed so different from the one we had been part of in the sixties and seventies. When our conversation finally returned to the issues we had been arguing about, the polarizations had receded into the past.

Over the next few years, Laura and I had discussions which ranged from the history of Prairie Fire and the Weather Underground to the dissolution

of the Soviet bloc and the strengths and weaknesses of the U.S. women's movement. We still disagreed about certain points, but we began to look to each other
as friends and political allies who were both committed to developing a relevant
framework for building work in the present. I brought Tony and Leila to visit
Laura and these visits were filled with eating and Scrabble, Yatzee and laughing
fun. Laura's playful energy enabled all of us to get beyond the stiff, stale visiting
room setting, and I carried some of that energy back outside with me when I left
the prison.

It wasn't only Laura's spirit that heartened me on my visits to Dublin.
When I visited Donna or Laura, I would always stop and chat for a few minutes with Alicia, Marilyn, or one of the others. I was introduced to women that
they were close to—Hamdiya and Danielle. The words that we exchanged were
sometimes no more than "how are you," but they were said with an inflection
of care that made me feel that we each truly understood the complex difficulties and sturdy determination that underlay our monosyllabic answers: "I'm
fine, fine!" I looked forward to the monthly visits; connecting with these women
anchored me in a way that people on the outside couldn't do at this particular
stage of my life.

Superficially, my life had begun to assume the same normalized con-
tours as those of my friends. Our relative privilege and the support we received
had allowed me to resume a viable life. I went to work; I took my kids to school,
to baseball games, and to playgroup; I did grocery shopping and cleaning; and
I squeezed in one or two meetings on week night evenings, and often an event
on the weekend. But inside I was driven by constant self-interrogation. What
should I be doing politically at this time? What would be most effective, given
the choices, given who I was? Was there any way to apply everything that I felt
I had learned from our history that didn't sound like a didactic lesson spouted
from an anachronistic past? These weren't just questions of philosophy or ideology. They were central to reconstructing my identity. I had considered myself a
revolutionary for the past twenty years. Now, the concept had been co-opted by
the advertising industry where everything from coca cola to a new hair product

was billed as "revolutionary"; or it had been flattened into the more conventional term of "activist" which encompassed all people who on some level tried to bring about social change. In this climate, the term revolutionary seemed grandiose and out-of-place and I could no longer use it, even in the privacy of my own mind. Activist seemed more appropriate, but it didn't get to the essence of how I saw myself.

When I went to Dublin, I knew that the women I visited were grappling with similar questions and dilemmas. They were removed not only from the era in which they had developed their political identities, but also from the physical communities that had nurtured those identities. When I came to visit, they barraged me with questions about what was going on. What was being done in the Bay Area to support the amnesty campaign for the Puerto Ricans? How was the work going with *Sparks Fly*, an annual cultural/educational event in the Bay Area that focused on the women political prisoners and raised money for their commissary needs. How could they as political prisoners best contribute to the campaign to stop Mumia Abu-Jamal from being executed? This last question took on the greatest urgency since, on June 1, 1995, Governor Tom Ridge of Pennsylvania had signed the death warrant for this brilliant Black leader.[3]

I hadn't known anything about Mumia when we were underground, even though he was facing execution on Pennyslvania's death row, the state that we were living in. Shortly after I arrived in Chicago, I attended an educational event about his case, where I learned how Mumia had begun his political involvement as the Minister of Information for the Black Panther Party at the age of fifteen. Mumia went on to become a prominent radio journalist in his hometown of Philadelphia, exposing the brutality of the Philadelphia police toward the Black community and the MOVE organization with which he was involved.[4] The Philadelphia police hated Mumia for calling them out. In 1981, he was framed for the murder of a Philadelphia police officer. His case was railroaded through the courts in a trial that relied on fabricated evidence, the disappearance of witnesses, and a racist judge. Judge Sabo was known as the "Hanging Judge" because he had sentenced more people to death than any other judge in the United States and the majority of those sentenced were Black and Latino.

Mumia had already been sitting on death row for three years when the city of Philadelphia bombed the MOVE organization on May 11, 1985, two weeks before I gave birth to Tony. The city killed eleven adults and children, but they didn't succeed in annihilating MOVE or in burying Mumia alive. Over time, MOVE and other organizations regrouped and began to build a movement to free Mumia. A legal team was pulled together to develop a strategy to overturn Mumia's conviction and The Prison Radio project began audiotaping Mumia's commentaries, "Live From Death Row."[5] Mumia's deep, sonorous voice began to be heard regularly on progressive radio shows, incisively analyzing every aspect of American society and especially its gulags: "Across a nation that claims to be the 'Land of the Free,' over a million souls sleep tonight in cages, consigned there by an improper process, kept there by political expediency, and destined to do so tomorrow because of the willing blindness of a sated and jaded citizenry…And the gulags continue to swell. *From Death Row, this is Mumia Abu-Jamal.*" [6]

Shortly after we moved back to San Francisco, in the wake of the recently announced execution date, Tony, Leila, and I went to a demonstration where thousands of people took over the streets of Oakland to protest this imminent threat to Mumia's life. Similar demonstrations occurred around the world. Political prisoners in Germany initiated a hunger strike for three days in solidarity with Mumia, and the strike was taken up by prisoners in Bolivia, Peru, France, and the United States. The power of the grassroots movement and the hard work of the legal team prevented the execution from happening on the proposed date. But everyone knew that the date had merely been postponed.

Political prisoner Alan Berkman[7] had met Mumia at Holmesburg Prison in Pennsylvania, where Mumia had helped to take care of him when Alan was undergoing cancer treatment. Alan spread the word about Mumia, and soon political prisoners across the country became convinced of the strategic priority of Mumia's case. They created an art show in solidarity with Mumia called "Art Against the Death Penalty," which premiered in New York City in December 1994. Over ninety political prisoners from different parts of the globe produced

drawings, paintings, sculpture, textiles, and poetry in order to educate about
Mumia and other political prisoners, and raise funds for Mumia's legal defense.
For the exhibition brochure, Mumia wrote:

> What is that old Latin saying? *Vita breva ars longa...*
> Life is brief, but art lasts. Like many of those dusty old say-
> ings, it has a good deal of truth. Art, by its very nature, is
> Against Death, ain't it? So the works that light up this exhibi-
> tion against the state's deadly designs are truly works of life, of
> resistance, of love.[8]

The Mumia Art Show had not yet been shown in the Bay Area and
the women at Dublin were eager to find outside collaborators who could help
bring the show to the Bay. Every time I visited, one woman or another would
mention the Art Show to me. I loved the concept of the show, especially since
we could use it to spotlight the artistry and vision of women political prisoners
if we held it in the Bay Area. But for months I couldn't figure out how I could
help initiate this event. Then Miranda Bergman, an extraordinary political artist
(who also was a dedicated friend and visitor of Marilyn Buck's), agreed to be the
curator, and her commitment to the project became the basis for pulling a group
together.

I had known Miranda since the seventies. We had worked together in
the early efforts to form a Women's Union, and we had been part of the same
Venceremos Brigade in 1977. During the years that I was gone, Miranda's
handprint became visible in murals all over San Francisco. Her work was part
of a mural movement, catalyzed by local Latino artists, which illuminated empty
walls of buildings with powerful representations of people's history, insisting
that San Francisco was still an active locale of resistance and international solidarity.

When I first returned to San Francisco, I was amazed to see the faces
of Marilyn Buck, Alejandrina Torres, Dylcia Pagán, Susan Rosenberg, Merle
Austin Africa, and Norma Jean Croy[9] proudly looking out from the façade of

The Women's Building in the Mission. The last time I had seen the Women's Building, which opened in 1979, its dingy exterior had given no indication of its liberatory mission or its place in history as the first women-owned building in the country. In 1994, Miranda and other muralistas[10] had transformed the walls of the Women's Building with their stunning "Maestrapeace" mural, a panoramic tribute to women's contributions and resistance that made the women political prisoners publically visible to all.

A dozen women (including myself) came together to form the "Mumia Art Show Women's Group," which collaborated with the women at Dublin to plan the exhibition. We found a venue at New College of California, gathered additional works from local artists, and planned a grand opening, as well as many smaller educational events. Laura designed a striking collage out of postage stamps that we used to publicize the show. People who had not worked together for years reconciled, argued, and reconciled again. Miranda was hanging art up until a few hours before the official opening on February 2, 1997. The Art Show was a great success. Crowds packed the opening event which featured ex-Black Liberation Army political prisoner Safiya Bukhari from New York, and we raised thousands of dollars for Mumia.[11]

For myself, it made me very happy to be able to work with the compañeras at Dublin, unleashing the power of their art "to defeat the state's deadly designs."

In March 1996, the recently formed California Coalition for Women Prisoners (CCWP) held an International Women's Day event in the Women's Building.[12] Karen had been one of the founding members of this group, together with women from the state prisons in Chowchilla who were plaintiffs in a class action lawsuit against the state of California for its failure to provide basic health care to the prisoners.[13] CCWP was created to build grassroots activism and mobilize people to fight beyond the courtroom. This was CCWP's first public event and Angela Davis was the keynote speaker. Hundreds of people poured into the

Women's Building to hear her speak, cramming the auditorium and spilling out into the lobby, far beyond the organizers' expectations.

Angela Davis was intricately tied to the history of the radical prison movement in California. I first heard her name when she was charged with conspiracy to commit murder in the Marin County Court House uprising of August 1970. Angela went underground and gained immediate notoriety when she was put on the *Ten Most Wanted* list. She was captured in New York City after a couple of months and extradited to California. Her trial became a focal point of political activity for the Communist Party USA (of which Angela was a member), as well as for many sectors of the left and the Black community.[14]

While she was in jail awaiting trial, Angela edited a book of essays by political prisoners titled *If They Come In The Morning*. In his introduction to the book, James Baldwin wrote "We must fight for your life as though it were our own—which it is—and render impassable with our bodies the corridor to the gas chamber. For if they take you in the morning, they will be coming for us that night."[15] George Jackson was murdered while she was in prison, and Angela's dedication to the book read "To all who have fallen in the liberation struggle... Now also for George, who fiercely resisted to the very end...Though his keepers sought to destroy him, George lives on, an example and inspiration for us all."[16]

Angela was acquitted of all charges in 1972, after a trial that lasted thirteen weeks. The case and her book had helped to shape national consciousness about the role of political prisoners within the movement. Although I had read other books by her since that time, I had lost track of her political work after the seventies and only knew that she was the chair of the History of Consciousness program at the University of California, Santa Cruz. Like the hundreds of other people at the event, I was very eager to hear what she would have to say about women prisoners, twenty-four years after her own incarceration.

Angela made a compelling speech, which was amplified by the comments of the CCWP organizers. Women had become the fastest growing sector of the prison population and California had the largest women's prisons in the world. The majority of women prisoners were Black and Brown, torn from the same oppressed communities as the ever increasing number of male prisoners.

When women were incarcerated, the impact rippled destructively throughout their communities, fracturing families, disorienting children, and further
destroying the fabric of life that was essential for preserving continuity and
resistance. Inside the prisons, women were subject to an array of institutional-
ized abuses, and sexual abuse had become incorporated as a central component
of their punishment. Gender structured the entire prison system, yet women
prisoners and their experiences were being left out of the public discourse about
prisons, and were also largely ignored by prison justice activists.

At the end of the event, many women signed up to become involved
with the California Coalition for Women Prisoners, and I was one of them.
CCWP took off after the International Women's Day event. The large meetings
we held every couple of weeks included women from a range of backgrounds,
experiences and motivations. There were former prisoners who were looking for
a way to advocate for the sisters they had left behind; there were radical activists
who saw women prisoners as a focal point for feminist anti-racist organizing;
and there were women who were new to politics but had been moved by the
description of abuse and wanted to help in some way. We wanted to build an organization that took direction from the women inside and offered a place where
former prisoners and women of color could develop their leadership. We wanted
to fight the racism that was central to the prison system. We wanted CCWP to
become a community as well as an organization. La Tonya, a former prisoner,
came up with a slogan to express this sensibility—*CCWP /Caring Collectively for
Women Prisoners*.

We organized visiting teams to go into the prisons on a regular basis
to meet with women and develop legal advocacy strategies based upon their
experiences with the prison system. Every visit was emotional, educational, and
galvanizing. When a visiting team walked through the multiple locking gates and
heard them click shut, when we looked up and realized that we too were encased
by miles of barbed wire fences, we got a tiny inkling of what it meant to be cut off
from the rest of the world under the daily, arbitrary control of men and women
with guns. Once we were in the visiting room, sitting face-to-face with a woman
who had a life sentence, or another who was anticipating her release in just a few

months, a small miracle occurred. A spark unlocked our voices. The gates and barbed wire receded for a few hours while we talked about the children they had left behind, the girlfriends they had found in prison, and the dreams and hopes they nurtured for the future. Our conversations usually began with the enormous difficulties of their lives inside, but they branched out to encompass our lives and dreams and hopes as well.

Some of the women carried an enormous weight of guilt about the offenses they had committed. Others told how they were railroaded through the system for so-called crimes that they never had committed, or which their boyfriends blamed on them. Many told about the racism of the guards and staff. All of them told about the horrors of the medical care system—the denial of services; the accusations that they were drug-seekers or were making up their symptoms in order to get out of work; the women who died because they couldn't even get an appointment to see a doctor. They weren't being treated like human beings, and they wanted to do something to make things change.

We needed to share these stories with the world outside. Together we decided to start a newsletter which would have articles from both the inside and the outside. We were debating what to name the newsletter when Dana, a former prisoner, suggested, *The Fire Inside.* It clicked. Not only would the newsletter be a vehicle for popular education, it would also nurture the fire of creativity and the resistance of women prisoners.

The first issue of *The Fire Inside* came out in the fall of 1996. It was dedicated to Joann Walker, an HIV-positive prisoner who had led the establishment of an HIV peer educator program at CCWF, and who continued to fight for basic medical treatment for incarcerated women with HIV/AIDS until her death in 1994. Joann wrote, "The system here is set up to oppress, depress, and stress out any incarcerated woman who wishes to fight back with a pen instead of her fist. I write all day long if need be." [17]

Over the years, The Fire Inside *has offered a space for narrative, education, philosophy, and art.* [18] *It has challenged the state's attempt to disappear prisoners behind an enveloping, deceitful cloak of criminality by revealing the human, social reality of the people caged inside. I have been honored to be part of this collective creative expression, which has sought not only to describe oppressive conditions but to transform them from the inside out.*

"Doña Isabel: The Unredeemed Homeland" (color pencil and pastel on paper) by Oscar Lopez Rivera, political prisoner. Doña Isabel Rosado was a Puerto Rican Nationalist leader who served more than a decade in prison and was active in the struggle in Vieques. www.boricuahumanrights.org.

CAN'T JAIL THE SPIRIT

SEPTEMBER 19, 1997 WAS OUR FIFTEENTH ANNIVERSARY. When Claude first went to prison, our relationship had been riddled with so many tensions, so many unsolvable questions, and so few moments of simple pleasure that it was difficult for me to imagine a future together. In our new San Francisco life, I liked living with the children in a house with other women, a welcome communal antidote to the years the four of us had spent as a nuclear family unit. And I loved meeting and working with radical queer people, most of whom were twenty years younger than me. They made me forget, sometimes, the decade divide between then and now. They provoked the question —was I meant to remain in a heterosexual relationship now that I had returned?

But over time, the relationships in our new household became strained, and I remembered that communal living, even in the seventies, had never been that easy. My fantasies about other relationship possibilities remained abstract and fleeting, while the long distance effort that Claude and I were making to rebuild our relationship was beginning to shift our frayed dynamic.

Every few months, I would go up to Sheridan to visit Claude by myself. During these special visits, we would forget the vending machines and ignore the barking of the loudspeaker. We would talk for hours, hardly even fidgeting in the hard plastic seats. We talked about what was happening with each of us; we tried to figure out what was really going on with the kids. We worked to untangle our unspoken resentments and dysfunctional habits, and to solidify the bonds that had always drawn us close. Between those weekends, separated from each other for months at a time, my feelings percolated beneath my daily preoccupations, and I began to envision a future with Claude.

In the beginning of September, Jody and Karen held a party to mark *their* twenty-fifth anniversary. It was an amazing occasion, a resounding affirmation of their love and partnership, sustained against all odds. When I first met them in 1973, they had just celebrated their first anniversary together. Since then, Karen and Jody had been a constant part of my life. After my second glass of wine, random memories drifted up—marching militantly through downtown San Francisco in support of Inez Garcia; arguing in our women's study group about feminism and Prairie Fire; rallying through the confusion and fear after the arrests in Houston; strategizing, analyzing, and finally deciding that we needed to go underground, that we could take on this project together.

In their words of welcome to the assembled group, Karen and Jody talked about their happiness at being able to celebrate this day amidst all of their old and new friends. They were no longer in hiding, no longer in isolation. Donna was now out of prison. Ericka, Zoe, Leila, and Tony were present along with all the other children who were part of their community. Except that part of their family, Claude, was still behind bars.

On the way back from the party, as we drove north on Highway One, a tiny sliver of sun spread a huge red aura on our left. Fifteen years before I had driven this same highway with Claude after a day together at the beach. Before Karen and Jody's party, I hadn't thought about *our* anniversary, hadn't registered the weight of fifteen years for Claude and me. Now, I remembered the nervous, confusing days leading up to our decision to sleep together—all the unspoken questions about how much of our attraction was determined by our constricted circumstances and what would happen, given these circumstances, if it didn't work out. Yet, once we allowed desire and hope to overcome our worries, once we made the irreversible leap and became lovers, the churning receded and we forgot the questions. For a while, we even put aside the many contradictions of our political project as we took days off to go to the beach, lie in the perfect September sun, and fall in love. That was a long time ago, and political decisions and their consequences seemed to dominate the trajectory of our relationship for most of the years since, making it difficult to discern the arc of love within it all.

That night, I wrote Claude a poem which sharpened my desire to make our relationship go forward.

To Claude in prison—
***Our* Fifteen Years**

Have I ever told you –
really told you
thru all the meandered tellings
of our fifteen odd years –
how I looked over
at you
one hot salt lake evening,
framed by the sunset
glowing thru our motel window
standing by your separate twin bed
(us two comrades sharing a room
on a political work trip)
and there it was,
the spark.
After all those years
of knowing you
in a different way,
after all those years
of my loving
in a different way,
I couldn't deny it,
you looked wonderful
framed in flames.
And just then it occurred to me –
why not
let something so possible,

so logical,
so desirable,
happen
amidst so much
that was none of the above.
Why not?

And so it happened,
not that night, but soon,
and for many years
you were one of the things
that made our life there
seem possible, semi-logical,
even if not desirable.

Now, fifteen years later
I watch you walk
thru the locked door,
framed by bars
but head up,
and you look wonderful!
In this place where nada
is logical
and not much is possible
you still are desirable.
So why not?
It will be worth the wait.

Feeling like I'm on a treadmill—lists, lists, and more
lists with no break in sight: events, files, parties, cards, letters,
phone calls, homework, visits all arrayed in random frenzy
in front, around, behind me and I cannot back off. My legs
ache, my back aches, my hips ache—I feel the accumulation of
stress lodged in each of those proliferating sore areas. My new
chiropractor asks, "So have you been under any stress?" and I
want to let loose in torrential sobs, *"yes, yes, yes!"* and hurl the
endless list of stress in her face. But instead I just say, "I guess
so" and remain in the closet with my particular set of stressors.
All the way home I promise myself that at least I have to make
time to put a few notes in my journal. At least I have to mark
the passage of the stages of return—from liberatory to coping;
from exhilarating rhythm and motion to stuck stiffness and
senseless schedules. (Journal entry, fall 1997)

I decided that the kids and I needed to move out of the communal
household where we had lived for the two years since our return to San Francisco. I wanted to get our own apartment, just the three of us, even though it meant
adding increased rent, cleaning, and childcare responsibilities to my already
full plate. But once we moved, being on our own somehow compensated for all
the rest. The apartment I found was kind of funky, but it was cheap enough and
had three small bedrooms so Tony and Leila no longer had to cram their very
distinct lives into one overcrowded space.

Now Tony could finally take out the books and baseball trophies that
had remained in boxes since we left Pittsburgh. I could hang out with him in
his new room after Leila went to bed and listen when he opened up. "I always
think—how could this all happen to me? Why me? I'm one in a million, billion
who grew up like this... And what if they had caught you all? What would have
happened to you? What would have happened to me and Leila?"

Leila settled gladly into her room, immediately arranging with fastidi-
ous organization her clothes, her books, her stuffed animals. In her new space,

she could play by herself or with friends for hours. Except at night, when her worries crept out. "I think I worry more than anyone in the world...I try to make my mind stop worrying but it won't...I worry that daddy is going to be in jail for as long as Mumia." I tell her, "No, he's getting out next July," then realize that for her it might as well be a thousand years away.

At school, Leila happily showed her teachers the scrapbooks filled with pictures of animals and vibrant African designs Claude periodically sent her. I was grateful that the teachers and families at Buena Vista made it so easy for her to be open about a father in prison. Tony, in contrast, only told a couple of special teachers at his middle school about Claude, reluctant to divulge any information about this charged subject. Yet he didn't hesitate to take every opportunity to include Mumia or Leonard Peltier in his poems or reports for school.

One evening Tony came to me with a question for a homework project. "What is our family's culture?" In the past, I had answered similar questions by saying our background was Jewish, but since we didn't celebrate Jewish holidays or even follow any Jewish customs, this was no longer enough for him. So, I tried to explain what I really felt: how the New Year's parties dedicated to women political prisoners, the El Grito de Lares commemorations, the Native sunrise ceremonies at Alcatraz, the Mission District Day of the Dead gatherings, the rallies at the gates of Dublin, the Mumia Art Show, and annual International Women's Day celebrations were all part of a culture of resistance that nourished my spirit and linked us with people who were struggling for justice around the world. As he and Leila got older, they could choose other forms of cultural or even religious expression if they wanted, but these were the traditions I had to share with them now. Tony listened closely. "Okay, but I can't put that in my homework," he said as he walked off to figure out what version of truth he wanted to represent for school.

That same year, when Leila was six, I took her to an International Women's Day event at the Yerba Buena Center for the Arts in downtown San Francisco. I remembered our IWD events in the seventies as marches and speeches sprinkled with musical interludes, dominated by white women. This IWD was entirely different. It focused on confronting violence against women through an amazing, synchronistic mélange of karate, dance, theater, spoken word, and drumming. The young women who had come together to create the event were almost all Black and Brown, and included queer people in drag as well. There were no speeches. Instead, the power and potential of young women of color exploded around us. Leila was transfixed.

When I was putting her to bed after the event, Leila told me she had a poem she needed to tell me. The words streamed from her:

> *I see women*
> *dressed all in white*
> *with words in yellow*
> *down their back,*
> *orange fire*
> *down their front,*
> *and colored fabric in their hair.*
> *They're getting ready to fight*
> *in their high heels.*

She repeated the poem a couple of times, changing a few words, and then we wrote it down so she could bring it to school to show her teacher.

In my dreams that night, gorgeous young women kicked and danced and embraced in an erotic, fierce, flowing *kata*. Suddenly, the stage where they were performing turned into a video screen and, as I watched, I was elated to see myself and Leila moving together in the midst of them all.

1998 was a freedom-bound year. While we were anxiously waiting for Claude to be released in July, I was working on the Jericho 98 national mobilization to demand freedom for all political prisoners held in the U.S. 1998 marked the hundred-year anniversary of the U.S. conquest of Puerto Rico and Hawaii,

and Jalil Muntaqim had put out a call to organize Jericho 98 to reinvigorate the
effort to win the release of political prisoners, appropriately placing them in
the framework of anti-colonial struggle. As Jalil explained in his call for Jericho
98: "The United States does not recognize the existence of political prisoners.
To do so would.... legitimize the existence of not only the individuals who are
incarcerated or have been captured but also those movements of which they are
a part."[1]

I knew Jalil from his time at San Quentin as a charismatic young
organizer of prisoners and their allies outside. Jalil had pushed and prodded, inspired and infatuated the young men and women of Prairie Fire who visited him
on a regular basis. He started the revolutionary prisoner journal *Arm the Spirit,*
which Prairie Fire helped publish for several years, and he launched the August
21st Coalition and the first Black August demonstration in front of San Quentin.

Jalil was 19 years old when he was arrested in August 1971 and charged
with the attempt to assassinate police officers, allegedly in response to George
Jackson's murder. He hadn't seen a day out of prison ever since. Yet his political energy and organizing initiative had continued unabated for all those years.
In 1997, he and Safiya Bukhari (a former political prisoner herself) developed
the proposal for Jericho 98, and in response Jericho committees began to form
around the country.

When Safiya came to speak at the Mumia Art Show, she raised the
idea of the Jericho mobilization. Fighting for the release of individual prisoners
within the confines of the legal system had won some victories, as in the cases
of Dhoruba Bin Wahad and Geronimo Ji Jaga Pratt[2] who were able to demonstrate, after decades of incarceration, that their convictions were due to the FBI's
COINTELPRO program. But there needed to be a movement that raised the
demand for collective amnesty based on international law which recognized
freedom fighters in anti-colonial struggles. From Ireland to South Africa, governments had been pushed to grant amnesty to political prisoners because of the
political nature of their cases. Jericho would build on this history and counter
the U.S. strategy of criminalizing all acts of resistance by reasserting the historic
role of the prisoners within their liberation movements.

The concept of Jericho was exciting to me. I wanted to place the day-to-day work I was doing with women prisoners in a broader framework. There was a direct link between the freedom movements of the sixties and seventies and the mass incarceration boom of the eighties and nineties that was warehousing ever increasing numbers of Black and Brown women and men. The older generation of Third World political leaders had paid for their militant resistance by being incarcerated in America's dungeons ever since. Now the younger generation was being bombarded by multiple strategies—drugs, police brutality, internal violence, failing schools—which demobilized them and tracked them into the prison system before they could even become socially conscious. Some hip hop artists gave props to Mumia, Leonard, and Assata, but for the most part the names of most of the political prisoners were unknown to the youth coming up. Safiya argued that in order to rebuild, the movement had to fight for its leaders in prison. "We need to build a strong movement that says to our youth…if you join this fight you will not be left alone to rot in prison. We will stand by you, we will fight for you, we will Free you! This is a wall to wall struggle!"[3]

Jericho's vision was strong, but implementing it was not an easy process. In the Bay Area, political debates about the definition of a political prisoner and the role of armed resistance immediately threatened to derail the committee. Personality conflicts among older generation activists who had worked together in the sixties and seventies flared up. Some individuals seemed determined to disrupt this fledgling group, fanning each disagreement into a boiling point of principle and attacking people instead of debating ideas. It shouldn't have been surprising, after my experience with the Puerto Rican community in Chicago, that Jericho was targeted from its founding, but it still was very disturbing to me and other members of the committee.

Fortunately, there was a critical mass of older and younger folks who were sufficiently dedicated to the project to stick with it and see it through. The leadership of Muhjah Shakir, Jericho's regional coordinator on the West Coast, was critical in sustaining the momentum.[4] Young Black and Latino youth from the Malcolm X Grassroots Movement and the Comité 98 brought unifying energy to the work, which helped keep the committee on track.[5]

On March 27, 1998, Jericho mobilized 5,000 people from many parts of the country to a day-long rally in Washington D.C. In the Bay Area, hundreds joined a march which brought the spirit of the political prisoners into the streets of Oakland—"Mumia esta presente! Oscar esta presente! Marilyn esta presente!" we chanted. And for those who didn't know who Mumia, Oscar, Marilyn, and the others were, we had a book filled with the biographies and pictures of U.S. political prisoners.

The fourth edition of *Can't Jail the Spirit* had been produced specifically for Jericho 98. In the forward, the editors explained, "The first edition of this book was produced in 1988 as a photocopied set of pages. Several of us in Chicago…had grown tired of the denials that there were no political prisoners. What better remedy to this, we thought, than to assemble the stories and photographs of these prisoners? If political prisoners did not exist, then who were these people?"[6]

It was a little eerie to see Claude's picture and story included in this edition, especially since he would be coming out in a few months. But I was glad that he had been able to contribute to the book. In his section, Claude wrote about the work he had done as a radio reporter and producer at KPFA in the sixties "exposing listeners to revolutionary voices ranging from Ho Chi Minh to George Jackson to Assata Shakur."[7] I knew that one of his dreams for the future was to be able to continue this work, using audio archives to educate about peoples' history that otherwise would be forgotten. Like many prison dreams, it was hard to know whether he would be able to transform this one into a reality once he got out. Claude closed his piece with a poem by Ho Chi Minh:

"My legs are tied with a rope, and my arms are bound at my side, but I smell the sweet perfume of woodland flowers and hear the birds. Impossible to keep these from me. Anyhow, now the road is not so long, and I am not alone."[8]

In June, a month before Claude was due to come home, Theresa Roxanne Cruz, a prisoner I had been working with, was unexpectedly released on bail after a judge overturned her conviction upon appeal. CCWP had started working on Theresa Cruz's case in 1996 after we read a letter from her children on the internet:

> Our names are Andrea, Antoinette, Carlitos, and Adriana (6 years old). We are children who are victims of Domestic Violence and suffer pain and terror too. We pray you will take time to read what we have to say:...Carlitos, 12—Our mother is a Battered Woman, serving a life-sentence at Frontera Prison. In 1991, our mother was sent to prison for Attempted Murder. My father was shot in the legs ,but my father is not crippled, maimed or dead. His life has continued while ours has been hurt and destroyed. Our mother moved five times in three years, my father beat her, stalked her and robbed her over and over again, and then made her believe that he was going to take me away from her and she would never ever see me again. This was not only a crime to us children, it was a tragedy.

I was immediately struck by the story and also by the involvement of Theresa's children in the fight for her release. CCWP contacted Theresa's mother, Theresa Azochar, and after learning more details of the case, we decided to join the effort to win her release.

Theresa Azochar was filled with a simmering anger. Theresa had wanted Roxanne (the name her family used for Theresa Cruz) to leave her boyfriend as soon as she found out about his abusive behavior and his encouragement of Roxanne's drug use. But when Roxanne finally left him, things only got worse. He stalked her, sent her obscene and violent messages, and finally initiated a custody suit to take their son, Carlitos, away from her. By then, Roxanne, was heavily medicated on prescription Xanax for depression and anxiety. One night before a scheduled custody hearing, she sat outside in a parked car while some friends of hers went to confront her ex. They ended up shooting him in the legs.

Four days later, while Roxanne and Carlitos were sitting in their car eating a Happy Meal, the police surrounded them and arrested her.

Initially Roxanne was charged with assault but the charge was later changed to conspiracy to commit murder, even though her ex recovered fully after the shooting. It was at this point that Theresa Azochar began to see that the legal system was stacked against her daughter. She sat through the trial in confusion, wondering at many points which side their lawyer really was on, since he failed to obtain copies of important transcripts, allowed the mother of a prosecuting attorney to sit on the jury, slept through much of the trial proceedings, and advised Roxanne against taking a deal where the maximum sentence would have been ten years because he thought she would get off with just probation. The Judge summarily dismissed any effort on the part of the lawyer to introduce evidence of the repeated abuse that had taken place prior to the shooting. Although this was a first offense, Roxanne ended up with a sentence of twenty-five years to life (later reduced to seven to life on appeal). Carlitos, who she had been struggling to protect, was sent to live with her abuser.

When I first heard the full story, I was shocked. I knew the criminal legal system was fundamentally unjust, but I still had little knowledge of the blatantly discriminatory practices that railroaded Brown and Black women and men to prison every day in California's courtrooms. The cases of battered women who resisted their abusers exposed the court's double standard regarding the constitutional right to self-defense.

I remembered the groundbreaking work that had been done in the seventies to support the right of women like Inez Garcia, Joanne Walker, and Dessie Woods to resist rape.[9] In CCWP, we hoped that Theresa Cruz's case could become a similar rallying point for the women's prison movement.

Over the next couple of years CCWP, Roxanne's family and her supporters held speak outs and rallies, appeared on TV talk shows, lobbied legislators in Sacramento, and wrote endless letters to the Parole Board and Governor to build support for her release. I visited Roxanne at CIW and came to know her kids and other members of the family when I stayed at their house in San Diego.

Adriana was Roxanne's youngest, born just before Roxanne was convicted and sent to prison. She only knew her mother through prison visits. Adriana's poems and letters were a poignant indictment of the system that kept her separated from her mother. In one letter to the Governor she wrote: "I wish I was a bird so I could fly to her prison and put my mommy on my wings and bring her home to us."[10]

Then the impossible seemed to happen. Roxanne's conviction was overturned by a federal judge because of the legal incompetence involved in the original trial. Another judge granted her bail, and I made plans to go down to San Diego to see her. The day before my scheduled visit, only sixteen days after she had been released, Roxanne's bail was revoked. The prosecutor had won an appeal of the bail claiming that she posed a danger to the "victim." Roxanne would have to turn herself in within the next couple of days.

I hadn't planned on spending Roxanne's last day of freedom with her and her family, but they all insisted that I come anyway, so I did. Roxanne looked beautiful in a flowering summer dress, and all four children took turns holding her hands, combing her hair, and vying for her attention. Andrea and Antoinette told me how Roxanne had already helped them find part-time jobs since she came home, Adriana boasted that her mommy had spent three afternoons at her school, and Carlitos gloated that his father had to let him spend time with his mother. But a few hours into the visit, the mood shifted, and the impending separation became a cold presence among us. While the grown ups talked about plans for new appeals and rallies to defend against hopelessness, one after another the kids broke down in their own ways. Finally, there was nothing to do but sob and hold one another.

Back in her cell, after she turned herself in, Roxanne wrote "It's so hard to believe that one moment I can touch, feel and love my children and the next minute it is all taken away so fast for no reason. When I sit in my cell I wonder was I ever really out, and the heartache of my children is here with me."[11] Andrea stopped talking for months and Carlitos became a wound up ball of rage.

I tried not to succumb to futile ruminations on the hoax of freedom. Claude was supposed to be coming home in three weeks, and the worry that had been just a tickle in my stomach became a prickling pain. Was Roxanne's loss of freedom a threatening portent of Claude's denial? Once Claude got out, would some quirk of fate send him back to prison? Or if he managed to preserve his freedom, wouldn't it be just another manifestation of white privilege?

Who deserved freedom, who got freedom, who got to keep freedom? I knew the answers of American history. I knew that it really wasn't about Claude and Roxanne in an individual sense. Yet, every time Leila would tell me another excited story about what we would do once daddy was out, the shadow of Adriana's tear-streaked face made it difficult for me to share her anticipation. Still, I had to believe that Claude would get out on July 30, and he would stay out. And some day Roxanne would get out of prison too.[12]

—∞∞∞—

Today is the day I have taken to organize my/our room for Claude's return. A week away now, accepting that it will be real, real enough to demand that a space in the closet be made, a drawer in the dresser be emptied… Three and a half years is a hefty amount of time, and yet it seems like the time has evaporated. Except then I think of the weight of new habits that have settled in my life—living on my own as a single mother. How will I open these habits up and rearrange them to include him in this tiny room, this stuffy house? How will it be for him, unlocking the habits of years of living in a cage? What will it be like, stepping through the prison gates, flying through the air, being back with us in San Francisco? How will it feel to stand at Land's End overlooking the ocean, at the very edge of this continent, and realize that somehow we made it back here together again? (Journal, July 23, 1998)

July 30 came and everything went as planned. Claude's friends, Jean and Ugo who lived in Portland, picked him up at the gates of Sheridan and drove him to the Portland airport. Claude called us before boarding the plane. His exit from the prison had been smooth and it had been wonderful to spend time with Jean and Ugo in the car. Only when he described the scene at airport, "This is a *very busy* place!" did I hear a note of strain and sense the over-the-top stimulation which other former prisoners had told me overwhelmed them when they first got out.

After his call, I made the kids do a last round of clean-up of the apartment, packed up the special platter of sushi that was one of Claude's favorite foods, and we drove to the airport. We didn't have to wait long, since the plane arrived early. "Just like dad to be early," Tony joked. Then there he was, looking thin but himself again in jeans and a plaid shirt instead of the prison khakis he had been wearing for the past three and a half years.

Leila jumped into Claude's arms, Tony threw his arms around him, and I was glad to be able to stand still and take in this moment. The moment was indeed short lived, because Claude had to make it to a halfway house in downtown San Francisco within the next couple of hours (no permission to even stop by our apartment on the way there), and it was impossible to relax until he had made this first, critical deadline.

Claude would be staying in a half-way house for the first four months as the condition for leaving Sheridan before his sentence was up. This was supposed to "ease" his transition from incarceration to freedom. We weren't prepared for the mockery the halfway house made of the concept of transition. The house was situated in the middle of San Francisco's drug-saturated Tenderloin neighborhood and the absurdity of this location was apparent even to Leila. "Why are there so many drunk people in the streets near daddy's new prison?" she whispered to me as we walked from our car to visit Claude the next day. It was hard not to trip over the people slumped in doorways, spreading out on to the sidewalk, and women and men openly passed each other bottles and drugs.

Claude was happy to see us and described how inside the atmosphere was chaotic. For many people coming out of prison, without family or friends to offer support, the temptation to immediately break every rule was enormous. People were constantly being hauled back to prison for minor violations and

even those who conscientiously followed every rule were threatened by acciden-
tal entanglement in the maelstrom of drama going on.

Claude immediately started to work twelve hour days at his new job
to avoid the house as much as possible. Before leaving Sheridan, a friend had
helped him find this job as an administrative coordinator at a non-profit agency,
and it was conveniently located in downtown San Francisco. After the first week,
he was allowed to come and visit us at home for a few hours each weekend day.
By the fourth week he had daily passes, but his 9 PM curfew left us breathlessly
driving back to the halfway house after a rushed dinner, crammed homework, and
truncated conversations. On the weekends, he could sleep over as long as he was
off the streets by 9 PM, a rule that was enforced by surprise late night phone calls
from the halfway house staff, which seemed to come just as we started to make
love or as we dropped off to sleep.

Former prisoners had all warned us not to expect this period to be easy.
It was both easier and harder than I expected. Claude immediately began reor-
ganizing the kitchen, the bathroom, and our cramped bedroom, creating space
where there had been clutter. It was so nice to tell each other what had happened
during our days at work for a few minutes on the drive back to the halfway house,
and on weekends it was wonderful to again share our bed that had been hauled
cross-country from Pittsburgh. But prison was still in Claude's bones. He woke
up at the slightest noise each night and couldn't go back to sleep for hours. He
became claustrophobic in crowded stores and movie theaters. And his need
for order, structure, and a clear plan for each day often collided with the more
laissez-faire style I had developed for me and the kids.

Within a couple of weeks, Claude had stopped being a miraculous appa-
rition among us. Leila's fantasy-daddy was replaced by a real daddy who wasn't
available to play all the time and also had expectations of her that she hadn't
counted on dealing with. It was easier for Tony to readapt to the dynamics among
the four of us. However, he hated conflict and shut himself in the walk-in closet
we had converted into a computer room whenever the rest of us began to argue.

One Sunday afternoon in October, after a weekend when family bickering had resumed its pre-prison level, Claude and I insisted on taking some time

for ourselves. We went to nearby La Raza park and sat on a bench listening to the conga drums. We looked at each other realizing that for the first time in the history of our relationship we could actually think of mapping out a future that was not framed by intolerable uncertainty or inevitable separation. The tensions of the weekend fell into perspective. It would take a while, but we could make this new stage work.

Claude was scheduled to complete his term in the halfway house at the end of November. As the date approached when we would all be living together full time, the limitations of our small apartment became more obvious. There was no room for Claude to put his tools, there was hardly any room for his clothes, and the faulty electrical wiring that I had ignored was a source of major concern for him. But how could we find a bigger place that we could afford in San Francisco's overheated housing market at the height of the dot.com boom? A few months before, we had been thousands of miles apart and one of us had been living in a cell, but still the issue of our living space took on great importance.

Then, one weekend afternoon, Claude went to see *Eyes of the Rainbow*, a Cuban video about Assata Shakur (which I had already seen).[13] The film was followed by a panel discussion and Claude was introduced as a former political prisoner. He talked briefly about his experiences inside and the difficulties prisoners have reestablishing their lives when they come out. After the discussion, a man in the audience came up to Claude and told him that he had a three bedroom house available to rent.

When Claude came home and told me, I assumed that the place was a dump or, worse yet, some type of set-up. What kind of landlord would go to an event about Assata Shakur and approach a recently released prisoner with an offer of a house to rent? However, Claude liked the owner, Colin, a quirky former hippie and Panther sympathizer from back in the day who had invested in real estate about twenty-five years ago. He convinced me that it was worth checking out the house. So, a few days later, we went over to the Bayview neighborhood where the house was located.

It was like walking into an enchanted space. On the first floor, a three story skylight sent sun pouring into the kitchen. There was a wood paneled living room and two bedrooms overlooking a garden. The second floor was a converted attic with sloping ceilings, a large open space, separate bedroom and study alcoves, three skylights, a second bathroom, a huge deck (with a hot tub!) and an amazing view of the bay. Every nook and cranny of this house, which had survived the 1906 earthquake, seemed perfect for us. The only catch was that there was no catch. Claude was already talking rent with Colin, who assured him that if we didn't have enough money now for a security deposit, we could pay it in installments. I was still in a state of disbelief, but there was no rational reason to resist the lure of this house. That night we signed the lease.

> This house is my half-century gift. Sitting here in the
> dusk, gazing out over the smokestacks, the cranes, and over
> to the rose-tinged blue of the bay with the twilight glitter of
> the East Bay hills beyond. Light pours in and surrounds us
> through every angle of this quirky, precious house. We are here
> and my worrying mind cannot corrupt the moment. Right now
> the house is still magic, but hopefully it will become just a part
> of our lives for a good while and the rest will grow and take
> shape within it. (Journal entry, December 14, 1998).

∞∞∞

Was it my imagination that the California sun was shining with more radiance than usual, casting its blessing on an event that few of us had expected to ever happen? Over a hundred people with flowers, flags, banners, and drums were gathered in front of the gates of FCI Dublin, this September 10. We were waiting to greet the four Puerto Rican compañeras—Alicia, Lucy, Carmen, and Dylcia—as they came through the gates of the prison. Although their release had been finalized by the White House and repeatedly discussed on radio and television shows, none of us could fully trust that it would occur without incident.

The month before a similar crowd had gathered in front of the same gates to greet Laura Whitehorn when she was released on parole on August 6. But Laura's release had been expected for years because it was based upon her official parole date. A couple of weeks after Laura was released, Silvia Baraldini, who was an Italian citizen, had been transferred to an Italian prison through a negotiated agreement after a massive national campaign in Italy calling for her repatriation.[14] These were important victories, but the release of 11 Puerto Rican political prisoners, which was occurring simultaneously in various locations around the country, felt more like a miracle, even though we knew that it was the result of years of astute strategizing and untiring work by the Puerto Rican independence movement and their allies around the world.

As we waited in front of the gates, the kids ran around and played, while the adults mulled over the rollercoaster events of the past several months that had culminated in our expectant vigil in front of Dublin this day. On April 19, 1999, a Puerto Rican civilian employee of the Navy, David Sanes Rodriguez, had been killed on the island of Vieques by a Navy bombing exercise that went off course. The Puerto Rican campaign against the U.S. Navy's occupation of Vieques, which had continued since the seventies, came to a boiling point in the aftermath of Sanes'death. The demand for the Navy to stop using Vieques in its bloody war games and return the land to Puerto Rican control was voiced by the Puerto Rican Governor, an array of U.S. Congressional representatives, and a demonstration of 50,000 people in Puerto Rico on July 4. The discovery by a special Puerto Rican commission that the Navy had used napalm and uranium-laced munitions on Vieques further fueled popular anger at the U.S. government and its military.

The growing outrage about Vieques converged with the accelerating campaign to free the political prisoners. In 1993, the prisoners had submitted an application to the White House for their unconditional release as a humanitarian gesture and an act of political reconciliation. Over the years, this application had been supported by tens of thousands. In the spring of 1999, petitions with 75,000 signatures had been sent to the White House. They had been signed by church leaders, politicians, and supporters including Archbishop Desmond

Tutu, Coretta Scott King, and Reverend Jesse Jackson, and they demanded the immediate release of the prisoners. At the same time, extensive discussions were being held with Clinton's chief counsel, Charles Ruff, about the possibility of clemency.

On August 11, after lengthy consideration, President Clinton officially offered a conditional commutation of the sentences for sixteen of the prisoners who were, according to his statement, serving excessively harsh and disproportionate sentences for their efforts to bring about independence for Puerto Rico. Although this was a significant victory, the prisoners objected to several terms of the offer. Eleven of them—Edwin Cortes, Elizam Escobar, Ricardo Jimenez, Adolfo Matos, Dylcia Pagán, Alberto Rodriguez, Alicia Rodriguz, Ida Luz Rodriguez, Luis Rosa, Alejandrina Torres, and Carmen Valentín—were being offered immediate release. However, Juan Segarra Palmer would need to serve five more years, Oscar Lopez would only have a few years shaved off of his sentence, Antonio Camacho Negron was just offered a commutation of his fine, and Carlos Alberto Torres was not offered release at all. The prisoners also opposed the strict parole restrictions they would have to abide by, especially those which severely restricted their travel and prohibited their association with each other and with other *independentistas* who had served time in prison. The demands of their campaign had been for unconditional release for all. They wanted to achieve this goal.[15]

Weeks of intense discussion and negotiation ensued. On August 18, the FBI, which had argued against the commutation prior to Clinton's decision, issued a slanderous, unsigned press release. It implied that the prisoners were planning to return to violence. Jan Susler, who was representing the prisoners, sharply pointed out that the FBI's attempt to undermine the commutation with disinformation was a continuation of its COINTELPRO program against the Puerto Rican independence movement.

On August 29, over 100,000 Puerto Ricans marched in San Juan to demand unconditional amnesty for the prisoners in an unprecedented display of unity. But Clinton wouldn't budge from his initial offer and issued a deadline for a decision to be made. We who had been breathlessly following the sequence of events understood that the decision was extremely complicated. It was crucial that the principled unity that the prisoners had maintained for nineteen years should not be fractured by the commutation offer. On the other hand, unity did not mean that each one had to decide in the same way. In the end, the eleven prisoners eligible for immediate release decided to accept the commutation, and Juan Segarra Palmer accepted commutation after five more years. Oscar Lopez declined the limited commutation, but affirmed his agreement with the others' decisions. Antonio Camacho Negron declined the waiver of his fine.

The eleven signed the commutation agreements on September 7, twenty years after Jimmy Carter had granted clemency to Lolita Lebron, Irving Flores, Rafael Cancel Miranda, and Oscar Collazo. The word went out in local papers, on the radio and the internet: "Meet the compañeros/as at the gates to welcome them home to their community." Now we were all here, trying not to let a few hours of waiting dampen our joy. Still, we couldn't help but wonder what besides prison bureaucracy, incompetence, and petty harassment could be causing the delay. Eventually, we received word that the logistics of departure were complicated by the requirement that they not "associate" with each other after release. These compañeras who had spent the past nineteen years in the closest possible proximity could not be allowed to walk out together.

Lucy and Alicia had been granted a special dispensation, since they were sisters, to travel together to Chicago where their family was anxiously awaiting them. They were driven from the prison on a back road and went directly to the airport in order not to miss their plane. Carmen and Dylcia's departures were staggered, but each was able to briefly stop by our welcoming party for a few minutes. As each arrived, a horde of reporters descended upon them. After ignoring their existence in this Bay Area prison for decades, the media vultures were now eager to cover this unprecedented event. Dylcia and Carmen each insisted on greeting the children and receiving the wilted flowers that the kids offered before consenting to speak briefly.

"I want to start a new life. I want to spend time with my son, and very shortly I will be landing in our motherland: Puerto Rico," said Dylcia, as she grasped her son, Guillermo, tightly. "I am going to continue to participate in the fight for independence. This I will do until the last day of my life," swore Carmen, holding her granddaughter Karina's hand.

As I listened to their unquenched fervor, I marveled at their capacity to maintain their belief, all these years, that the Puerto Rican movement would someday free them. Through barren stretches when nothing seemed to move forward, and intermittent surges when release seemed to be around the corner, all of the Puerto Rican prisoners had insisted on a vision of freedom that seemed impossible given the confines of their daily existence. They had struggled to live *with eyes not yet born.*

Each woman made it clear when she spoke that part of her heart remained with the prisoners left behind—Marilyn and Linda, plus thousands of others. As the drums beat and the banners waved in the breeze, I gripped Leila's hand and squeezed Tony's shoulder. Someone began to chant and together we all turned our voices in the direction of the prison. *"Libertad, libertad, libertad, libertad!"* we shouted loudly, uproariously, defiantly, so that all of the women on the other side of the razor wire could hear and take hope.

Members of the San Francisco 8 with their family, friends, and supporters after most of them were released on bail in September 2007. Photo by Scott Braley, www.scottbraley.com.

EPILOGUE

A LUTA CONTINUA! [1]
(THE STRUGGLE CONTINUES!)

AS THIS BOOK DREW TO A CLOSE, it was tempting to craft a storybook ending. Eleven Puerto Ricans walked out of prison. A circle completed. Freedom, Victory, Can't Jail the Spirit! But real life bitterly contests facile conclusions. The struggle continues in every dimension of life on this planet. One of the state's nefarious projects has been to obliterate the living reminders of militant resistance, attempting to reconfigure historic victories as portents of ultimate defeat.

On September 23, 2005, the FBI chose El Grito de Lares, one of the most celebrated days in the Puerto Rican independence movement, as the day to assassinate seventy-two year old Filiberto Ojeda Rios, a founder and leader of Los Macheteros. El Grito de Lares commemorates the uprising of the people of Lares, Puerto Rico against Spanish colonial rule in 1868. On this revered day, the FBI fired more than one hundred shots into the small house in Hormigueros where Filiberto and his life partner, Elma Beatriz Rosado Barbosa, lived in clandestinity. In 1985, the FBI had almost killed Filiberto when he was arrested and charged with participating in the 1983 expropriation of $7.5 million from Wells Fargo.[2] Released on bail, Ojeda had managed to remain underground for the next fifteen years until the FBI discovered him. After fatally shooting him, the FBI left Filiberto to bleed to death, preventing medical teams from entering the house for hours. Elma reported that Filiberto's last words were *"Pa'lante siempre!"* (forever onward).[3]

Filiberto's assassination was met by an outpouring of fury in Puerto Rico. The Governor of Puerto Rico, Puerto Rican members of the U.S. Congress, and Amnesty International all called for an investigation. "FBI out of Puerto Rico!" became the popular rallying cry for mass outrage. But after a so-called investigation that exonerated the FBI of all wrong-doing, the U.S. government launched a counter-offensive using grand jury witch hunts to target a new generation of independentistas on the island and the U.S. mainland. In February 2008, the FBI captured another fugitive wanted in the Wells Fargo expropriation, Avelino González Claudio, 65. In a statement made from prison shortly after he was arrested, González Claudio expressed the resolute resistance that has characterized all of the Puerto Rican political prisoners: "Pandora left desperation out of her box, and because of this they may chain and imprison my body, but never my spirit and my ideas."[4]

In January 2007, another piece of history was dragged into the present when the state of California charged eight Black elders, most of whom were former Black Panthers, with the 1971 killing of a police officer at the San Francisco, Ingleside station. They also charged them with a sweeping conspiracy, alleging their involvement in Black Liberation Army activities between 1968 and 1973. Ray Boudreaux, Richard Brown, Hank Jones, Richard O'Neal, Harold Taylor, and Francisco Torres (ranging in age from 57 to 70) were arrested in California, New York, and Florida. Herman Bell and Jalil Muntaqim were notified of the charges in New York state prisons, where they had already been serving time for thirty years on other politically related charges.[5]

On the morning of January 23, when I picked up the phone and heard about the arrests around the country, I felt like the line between past and present was blurring in a haunted circular continuum. How could the government attempt to try a case that was thirty-six years old? How could they revive charges that were based on torture-coerced confessions, charges that had been thrown out of court in the seventies? How could they pluck the men out of their peaceful, productive lives and throw their families into turmoil? What macabre script, what twisted mentality could legitimize these arrests as a form of justice?

The arrests didn't come as a complete surprise, but they still were profoundly disturbing. Since 2003, the men had been hounded by the FBI and detectives from the San Francisco police department; the investigation into the 1971 case had been reopened using funds made available by Homeland Security's post-911 war against terrorism. Detectives made repeated, threatening visits to dozens of people around the country, hoping that someone would collaborate and become a witness against the others. When that didn't work, they subpoenaed five men (Jones, Brown, Taylor, Boudreaux, and John Bowman, since deceased) to a San Francisco grand jury in the fall of 2005. They all refused to testify, were held in contempt of court, and jailed. Defiantly, despite the discomfort of jail, despite their health problems and the disruptions their families were facing, they all stood their ground. When they were released at the expiration of the grand jury term in October 2005, they emerged with a newly forged group unity and sense of purpose. They formed the Committee for the Defense of Human Rights and began to organize.[6]

Claude and Freedom Archives worked with them to produce a video telling their side of the story. In 1973, Harold Taylor and John Bowman had been arrested and tortured in New Orleans. New Orleans police, aided by San Francisco detectives, had used electric shock, cattle prods, beatings and sensory deprivation to elicit "confessions" from them. Subsequently, the case had been thrown out by a San Francisco judge because the confessions were based on torture (illegal in those days). Thirty years later, it was chilling for the men to see the same detectives who had participated in their torture knock on their doors wanting to have a conversation about the past. The video, called *Legacy of Torture*, was scheduled to premiere when state Attorney General Jerry Brown filed charges, based on the old tortured confessions, and the men were arrested. Following a week of sensationalized media coverage of the case, hundreds of people lined up to get into the Roxie theater to see the video, and we had to add an extra showing to accommodate the crowds.

To those of us who had lived through the height of COINTELPRO, it was clear that this case was a continuation of that program and was intended to send a frightening, paralyzing message to a new generation about the price of resistance. The men had an outstanding legal team; what was critically needed was grassroots support. We quickly formed a defense committee in which former Panthers and Prairie Fire members were joined by younger representatives of organizations like the Malcolm X Grassroots Movement, Critical Resistance, and the Eastside Arts Alliance.[7] We mobilized people to come to court, organized regular visits to the men in San Francisco County Jail, developed a website and an email listserve, and held showings of *Legacy of Torture*. The *San Francisco Bay View* newspaper ran regular articles and commentaries about the case and helped spread the word throughout the country.[8]

A major breakthrough occurred when Judge Moscone was appointed to the case and he significantly reduced the bail from an outrageous $3 million each to figures ranging from $200,000 to $650,000. Within a month, family members and political allies put up enough property to bail all six of them out, successfully raising the total of $2,605,000. It was particularly moving to me that many former Prairie Fire members who owned houses stepped forward and put them up as collateral for the bail.

As New York state prisoners, neither Jalil Muntaqim nor Herman Bell were eligible for bail. After spending over twenty-five years in New York prisons, they had been hauled across country to face these decades-old charges in San Francisco. Back in the day, when Prairie Fire members visited San Quentin regularly, Jalil was known as Tony Bottom, and his ideas and energy were behind much of the prison work that we undertook. I myself had never visited him in that era, but I had followed his political path over the decades and knew that he had never had stopped fighting for the freedom of all political prisoners and for his own release.[9]

I finally met Jalil in 2004, when I accompanied my son, Tony, on a visit to Auburn prison in upstate New York where Jalil was incarcerated. When Tony started attending nearby Cornell University, he began to visit Jalil and they became quite close. Ironically, at the same time Tony was graduating and moving back to San Francisco, Jalil was being forcibly returned to the area where he had grown up. Jalil had been arrested on August 28, 1971 a couple of months before his twentieth birthday and had lived inside one prison or another ever since. He hadn't been on the streets of his home town since he was a teenager.

What is return like when you are driven through the city in shackles? Jalil told me in a letter, "In my youth I rode my bicycle in every part of the City, enjoying all of its differences in wealth, culture, atmosphere, and texture. I had a genuine love for S.F., but unfortunately I no longer view it as my city. It has lost its vibrancy and the ideal that all was possible." I cannot argue. For Black people especially, San Francisco has become a dangerous place to live. 60% of the prisoners in San Francisco County Jail, where the SF8 have been held, are Black in a city whose Black population has declined to 6.7%.[10] Gentrification is driving out record numbers of Black families, and impending redevelopment plans threaten an even more total ethnic cleansing. Is it any wonder that the few Black neighborhoods that remain are imploding with violence? My daughter brings home constant, traumatic stories of Black friends in her high school who have been arrested, injured, or killed. For most Black youth, San Francisco is not a good place to grow up.

Yet, there are multiple, parallel realities in San Francisco, as there are all over America. San Francisco is my home, now even more than when I left to go underground. I am attached to the crests of hills, the random architecture of fog, the scent of eucalyptus, the brilliance of the bougainvilleas, the cleansing crash of ocean at the edge of the city. My children have gone to school here. They have learned to drive navigating San Francisco's steep and winding streets. They have absorbed the disparate, complementary, contradictory dimensions of its culture and its politics. They have developed consciousness here. It is their home.

Claude has taken his prison dream of an audio archive and transformed it into The Freedom Archives, a center for radical media and educational work, based in San Francisco's Mission district and known to many around the country. Its mission, to preserve the past, illuminate the present, shape the future, has been put into practice through its production of historically oriented CD's and videos. The Freedom Archives also trains youth to produce their own audio and video works, assisting them in "unearthing lessons of the recent past even as they raise new concerns of their own." [11]

In September 2007, Claude and I marked our twenty-fifth anniversary and were finally able to celebrate our relationship at a collective gathering of family, friends, and our extended community. We shared the story of our absurd marriage ceremony when I couldn't stop laughing hysterically. We were able to express our gratitude to the many layers of community that had made it possible for us to reconstruct our lives in the Bay Area. I was honored to have elder friends at the party who model the continuation of an activist life into one's sixties, seventies, and even eighties. I was particularly moved by the presence of the people I work with in CCWP— Hamdiya, CCWP's Director, who I had first met when she was inside Dublin prison, and the young activists who are committed to the work for women prisoners. They presented a plaque to me and Claude that read: "On behalf of all the members of CCWP, we congratulate both of you for your commitment to each other and to the struggle for justice for all people. We love you and sincerely hope you enjoy another twenty-five years together."

We are fortunate indeed!

Still, some mornings as I skim the paper at breakfast or listen to the radio while driving to work, I hear the names Guantanamo and Abu Ghraib— those international symbols of detention, torture, isolation, and punishment— and realize that they have now become household words, assimilated into the fabric of our daily lives. They are the visible tip of a geopolitical iceberg that is not melting—the global convergence of the military and prison industrial complexes which includes the 2.3 million people in prisons and jails in the United States and the thirty-six "golden gulags"that scar the California landscape. [12] I hear reports about the Green Scare prisoners on KPFA and realize that most of the public, and even the left, is unaware of the sweeping government offensive, Operation Backfire, that has targeted dozens of environmental and animal rights activists over the past several years. [13] Grand juries, agent provocateurs, arrests, indictments, terrorist enhancements have all been part of the arsenal used against these young, primarily white activists. Some have broken under the strain and betrayed each other. Others have withstood the pressure and have received unprecedented, draconian sentences. The government's Green Scare campaign, like the Red Scare in the fifties, is not only meant to snuff the environmental and animal rights movements but to send a menacing warning to all political activists.

What will it take to dismantle this gargantuan repression and punishment complex and the larger system of imperialism it is designed to protect? How not to despair? How to hang on to that other, still struggling, fundamental side of the human spirit that insists on liberation? A luta continua, without assurances or guarantees.

Some of my most probing discussions about such political and philosophical questions—about the forms, the organization, the culture of resistance—still take place with the political prisoners I visit. I ask Jalil what the phrase "Arm the Spirit" means to him after all these years. He writes, "The call to Arm the Spirit is for revolutionaries to comprehend their capacity to love, to give themselves to humanity, to know one's purpose in the course of building and sustaining the revolutionary struggle." To Jalil, this is a self-evident truth, the mandate that guides him as he continues to live, dream, and strategize a different reality from behind bars.

I talk with Marilyn Buck (still at FCI Dublin) about politics, philosophy, literature, poetry. She writes raw, unnerving, poems and essays.[14] I admire her language, her penchant for intricacy, her commitment to women, her ability to name contradictions, her capacity to keep writing, to keep living, to keep struggling. We both believe in the power of words. We both marvel at their capacity to fire connection, transformation, resistance. Marilyn writes:

> *words stretch*
> *into spaces*
> *beyond bars and walls...*

words holler
scream love songs
  chant
refuse to conform
indict cruelty
resist dying[15]

A Luta Continua! Pa'lante Siempre! Arm the Spirit!

holler, chant, indict

Carry it on, in whatever way you can.

"Marilyn Buck" painting by Tom Manning, political
prisoner captured in 1985 as part of the Ohio 7. www.
geocities.com/tom-manning.

ENDNOTES

Introduction

[1] Fidel Castro, quoted in *Prairie Fire*, 9.
[2] Assata Shakur, *Assata*, 2.

Escape

[1] The "need-to-know" principle is basic to organizations and groups that are structured to maximize security. People only have as much information as they need to know to accomplish their specific responsibility.
[2] The MOVE organization was started by John Africa who wrote "The Guidelines" to explain MOVE beliefs. See www.onamove.org for more information. For a fictionalized reflection on the 1985 bombing of MOVE, see *Philadelphia Fire* by John Edgar Wideman.
[3] In August, 1978, nine MOVE members were arrested following a major police assault on their home in Powelton Village, Philadelphia. They were convicted as a "family" for the death of a police officer during the assault. They remain in prison except for Merle Africa who died in prison in 1998.
[4] Susan Rosenberg and Tim Blunk were arrested in 1984 and charged with possession of explosives. They were both later charged in 1988 as part of the Resistance Conspiracy case.
[5] Alan Berkman was arrested on weapons and conspiracy charges and indicted in 1988 as part of the Resistance Conspiracy case, in which he and six others were charged with the bombing of the U.S. Capitol and other military installations. These acts were done as forms of resistance to U.S. domestic and international warfare.
[6] Assata Shakur was a Black Panther leader who became a target of the FBI's COINTELPRO program. She was arrested in 1973 and charged with numerous offenses including the murder of a state trooper during the incident for which she was arrested. Three charges were eventually dismissed and she was acquitted in four trials. In the fifth trial, in 1977, she was convicted by an all-white jury and sentenced to life plus thirty-three years. In 1979, she escaped from prison and, in 1984, she was granted political asylum by Cuba, where she has lived in exile ever since. The U.S. government has placed a $1million bounty on her head. See *Assata: an Autobiography* for her moving narrative of her life through her time in prison. See www.handsoffassata.org and www.assashakur.org for current information about her.
[7] After being released from prison in the seventies, Kamau Sadiki (aka Fred Hilton) lived without incident for twenty-five years. In 2002 he was charged and later convicted of the 1972 murder of a police officer after he refused to cooperate with the government's effort to apprehend Assata. See www.itsabouttimebpp.com for more about his case.

Fugitive Deconstructions

[1] *Newsweek*, July 1, 1985, 38.

[2] Donna had been part of the Weather Underground also.

[3] See Dan Berger's *Outlaws of America* for a comprehensive history of the Weather Underground Organization, and also Ron Jacob's *The Way the Wind Blew*. Good sources for overviews of the Black Panther Party include, *Up Against the Wall: Violence in the Making and Unmaking of the Black Panther Party*, Curtis Austin; *Liberation, Imagination, and the Black Panther Party: A New Look at the Panthers and their Legacy*, Kathleen Cleaver and George Katsiaficas, eds; *The Black Panthers Speak*, Philip Foner, ed.; and *The Black Panther Party Reconsidered*, Charles Jones, ed.

[4] COINTELPRO was the FBI's covert counterintelligence program to suppress political dissent from the fifties through the seventies. One of the first targets of COINTELPRO in the fifties was the Puerto Rican Independence Movement and the leaders of the Nationalist Party (including Pedro Albizu Campos and Juan Antonio Corretjer). See http://www.icdc.com/~paulwolf/cointelpro/pr.htm for a description of this effort.

In the sixties, the Black Panther Party was identified as one of its most important targets. Under COINTELPRO, FBI activities against the Panthers included infiltration, psychological warfare, legal attacks, break-ins, and assassinations. See Brian Glick's, *The War at Home,* and Ward Churchill and Jim Vander Wall's, *COINTELPRO Papers,* for excellent material on COINTELPRO.

[5] The Ohio 7 were members of an anti-imperialist clandestine group, the United Freedom Front, that carried out attacks primarily in opposition to U.S. policy in Central America and Southern Africa. They were arrested in 1984.

[6] Margaret Randall, *Sandino's Daughters.*

[7] Ibid. 122.

[8] Los Macheteros (the machete-wielders or the canecutters), was the popular name for *El Ejercito Boricua Popular*, one of several active clandestine groups based in Puerto Rico during the seventies and eighties.

[9] Good resources on the struggle in Haiti include, *Uses of Haiti,* by Paul Farmer; *Hidden From the Headlines,* Haiti Action Committee; and *Eyes of the Heart,* by Jean-Bertrand Aristide

[10] Two interesting books on the Phillipines are Ninotchka Rosca's, *Endgame: The Fall of Marcos;* and *Jose Maria Sison: At Home in the World: Portrait of a Revolutionary*, edited by Ninotchka Rosca and Richard Koritz.

[11] Oscar Lopez Rivera is a Puerto Rican *independentista* who was arrested in 1981 convicted of seditious conspiracy and sentenced to fifty-five years in prison. He was later given an additional fifteen years for his alleged escape attempt. He remains a political prisoner today.

[12] In January 1988, Oscar Lopez and three others were convicted of the conspiracy to free him from prison.

New World Coming

[1] Nina Simone, "New World Coming," from the album *Here Comes the Sun,* released in 1971.

[2] George Jackson, *Soledad Brother,* 32. See *Soledad Brother* and *Blood in My Eye* by Jackson

for a history of his life and an understanding of his brilliant theoretical contributions to the radical prison movement.

[3] Susan Brownmiller became a leading theoretician of the anti-rape movement. In 1975, she published an extensively researched but controversial book, *Against Our Will: Men, Women and Rape.*

[4] See New York Radical Feminists, *Rape: the First Sourcebook for Women,* Noreen Connell and Cassandra Wilson,eds.

[5] Gerda Lerner's book, *Black Women in White America,* was one of the first to document the racist use of the rape charge against Black men throughout U.S. history.

[6] From 1974 SFWAR classroom presentation tape. Author's personal archive.

[7] Inez Garcia was found guilty of second degree murder in 1974, but her conviction was overturned in 1975 on a technicality. She was acquitted in her second trial in 1977. For more information on Inez Garcia see Kenneth W. Salter, ed., *The Trial of Inez García.* Other women of color also resisted sexual assault. Joanne Little was a Black prisoner accused of killing a white guard who sexually assaulted her in a North Carolina jail in 1974, where she was the only woman prisoner. She was acquitted of all charges in 1975. See Angela Davis, "Joanne Little: The Dialectics of Rape," MS Magazine, June 1975. Yvonne Wanrowe was a Colville Indian who was convicted in 1972 of killing a white man who tried to molest her son. Her appeal was taken to the Washington Supreme Court and finally, in 1979, an agreement was reached which allowed her to be released.

[8] For critiques of Brownmiller's positions see Angela Davis, "The Racist Use of the Rape Charge," in *Women, Race and Class;* and Alison Edwards, *Rape, Racism and the White Women's Movement: An Answer to Susan Brownmiller.*

[9] See http://www.sfwar.org for current information about San Francisco Women Against Rape.

[10] Judy Grahn, *The Common Woman* (chapbook), 4.

[11] Robin Morgan was the editor of the groundbreaking 1970 feminist anthology, *Sisterhood is Powerful,* and has written many other books since.

[12] Today, anti-transgender prejudices are being vehemently challenged by gender queer people and their allies.

[13] In her book, *Sex and Sensibility: Stories of a Lesbian Generation,* Arlene Stein notes that this conference came to symbolize the difficulties of devising a collective conception of lesbian sisterhood. See p. 107. In interviews she did with L.A. and Bay Area lesbians fifteen years later, they still made frequent references to the disputes at the conference when explaining the challenges of building movement among lesbians.

Riding the Tempest

[1] See www.janenorling.com for a listing of Jane's works over the past decades.

[2] Arlene Eisen-Bergman, *Women of Viet Nam,* 30

[3] Ibid. 216

[4] Ibid.

[5] For a comprehensive description of this innovative project see Karlene Faith's *Unruly Women,* "Education for Empowerment," Chapter 7.

[6] The pamphlet was called, *From Women in Prison Here to Women in Viet Nam: We Are*

Sisters. Author's personal archive.

[7] Humberto Solas, *Lucia,* Cuba 1968.

[8] Among the numerous materials available on the Chilean coup and its surrounding history, a few excellent recent resources include *Chile:The Other September 11th,* Aquilera, Dorfman, Fredes, eds.; *Chile: Promise of Freedom,* Freedom Archives, Audio CD; and Ariel Dorfman, *Heading South, Looking North: A Bilingual Journey.*

[9] Dan Berger, *Outlaws of America,* 331.

[10] The first action that was claimed by the SLA was the 1973 murder of Marcus Foster, the first Black Superintendent of Education for the Oakland school system. The SLA accused Foster of supporting a school wide ID system for students and police in the schools (although it is not clear that he did support these policies). Foster's murder was almost universally condemned and the alleged SLA perpetrators were quickly caught and convicted (one of the convictions was later overturned on appeal). I disagreed with the Foster murder and couldn't see any positive political purpose to it, but thought the Hearst kidnapping needed to be evaluated separately.

[11] Communiqué, February 13, 1974, Freedom Archives collection

[12] Communiqué from *Sisters of the Symbionese Liberation Army* date unknown, Freedom Archives collection.

[13] Lenin's "Left-wing Communism, an Infantile Disorder" was used by many Marxist-Leninist groups, often in an arbitrary way, to critique and denounce other groups' actions that they considered extremist.

[14] Statement by the San Francisco Marxist-Leninist Organization, Freedom Archives collection.

[15] WUO communiqué on the SLA, Freedom Archives collection.

[16] WUO poem, Freedom Archives collection.

[17] Tania was the guerrilla name of Tamara Bunke who was active in the Cuban revolution and later fought in Bolivia with Che Guevara. Leftist Regis Debray, who was a friend and political associate of Tamara Bunke, sent a public letter to Patricia Hearst questioning the authenticity of her choice in adopting this name.

[18] Tom Hayden, *The Los Angeles Times,* May 26, 1974.

[19] Anonymous, Freedom Archives collection. Ruchell refers to Ruchell Cinque Magee who has been incarcerated since 1963. He was convicted in the Marin County uprising of 1970, where Jonathan Jackson took over the courthouse to demand the freedom of the Soledad Brothers (who included Jonathan's brother George) and expose the deplorable conditions in California prisons.

A Single Spark

[1] From a letter written by Mao, Jan 5, 1930.

[2] The Weather Underground, *Prairie Fire,* 2.

[3] Ibid., 1.

[4] Ibid., 10.

[5] Ibid., 10.

[6] Ibid., 10.

[7] Ibid, 28.

[8] Ibid, 14.

[9] The militant direct actions of the "Days of Rage" took place in Chicago in October 1969 and coincided with the beginning of the Chicago 8 conspiracy trial. See *Outlaws of America,* 107–114, *Flying Close to the Sun,* and *Fugitive Days* for descriptions of the "Days of Rage." The townhouse explosion occurred on March 6, 1970. Three Weather members, Ted Gold, Terry Robbins, and Diana Oughton were killed in the process of constructing an explosive device, and two other members, Kathy Boudin and Cathy Wilkerson escaped from the explosion. Also see books listed above for detailed descriptions of the tragedy.

[10] TIS is an amalgam of various Marxist-Leninist organizations working the Bay Area in that period. However, the political positions attributed to TIS reflect actual statements and papers that were published at the time.

[11] *Prairie Fire,* 144.

[12] For more information on the community control struggle in New York see, *Justice, Justice: School Politics and the Eclipse of Liberalism,* Perlstein, Sadovnik, and Semel, eds.

[13] The term "cadre" was used by many revolutionary groups in the period to describe their members, indicating that they were trained and wholly dedicated to the organization and political project.

[14] See Max Elbaum, *Revolution in the Air,* chapter 10, for an overview of the relationship between the new communist movement in the U.S. and China.

[15] The Chinese criticized the Soviet Union for advocating "peaceful coexistence" between capitalism and socialism; for reinstituting many capitalism structures as "state capitalism"; and for "revising" all the fundamental tenets of Marxism-Leninism.

[16] The term "petit-bourgeois individualism" was commonly used by left organizations to criticize people's tendencies to put individual needs and desires above the collective good.

[17] *Prairie Fire,* 165.

[18] Women of the Weather Underground, *Sing A Battlesong,* 1.

[19] Ibid., 2.

Venceremos

[1] Clayton Van Lydegraf, *The Object is to Win,* http://vanlydegraf.hostingweb.us.

[2] The Black-Belt south is a region where Black people have historically been the majority of the population, (between 100-200 counties in the Southeastern portion of the United States).

[3] See Dan Berger's description of *Osawatomie* in *Outlaws of America,* 207–210.

[4] See the description of the Hard Times Conference in chapter 10, *Outlaws of America.*

[5] The Republic of New Afrika (RNA) was formed in 1968 and called for the formation of a sovereign, politically independent government based in the Black-majority national territory consisting of Louisiana, Mississippi, Alabama, Georgia, and South Carolina, and the Black-majority counties adjacent to this area in Arkansas, Tennessee and Florida. The RNA quickly became a target of the FBI's COINTELPRO program which considered it to be a seditious group. The RNA was subject to repeated harassment, raids, and imprisonment of its leaders.

[6] See *Outlaws of America* on the inversion strategy, 215–217.

[7] "Speaking Bitterness" was a term used in the Chinese Revolution when people gave testi-

mony about oppressive conditions they have experienced in the past.

[8] *The Split in the Weather Underground Organization: Struggling Against White and Male Supremacy*, John Brown Book Club, ed. Author's personal archive.

[9] The Bay of Pigs Invasion (Playa Girón), was an unsuccessful attempt, in April 1961, by a U.S.-trained force of Cuban exiles to invade south-west Cuba and overthrow the new Cuban government, established in 1959.

[10] A shotgun used in the Marin County Courthouse uprising in August 1970 was registered in Angela Davis' name and she was charged with conspiracy, kidnapping, and murder connected to the uprising. She was acquitted in 1972 of all the charges.

[11] Assata Shakur, "Open Letter," April 1998 in *Sparks Fly*, pamphlet. Author's personal archive.

Claim No Easy Victories

[1] Amilcar Cabral, 1965.

[2] Yvonne Wanrowe was a Colville Indian convicted by an all-white jury for the self-defense killing of a man who molested her nine-year old son. Susan Saxe was a lesbian revolutionary, serving time for manslaughter and armed robbery in connection with a bank expropriation. Lolita Lebron was the Puerto Rican Nationalist who had attacked the U.S. Congress in 1954 to protest U.S. colonial control of her country. Marilyn Buck was a white anti-imperialist who had been convicted in 1973 for purchasing two boxes of ammunition allegedly for the use of the Black Liberation Army. Assata Shakur was the Black revolutionary prisoner whose buttons I had distributed all over Cuba.

[3] *Breakthrough*, vol 1, no. 3–4, 1977

[4] *"The Phyllis Schlafly Report"*quoted in *SHOWDOWN AT HOUSTON,* 1977 broadside. Author's personal archive.

[5] *Los Angeles Times*, October 23, 1977, quoted in *SHOWDOWN AT HOUSTON.*

[6] *Christian Science Monitor,* "Women's Year Clash: Anti-Feminists Gird for Texas Battle," quoted in *SHOWDOWN AT HOUSTON.*

[7] *Breakthrough*, vol. 2, no. 1, Spring 1978.

[8] *Outlaws of America*, 236.

Chimurenga

[1] Holly Near,"It Could Have Been Me" on *A Live Album,* 1974.

[2] *New York Times*, December 12, 1977.

[3] The Combahee River Collective included prominent Black feminist authors Barbara Smith, Audre Lorde, and Cheryl Clarke.

[4] Cherríe Moraga and Gloria Anzaldúa, *This Bridge Called My Back*, 210.

[5] Ibid 216.

[6] One notable exception was our work on the BASTA! conference which took place in Oakland in August 1980. The conference was convened by three Bay Area organizations—The Feminist Women's Health Center, The Black Women's Revolutionary Council, and the Eleventh Hour Battallion. Black lesbian feminist poet and activist Pat Parker was a leader in all three of these organizations and a key organizer of BASTA! As one of Prairie Fire's representatives to the organizing coalition, I was very happy to be working on a confer-

ence whose explicit goal was to develop an anti-imperialist, anti-racist, revolutionary women's agenda. Unfortunately, little joint organizing between these groups continued after the conference ended.

[7] *Breakthrough*, vol. 1, no.3–4, Oct–Dec 1977, 9.

[8] *Breakthrough*, vol. 1, no.3–4, Oct–Dec 1977, Ibid, 10.

[9] PFOC, *Women's Liberation in the Zimbabwean Revolution*, 30.

[10] Ibid 35–36.

Repression Breeds Resistance

[1] James Baldwin, *The Fire Next Time*, 19–20.

[2] The African Peoples Socialist Party (APSP) was founded in 1972 in Gainesville Florida and still exists today. See www.apspuhuru.org. The Afrikan Peoples Party (APP) was established in the sixties in Los Angeles and published a journal called *SOULBOOK* for several years. The Republic of New Afrika (RNA) was formed in 1968 in Detroit, Michigan, and exists today. See *We Will Return in the Whirlwind: Black Organizations 1960–1975*, by Muhammad Ahmad (Max Stanford, Jr.) for a history of some of the lesser known radical Black organizations of the sixties and early seventies.

[3] *Notes from an Afrikan P.O.W.*, Book 1, 14–15.

[4] The Nationalists had wanted to make the continued colonization of Puerto Rico visible to the world. After unfurling a Puerto Rican flag in the middle of a session of Congress, Lolita Lebron shouted "Que Viva Puerto Rico Libre!" and the four proceeded to fire thirty shots, wounding one representative. The four were charged with attempted murder and sentenced to death. The sentence was later changed to life in prison.

[5] FALN communiqué, October 1974.

[6] *Breakthrough*, Vol 2, No.1, Spring 1978, 68.

[7] Ibid., 69.

[8] The term Chicano/Mejicano was used to describe Mexican people living within U.S. borders. The demand of the MLN was reunification of U.S.-controlled Mexico with the rest of Mexico.

[9] Because Puerto Rico is a Commonwealth of the United States, residents of Puerto Rico are prohibited from voting in federal elections.

[10] The Trilateral Commission was formed in 1973 by representatives of Japan, Europe, and the United States to "control change in the international system."

[11] Samuel Huntington, Michael Crozier & Joji Watanuki (Trilateral Commission),*The Crisis of Democracy*,1975.

[12] These themes were discussed in *Breakthrough* repeatedly. In particular, see "Law and Order: Blueprint for Fascism", Breakthrough Vol.4, No. 1, Winter 1980; and "'Gentrification'—Or Genocide? The Price of Urban Renaissance", *Breakthrough*, Vol. 5, No.1, Spring 1981.

[13] Cerro Maravilla came to symbolize unbridled U.S. repression of the Puerto Rican independence movement. Initial U.S. investigations cleared the FBI agents and Puerto Rican police of all wrong doing, but subsequent investigations by Puerto Rican legislators and local agencies convicted ten officers of perjury, destruction of evidence, obstruction of justice, and second-degree murder.

[14] Morales was able to avoid capture until 1983, when he was caught in Mexico. After a complicated set of negotiations, he was allowed to leave for Cuba, where he was granted political asylum.

[15] *Libertad* Vol. 1, No. 1, 1979, Freedom Archives collection.

[16] Lolita Lebron, Rafael Cancel Miranda, Irving Flores, and Oscar Collazo were released in 1979. The fifth Nationalist prisoner, Andres Figueroa Cordero had already had his sentence commuted by Carter on Oct. 6, 1977, because he had terminal cancer.

[17] Cuba agreed to release six U.S. citizens held in Cuban jails as part of the negotiations.

This Is The Time

[1] Josina Machel was a Mozambican freedom fighter who died in combat against the Portuguese in April 1970. Poem from the author's personal archive.

[2] Nina Simone, "That's All I Want From You," from the album *Baltimore.*

[3] *Breakthrough*, 13–15, Vol. 4, No.1, Winter 1980.

[4] Ibid. 12.

[5] Regis Debray, *Revolution in the Revolution?.*

[6] Nadine Gordimer, *Burger's Daughter.*

[7] *Ibid.,* 332

[8] In June 1976, students in Soweto went on strike to protest a decree mandating instruction in the Afrikaans language of the ruling settler colonialists. A police massacre occurred at a rally of 10,000 people on June 16 and, in the next few days, over 500 people were killed and several thousand arrested.

[9] The FALN 11 were Elizam Escobar, Ricardo Jimenez, Adolfo Matos, Dylcia Pagán, Alberto Rodriguez, Alicia Rodriguez, Ida Luz Rodriguez, Luis Rosa, Carlos Alberto Torres, Haydee Beltrán Torres, and Carmen Valentín.

[10] After Dylcia's arrest, Guillermo was sent to Mexico by friends in the movement and was raised by a Mexican family. The film, *The Double Life of Ernesto Gomez Gomez*, tells the story of Guillermo, aka Ernesto, and his reunion, when he is fifteen years old, with his mother who is still in prison.

[11] Salisbury's name had not yet been changed to Harare.

[12] Horace Campbell's essay, "The Night the British flag was lowered in Rhodesia," in *Reclaiming Zimbabwe,* provided factual information about the sequence of events during the celebration that supplemented my memory of that evening.

[13] Bob Marley, *Africans a liberate Zimbabwe.*

[14] Horace Campbell, *Reclaiming Zimbabwe.*

[15] Ibid., 2.

[16] Ibid., 284.

[17] Patricia McFadden, *Women in Action*, Issue 1, 1997, http://www.hartford-hwp.com/archives/30/152.html.

[18] Ronald Fernandez, *Prisoners of Colonialism*, 224.

[19] The Frente Farabundo Martí para la Liberación Nacional (FMLN), was formed in 1980 to liberate El Salvador from the U.S.-backed military dictatorship.

[20] A Brink's truck making a cash delivery was surrounded in Nyack, New York in October 1981 by political activists who intended to use the funds for the Black Liberation Move-

ment. One Brink's guard and two police officers were killed, one Black activist was killed, and four people involved in the expropriation were arrested. See Chapter 11 of *Outlaws of America* for an excellent overview of the Brink's incident and its aftermath.

America's Most Wanted

[1] Constantin Costa-Gavras, *Missing*, 1982.
[2] See "Riding the Tempest," in this book, for more on the SLA.

Risking a Somersault in the Air

[1] Margaret Randall, *Risking a Somersault in the Air*, 2.
[2] Ibid. 117.
[3] *Sinister Wisdom*, # 28, Winter 1985.
[4] *Risking a Somersault in the Air*, 215.

No Hay Camino

[1] Antonio Machado, *Campos de Castilla*, 1912.
[2] Marilyn Buck, *State of Exile*, vii–viii. Cristina Peri Rossi wrote the poems in this book in 1974, shortly after being exiled from Uruguay. They weren't published in Spanish until 2003. Marilyn Buck undertook the project of translating the book into English as part of her Master's thesis completed inside prison in 2005.
[3] Ibid. xii.
[4] Ibid. 28.
[5] Giaconda Belli, *The Country Under My Skin*, 353.
[6] The Frente Sandinista de Liberación Nacional (FSLN), popularly known as the Sandinistas was the front that won against the U.S.-backed Somoza military dictatorship in 1979.
[7] Contragate, or the Iran-Contra affair, was initially the exposure of illegal CIA weapons sales to Iran that were used to fund the Contas in Nicaragua. Over time, it was further exposed that the CIA had also supported Contra drug trafficking in the U.S. as a means of raising funds. In 1996, a reporter for the *San Jose Mercury News*, Gary Webb published a series of reports that showed how the CIA and the Contras had initiated the crack cocaine epidemic in Los Angeles through their drug trafficking. Webb later published the reports as a book: *Dark Alliance—The CIA, the Contras and the Crack Cocaine Epidemic*. In 2004, Gary Webb was found dead with two gunshot wounds to the head, deemed a suicide but questioned by many.
[8] Antonio Machado was an early twentieth-century Spanish poet who we had studied in class. "No Hay Camino," from his book, *Campos de Castilla*, is one of his most well known poems.
[9] See Roxanne Dunbar-Ortiz's political memoir, *Blood on the Border*, for an excellent analysis of the Sandinista mistakes regarding the Miskitu and their many efforts to rectify these mistakes over the years.
[10] Margaret Randall, *Gathering Rage: The Failure of 20th Century Revolutions to Develop a Feminist Agenda*, 22.

[11] Ibid. 57.

[12] The situation of Nicaraguan women and the country as a whole steadily deteriorated in all areas after the Sandinista loss. Within two years, the new economic plan brought in by UNO forced 20,000 women into unemployment, and the majority of rural infant service centers were closed. In the wake of these problems, Nicaraguan feminists took the lead in regional efforts in Central America to define a feminist agenda for Latin American women that includes abortion, domestic violence, lesbianism, and prostitution, as well as worker's rights, health care, and education.

With Eyes Not Yet Born

[1] Otto René Castillo, "Before the Scales Tomorrow," in *Tomorrow Triumphant*. Otto René Castillo was a Guatemalan revolutionary and poet. He was captured, tortured and immolated by the Guatemalan army in 1967.

[2] The U.S. invaded Panama in December 1989 in order to depose military dictator Manuel Noriega, who was no longer cooperating fully with their agenda. The U.S. replaced Noriega with a "better" puppet leader, Guillermo Endara. Noriega was arrested and convicted in 1992 of drug trafficking and racketeering. He is currently incarcerated in a U.S. prison.

[3] ACT UP, The AIDS Coalition To Unleash Power, was started in 1987 to develop direct action targeting government gross mismanagement of the AIDS crisis and the profiteering of drug companies from AIDS.

[4] In 1987, six gay activists in New York formed the "Silence=Death" project. It drew parallels between the Nazi period and the AIDS crisis, declaring that "silence about the oppression and annihilation of gay people, then and now, must be broken as a matter of our survival." The slogan was adopted by ACT-UP and became one of the best known slogans of the AIDS activist movement.

[5] The ACT UP/NY Women & AIDS Book Group, *Women, AIDS & Activism*.

[6] Leila Khaled, *My People Shall Live*, 21.

[7] Ibid., 22.

[8] Jeanette Winter, *Follow the Drinking Gourd*.

Interrogating Surrender

[1] Nazim Hikmet, from the poem, "It's This Way," in *Selected Poetry*. The poem was written in a Turkish prison by Hikmet in 1948, where he was incarcerated for being a communist and writing incendiary poetry.

[2] See Ronald Fernandez, *Prisoners of Colonialism*, for the application of this principle by Puerto Rican *independentistas* in the United States.

[3] See Chapter 11 of *Outlaws of America* for an excellent overview of the Brink's incident and its aftermath.

[4] Los Macheteros or El Ejercito Popular Boricua was a clandestine political military organization based on the island of Puerto Rico. One of their most famous actions was the expropriation of $7 million from Wells Fargo in 1983. See the chapter on "Los Macheteros" in *Prisoners of Colonialism* for a description of their history in the seventies and eighties.

[5] Silvia Baraldini is an Italian national who lived in the United States from the time she was

sixteen. She was arrested in 1982 and convicted of conspiracy against the U.S. Government, including assistance with the escape of Assata Shakur. She was sentenced to forty-three years in prison. In 1999, she was transferred to Italy as a result of massive campaign. In 2006, she was pardoned and released by the Italian government. Susan Rosenberg was arrested in 1984 and sentenced to fifty-eight years for possession of false identification papers, explosives, and other weapons. Her sentence was commuted by President Clinton in 2001 just before he left office. Alejandrina Torres, a Puerto Rican, was arrested in 1983, convicted of seditious conspiracy and sentenced to thirty-five years. Her sentence was commuted by President Clinton in September 1999.

[6] The decision in favor of the women was eventually overturned. The Lexington Control Unit was shut down, but replaced by a new larger "control unit" called Shawnee, within Marianna prison in Florida—which held nine times as many cells as the Lexington experiment. All three political prisoners in Lexington—Torres, Rosenberg, and Baraldini were transferred there for a time.

[7] *Living in Secret,* Cristina Salat.

Return

[1] Joyce Block, *Family Myths*, dedication.

[2] Mariana Bracetti was a leader of the Puerto Rico independence movement in the 1860s. Pedro Albizu Campos was a preeminent Puerto Rican independence leader from the 1930's until his death in 1965. He was the founder and president of the Puerto Rican Nationalist Party and served many years as a political prisoner inside U.S. prisons. Lolita Lebron was one of the five Puerto Rican Nationalist prisoners (see "Repression Breeds Resistance," in this book, for more about the Nationalists).

[3] *New York Times,* December 8, 1994.

Light Will Always Be Showing

[1] A *bohio* was a small hut-type house common in the Cuban countryside.

[2] KPFA is the Bay Area Pacifica radio station, the first one established in 1949 in Berkeley. During the sixties and seventies Claude had been a radio journalist with KPFA, hosting several different radio shows and serving as the station's production director for a few years.

[3] *El Pito* can be translated as "whistleblower."

Reconstructing Memory

[1] The term "non-profit industrial complex" was popularized a number of years later by the group INCITE—Women of Color Against Violence. *The Revolution Will Not Be Funded,* edited by INCITE in 2007, extensively documents and analyzes the non-profit phenomenon that I began to observe when I returned to the Bay Area in the nineties.

[2] For extensive description of this case and its impact on the Rosenberg's children, see two autobiographical books: *An Execution in the Family,* Robert Meeropol, and *We Are Your Sons,* by Michael and Robert Meeropol.

The Fire Inside

[1] Laura's life and politics are vividly described in the video, *Out—The Making of a Revolutionary*, directed by Sonja Devries and Rhonda Collins, 2000.

[2] *Hauling Up the Morning* was edited by two political prisoners, Tim Blunk and Ray Levasseur, and was a powerful compilation of poetry, essays, and pictures created by political prisoners across the U.S.

[3] Mumia Abu-Jamal has written innumerable commentaries and several books. There are also a number of excellent books written about him (see bibliography). One of them, *On a Move* was written by Terry Bisson, who edited this book.

[4] In particular, Mumia exposed the police role in the 1978 assault on MOVE and was active defending the MOVE 9. See endnotes 2 and 3 for "Escape" in this book for more on MOVE 9.

[5] See http://www.prisonradio.org.

[6] "Gulag America," commentary, 1998 from www.flashpoints.net.

[7] See endnotes for "Escape" in this book for more about Alan Berkman.

[8] Brochure for "Art Against the Death Penalty," 1994. Author's personal archive.

[9] Norma Jean Croy was a Native American political prisoner who was unjustly convicted of the murder of an FBI agent and spent eighteen years in prison. She was finally released in 1997.

[10] Juana Alicia, Edythe Boone, Susan Kelk Cervantes, Meera Desai, Irene Perez, and Yvonne Littleton were the muralistas who created the mural with Miranda. See the pamphlet, *Maestrapeace—A Guide to the Mural on the San Francisco Women's Building*, for more information on the mural.

[11] Safiya Bukhari was a Black Panther and Black Liberation Army member. She spent nine years in prison, was the founder of the New York Coalition to Free Mumia Abu-Jamal, and a co-founder of the Jericho Movement. She died in 2003.

[12] For more information about CCWP, see www.womenprisoners.org.

[13] The video, *Fighting for Our Lives*, produced by Freedom Archives, tells the story of Charisse Shumate, the lead plaintiff in the lawsuit and a founding member of CCWP.

[14] See *Angela Davis, An Autobiography*, for an in depth description of the story of her trial.

[15] *If They Come in the Morning*, Angela Davis, 23.

[16] Ibid., dedication page.

[17] Joann Walker, "Medical Treatment at Chowchilla," in *Criminal Injustice*, Elihu Rosenblatt, ed., 124.

[18] See "The Fire Inside" in *NWSA Journal*, Vol. 20, No. 2, Summer 2008, for a history of the evolution of *The Fire Inside* and a compilation of its writings.

Can't Jail the Spirit

[1] Jalil Muntaquim, Jericho 98 call quoted in *Can't Jail the Spirit*, 4th edition, 101.

[2] Dhoruba Bin Wahad was a Black Panther and BLA leader who was convicted of murder of two police officers and sentenced to twenty-five years to life in prison in 1973. In 1975,

Dhoruba filed a lawsuit against the FBI and, the New York police and over the course of the next fifteen years, he obtained thousands of pages of FBI documents which became the basis for the appeal of his conviction. In 1990, his conviction was overturned and he was released. In 1995, he settled his lawsuit against the FBI for $400,000. His history and case was the subject of a documentary, *Passin' it On—The Black Panthers Search for Justice*, directed by Jon Valadez. Geronimo Ji Jaga Pratt was a leader of the Black Panther Party in Los Angeles. He was convicted of the 1968 murder of a Santa Monica woman and spent twenty-seven years in prison, eight in solitary confinement. His conviction was finally overturned in 1997, because the prosecution had not disclosed that a key witness in his case, Julio Butler, was an informant working for the L.A. police department and the FBI. See Jack Olsen's biography of Geronimo, *Last Man Standing*, for a history of his life and the case.

[3] *Can't Jail the Spirit*, 12, 4th edition, March 1998.

[4] Muhjah Shakir had been a leading member of the Geronimo Defense Committee for many years and was also active in the Republic of New Afrika (RNA). Her leadership in the Jericho movement and her friendship were very important to me personally and politically in this period.

[5] "The Malcolm X Grassroots Movement is an organization of Afrikans in America/New Afrikans whose mission is to defend the human rights of our people and promote self-determination in our community," from their website, http://mxgm.org. Comité 98 was a group of Bay Area Borinqueños, primarily from UC Berkeley, who visited the Puerto Rican compañeras at Dublin. They formed the Comité to mark the centennial of Puerto Rican colonization and worked with Jericho 98.

[6] *Can't Jail the Spirit*, 5, 1998, 4th edition. *Can't Jail the Spirit* was edited by the Committee to End the Marion Lockdown (CEML), based in Chicago. As part of CEML, Nancy Kurshan and Steve Whitman worked on each edition, including the fifth edition produced in 2002.

[7] Ibid., 187.

[8] Ibid., 188.

[9] For more about Inez Garcia's case see "New World Coming" in this book.

[10] *The Fire Inside*, Issue #15, August 2000.

[11] Ibid., Issue #9, September 1998.

[12] Theresa Cruz was finally released eight years later in April 2006 by the Board of Parole Hearings. Sadly, her mother didn't live to see Roxanne's freedom. Theresa Azochar died in December 2004.

[13] Cuban videographer, Gloria Rolanda directed *Eyes of the Rainbow*, a beautiful, poetically narrated film about Assata, released in 1997.

[14] In 2001, Silvia was released to house arrest. In September 2006, she was unconditionally released based upon a general pardon law passed by the Italian Parliament.

[15] In 1979, President Carter had released the Nationalists unconditionally.

A Luta Continua

[1] This slogan was popularized by Samora Machel, leader of Mozambican liberation struggle and first president of independent Mozambique. It was commonly referred to during the seventies within the U.S. left.

[2] See "Fugitive Deconstructions" in this book for previous mention of the Wells Fargo expropriation.

[3] See http://nyc.indymedia.org/en/2005/09/57857.html.

[4] Friends and Family of Avelino González Claudio, "Avelino González... A Tireless Fighter," http://prolibertadweb.tripod.com/id9.html.

[5] Jalil Muntaqim and Herman Bell have both been serving life sentences in New York state for various alleged offenses, including the assassination of two New York City police officers. Jalil, Herman, and Albert Nuh Washington (deceased) are known as the New York 3, and they consistently maintained that their convictions are a result of the FBI's COINTELPRO program. According to Herman, "We've continued to fight to re-open our case based on evidence which proves that our trial was entirely unfair and prejudicially reviewed. We have specific proof of police perjury, concealment, destruction of evidence, and serious judicial misconduct in our case. While public awareness and support is essential to win a new trial for us, such support and awareness are also essential to protect against use of similar repressive techniques on today's young activists." http://www.prisonactivist.org/archive/pps+pows/ny3_update.html

[6] See http://www.freethesf8.org for comprehensive information on the Committee for the Defense of Human Rights and the San Francisco 8.

[7] See www.mxgm.org; www.criticalresistance.org; and www.eastsideartsalliance.com for more information about these organizations.

[8] The *San Francisco Bay View* newspaper was founded in 1976 and continued to publish weekly until August 2008 when it was forced to stop its print edition due to financial strain. For decades it was a preeminent national Black independent newspaper, "a communications network for the Black community worldwide." It consistently gave voice to prisoners and political prisoners across the country. It continues to maintain an informative website, www.sfbayview.com.

[9] See "Repression Breeds Resistance" and "Can't Jail the Spirit" in this book for more on Jalil.

[10] Study reported in *The San Francisco Chronicle*, May 6, 2008.

[11] See www.freedomarchives.org for information on the archives.

[12] See Ruthie Gilmore's book, *Golden Gulag*, for a comprehensive look into the political economy of California's prisons.

[13] See www.greenscare.org for information on this repressive government campaign. According to the website, the term *Green Scare* was first used to define "the tactics that the US government and all their tentacles (FBI, IRS, BATF, Joint Terrorism Task Forces, local police, the court system) are using to attack the ELF/ALF (Earth Liberation Front and Animal Liberation Front) and specifically those who publicly support them."

[14] Marilyn received a PEN American Center prize for poetry in 2001. In addition to *Rescue the Word*, her poetry is available on the CD *Wild Poppies*, produced by Freedom Archives in 2004. Her poetry and essays have been reprinted in several anthologies and a variety of journals and magazines.

[15] Marilyn Buck, *Rescue the Word*, 2. *Friends of Marilyn Buck*, San Francisco 2001.

BIBLIOGRAPHY

Abu-Jamal, Mumia with Noelle Hanrahan, ed. *All Things Censored.* New York: Seven Stories Press, 2000.

Abu-Jamal, Mumia. *Death Blossoms: Reflections From a Prisoner of Conscience.* Farmington, Pennsylvania: Plough Publishing, 1997.

Abu-Jamal, Mumia. *We Want Freedom: A Life in the Black Panther Party.* Cambridge: South End Press, 2000.

ACE Program Women, Bedford Hills Correctional Facility. *Breaking the Walls of Silence: AIDS and Women in a New York State Maximum-Security Prison.* Woodstock, New York: Overlook Press, 1998.

ACT-UP/NY Women & AIDS Book Group. *Women, AIDS & Activism.* Boston: South End Press, 1990.

Ahmad, Muhammad (Max Stanford, Jr.). *We Will Return in the Whirlwind: Black Radical Organizations 1960-1975.* Chicago: Charles H. Kerr Publishing, 2007.

Anderson, S.E and Tony Medina, eds. *In Defense of Mumia: An Anthology of Prose, Poetry and Art.* New York: Writers and Readers Publishing, 1996.

Aristide, Jean-Bertrand. *Eyes of the Heart: Seeking a Path for the Poor in the Age of Globalization.* Monroe, Maine: Common Courage Press, 2000.

Austin, Curtis. *Up Against the Wall: Violence in the Making and Unmaking of the Black Panther Party.* Fayetteville: University of Arkansas Press, 2006.

Ayers, Bill. *Fugitive Days: A Memoir.* Boston: Beacon Press, 2001.

Baldwin, James. *The Fire Next Time.* New York: Dial Press, 1963.

Bauer, Karin, ed. *Everybody Talks About the Weather...We Don't: The Writings of Ulrike Meinhof.* New York: Seven Stories Press, 2008.

Belli, Gioconda. *The Country Under My Skin: A Memoir of Love and War.* New York: Alfred Knopf, 2002.

Berger, Dan. *Outlaws of America: The Weather Underground and the Politics of Solidarity.* Oakland: AK Press, 2006.

Berger, Dan, Chesa Boudin and Kenyon Farrow, eds. *Letters from Young Activists: Today's Rebels Speak Out.* New York: Nation Books, 2005.

Bisson, Terry. *On A Move: The Story of Mumia Abu-Jamal.* Litmus Books, 2000.

Block, Joyce. *Family Myths.* New York: Simon & Schuster, 1994.

Blunk, Tim, and Raymond Luc Levasseur, eds. 1990. *Hauling Up the Morning: Writings and Art by Political Prisoners and Prisoners of War in the U.S.* Trenton, New Jersey: Red Sea Press, 1990.

Brownmiller, Susan. *Against Our Will: Men, Women and Rape.* New York: Ballantine Books, 1975.

Buck, Marilyn. *Rescue the Word* (chapbook). San Francisco: Friends of Marilyn Buck, 2001.

Buck, Marilyn, David Gilbert and Laura Whitehorn. *Enemies of the State* (pamphlet). Montreal: Abraham Guillen Press and Arm the Spirit, 2002.

California Coalition for Women Prisoners. *The Fire Inside* (newsletter). San Francisco: 1996-2008. www.womenprisoners.org.

Campbell, Horace. *Reclaiming Zimbabwe: The Exhaustion of the Patriarchal Model of Liberation.* Trenton, New Jersey: Africa World Press, 2003.

Castillo, Otto René. *Tomorrow Triumphant.* San Francisco: Night Horn Books, 1984.

Chinosole, ed. *Schooling the Generations in the Politics of Prison.* Berkeley: New Earth Publications, 1996.

Churchill, Ward and Jim Vander Wall. *Agents of Repression: The FBI's Secret War Against the Black Panther Party and the American Indian Movement.* Boston: South End Press, 1988.

Churchill, Ward and Jim Vander Wall, eds. *Cages of Steel: The Politics of Imprisonment.* Washington, D.C.: Maisonneuve Press, 1992.

Churchill, Ward and Jim Vander Wall. *The COINTELPRO Papers: Documents from the FBI's Secret War Against Dissent in the United States.* Boston: South End Press, 1990.

Cleaver, Kathleen and George Katsiaficas, eds. *Liberation, Imagination and the Black*

Panther Party: A New Look at the Panthers and their Legacy. New York: Routledge: 2001.

Cohn, Roy M. *Outlaws of Amerika: The Weather Underground Organization.* Alexandria, Virginia: Western Goals, 1982.

Committee to End the Marion Lockdown, ed. *Can't Jail the Spirit: Political Prisoners in the U.S.* Chicago: Editorial Coqui Publishers, Fourth Edition, 1998.

Crozier, Michael, Samuel Huntington and Joji Watanuki. *The Crisis of Democracy: Report on the Governability of Democracy to the Trilateral Commission.* New York: New York University Press, 1975.

Davis, Angela Y. *Angela Davis: An Autobiography.* New York: International Publishers, 1988.

Davis, Angela Y. *If They Come in the Morning.* New York: Signet, 1971.

Davis, Angela Y. "Joann Little: The Dialectics of Rape," from *Ms Magazine*, June 1975. Reprinted in *Save Joann Little* (pamphlet). Oakland: Women's Press Collective, 1975.

Davis, Angela Y. *Women Race and Class.* New York: Random House, 1981.

Debray, Régis. *The Revolution in the Revolution?* New York: Grove Press, 1967.

Devries, Sonja and Collins, Rhonda, dirs. *OUT: The Making of a Revolutionary* (video documentary). 2000.

Dorfman, Ariel with Pilar Aquilera, and Ricardo Fredes, eds. *Chile: The Other September 11: An Anthology of Reflections on the 1973 Coup.* New York: Ocean Press, 2006.

Dorfman, Ariel. *Heading South, Looking North: A Bilingual Journey.* New York: Farrar, Straus & Giroux, 1998.

Dunbar-Ortiz, Roxanne. *Blood on the Border: A Memoir of the Contra War.* Cambridge: South End Press, 2005.

Dunbar-Ortiz, Roxanne. *Outlaw Woman: A Memoir of the War Years, 1960-1975.* San Francisco: City Lights, 2001.

Edwards, Alison. *Rape, Racism and the White Women's Movement: An Answer to Susan Brownmiller* (pamphlet). Chicago: Sojourner Truth Organization, 1979.

Eisen-Bergman, Arlene. *From Women in Prison Here To Women of Viet Nam: We Are Sisters* (pamphlet). San Francisco: Peoples Press, 1975.

Eisen-Bergman, Arlene. *Women of Viet Nam*. San Francisco: Peoples Press, 1974.

Elbaum, Max. *Revolution in the Air: Sixties Radicals turn to Lenin, Mao and Che.* London: Verso, 2002.

Faith, Karlene. *Unruly Women, The Politics of Confinement and Resistance.* Vancouver: Press Gang Publishers,1993.

Farmer, Paul. *The Uses of Haiti.* Monroe, Maine: Common Courage Press, 2005.

Fernandez, Ronald. *Prisoners of Colonialism:The Struggle for Justice in Puerto Rico.* Monroe, Maine: Common Courage Press, 1994.

Fire Inside Collective. *The Fire Inside* (newsletter).San Francisco: The California Coalition for Women Prisoners,1996-2008. http://womenprisoners.org/fire.

Fire Inside Collective. "The Fire Inside: Newsletter of the California Coalition for Women Prisoners," in NWSA Journal,Vol 20, No. 2, Summer 2008.

Foner, Philip S.,ed. *The Black Panthers Speak.* New York: DaCapo Press, 2002.

Forman, James. *The Making of Black Revolutionaries.* Seattle: University of Washington Press, 2000.

Freedom Archives, producer. *Chile: Promise of Freedom* (audio CD). San Francisco: Freedom Archvies, 2003. www.freedomarchives.org.

Freedom Archives, producer. *Wild Poppies: A Poetry Jam Across Prison Walls - Poets And Musicians Honor Poet And Political Prisoner Marilyn Buck* (audio CD). San Francisco: Freedom Archives, 2004. www.freedomarchives.org.

Freedom Archives, producer. *Legacy of Torture: The War on the Black Liberation Movement* (video). San Francisco: Freedom Archives, 2007. www.freedomarchives.org.

Fujino, Diane. *Heartbeat of Struggle: The Revolutionary Life of Yuri Kochiyama.* Minneapolis: University of Minnesota Press, 2005.

Gilbert, David. *No Surrender: Writings from an Anti-Imperialist Political Prisoner.* Montreal: Abraham Guillen Press and Arm the Spirit, 2004.

Gilmore, Ruth Wilson. *Golden Gulag: Prisons, Surplus, Crisis, and Opposition in Globalizing California.* Berkeley: University of California Press, 2007.

Glick, Brian. *War at Home: Covert Action Against U.S. Activists and What We Can Do About It.* Cambridge: South End Press, 1989.

Goldberg, Eve & Claude Marks, dirs. Charisse Shumate: *Fighting for our Lives* (video documentary). San Francisco: Freedom Archives, 2003. www.freedomarchives.org.

Gordimer, Nadine. *Burger's Daughter.* London: Penguin Books, 1979.

Grahn, Judy. *The Common Woman* (chapbook).Oakland: Women's Press Collective, 1972.

Green, Sam and Bill Siegel, dirs. *The Weather Underground* (documentary film). San Francisco: The Free History Project, 2003.

Haiti Action Committee. *Hidden From the Headlines: The U.S. War Against Haiti,* (pamphlet). Berkeley: Haiti Action Committee, 2004.

Harlow, Barbara. *Women, Writing and Political Detention.* Hanover, New Hampshire: Wesleyan University Press, 1992.

Hikmet, Nazim. *Selected Poetry.* New York: Persea Books,1986.

Hull, Gloria, Patricia Bell Scott and Barbara Smith. *But Some of Us Are Brave: Black Women's Studies.* Old Westbury: The Feminist Press, 1982.

INCITE! Women of Color Against Violence,ed. *The Revolution Will Not Be Funded: Beyond the Non-Profit Industrial Complex.* Cambridge: South End Press, 2007.

Jackson, George. *Blood in My Eye.* Baltimore: Black Classic Press, 1990.

Jackson, George. *Soledad Brother: The Prison Letters of George Jackson.* New York: Bantam Books, 1970.

Jacobs, Ron. *The Way The Wind Blew: A History of the Weather Underground.* London: Verso, 1997.

James, Joy, ed. *Imprisoned Intellectuals: America's Political Prisoners Write on Life, Liberation, and Rebellion.* Lanham, Maryland: Rowman & Littlefield, 2003.

James, Joy,ed. *The New Abolitionists: (Neo)slave Narratives And Contemporary Prison Writings.* New York: SUNY Press, 2005.

James, Joy. *Resisting State Violence: Radicalism, Gender and Race in U.S. Culture.* Minneapolis: University of Minnesota Press, 1996.

James, Joy, ed. *States of Confinement: Policing, Detention and Prisons.* New York: St. Martin's Press, 2000.

John Brown Book Club, ed. *The Split in the Weather Underground: Struggling Against White and Male Supremacy* (pamphlet). Seattle: John Brown Book Club, 1977.

Jones, Charles,ed. *The Black Panther Party Reconsidered.* Baltimore: Black Classic Press, 1998.

Jones, Thai. *A Radical Line: From the Labor Movement to the Weather Underground, One Family's Century of Conscience.* New York: Free Press, 2004.

Kelley, Robin, D.G. *Freedom Dreams: The Black Radical Imagination.* Boston: Beacon Press, 2002.

Khaled, Leila as told to George Hajjar. *My People Shall Live: The Autobiography of a Revolutionary.* London: Hodder and Stoughton, 1973.

Lenin, V.I. *Left-Wing Communism, an Infantile Disorder: A Popular Essay in Marxian Strategy and Tactics.* International Publishers Company, 1940.

Lenin, V. I., Service, Robert, ed. *The State and Revolution.* New York: Penguin Group, 1993.

Lerner, Gerda, ed. *Black Women in White America: A Documentary History.* New York: Knopf, 1992.

Machel, Samora. *Imperialist Strategy in Zimbabwe and Southern Africa* (pamphlet). New York: May 19th Communist Organization, 1979.

Machado, Antonio with translation by Mary Berg and Dennis Maloney. *Campos de Castilla.* Buffalo: White Pine Press, 2005.

Mann, Eric. *Comrade George: An Investigation into the Life, Political Thought and Assassination of George Jackson.* New York: Perennial Library, 1974.

Meeropol, Michael and Robert Meeropol. *We Are Your Sons.* Boston: Houghton Mifflin Company, 1975.

Meeropol, Robert. *An Execution in the Family.* New York: St. Martin's Press, 2003.

Meyer, Matt, ed. *Let Freedom Ring: A Collection of Documents from the Movements to Free U.S. Political Prisoners.* Oakland and Montreal: PM Press and Kersplebedeb, 2008.

Moraga, Cherríe and Gloria Anzaldúa, eds. *This Bridge Called My Back: Writings by*

Radical Women of Color. New York: Kitchen Table: Women of Color Press, 1983.

Morgan, Robin, ed. *Sisterhood is Powerful.* New York: Vintage Books, 1970.

MOVE Organization. *25 Years On The Move* (pamphlet). MOVE Organization, 1996.

Muntaqim, Jalil. *We Are Our Own Liberators! Selected Prison Writings.* Abraham Guillen Press and Arm the Spirit, 2003.

Movimiento de Liberación Nacional Puertorriqueño(MLN). *Program and Ideology of the MLN* (pamphlet). Chicago: MLN, 1987.

New York Radical Feminists with Connell, Noreen and Wilson, Cassandra, eds. *Rape: the First Sourcebook for Women.* New York: New American Library, 1974.

Olsen, Jack. *Last Man Standing: The Tragedy and Triumph of Geronimo Pratt.* New York: Doubleday, 2000.

Out of Control: Lesbian Committee to Support Women Political Prisoners and Prisoners of War, ed. *Sparks Fly: Women Political Prisoners and Prisoners of War in the U.S.*(pamphlet). Berkeley:Agit Press, 1998.

Parenti, Christian. *Lockdown America: Police and Prisons in the Age of Crisis.* London: Verso, 1999.

Parker, Pat. *Movement in Black.* Ithaca: Firebrand Books, 1999.

Peoples Press Puerto Rico Project. *Puerto Rico the Flame of Resistance.* San Francisco: Peoples Press, 1977.

Peri Rossi, Cristina with translation and introduction by Marilyn Buck. *State of Exile.* San Francisco: City Lights, Pocket Poets #58, 2008.

Perlstein, Daniel with Alan Sadovnik, and Susan Semel, eds. *Justice, Justice: School Politics and the Eclipse of Liberalism.* New York: Peter Lang, Inc. 2004.

Prairie Fire Organizing Committee. *Breakthrough* (political journal). San Francisco: 1976-1995.

Prairie Fire Organizing Committee. *Women's Liberation and Imperialism.* San Francisco: 1977.

Prairie Fire Organizing Committee. *Women's Liberation in the Zimbabwean Revolution* (pamphlet). San Francisco: John Brown Book Club, 1979.

Ramos-Zayas, Ana. *National Performances: The Politics of Class, Race and Space in Puerto Rican Chicago.* Chicago: University of Chicago Press, 2003.

Randall, Margaret. *Cuban Women Now.* Toronto: The Women's Press, 1974.

Randall, Margaret. *Gathering Rage – The Failure of 20th Century Revolutions to Develop a Feminist Agenda.* New York: Monthly Review Press, 1992.

Randall, Margaret. *Sandino's Daughters: Testimonies of Nicaraguan Women in Struggle.* London: Zed Press, 1981.

Randall, Margaret. *Sandino's Daughters Revisited: Feminism in Nicaragua.* New Brunswick: Rutgers University Press, 1994.

Randall, Margaret. *Risking a Somersault in the Air: Conversations with Nicaraguan Writers.* San Francisco: Solidarity Publications, 1984.

Rieder, Ines and Patricia Ruppelt, eds. *AIDS: The Women.* San Francisco and Pittsburgh: Cleis Press, 1988.

Rolando,Gloria, dir. *Eyes of the Rainbow* (video). Havana: Imagines del Caribe, 1997.

Rosca, Ninotchka. *Endgame: The Fall of Marcos.* Scholastic Library Publishing, 1987.

Rosca, Ninotchka and Richard A. Koritz, eds. *Jose Maria Sison: At Home in the World: Portrait of a Revolutionary.* Greensboro, North Carolina : Open Hand Publishing, 2004.

Rosenblatt, Elihu,ed. *Criminal Injustice: Confronting the Prison Crisis.* Boston: South End Press, 1996.

Rosenblum, Nina, dir. *Through the Wire* (documentary film). Daedalus Productions, 1990.

Rowbotham, Sheila. *Women Resistance & Revolution.* New York: Vintage, 1974.

Ryan, Cathy and Weimberg, Gary, dirs. *The Double Life of Ernesto Gomez Gomez.* Berkeley: Luna Productions, 1999.

Salat, Cristina. *Living in Secret.* New York: Bantam, 1993.

Salter, Kenneth W.,ed. *The Trial of Inez García.* Berkeley: Editorial Justa Publications, 1976.

Scheffler, Judith A., ed. *Wall Tappings: Women's Prison Writings.* New York: The Feminist Press at CUNY, 2002.

Segrest, Mab. *Memoir of a Race Traitor.* Boston: South End Press, 1994.

Shakur, Assata. *Assata: An Autobiography.* Chicago: Lawrence Hill Books, 1987.

Smith, Chip. *The Cost of Privilege: Taking on the System of White Supremacy and Racism.* Fayetteville, North Carolina: Camino Press, 2007.

Springer, Kimberly. *Living for the Revolution: Black Feminist Organizations, 1968-1980.* Durham: Duke University Press, 2005.

Stateville Prisoner Organization. *Notes from a New Afrikan P.O.W. Journal.* Illinois: 1978-1981.

Stein, Arlene. *Sex and Sensibility: Stories of a Lesbian Generation.* Berkeley: University of California Press, 1997.

Sudbury, Julia, ed. *Global Lockdown: Race, Gender and the Prison Industrial Complex.* London: Routledge, 2005.

Talvi, Silja J.A. *Women Behind Bars: The Crisis of Women in the U.S. Prison System.* Emeryville: Seal Press, 2007.

Thompson, Becky. *A Promise and a Way of Life: White Antiracist Activism.* Minnesota: University of Minnesota Press, 2001.

Torres, Andrés and Velázquez, José E., eds. *The Puerto Rican Movement: Voices from the Diaspora.* Philadelphia: Temple University, 1998.

Valadez, Jon, dir. *Passin' It On – The Black Panthers Search for Justice* (video documentary). 2003.

Van Lydegraf, Clayton. *The Object is to Win* (pamphlet). 1971, third edition. http://vanlydegraf.hostingweb.us.

Varon, Jeremy. *Bringing the War Home: The Weather Underground, The Red Army Faction, and Revolutionary Violence in the Sixties and Seventies.* Berkeley: University of California Press, 2004.

Webb, Gary. *Dark Alliance:The CIA, The Contras and the Crack Cocaine Epidemic.* New York: Seven Stories Press, 1998.

Weather Underground. *Prairie Fire: The Politics of Revolutionary Anti-Imperialism.* Communications Co., 1974.

Weather Underground. *Osawatomie* (political journal). 1975-1976.

Wideman, John Edgar. *Philadelphia Fire*. New York: Vintage Books, 1991.

Wilkerson, Cathy. *Flying Close to the Sun: My Life and Times As A Weatherman*. New York: Seven Stories Press, 2007.

Williams, Evelyn. *Inadmissible Evidence: The Story of the African-American Trial Lawyer Who Defended the Black Liberation Army*. New York: Lawrence Hill Books, 1993.

Winter, Jeanette. *Follow the Drinking Gourd*. New York: Knopf, 1988.

Women in the Weather Underground Organization. *Sing a Battlesong* (pamphlet). Inkworks, 1975.

INDEX